SPEAKING FROM THE DEPTHS

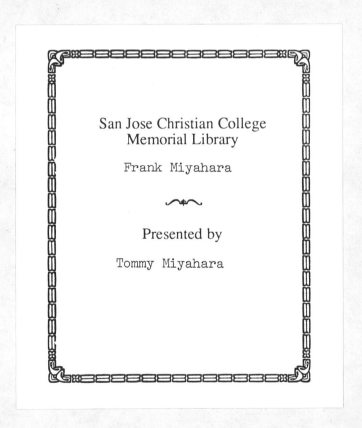

Speaking from the Depths

*Alfred North Whitehead's Hermeneutical Metaphysics of
Propositions, Experience, Symbolism,
Language, and Religion*

Stephen T. Franklin

William B. Eerdmans Publishing Company
Grand Rapids, Michigan

Copyright © 1990 by Wm. B. Eerdmans Publishing Co.
255 Jefferson Ave. S.E., Grand Rapids, Mich. 49503

Printed in the United States of America

Library of Congress Cataloging-in-Publication Data

Franklin, Stephen T.
    Speaking from the depths: Alfred North Whitehead's hermeneutical
metaphysics of propositions, experience, symbolism, language, and
religion / Stephen T. Franklin.
        p.   cm.
    Bibliography: p. 381
    ISBN 0-8028-0370-9
    1. Whitehead, Alfred North, 1861–1947. I. Title.
B1674.W354F7   1990
192—dc19
                                                     89-1204
                                                      CIP

To my family—
My parents, the Reverend Theodore E. and Marion V. Franklin;
my wife, Martha J. Franklin;
and my children, Elizabeth J. and David S. Franklin;
each of them members of my earthly family
and also members of the family of faith in Jesus Christ—
with love.

Acknowledgments

The author and publisher gratefully acknowledge permission granted by the following publishers to use extended quotations from copyrighted works of Alfred North Whitehead.

From *Adventures of Ideas*

Reprinted with permission of Macmillan Publishing Company. Copyright © 1933 by Macmillan Publishing Company; renewed 1961 by Evelyn Whitehead. (for USA and Canada)

Reprinted with permission of Cambridge University Press. Copyright © 1933 by Cambridge University Press; renewed 1961 by Evelyn Whitehead. (for world rights)

From *Modes of Thought*

Reprinted with permission of Macmillan Publishing Company. Copyright © 1938 by Macmillan Publishing Company; renewed 1966 by T. North Whitehead. (for USA and Canada)

Reprinted with permission of Cambridge University Press. Copyright © 1938 by Cambridge University Press; renewed 1966 by T. North Whitehead. (for world rights)

From *Process and Reality*

Reprinted with permission of Macmillan Publishing Company. Copyright © 1929 by Macmillan Publishing Company; renewed 1957 by Evelyn Whitehead.

From *Religion in the Making*

Reprinted with permission of Macmillan Publishing Company. Copyright © 1926 by Macmillan Publishing Company; renewed 1954 by Evelyn Whitehead. (for USA and Canada)

Reprinted with permission of Cambridge University Press. Copyright © 1926 by Cambridge University Press; renewed 1954 by Evelyn Whitehead. (for world rights)

From *Science and the Modern World*

Reprinted with permission of Macmillan Publishing Company. Copyright © 1925 by Macmillan Publishing Company; renewed 1953 by Evelyn Whitehead. (for USA and Canada)

From *Symbolism; Its Meaning and Effect*

Reprinted with permission of Macmillan Publishing Company. Copyright © 1927 by Macmillan Publishing Company; renewed 1955 by Evelyn Whitehead. (for USA and Canada)

Reprinted with permission of Cambridge University Press. Copyright © 1927 by Cambridge University Press; renewed 1955 by Evelyn Whitehead. (for world rights)

Contents

PART FOUR: RELIGION

Preface

EVERY BOOK HAS A HISTORY. The origins of this book rest in my quest to find a way of explaining how human language can speak of God. As I began to read Whitehead's philosophy, I discovered a profound metaphysical vision which allowed for the possibility of God-language conveying genuine claims about what is the case. His view of God-language was set in a nuanced description of human language in general.

Three points especially impressed me. First, Whitehead emphasized that human language has many functions beyond that of describing what is the case. In fact, in his view, these other uses are far more foundational than that of conveying information. Second, Whitehead embedded his description of language in the entirety of his metaphysical vision. To fail to understand the metaphysical context is to turn Whitehead's views on language into either baffling incomprehensibility or a rather disconnected series of cliches and trivialities. Lastly, the more I studied Whitehead's philosophy, the more it became clear that his theory of language was but one part of a larger hermeneutical vision.

By hermeneutics, I mean a philosophy that offers an explanation of the act of understanding, especially as understanding requires interpretation. A hermeneutical philosophy, at least since Schleiermacher, has therefore included a description of human persons such that the act of interpretation is seen as necessary as well as possible, and it has drawn out the implications of this view of interpretation for the nature of human understanding. Whitehead provides us with such a description—a description which I have found to possess great beauty and persuasiveness. Whitehead goes beyond this, however, and roots his philosophy of human persons in the character of nature, that is, in reality as a whole. Exactly how Whitehead does this gets into the heart of the book and cannot be developed in this Preface.[1]

---

1. Whitehead argues that all human understanding requires acts such as deciding and simplifying. The acts of deciding and simplifying *are* interpretations of our world.

The heart of this book is an analysis of four topics in Whitehead's philosophy: propositions, symbolism, language, and religion. I begin in Part One with propositions because in Whitehead's system propositions are more primitive than either symbolism or language. Also, it is a relatively straightforward matter to root propositions within the broad contours of his entire metaphysical system, including the foundations of experience and the nature of reality (what Whitehead calls 'concrescence'). Part One, therefore, deals with many of the "big" questions of metaphysics. It also introduces the technical vocabulary which will be employed in the rest of the book. Because of the introduction of this technical vocabulary, most readers will find Chapter One the most time-consuming chapter in the book.

Part Two focuses on symbolism. For Whitehead, all sense experience has a symbolic character, and so Part Two also discusses human sense experience. In addition, Part Two covers the topics of causality, space, and time.

Part Three, which presents Whitehead's theory of language, is the pivot of the book. Whitehead's theory of language is a special case of his larger theory of symbolism. It also presupposes his theory of propositions and his larger metaphysical vision. Part Three, therefore, builds on the first two parts. In Part Three, there is a consideration of the relation between ordinary and metaphysical language as well as the relation of language to our social and personal experience. A central thesis of Part Three is that our experience of the world is partially but not totally structured by language. Our experience of the world comes first, and our linguistic structuring of that world comes second, and we never completely lose that foundational experience of the world. We can compare our linguistically-structured world with the world as it is present in our pre-linguistic, foundational experience. The first three parts of the book, therefore, present the hermeneutical side of Whitehead's philosophy.

Part Four applies Whitehead's hermeneutical vision to the special case of religion. For Whitehead the term "religion" has to do with the coordination of values and not just with our human interaction with God. Part Four shows how Whitehead's metaphysics of experience, propositions, symbolism, and language shape his view of religion. Religion is thus a test case for the adequacy of Whitehead's metaphysical vision, and especially of the hermeneutical themes in that vision. In Whitehead's opinion, we live our lives on the basis of our pre-linguistic, foundational experience, where religious experience is rooted in this pre-linguistic, foundational experience. One function of religious lan-

---

Human acts such as those of deciding and simplifying, however, are but very sophisticated developments of certain generic characteristics which apply to any genuinely real thing. The book as a whole is our explanation of these claims.

guage, nevertheless, is to elicit our religious experiences into the realm of ordinary, conscious experience. I also investigate how religious language shapes our experience of the world, making us more alert to dimensions of experience which we might have otherwise overlooked. I examine the role of religious language in maintaining a religious form of life and a religious community. I ask what Whitehead means when he says that religious language works *ex opere operato*. I consider the relation between popular religious language (such as the New Testament stories by and about Jesus) and the metaphysical language of speculative philosophy. Lastly, I engage in a literary experiment in which I ask how to explicate from a Whiteheadian point of view the Biblical claim that God creates the world through his word.

There are two things which this book is not. First, it is not a general survey of modern hermeneutical thinking. At one stage in the book's development, I wrote several chapters in which I related Whitehead's hermeneutical vision to that of Schleiermacher, Heidegger, Gadamer, and others. The results were completely unsatisfactory because there is no adequate exposition of these hermeneutical motifs in Whitehead. If I made my exposition of Whitehead simple enough to be intelligible to most readers, I ended up trivializing his views. If I made my discussion of Whitehead sophisticated enough to be a serious presentation of his view, my chapters became far too complex. As I wrote, I became keenly aware of the utter lack of an adequate exposition of these hermeneutical motifs in Whitehead. I chose to write a serious exposition of Whitehead's theory of experience, propositions, language, and religion. My hope is that the appearance of this book provides a solid basis for including Whiteheadian motifs in the contemporary discussion of hermeneutics.

Second, this book is not an introduction to Whitehead's metaphysics; rather it presupposes an elementary knowledge of his system. I also tried writing some preliminary chapters to introduce Whitehead's metaphysics, and I discovered that, to be satisfactory, a book must focus on either introducing Whitehead's system as a whole or developing in depth the hermeneutical stream in his writings. I chose to elaborate fully this hermeneutical stream because it has never been done.

In my classes I have used three books to introduce Whitehead to my students: William Christian's *An Interpretation of Whitehead's Metaphysics*; Elizabeth Kraus's *The Metaphysics of Experience: A Companion to Whitehead's "Process and Reality"*; and Ivor Leclerc's *Whitehead's Metaphysics: An Introductory Exposition*. All three have merit, but the students have tended to find Leclerc's work the most helpful entrance into the world of Whiteheadian thought. (Christian's and Leclerc's works are quite old, and Kraus's work is a bit difficult to serve as an introduction to the complete neophyte. There is need for a comprehensive and up-to-date introduction to Whitehead's metaphysics.) My goal in writing this book is to make a contribution to the literature on Whitehead that is useful both to the reader who knows Whitehead only "somewhat" and to the Whiteheadian expert who may have never approached Whitehead from this linguistic/hermeneutical perspective.

During the composition of this book, Lewis Ford's book, *The Emergence of Whitehead's Metaphysics* appeared (1984). Lewis's book, which deals with the many stages in the development of Whitehead's thinking, implied that I had been writing my book from the standpoint of what he calls Whitehead's "final philosophy" (p. xii). For the most part, it is not particularly useful to complicate my book by reference to the history of Whitehead's personal development. Where a discussion of Whitehead's personal philosophical journey does illumine his "final position," however, I have freely drawn on Lewis's work.

Much earlier (1978), David Ray Griffin and Donald W. Sherburne's corrected edition of Whitehead's central work *Process and Reality* appeared. This corrected edition was necessary because the original editions, published by the Macmillan Company in the United States and Cambridge University Press in Great Britain, contain many, many typographical errors. Earlier still, in 1963, George Kline had already identified many of the errors in the text of *Process and Reality*. Kline conveniently divided these errors into three categories, running from the most obvious to the most conjectural. Griffin and Sherburne's edition of *Process and Reality* takes this resource into account. Our quotations from *Process and Reality* follow the corrections made by Griffin and Sherburne. We have noted in the footnotes one or two places where Griffin and Sherburne's corrections differ from Kline's suggested corrections.

For technical reasons the pagination in Griffin and Sherburne's edition of *Process and Reality* differs entirely from that in the original Macmillan edition. Thus from the start of my project I was confronted with the choice of which edition to cite. I chose to cite the original because the corrected edition includes the page numbers of the original edition in its text. Citation of the original edition allows readers of both the original edition and the corrected edition to find the indicated passage, whereas citation of the corrected edition would have allowed a reader to find the indicated passage only in the corrected edition.

Whitehead's works have been published in many different editions over the years. In this book, I have tried to refer to those which the reader will find readily available on the market. In cases where two different editions may be purchased, I have chosen that which has the pagination of the original edition. Since I cite some books repeatedly, I have found it convenient to use the following abbreviations, recommended by the journal *Process Studies*, for them. (Full bibliographical information for each book may be obtained in the bibliography, which gives the publication data both for the original edition and for the edition cited in this book [note especially SMW].)

AI   *Adventures of Ideas*
CN   *Concept of Nature*
IM   *An Introduction to Mathematics*
MT   *Modes of Thought*
PR   *Process and Reality: An Essay in Cosmology*
RM   *Religion in the Making*
S   *Symbolism: Its Meaning and Effects*
SMW   *Science and the Modern World*

The references to Whitehead's books have lowercase letters after the page numbers: for example, 173b or 479a. Such a letter refers to a specific paragraph on the page in question. The letter "a" refers to the first paragraph on a page, regardless of whether that paragraph begins on the page in question or was carried over from the previous page. The letter "b" refers to the second paragraph, and so forth. Thus PR 158f refers to the sixth paragraph on page 158 of *Process and Reality*, while S 9a refers to the first paragraph on page 9 of *Symbolism*.

For the sake of clarity, I have introduced some stylistic peculiarities. Single quotes set off technical terms which have an unusual meaning in Whitehead's own writings. The reader will find, for example, 'concrescence', 'prehension', and 'proposition'. We use double quotes for other technical terms — both for those which are common in the larger philosophical tradition and those which I have introduced. The reader will find, therefore, "ordinary language," "necessity," and "reality." Many words, however, will have both a special meaning in Whitehead's system and another (usually more general) meaning. The reader will find 'truth' and "truth," 'proposition' and "proposition," and 'reality' and "reality." When 'truth' occurs in the text, the reader will know that the reference is to Whitehead's notion of truth. When "truth" occurs, the reader will know that the reference is to some notion of truth which is not limited to Whitehead's technical definition. In this regard, it is to be noted that Whitehead sets a word off in quotation marks not only to mention the word, but also to remind the reader that the word in question is being used in a technical or extended sense. I have followed Whitehead's example in this.

There is a second use for single quotes: to set off eternal objects. 'Red' refers thus to an eternal object, whereas "red" refers to the ordinary color as it is extended in space and time.

Lastly, in the body of this book I have used the editorial "we" except when offering my own personal history as an example of some point. Thus "we" present "our" interpretation of the linguistic/hermeneutical stream of Whitehead's philosophy, but the difficulty of an adult's learning a second language may be illustrated by "my" struggles with learning Japanese when "I" was in my mid-thirties.

I hope that this book proves useful to a variety of readers and that it stimulates additional development both in the area of Whiteheadian studies and in the broader circles of hermeneutical discussion. It is my further hope that through this book I can share, not uncritically, something of the beauty and power of the Whiteheadian vision.

Ad Majorem Gloriam Dei

PART ONE: PROPOSITIONS

Part one presents a systematic survey of Alfred North Whitehead's theory of propositions. We place our presentation of propositions within the context of several other issues, such as the nature of truth, consciousness, and actuality. The completeness of this survey, however, will be limited. We will not discuss the implications of Whitehead's theory of propositions for his theories of sense experience, language, or religion. Those are the topics for the remaining parts of our book.

1 The Stages of Concrescence as the Context for Propositional and Intellectual Feelings

WHITEHEAD DEVELOPS HIS THEORY OF PROPOSITIONS in a language created specifically for this purpose. An effective way of introducing his technical vocabulary is to organize the presentation around the notion of concrescence. This is especially appropriate since Whitehead himself uses this principle of organization in one of his discussions of propositions in *Process and Reality*.[1]

The concrescence of an actual entity can be divided into phases. In *Process and Reality*, there is no set number of these phases; rather, the number varies according to the expository goal Whitehead has in mind. For our purposes, it will be convenient to divide the concrescence into five phases. They are (1) the conformal phase, (2) the conceptual phase, (3) the comparative phase, (4) the intellectual phase, and (5) the satisfaction. Not all entities attain the intellectual phase, although all actual entities must arrive at a satisfaction of some sort (PR 39b, 335c).

I

In the conformal stage, a concrescing actual entity prehends, directly or indirectly,[2] every actual entity in its past (PR 366a).[3] These are physical

---

1. One of the chapters in *Process and Reality* which is devoted to propositions is Chapter IV of Part III. Part III, however, is a discussion of the concrescence of an actual entity. Thus Whitehead sets his theory of propositions in the context of the concrescence of an actual entity.
2. For a discussion of the distinction between direct and indirect prehensions, see PR 345b-c, 435c, and 468c-69a. It must be noted that Whitehead's terminology at this point is quite fluid. Sometimes he uses the words 'immediate' and 'mediate' in place of 'direct' and 'indirect', giving the latter two terms still other meanings. For an example of one of these other meanings for 'direct' and 'indirect' see pages below, pp. 15-17.
3. We discuss this point further in Chapter Three, Section V, pp. 87-90.

prehensions. The prehension by the concrescing actual entity of a single past actual entity is called a 'simple physical feeling' (PR 361a). (A 'simple physical feeling' may also be called a 'simple physical prehension'.) This first stage is the stage of simple physical feelings; the concrescence begins[4] as a collection of simple physical prehensions destined for integration into one determinate satisfaction (PR 362b; cf. PR 66a). These simple feelings are the means whereby the past is included in the present. The past actual entity is included in the concrescing actual entity, not merely in the sense that the past actual entity is mirrored in the present actual entity, but also in the sense that the past actual entity becomes a part of the very nature, of the 'real internal constitution', of the concrescing actual entity.[5] And in addition to this inclusion of the past actual entity in the present one, the present actual entity feels the past actual entity with a subjective form which reenacts the nature of the prehended actual entity. For example, if the past actual entity was prehended as a green item, then the prehending actual entity will not only have a green item as the datum of that prehension, but in addition the subjective form of the prehension of that green item will itself have a greenish nature. In other words, the eternal object green will not only be a determinant of the datum of that prehension, but it will also function as a determinate of the subjective form of that prehension (PR 364c). At this first stage, therefore, the present must conform to the past. Simple physical feelings are conformal feelings (PR 364c).

II

The second phase is the conceptual stage. In the conceptual stage, "feelings emerge which have eternal objects as their data."[6] These conceptual prehensions, however, do not arise at random. They are formed in accordance with the fourth categoreal obligation, The Category of Conceptual Valuation, which reads as follows:

> From each physical feeling there is the derivation of a purely conceptual feeling whose datum is the eternal object determinant of the definiteness of the actual entity, or of the nexus, physically felt (PR 39i-40a).

Thus in our example in the previous paragraph, the simple physical prehension of the green past actual entity gives rise, in the prehending actual entity, to a conceptual prehension with the eternal object green as

---

4. In Chapter Two, Section II, pp. 42-51, we will discuss the meanings of the terms "begin," "end," "before," and "later" as they apply to the concrescence of an actual entity.

5. In Chapter Three, Section II, pp. 65-76, we will defend our interpretation of the act of concrescence, according to which the past is included or incorporated into the present concrescence.

6. Spencer, "The Ethics of Alfred North Whitehead," 66.

its datum. It is not our purpose in this chapter to give an analysis of the notion of an eternal object; nor will we analyze the notion of mentality which is closely associated with it. Suffice it to say that an eternal object is a potential—Whitehead calls it a "pure potential" (PR 32i). It is a potential for the determination of fact. Consider the eternal object which is a specific shade of green. This green might be one of the characteristics of *any* actual entity; that is, as far as the eternal object itself is concerned, there is no actual entity which this shade of green might not characterize. Of course, in the real world, there are limitations on the kinds of entities which actually are characterized by this shade of green. For example, green will not be among the characteristics of the actual entities which constitute the hair of a horse. But, and this is the important point, the reasons why a horse cannot be green have to do with the laws of nature and the patterns of relevance among eternal objects established by God; and these reasons are all external to the essence of that shade of green. In terms of the eternal object itself, there is no reason why that eternal object, that shade of green, might not characterize the actual entities making up the hair of the horse. Again, the actual entities making up the wall of my study are colored a certain shade of gold. As such, those actual entities constituting my study wall cannot also be characterized by the particular shade of green in question, at least not in the same way as they are characterized by the gold. There is, however, nothing internal to the eternal object of that shade of green which rules out the possibility of the walls of my study being green; it is an external fact that the walls are gold, and *that* is the reason why they cannot be green. In sum, eternal objects are the *pure potentials* for the determination (i.e., characterization) of fact.[7]

Rather than formally discussing the nature of a conceptual prehension, we present the chart on the following page, which shows some of the ways in which Whitehead distinguishes between the physical aspects and the conceptual and mental aspects of our world. By observing the range of notions with which Whitehead associates the term 'physical' and the range he associates with 'conceptual' and 'mental', it is possible to gain a rather clear and synoptic view of his understanding of these terms.

A lengthy paper could be written on the precise content which Whitehead gives to each of these contrasts. For example, in number 12 Whitehead makes it very clear that one particular can enter into the description of another particular (PR 79c-80a), while even a universal has its individual essence (SMW 165a). Nonetheless, a useful picture does emerge of Whitehead's general understanding of these terms.

---

7. In Whitehead's philosophy, the same basic point is made by the ontological principle which states that actual entities are the only reasons. Therefore, the reason why my wall is gold must stem, according to the ontological principle, from the nature of some set of actual entities and not from an eternal object considered in abstraction from actual entities. See PR 28b.

Physical	*Conceptual/Mental*
1. Determinate	1. Indeterminate
2. Fact	2. Ideal
3. Identity	3. Contrast
4. Repetition	4. Novelty
5. Efficient Cause	5. Final Cause
6. Force	6. Persuasion
7. Conformity	7. Autonomy
8. Actual	8. Potential
9. Public	9. Private
10. Temporal	10. Eternal
11. Spatial	11. Transpatial
12. Particular	12. Universal

It is in the realm of the conceptual and mental, according to contrast number 4 above, that novelty enters the world. And yet if the data of
every conceptual prehension were totally derived from its corresponding
previous simple physical prehension, then there would be no real novelty—the universe would simply repeat itself forever. To meet this need for
prehensions of novel eternal objects, Whitehead introduces reversion. He
describes reversion this way:

> There is secondary origination of conceptual feelings with data which are
> partially identical with, and partially diverse from, the eternal objects
> forming the data in the first phase of the mental pole. The diversity is a rel-
> evant diversity determined by the subjective aim (PR 40b).

In other words, the conceptual prehensions which were derived from the
simple physical feelings give rise in turn to still other prehensions, these
other prehensions being conceptual prehensions of new eternal objects.
These "new" eternal objects are, however, new only in relation to the actual world of the prehending actual entity. In themselves eternal objects are
timeless and gain their being, their status in reality, from the fact that they
are the objects of God's eternal conceptual prehensions of all eternal objects
(PR 73a-b).[8] In short, it is the concrescing actual entity's simple physical
feeling of God at the first conformal stage which makes the reverted conceptual feelings possible at this second, conceptual stage (PR 377d).

The introduction of the notion of a 'simple physical prehension of
God' requires the concomitant introduction of the notion of a 'hybrid

8. In this book, we will always understand Whitehead as considering God a single
actual entity. This seems to be quite clearly stated in passages such as PR 28a and PR 521c.
Some scholars hold that, on his own principles, Whitehead *ought* to have considered God a
society of actual entities; but even these men typically agree that Whitehead himself saw God
as *an* actual entity. See, for example, Cobb, *A Christian Natural Theology,* 188. We shall, therefore, consider, without further comment, Whitehead's God *an* actual entity.

prehension'. When one actual entity, say A, prehends a past actual entity, say B, actual entity A never prehends the entire actual entity B. Rather, only a part of B is included in the 'real internal constitution' of A; as Whitehead says, "Objectification involves elimination" (PR 517b).[9] A can, therefore, include in itself (i.e., positively prehend) only a part of B. The parts of B are, however, nothing but prehensions. Now if A prehends B by means of one of B's own physical prehensions, then A has a 'pure physical prehension' of B (PR 375b). If, on the other hand, A prehends B by means of one of B's own conceptual prehensions, then A has a 'hybrid physical prehension' of B (PR 376b). Obviously, the concrescing actual entity will prehend God in the first, conformal stage by means of a hybrid physical prehension, since the data in the concrescing actual entity's prehension of God are eternal objects.[10]

We note the following points. First, a *simple* physical prehension may be either pure or hybrid, and yet remain simple. The criterion for a simple physical prehension is that it be a prehension of a single past actual entity. It makes no difference if that single past entity be prehended by means of one of its own physical prehensions or by means of one of its own conceptual prehensions; the concrescing actual entity is still prehending that past actual entity by means of a simple physical prehension.[11] Second, it should also be noted that the later stages of concrescence of an actual entity involve the integration of physical and conceptual prehensions, and these later integrations are also called prehensions. Now it is possible for a concrescing actual entity, A, to prehend a past actual entity, B, by means of one of B's later integrative prehensions. Such a prehension by A will necessarily be a hybrid prehension of B.[12]

9. Every finite entity's prehension of God therefore involves the elimination from positive feeling of some portion of God. For support of this claim, we may point to Ford, "Is There a Distinct Superjective Nature?" 228. The converse, however, may not hold: namely, it may be that in prehending a finite entity in the world, God is not required to eliminate any portion of that finite entity from positive feeling. We will discuss this issue further in Part Four, Chapter Nineteen.

10. More precisely, the new actual entity derives its subjective aim from this prehension of God. The subjective aim will be considered in greater detail in Chapter Two, Section III, pp. 51-61. The point to note is this. As we shall see in the next paragraph, conceptual feelings can be either pure or impure. The concrescing entity A, therefore, may feel either a pure or an impure conceptual feeling in past entity B, and still A has a *hybrid* physical prehension of B.

11. Thus Spencer is in error when he presents simple physical prehensions and hybrid physical prehensions as disjunctive alternatives ("The Ethics of Alfred North Whitehead," 65). It is quite possible to have a simple hybrid physical prehension.

12. Whitehead sometimes uses the term 'physical' in an extended sense. For example, see PR 474b, where presentational immediacy is called a physical feeling. We will present a full discussion of Whitehead's concept of 'presentational immediacy' in Part Two, Chapter Ten. The point to note here is that presentational immediacy, as we shall see, is not a physical feeling in the obvious sense that we are using in the main text.

Likewise, Whitehead sometimes uses the term 'conceptual' in an extended sense.

III

The third stage is the comparative stage. In this phase, the concrescing actual entity integrates conceptual feelings with physical feelings. These integrative feelings consist of comparisons of the data of the conceptual feelings with the data of the physical feelings.

A

It is at this stage that transmutation takes place. Transmutation is defined as follows: when, in accordance with conceptual valuation (i.e., the derivation of a conceptual feeling at stage two from its corresponding physical prehension at stage one) or with reversion (i.e., the derivation at stage two of additional conceptual prehensions),

> . . . one, and the same, conceptual feeling is derived impartially by a prehending subject from its analogous simple physical feelings of various actual entities, then in a subsequent phase of integration—of these simple physical feelings together with the derivate conceptual feeling—the prehending subject may transmute the datum of this conceptual feeling into a contrast with the nexus of those prehended actual entities, or of some part of that nexus; so that the nexus (or its part), thus qualified, is the objective datum of a feeling entertained by this prehending subject (PR 384a).

This extended use of 'conceptual' is much rarer than the extended use of 'physical', but it is found. For example, "This conceptual feeling, by its reference to definite regions, belongs to the secondary type termed 'propositional feelings'" (PR 477b). The point to note is that, properly speaking, a propositional feeling is an integrative feeling and not a conceptual one. Yet Whitehead can, when wishing to draw attention to certain aspects of propositional feelings, call them conceptual feelings.

Whitehead also speaks of impure physical prehensions. An impure physical prehension is an integrative prehension which involves both physical and conceptual prehensions. An impure physical prehension is 'impure' because it does not draw only upon prior physical prehensions but draws upon conceptual prehensions as well. Whitehead calls such a proposition 'physical' when he wishes to focus attention upon its subordinate physical prehensions or when he wishes to emphasize how the proposition is functioning in some particular situation as a physical prehension. There are also impure conceptual prehensions. Whitehead describes an integrative prehension as an impure conceptual prehension when he wishes to draw attention to the subordinate conceptual prehensions or to emphasize how it is functioning as a conceptual prehension. In the last analysis, every impure physical prehension is also an impure conceptual prehension, and the choice between calling it a physical or a conceptual prehension is really a matter of emphasis.

Perhaps we should also note the difference between a hybrid physical prehension and an impure physical prehension. Basically, a hybrid physical prehension occurs at the first stage of the concrescence of a new entity. It is a *physical* prehension because it is a prehension of a past *actual entity*—as opposed to a prehension of an eternal object. And it is a *hybrid* prehension because its dative prehension (i.e., the part of the past entity which is felt by the new entity) is either a pure or an impure conceptual feeling—as opposed to a pure physical feeling. In distinction to this, an impure physical feeling is an integrative feeling which can occur only at a later stage within the concrescing entity.

The wording here is somewhat complicated, to say the least. The idea of transmutation itself, however, is quite simple. For an explanation of transmutation, consider diagram 1.[13] The rectangular boxes are the dative past actual entities. L, M, and N are simple physical prehensions of those entities. The diagram has "pipes" from L, M, and N to their respective past actual entities. The pipes indicate that L, M, and N "include" the past actual entities.[14] The pipes represent either pure or hybrid physical prehensions. L, M, and N, along with all other simple physical prehensions (which are not shown), constitute the first, conformal stage of concrescence. Each of these simple physical prehensions gives rise to a conceptual prehension of an eternal object. These relationships are represented in diagram 1 by additional pipes from L, M, and N to O. The use of pipes indicates that the eternal object prehended at O is present at L, M, and N and was not "pulled out of thin air." In the diagram, simple physical prehensions L, M, and N all give rise to a conceptual prehension of the same eternal object. We have labeled this conceptual prehension O. O and all the other pure conceptual prehensions derivative from simple physical prehensions constitute the second stage of concrescence. In the third stage, the concrescing actual entity now applies, at T, the eternal object which is the datum of the conceptual prehension O and which is derived from L, M, and N individually to the dative actual entities, x, y, and z, considered as a group, as a whole, as a unit, as a nexus. Thus the set of actual entities x, y, and z will now be viewed by the concrescing actual entity as one unit which is actually and concretely characterized by that eternal object which is the datum for conceptual prehension O. We may elaborate this last point by saying that in the transmutation, the eternal object felt at O is applied to the nexus *physically* (PR 384b). The concrescing entity thus feels the nexus composed of x, y, and z as though *it* (that is, the nexus as a whole) were the *source* of the eternal object felt at O. In other words, the concrescing entity feels the transmuted nexus as though that nexus were a genuine unit in the world, concretely characterized by the eternal object in question.

Diagram 2 illustrates transmutation with reversion. For the sake of simplicity we have drawn lines rather than pipes between the prehensions and their respective data. The reader must be careful not to be misled by the use of lines. The prehensions do *not* first exist and then establish a rela-

---

13. In endpaper. Donald W. Sherburne uses diagrams to illustrate Whitehead's discussion of concrescence. I have found his diagrams to be extremely helpful and hope the diagrams in this book prove to be equally useful. The diagrams in this book are original and, therefore, different. For additional pictorial guidance to the stages of concrescence, the reader may wish to consult Sherburne's book, *A Whiteheadian Aesthetic: Some Implications of Whitehead's Metaphysical Speculation*, 41-71.

14. We will consider this theme of "inclusion" throughout the book. The discussion of diagram 4 provides a preliminary orientation.

tion to the data. The prehension *is* the new actual entity's inclusion of that data. In this diagram, we have used solid lines to indicate that L, M, and N are physical prehensions, and we have used broken lines to indicate that O and P are conceptual prehensions.

The situation in diagram 2 is basically the same as that in diagram 1, except that at the second stage the conceptual prehension O gives rise to an additional conceptual prehension P. The difference between the eternal objects prehended by O and P may be small and unimportant or it may be large and vital, but they will differ. In the transmutation, represented by T, it is the eternal object prehended by P which is predicated of the group of actual entities x, y, and z. Since the eternal object prehended at P is not to be found in x, y, and z, individually or collectively, it follows that the concrescing actual entity will not be accurate in its feeling of the nexus composed of x, y, and z. It must be noted, however, that this inaccuracy may be felicitous as well as infelicitous.

We have three comments on transmutation. First, in both diagrams, we have drawn the bracket for L, M, and N inside stage one. This is to emphasize that transmutation feels the nexus of x, y, and z as a physical reality, definitely and concretely characterized by the eternal object prehended at O or at P, as the case may be. The transmuted nexus is felt as a real fact in the real world (PR 355a). Second, it is through transmutation that people, houses, stones, parliaments, and books emerge as unified "objects" from the multitude of separate and distinct actual entities (PR 98a-99c). Lastly, transmutation is the master principle of order. That is, the patterns in the world are lost in the pullulating swarm of separate actual entities. But simplified by transmutation, the order inherent in the seemingly chaotic jungle of actual entities begins to stand out from its background; the order is emphasized; and in conscious experience (which appears only later in the concrescence), we find ourselves able to apprehend the world as a realm of order and pattern (PR 383b).

B

It is in this third stage, the comparative stage, that physical purposes and propositional prehensions arise.[15] Whitehead considers propositional prehensions more advanced than physical purposes, the idea being that propositions are an evolutionary development out of physical purposes. In our discussion of these two entities, however, we will first consider the more ad-

15. Propositional prehensions are not normally called comparative feelings. So it may seem a bit odd to stress their appearance during this third, comparative, phase of concrescence. As we shall see in the following pages, however, a propositional feeling certainly does feel a contrast — a contrast between the logical subject(s) and the predicate of the proposition. It is not, therefore, idiosyncratic to introduce propositions under the phase of concrescence called "the comparative stage."

vanced propositions and turn afterwards to the more primitive physical purposes. The reason for this reverse order is that it is easier to describe how physical purposes lack certain characteristics of propositions than it is to describe physical purposes in their own right. It is in this third stage, the comparative stage, that propositions arise. Now propositions are the data of propositional feelings (PR 287c, 391a-b). We will start our analysis of propositions, therefore, by observing the genesis of propositional feelings. There are two types of propositional feelings: perceptive feelings and imaginative feelings (PR 399c). We will consider perceptive feelings first since they are simpler. Diagram 3 will guide our discussion of perceptive feelings. Here the concrescing actual entity has a simple physical feeling of a past actual entity labeled y; the simple physical feeling is L in our diagram. L, in accordance with the principle of conceptual valuation, in turn gives rise to conceptual prehension O. Now P.F. is a feeling of a contrast between the eternal object felt at O and the actual entity felt at L; but in this contrast, the data of both L and O are modified by P.F. For example, the datum at L is felt by P.F. as an abstraction, as a bare 'it'. To explain how the datum at L is felt by P.F. as a bare 'it', we must take a closer look at the nature of a prehension. Whitehead divides a positive prehension into five parts:

> A feeling—that is, a positive prehension—is essentially a transition effecting a concrescence. Its complex constitution is analysable into five factors which express what that transition consists of, and effects. The factors are: (i) the 'subject' which feels, (ii) the 'initial data' which are to be felt, (iii) the 'elimination' in virtue of negative prehensions, (iv) the 'objective datum' which is felt, (v) 'the subjective form' which is *how* that subject feels that objective datum (PR 337d-38a).

In other words, there is usually[16] more in the datum than can be incorporated into the prehension, and as a result there is the need to eliminate some of the contents of the datum. Diagram 4 will help illustrate this point. In diagram 4, the datum has been divided (arbitrarily) into five parts.[17] β is a prehension within a concrescing actual entity. Now the concrescing actual entity has no use for parts i, ii, iv, and v in its later integrative prehensions, so they are eliminated by negative prehensions. The negative prehensions are indicated by the lines of dots. This means that the contents of i, ii, iv, and v are not included in the later integrations of the concrescing actual entity. But part iii is useful to the concrescing entity; therefore, it is positively prehended—that is, the contents of iii are included in the concrescing entity. In fact, prehension β is nothing other than the act of including part iii in the concrescing entity. Part iii is now internal to the concrescing entity. The datum which includes all five parts is called, thus,

---

16. God's prehensions of finite actual entities are an exception. See Part Four, Chapter Nineteen, Section I, pp. 333-34.

17. The 'parts' are subordinate prehensions constitutive of the datum.

the 'initial datum', while the part of the datum which is positively included in β, that is, part iii, is called the 'objective datum'.

It may be well to note the limitations of diagram 4 before continuing. First, the diagram does not show the subject of β. Second, the diagram does not illustrate the subjective form of β. Since the content of β and part iii are one and the same reality, it is only the subjective form of β which distinguishes the prehension β from the objective datum, that is, from part iii of the initial datum.

We return now to our discussion of diagram 3. We were discussing how P.F. modified the contents of both L and O. Thus P.F. prehends the datum of L; but through negative prehensions, all the content of this datum of L has been eliminated except (A) the fact that this datum of L is real and (B) the location of this datum of L. To be more precise, since L itself is the positive inclusion (in the concrescing actual entity) of some portion of the past actual entity y, it follows that P.F. is feeling the past actual entity y with all of y's content eliminated except (A) the fact that y is an actuality and (B) the location of y. In diagram 3, the fact that P.F. feels y (which is the datum of L) as a bare 'it' is indicated by the inclusion of a square ⃞L in the lower arm. ⃞L is placed in the third phase to indicate that P.F. effects the reduction of y to a bare 'it'.

In diagram 3, the original conceptual feeling O has as its datum an eternal object. Let p be the eternal object which O prehends. O, therefore, prehends p in p's full generality as a possible character of *any* actual entity. On the other hand P.F. alters the status of p when it prehends O; P.F. limits the generality of p's status as a possible character of *any* actual entity to the much narrower status of being a possible character of y, where y has been reduced to a bare 'it'. In short, the potentiality of p is no longer pure; rather p's potentiality has been reduced to the potentiality of being a determinant of y.

The contrast felt by P.F. between p and y, where y is an actual entity reduced to a status as a bare 'it' and where p's potentiality has been focused on y, is called a proposition. P.F. feels a proposition.

The introduction of some additional terminology will be necessary for our later discussion of propositions and propositional feelings. First, in the above discussion, p is the 'predicative pattern'. The predicative pattern may be simple (e.g., 'being a specific shade of green') or it may be complicated (e.g., 'being subject to the wrath of God excepting in the case where there was a reconciliation to him through Christ'). But in either case, the predicative pattern is an eternal object with its potentiality for being a determinant of fact, focused upon a specified set of actual entities.[18]

18. The limiting case, of course, would be a set consisting of one actual entity. For the sake of simplicity, the discussion so far in this paper has been in terms of a single actual entity serving as the logical subject. Cf. PR 393b-94a.

Second, the conceptual feeling whose datum is the predicative pattern (in its full generality as an eternal object, potentially determining any actual entity) is called the 'predicative feeling'. In diagram 3, O is the predicative feeling (PR 398a). Third, the physical feeling from which the predicative feeling was derived is called the 'physical recollection'. In our illustration, L is the physical recollection (PR 397d). (It may be noted that in place of 'physical recollection' Whitehead also uses the term 'physical recognition'; these two phrases seem to be completely interchangeable.) Fourth, the actual entities upon which the predicative pattern is focused are called the 'logical subjects' (PR 36a, 283c). In a proposition, however, the predicative pattern is focused upon a set of actual entities only insofar as those entities are considered bare 'its'. Thus in diagram 3 actual entity y is the logical subject, but it is the logical subject only insofar as it has been reduced to a bare 'it' by means of negative prehensions at P.F. Fifth, the physical prehension through which the logical subjects enter the concrescing actual entity is called the 'indicative feeling'. In diagram 3, L is the indicative feeling (PR 397d).

It will be observed that in diagram 3 L is both the physical recognition and the indicative feeling. Thus P.F. is a perceptive feeling, since a perceptive feeling is defined as a propositional feeling in which the physical recognition and the indicative feeling are identical (PR 400b). There are, however, two sorts of perceptive feelings. The first is an authentic perceptive feeling. In an authentic perceptive feeling, there is no reversion in the concrescing actual entity which is the subject (PR 400d-401a, 410a). That is, the predicative pattern is derived from the predicative feeling (i.e., O) which in turn is derived from the physical recognition (i.e., L), all without reversion. Diagram 3 outlines the genesis of an authentic perceptive feeling. (There are two subvarieties of authentic perceptive feelings: direct authentic perceptive feelings and indirect authentic perceptive feelings. It will be convenient to postpone our discussion of them, however.) The second type of perceptive feeling is an unauthentic perceptive feeling. Diagram 5 outlines an unauthentic perceptive feeling. In diagram 5, we assign basically the same meanings to the symbols as we did in diagram 3. Thus in diagram 5, y is the initial datum for simple physical prehension L. L is both the indicative feeling and the physical recollection. L gives rise to conceptual feeling O, which in turn by reversion gives rise to conceptual feeling P. P is the predicative feeling; this is because the integrative feeling P.F. takes the eternal object which is the datum of P and focuses its potentiality upon y considered as a bare 'it'. The status of y as a bare 'it' for P.F. is indicated in the chart by $\boxed{L}$. The logical subject is y. P.F. is a *perceptive* feeling because L serves both as the indicative feeling as well as the physical recollection. Moreover, P.F. is an *unauthentic* perceptive feeling because the predicative feeling P is derived by means of reversion from the physical recollection L (PR 399d-400a).[19]

The other main form of propositional feeling is the imaginative feeling. Thus perceptive feelings and imaginative feelings together form the set of propositional feelings. An imaginative feeling is defined as a propositional feeling in which the physical recollection is distinct from the indicative feeling (PR 400c). This is illustrated by diagram 6. Here y—reduced to a bare 'it', as indicated by $\boxed{\text{M}}$—is the logical subject, and M is the indicative feeling since it is through M that y enters into the concrescence. O is the predicative feeling from which feeling I.F. derives the predicative pattern. But O is derived not from M, the indicative feeling, but from L, where L is separate and distinct from M. Thus L is the physical recollection, and this physical recollection is quite distinct from the indicative feeling. I.F., therefore, has met the criterion for being an imaginative feeling.

It may be observed that there is a basic similarity of an imaginative feeling to an unauthentic perceptive feeling. In both cases the logical subject is contrasted with an eternal object which did not directly derive from that logical subject. In other words, in both cases the concrescing entity characterizes the logical subject (y in both diagrams 5 and 6) by means of a predicate whose source is not that logical subject (i.e., y).

It may also be noted that in an imaginative feeling, the presence or absence of reversion in the concrescing actual entity is normally a matter of little consequence. The reason for this may be readily observed by adding a reversion to diagram 6. This new situation is illustrated in diagram 7. In diagram 7, the conceptual feeling O has given rise to a reverted conceptual feeling P, and this P serves as the predicative feeling for I.F.—that is, the predicative pattern, which I.F. contrasts with the logical subject y, has been derived from P instead of O. Now it will be observed that O itself does not derive from y. (It derives from x.) The eternal object prehended at O, therefore, may be just as remote from the eternal objects which actually characterize y as the eternal object prehended at P; in fact, there is no reason in theory why the eternal object obtained by reversion at P might not be *more* similar to the eternal objects characterizing y than the eternal object prehended at O.

Let us give a concrete example. Suppose that, in both diagrams 6 and 7, actual entity x is characterized by a deep red and that actual entity y is characterized by a deep blue. L and M, of course, are simple physical prehensions of x and y respectively. Further suppose that in both diagrams 6 and 7, L gives rise to O, which prehends the eternal object 'deep red of

19. The paragraph cited in the text (PR 399d-400a) is misplaced, according to Kline, "Corrigenda for *Process and Reality*," 206. It belongs between PR 401b and PR 401c, where it has been placed in the corrected edition of *Process and Reality*.

the specified sort', and M gives rise to Q, which prehends the eternal object 'deep blue of the specified sort'. Now, in diagram 6, I.F. feels the logical subject y (reduced to a mere 'it') as potentially deep red (while in fact, y is deep blue). In addition, let us suppose that, in diagram 7, the conceptual feeling O (which has the eternal object 'deep red' as its datum) gives rise to a reverted conceptual feeling P whose datum is the eternal object 'light blue of the specified sort'. Then in diagram 7, I.F. feels the logical subject y as potentially light blue (while in fact, it is deep blue). Thus it accidentally happens that the I.F. of diagram 7 is closer to the truth (i.e., the actual character of y) than the I.F. of diagram 6. Further, it is clear that by altering the eternal object prehended at P in diagram 7, we can make the resulting I.F. either still closer to the truth about the way y is actually characterized (e.g., let the datum for P be the precise deep blue which characterized y) or more remote from the way that y is characterized (e.g., let the datum for P be a light green). Thus in an imaginative feeling, reversion in the subject may or may not cause the predicative pattern to be less similar to those eternal objects actually characterizing y. And so it serves no useful purpose to distinguish between an imaginative feeling which has reversion in its genesis and one which does not have reversion in its genesis.

Up to this point our discussion has been artificially simple. We have discussed propositional feelings in which a single actual entity served as the logical subject. But in fact, many propositional feelings have a group (or even many groups) of actual entities, all serving as logical subjects.[20] For example, when we say, "Socrates is mortal," the logical subjects of that proposition are all those actual entities which together constituted that enduring object, that society, which we call Socrates (PR 404a-5a).[21] Since Whitehead claims that, almost without exception, only transmuted physical feelings ever enter consciousness (PR 362a), we will consider a propositional feeling which has many actual entities serving as logical subjects, bound together into a single group by means of the mechanism of transmutation.[22] Our discussion will be conducted in terms of diagram 8.

20. Propositions which become components in a conscious feeling are especially likely to have a multitude of actual entities as logical subjects. Cf. PR 362a, c.

21. In this sentence we call Socrates (including his body) an enduring object. We may note that Whitehead uses the term 'enduring object' ambiguously. In one sense, an enduring object is a society which has personal order—that is, a society where only one actual entity in that society may exist at any one time (PR 50b-52a). In this sense, Socrates, including his body, cannot be an enduring object since many of the actual entities will exist simultaneously with the other actual entities in his body. On the other hand, Whitehead sometimes uses the term "enduring object" to refer to any of those "societies" which traditionally have been called substances. For example, Whitehead lists tables, animal bodies, and stars as enduring objects (AI 265b). In this book we will use the term 'enduring object' in this extended sense, and we will consider a society which has only one member existing at any one time to be a limiting case of an enduring object.

22. Even the proposition to be considered is, however, relatively simple. For a proposition which is genuinely complicated in terms of its logical subjects, consider this:

In one sense, in diagram 8, the indicative feeling is the set of simple physical feelings L, M, and N; but in another sense the indicative feeling is T. P.F. is, clearly, a perceptive feeling. But here P.F. feels the potentiality of the eternal object prehended at O to be a determinant of the *nexus* of actual entities x, y, and z; that is, P.F. applies the eternal object prehended at O to the unit, the whole, the group of actual entities x, y, and z. P.F. is able to consider x, y, and z as a unit because of the transmutation at T. We have two comments on diagram 8. First, an analogous diagram could be drawn for an imaginative feeling. Second, a transmutation of only three actual entities will be very rare; more often the numbers of actual entities transmuted will be in the millions or billions.[23]

Another way, however, in which transmutation can be related to propositional feelings is that in which the transmutation has already taken place in the initial data. Once again, we shall illustrate our discussion in terms of a diagram.

In diagram 9, actual entity A is the concrescing actual entity and K is one of its simple physical feelings. (Actual entity A has other simple physical feelings which are not shown.) From K the concrescing actual entity derives the conceptual feeling W; this allows P.F. to feel the contrast between K (reduced to a bare 'it', as indicated by $\boxed{K}$) and the eternal object which is prehended at W (and which eternal object is focused upon $\boxed{K}$). In diagram 9, actual entity B is in the past of the concrescing entity A; and x, y, z are actual entities in the past of B. In actual entity B, simple prehensions L, M, and N have all given rise to conceptual feeling O, which in turn has given rise to the reverted conceptual feeling P. Lastly, entity B has transmuted the eternal object obtained at P into a determinate of x, y, and z considered as a unity, as a nexus.

In diagram 9, P.F. is a perceptive feeling; this is because K serves both as the indicative feeling and as the physical recollection. Moreover, since there was, within the concrescing actual entity A, no reversion in the genesis of P.F., it follows that P.F. is an authentic perceptive feeling. Previously, on page 12, we mentioned that Whitehead divided authentic perceptive feelings into two types, but we postponed discussing that distinction. We are now in a position to explain the distinction between the

---

"Some of the pre-Christian ancient men reached an age of eighty or more." Clearly the logical subjects are all pre-Christian men. But each of these men is a society of actual entities. We are, thus, considering as logical subjects an indeterminate number of societies (i.e., the men) each of which is a vast multitude of actual entities. Moreover, the proposition is saying that *some* of these societies have the characteristic of reaching eighty years old. And, of course, we are considering each of these actual entities, and each society of them (each man), as reduced to a bare 'it' with only enough character left to locate each actual entity and each nexus (each man) in space and time.

23. Whitehead never states this explicitly. But it is a reasonable doctrine when one remembers that Whitehead does state that it is by means of transmutation that our perceptions of such items as horses emerge.

two types of authentic perceptive feelings, 'direct' and 'indirect'. In a 'direct authentic perceptive feeling' there is no reversion in the genesis of the perceptive feeling within the concrescing actual entity and neither is there reversion in the dative actual entity. In an 'indirect authentic perceptive feeling' there is no reversion in the genesis of the perceptive feeling within the concrescing actual entity, but there is reversion in the dative actual entity (PR 399c-401c, 410a). Diagram 9, therefore, illustrates one type of an 'indirect authentic perceptive feeling'. It is indirect because actual entity B, the dative entity, includes a reverted transmutation of actual entities x, y, and z; the reversion occurs in the derivation of P from O. Since actual entity A prehends B by means of T, it follows that A has "picked up" the transmutation from B and incorporated it into itself. Since ultimately actual entity A is prehending the nexus composed of x, y, and z, the "error" introduced in the reversion from O to P in entity B is carried into A; thus A prehends the nexus x, y, and z as characterized by the eternal object introduced at P, and not by means of the eternal objects genuinely present in the nexus x, y, and z.

In a 'direct authentic perceptive feeling' there is no reversion in the datum. Diagram 9 could easily be changed to an outline of a direct authentic perceptive feeling. All that is required is to eliminate P from the second stage of actual entity B and then to alter T so that its upper arm extends to O in place of P. Since this change eliminates the reversion in the dative actual entity B, it follows that P.F. would now be a direct authentic perceptive feeling. Our discussion of perceptive feelings may be summarized as follows.

Perceptive Feelings: The indicative feeling and the physical recollection are one and the same feeling.

I. Authentic Perceptive Feelings: No reversion in the concrescing actual entity.
    A. Direct Authentic Perceptive Feelings. No reversion in the dative actual entity.
    B. Indirect Authentic Perceptive Feelings. Reversion in the dative actual entity.
II. Unauthentic Perceptive Feelings: Reversion in the concrescing actual entity.[24]

Before continuing, it may be appropriate to make two observations about imaginative feelings. First, as in perceptive feelings, imaginative

24. We have two final comments on perceptive feelings. First, while diagram 3 depicts an authentic perceptive feeling, there is no way of telling from the diagram whether that authentic perceptive feeling is direct or indirect since no information about the contents of y is provided. Second, there are many ways in which reversion can enter into a propositional feeling other than in connection with transmutation—ways which we have not discussed.

feelings also commonly have many logical subjects. And second, one common method for the many logical subjects to enter into the imaginative feeling is through the mechanism of transmutation, either in the concrescing entity or in a dative actual entity. We will not construct another diagram to illustrate this point. To illustrate one way in which many logical subjects might enter into an imaginative feeling, all one would need to do is to take our diagram 6 and then enlarge the actual entity labeled y to show transmutation occurring within y; in other words, the portions of diagram 9 which are labeled "Data in the Past of B" and "Actual Entity B" would be disconnected from K in diagram 9 and connected to M in diagram 6.

C

Propositions are the contrasts felt by propositional feelings. Nonetheless, it is possible to abstract the proposition from its feeling and discuss the proposition in its own identity. Whitehead gives many definitions of propositions, but perhaps the most basic is that a proposition is a 'lure for feeling' (PR 281a-c, 395c). The role of a proposition as grist for the logician's judgment of it as true or false is secondary to the ability of a proposition to elicit feeling on the part of the subject which is prehending the proposition. Not all prehensions of propositions involve consciousness, but it may be easier to grasp Whitehead's thinking on this issue if we consider some propositions as they are part of consciousness. Whitehead suggests that a Christian meditating on the Gospel may not always be consciously making judgments of true or false for each of the propositions in the Gospel; rather he may well be entertaining the propositions for no other reason than to enjoy their powerful impact on his feelings. In fact, he may even eventually judge the Gospel's propositions to be true because of their ability to elicit powerful emotions (PR 281b).

Propositions have such power to evoke feeling because they introduce potentiality into the concrescing actual entity. But it is not potentiality in the abstract which serves as the lure; it is potentiality as it applies to specific elements in the environment. At the simplest level, a proposition is the potentiality of *that* being a wall and blue (or of *that* being a blue wall, or of *that* wall being blue), or of *this* being a table, or of *that* being my wife's reddish-blond hair. Whereas the potentiality of an eternal object is completely general, the potentiality of a proposition is concrete.

A proposition gains its concrete potentiality by modifying both the eternal object ingredient in it (i.e., the predicative pattern) and the actual entities ingredient in it (i.e., the logical subjects). We have already discussed the modification of the actual entities—they are reduced to the status of mere 'its'. And we have also discussed the modification of the eternal object—the complete generality of the potentiality of the eternal object is focused down onto a specific set of actual entities. However, the contrast between an eternal object thus modified and a set of actual entities thus modified *is* a proposition. It is for this reason that Whitehead calls a proposition a hybrid form of entity.

"A proposition is a new kind of entity. It is a hybrid between pure potentialities and actualities" (PR 282c). Whitehead's own summary runs as follows:

> A proposition shares with an eternal object the character of indeterminateness, in that both are definite potentialities *for* actuality with undetermined realization *in* actuality. But they differ in that an eternal object refers to actuality with absolute generality, whereas a proposition refers to indicated logical subjects (PR 395b).

Whitehead also says that propositions "are the tales that perhaps might be told about particular actualities" (PR 392a). What Whitehead apparently has in mind is this. Given that the logical subjects have been stripped of their characteristics, it follows that *any* eternal object may be focused upon them.[25] As such, any proposition with those particular logical subjects is a tale which *might* be told about them.

Someone might object, however, to Whitehead's emphasis on propositions as tales which might be told, as follows. Imagine, says our objector, a proposition about a specified set of actual entities; further imagine that the predicate of this proposition just happens to be an eternal object which in fact does characterize the actual entities which are the subjects of the proposition. In such a case, concludes our objector, it would be incorrect to call that particular proposition a potentiality or a tale which *might* be told, for in concrete fact this proposition tells what *is* the case; this proposition tells not of potentialities but of actualities. Our response to such an objector is to remind him that in a proposition the actual entities are reduced to barren 'its' without character. Thus even if the predicate of the proposition is an eternal object already present in those entities, the element of potentiality is not lost because the proposition *is* the comparison of that predicate with the *barren* logical subjects. The presence or absence of the predicate in the actual entities considered in themselves, before their abstraction into their role as logical subjects, is a matter which is external to the proposition. Thus a proposition is a form of potentiality, regardless of whether that potentiality is actualized or not.

A proposition, then, has an identity and status within Whitehead's metaphysics. Although propositions are found only as the data of propositional prehensions, propositions can be identified and discussed in

25. This will hold providing that there are enough logical subjects to support the predicate. There is something wrong, for example, in focusing the eternal object, 'constituting a set of diverse actual entities', upon a set of logical subjects which has only one member.

abstraction from those prehensions. We have already done so when we discussed propositions as 'lures for feelings', 'hybrid entities', and 'tales which might be told'; Whitehead is clear that it is propositions which are lures for feelings, and not propositional feelings. The following observations will further demonstrate the way in which propositions have an identity and status of their own in Whitehead's system.

One and the same proposition can be the datum for both a perceptive feeling and an imaginative feeling. The difference between a perceptive feeling and an imaginative feeling lies not in the proposition felt but in (A) the difference between their modes of genesis and (B) the difference in their subjective forms. Consider a specific nexus of actual entities; let us call that nexus N. Let us also consider an eternal object p. Then we can construct a proposition of the following sort: "N having characteristic p." Let us call this proposition P. Now P might be the datum in a perceptive feeling if the indicative feeling whereby the concrescing actual entity derives the nexus N is the same as the physical recollection. But P might also be the datum of an imaginative feeling if the indicative feeling is separate and distinct from the physical recollection. Here in the imaginative feeling, even though the predicate p was not derived directly or indirectly from the same feeling as that which provided the nexus N, yet this imaginative feeling is still prehending the contrast between predicate p and nexus N—that is, the imaginative feeling is still feeling proposition P, "N having characteristic p." Thus, the difference between a perceptive feeling of P and an imaginative feeling of P lies not with P but in their diverse geneses. In addition, because of their distinct origins, a perceptive feeling of P and an imaginative feeling of P will likely have different subjective forms. For example, since in a perceptive feeling the indicative feeling is the same as the physical recollection, the perceptive feeling of P will probably prehend P as closely tied to the actual world, whereas, given the diversity of the indicative feeling from the physical recollection in an imaginative feeling, it follows that an imaginative feeling of P will probably prehend P in a more speculative manner. In either case, P remains the same despite the diversity in the subjective forms in the prehensions of P (PR 402a, 417a).[26]

Whitehead also claims that often the same proposition may be felt by more than one actual entity (PR 395c). This is closely related to the position discussed in the above paragraph. There, however, we were observing that the same proposition may be felt as a datum in diverse types of propositional feelings, while here we are observing that the same proposi-

26. It may be worth observing that the identity of propositions, which we have been discussing, may be obtained only via a double abstraction. First, we must lift the propositional feeling out of its context as a subordinate prehension belonging to a specific actual entity. Second, we must then pry the proposition loose from its status as the datum of a propositional feeling (cf. PR 293b).

tion may be found in diverse actual entities. There are, however, certain limitations on which propositions any one particular actual entity can entertain; later we will discuss these limitations.

The same proposition may be judged diversely by various actual entities without that proposition losing its identity (PR 293b). To understand this point, and how it differs from the previous two points, it is necessary to observe that, while all propositions exist only insofar as they are data in propositional feelings, very few of these propositional feelings ever enter into consciousness. But if the same proposition should enter into consciousness in two or more different actual entities, then that one and the same proposition may be judged to be true by one actual entity, false by another, and simply interesting by a third.

The fourth way in which the self-identity and independent status of a proposition may be illustrated from Whitehead's text is this:

> Thus the proposition is in fact true, or false. But its own truth, or its own falsity, is no business of a proposition. That question concerns only a subject entertaining a propositional feeling with that proposition for its datum. Such an actual entity is termed a 'prehending subject' of the proposition (PR 394b-95a).

A proposition is said to be true if its predicative pattern, which in the proposition is applied to the 'stripped' logical subjects, to mere 'its', also characterizes the logical subjects as they exist in their own right, "out-there," before being reduced to mere 'its'. A proposition whose predicative pattern lacks this relation to its logical subjects is false. The truth or falsity of a proposition may be obtained only through a comparison of the role of the predicative pattern within the proposition, as characterizing the stripped logical subjects, with its role outside the proposition, as characterizing or not characterizing the logical subjects as they exist in themselves before being reduced to mere 'its'. Thus the truth or falsity of a proposition is not a part of the proposition itself. The proposition has an identity and status which is not dependent on its truth or falsity. As Whitehead repeatedly states, it is more important that a proposition be interesting than that it be true.

D

In *Process and Reality*, Whitehead's discussion of propositions is limited by the fact that he only considers propositions about the past. Whitehead always assumes that the logical subjects of a proposition are in the past of the actual entity prehending that proposition. For example, we read:

> Thus no actual entity can feel a proposition, if its actual world does not include the logical subjects of that proposition. The proposition 'Caesar

> crossed the Rubicon' could not be felt by Hannibal in any occasion of his
> existence on earth (PR 396b).
>
>> The actual entities whose actual worlds include the logical subjects
>> of a proposition will be said to fall within the 'locus' of that proposition.
>> The proposition is prehensible by them (PR 397b).

In one passage in *Process and Reality*, however, Whitehead does indicate
that he is aware that this position creates a problem for the status of propositions about the future (and, by implication, a problem for the status of
propositions about the present as well).

>> The presupposed logical subjects may not be in the actual world of
>> some actual entity. In this case, the proposition does not exist for that ac-
>> tual entity. The pure concept of *such* a proposition refers in the hypotheti-
>> cal future beyond that actual entity. The proposition itself awaits its logi-
>> cal subjects (PR 286e-87a).

Unfortunately, in *Process and Reality* Whitehead never explains what he
means by "the pure concept of *such* a proposition."

In *Adventures of Ideas* there is an additional discussion of propositions about the future (AI 248a-51a). Although this discussion is somewhat
more complete than the one in *Process and Reality*, it is still quite sketchy.
Therefore, we must be somewhat speculative in our reconstruction of
Whitehead's position on propositions about the future (as well as about
the present)—although we may be guided to some extent by his discussion in *Adventures of Ideas*.

Our interpretation of Whitehead's theory of present and future
propositions makes the following assumptions, which we will summari-
ly state, leaving their defense and full explication until Chapter Eight of
Part Two.

1. Each new actual entity prehends the entire set of relata and relations in the extensive continuum, including those portions of it which are
past, present, and future to that new entity.

2. Although from one point of view, the relata and relations of the
extensive continuum may be considered an incredibly complicated eternal object (or, alternatively, a series of eternal objects), nevertheless, the
continuum must also be understood as infected by a sense of "particularity" and "concreteness" because of its association with actual entities. The continuum is, therefore, more than merely a series of eternal objects. That is, because all the relata and relations which constitute the
continuum have been prehended by all actual entities, and because the
continuum has been exemplified by all actual entities (except God), it follows that the continuum is not merely an abstract possibility for the new
entity but is a physical fact in the real world.

3. The basic unit in the extensive continuum is a 'region'. Each actual entity occupies a region, and each region is the possible site for the

concrescence of an actual entity. Thus the relata of the continuum are these regions, and the relations in the continuum are the relations between the regions.

4. Contemporary and future actual entities are present in the concrescing actual entity only as regions. That is, any finite entity must prehend some portion of every other actual entity negatively. No past entity, for example, is completely present in the concrescing entity; rather, some portion of that past entity must be eliminated from positive inclusion in the new entity. In a similar fashion, we may consider every contemporary and future entity reduced to the region it occupies, where it is only this region which is positively included in the new entity, and where every other aspect of such a contemporary entity or future entity is excluded from the concrescing entity.

5. The fact that the contemporary and future entities are present in the new concrescence only as regions does not mean that they are present only as eternal objects. Of course, the regions are, from one point of view, eternal objects. Consequently, the contemporary and future entities are present in the new entity *at least* as eternal objects. But the contemporary and future actual entities are *not* present *only* as eternal objects because the regions of the extensive continuum are "infected" with the particularity which stems from continuum's exemplification in actuality. And because the entire continuum is infected with such particularity, it therefore follows that, when contemporary and future entities are present in the new entity as regions, they are thereby truly present in the new entity as genuine actual entities with their own sense of particularity.

We may now state our understanding of the nature of propositions about the present and the future. Like propositions about the past, propositions about the present and the future must have an eternal object serving as the predicate as well as a set of actual entities serving as the logical subjects. In such a proposition, the role of the predicate is the same as it is in a proposition about the past, but the actual entities serving as the logical subjects are present in the new entity merely as regions. In this regard, therefore, there is a genuine difference from propositions about the past—because the actual entities serving as logical subjects in past propositions entered the prehending entity with far more identity than merely being regions in the continuum. But while this difference of past propositions from present and future propositions is genuine, its importance may be easily overestimated. In the case of past propositions, the actual entities serving as logical subjects must be reduced to mere 'its', retaining merely enough identity to locate them. But in the case of contemporary and future propositions, we may consider the actual entities serving as the logical subjects to have entered the concrescing entity *already* reduced to mere 'its'; (and since these 'its' are regions in the continuum, they clearly are locatable). In sum, we may say that in the case of propositions about the present and the future, the logical subjects enter the concrescence already reduced to mere 'its' with a location. Thus present and future propositions are the attribution of a predicate to certain contemporary or future actual entities insofar as these entities have been reduced to mere locations in the extensive continuum.

At this point, an objector to our interpretation might raise the following question: Since a region in the extensive continuum is an eternal object, does it not follow that a "proposition" about the present or future is nothing but the attribution of one eternal object (the predicate) to another eternal object (the regions)? And, continues the objector, the attribution of one eternal object to another eternal object is not a proposition; it is merely another, more complex eternal object. In response to the objector, we may note (as we did in assumptions 2 and 5 above) that the extensive continuum is "infected" with a sense of particularity stemming from the fact that it has been exemplified in concrete actuality. This particularity extends to the regions in the continuum (as it must if the basic building blocks of the continuum *are* those regions and their relations). And it is this particularity of the regions of the continuum which makes them more than merely eternal objects—although they are at least eternal objects. As we shall see in Chapter Three of this Part One, this particularity is the result of (and in one sense it is the same as) actuality. Thus to the extent that the regions of the continuum are infected with particularity, they are also associated with actuality. And as a result of their association with actuality, we may say that the regions of the continuum are (at least in an extended and analogous sense) actual entities. Therefore, we may conclude that propositions about the present and the future are more than merely the attribution of one eternal object to another; rather they are the attribution of an eternal object to a set of actual entities—although these "actual entities" are actual only by analogy and by extension.

In *Adventures of Ideas* Whitehead discusses propositions about the future. In this book, he is not, however, primarily interested in using his metaphysical system to explain how propositions about the future are possible. Rather, he is concerned to show how—assuming that propositions about the future are possible—we are not left in total ignorance about that future. His position may be summarized as follows. It is metaphysically necessary (A) that each concrescing entity prehend its past actual entities, (B) that each concrescing entity conform, to some extent, to these past entities, and (C) that each concrescing entity, in its turn, be succeeded by still later actual entities. From these considerations it follows that for any actual entity—call it X—there will be future actual entities which must conform to X. Therefore—assuming that X can reach consciousness—it follows that X can know something about the future simply by knowing its *own* identity. Of course, to the extent that the future entities are free to choose how they will conform to X, it follows that X will only know those future entities in outline. Nevertheless, X's knowledge of the future is real and genuine. The important point, however, is this: X knows the future by knowing its own identity.

> It is now possible to determine the sense in which the future is immanent in the present. The future is immanent in the present by reason of the fact that the present bears in its own essence the relationships which it will have to the future. It thereby includes in its essence the necessities to which the future must conform. The future is there in the present, as a general fact belonging to the nature of things. It is also there with such general determinations as it lies in the nature of the particular present to impose upon the particular future which must succeed it (AI 250b).

> But there are no actual occasions in the future, already constituted. Thus there are no actual occasions in the future to exercise efficient causation in the present. What is objective in the present is the necessity of a future of actual occasions, and the necessity that these future occasions conform to the conditions inherent in the essence of the present occasion. The future belongs to the essence of the present fact, and has no actuality other than the actuality of present fact. But its particular relationships to present fact are already realized in the nature of the present fact (AI 251a).

Within this discourse about the immanence of the future in the present Whitehead discusses propositions about the future; he calls them anticipatory propositions. And at this point Whitehead—to some extent —confirms our analysis of propositions about the future. We hold to the interpretation that propositions about the future (as well as the present) have regions in the extensive continuum serving as their logical subjects. Now, as we shall demonstrate in Chapter Eight of Part Two, the extensive continuum as a whole is present in each new entity as a part of the very identity of that new entity. Consequently, the regions in the continuum, which truly *are* the future actual entities, also are a part of the present entity. This, in turn, leads us to the conclusion that in constructing propositions about the future, an actual entity is thereby also constructing propositions about itself! But this is exactly Whitehead's claim.

> In this sense, the future is immanent in each present occasion, with its particular relations to the present settled in various degrees of dominance. But no future individual occasion is in existence. The anticipatory propositions all concern the constitution of the present occasion and the necessities inherent in it. This constitution necessitates that there be a future, and necessitates a quota of contributions for re-enaction in the primary phases of future occasions (AI 249a).

We will complete this section on propositions about the future (and present) with the following observation. One major advantage of Whitehead's theory of propositions—at least as we have extended it—is that propositions about the future are not true or false at the time they are being entertained. That is, granted our interpretation in which the logical subjects of these propositions are (A) regions in the extensive continuum which, nevertheless, are (B) also future actual entities, it follows that the proposition is neither true nor false. Such a proposition we may call "possible," where possibility applies directly to the proposition and not to our human ignorance of the truth value of that proposition. In this regard, propositions about the past are quite unlike propositions about future; this is because when we say that a proposition about the past is possible, we mean that the proposition is literally true or false, but due to our human limitations, we do not know which. When we assert that a proposition about the future is possible, we are not saying that we are ignorant of its truth value; rather we are claiming that the proposition depicts a situation which is not yet actualized. And since the situation is not yet actualized, a proposition about that situation cannot be either true or false. We explain as follows.

In a true proposition about the past, the truth of that proposition literally *is* the two-way functioning of an eternal object as (A) the predicate of the proposition and (B) as a character of the logical subjects as they exist as actual entities before being reduced to mere 'its'; and in a false proposition about the past, the eternal object which is the predicate of the proposition is definitely excluded from characterizing the logical subjects before their reduction to mere 'its'. Now let us turn to propositions about the future. In propositions about the future, the logical subjects are regions in the extensive continuum, and, therefore, these future actual entities can neither possess nor fail to possess any additional characteristics beyond those inherent in their status as regions in the continuum. Consequently, at the time a proposition about the future is being entertained by a concrescing actual entity, the predicate of that proposition does not, and cannot, definitely characterize the future natures of the logical subjects nor does it definitely not characterize them. And so, the predicate of a proposition about the future is merely a potential character of those future actual entities. In conclusion we may assert that a proposition about the future *cannot* be true—because its predicate, *at the time that the proposition is being entertained by the concrescing entity,* is not, and cannot, be serving as a genuine and concrete characteristic of those *future* logical subjects, where Whitehead's definition of truth requires that the predicate of the proposition actually *be* such a characteristic of the logical subjects. Nor can that proposition about the future be false—because its predicate is not definitely excluded from serving as a genuine character of the logical subjects, as Whitehead's definition of falsity requires. Such a proposition about the future can only be possible—because its predicate is merely a potential character of the future logical subjects.

E

In our discussion of the third, comparative stage, we have covered transmutations, propositional feelings, and propositions. Before leaving this section, however, we should make good our earlier promise (pp. 9-10) to discuss physical purposes, which we described as a type of inchoate or primitive propositional feeling. Consider diagrams 10 and 11, which show two typical physical purposes.

In these diagrams, x, y, and z are the dative actual entities. M is a simple physical prehension of y, and O is the resulting conceptual prehension. In diagram 11, P is obtained from O by reversion. In both diagrams, P.P. is the physical purpose. Thus a physical purpose feels a contrast between an eternal object (derived from O in diagram 10 and from P in diagram 11) and an actual entity (y in the diagrams) as presented to the concrescing entity through a simple physical feeling (M in the diagrams). In contrast to the situation in earlier discussions, in a physical purpose y is not reduced to a mere 'it'. Rather, the comparison is of the eternal object with the whole, fully characterized, actual entity (or, more precisely, with as much of the actual entity y as is present in M and which has not been eliminated at M by negative prehensions). That is, in diagram 10, the eternal object which was pried loose from M at O sinks back into immanence with M at P.P. In the second diagram the eternal object which was prehended in its transcendent role at P is collapsed by the physical purpose P.P. into immanence with M (PR 422b). In both diagrams, the fact that M is incorporated into P.P. without being reduced to a mere 'it' is indicated by the absence of the abstractive square for M (i.e., $\boxed{M}$; cf. diagrams 3, 5, 6, 7, 8, 9) in the lower arm of the bracket.

Once again, it is worth noting that the case in which there is only one dative actual entity for a physical purpose is rare. More commonly, we find nexuses of actual entities serving this role. The diagrams could be altered to show such a nexus; diagrams 8 and 9 illustrate how this might be done.

The primary value of a physical purpose to a concrescing actual entity is this: a prehension of a past actual entity by means of a physical purpose makes available to the concrescing entity a wider variety of subjective forms than an ordinary physical prehension would make available. In terms of our diagrams, P.P. has a wider range of potential subjective forms than does M. This is due to the greater freedom associated with conceptual prehensions such as O and P, which are reintegrated into M. Moreover, this greater range of subjective forms is gained without recourse to the more sophisticated structures of the propositional feeling. Indeed, it seems to be an empirical fact that the vast majority of actual entities in our cosmic epoch do not have the requisite complexity of structure and environment to support the production of important propositional feelings. But our epoch's actual entities are sufficiently endowed to support physical purposes (PR 421b). Whitehead suggests that the actual entities which constitute electrons and protons maintain themselves by means of physical purposes (cf PR 470b-71d).

We have two last comments on physical purposes. First, it is the widespread existence of physical purposes, it would seem, which makes possible the creation of propositional prehensions. A physical purpose feels a contrast between the eternal object and the past actual entities from which it came. This contrast, while not as sharp as in a proposition where the past actual entity has been reduced to a mere 'it', nevertheless is real and provides material in the past environment of the concrescing actual entity which tends in the direction of true propositions. When the concrescing actual entity thus creates a proposition—even when none exists in its recent past—it is still "in sync" with the general tendencies of the surrounding universe. Second, there is a continuum between physical purposes and propositional prehensions, with physical purposes gradually merging into propositional feelings. This is particularly the case if we think of the reduction of a proposition's logical subjects to mere 'its' as a matter of degree. Sometimes just a few of the characteristics are "stripped" from the logical subjects, while at other times all the characteristics except location in the region are stripped away from the logical subjects. When just a few of the characteristics of the past actual entities are taken away, we are dealing with physical purposes. When they all are stripped away, we are dealing with propositional prehensions.

IV

There are five possible phases in the concrescence of an actual entity, as we have analyzed it.[27] Thus far, we have discussed three of them. The fourth phase is the intellectual stage, in which consciousness emerges. In Whitehead's metaphysics, consciousness is intimately linked with propositions because consciousness cannot exist except upon a foundation of propositional feelings. Thus we should not be surprised to discover that there are two basic types of intellectual feelings, corresponding to the two types of propositional feelings. These two types are 'conscious perceptions' and 'intuitive judgments'. A conscious perception is the feeling of a contrast between the proposition felt in a perceptive feeling and the actual entities from which it derives (PR 409b-d). An intuitive judgment is the feeling of a contrast between the proposition felt in an imaginative feeling and the actual entities from which it derives (PR 413c-14b).

---

27. Nothing in Whitehead's system requires that every actual entity pass through all five stages. The fourth stage, in particular, is bypassed in many entities.

Diagram 12 shows the development of a conscious perception. The structure of this diagram from M through P.F. is identical to that of diagram 5; P.F. is an authentic perceptive feeling. C.P. is the contrast of the proposition felt at P.F. with actual entity y as prehended at M. In the lower arm of the bracket leading to C.P., y is felt as a fully clothed actual entity, and not as reduced to a mere 'it'; y is felt as an actuality characterized by definite eternal objects.

Diagram 13 shows the development of an intuitive judgment. I.J. is an intuitive judgment; it feels the contrast between the proposition felt by an imaginative feeling (I.F. in the diagram) and the actual entity felt by its corresponding indicative feeling (y as prehended at M in this case). Clearly diagram 13 is the same as diagram 12 except that an imaginative feeling has been substituted for a perceptive feeling.

This leads us to the important issue of consciousness. According to Whitehead, consciousness lurks in the subjective forms of conscious perceptions and intuitive judgments. The vast majority of actual entities, including those having propositional feelings, never achieve this fourth stage, and thus they never are conscious. When consciousness is achieved, however, it emerges in the subjective forms of conscious perceptions and intuitive judgments.

It is reasonable to ask Whitehead, "Why?" Why does he hold that consciousness lurks in the subjective form of these feelings? What is there about the contrast between a proposition and its logical subjects (as present "fully clothed" in the indicative feeling) which leads Whitehead to insist that only such contrasts have the power to generate consciousness? The answer lies in the fact that for Whitehead the contrast between a proposition and its "fully clothed" logical subjects is the contrast between potentiality and actuality. The actual entities serving as the logical subjects (as inducted into the concrescing entity via the indicative feeling) are what is the case. The proposition is what might be the case; and even when the proposition is literally and wholly true, the element of potentiality is not lost (cf. pages 22-23, above). The feeling of an actuality is an affirmation; the feeling of a potentiality is a negation of that actuality. Thus consciousness is the subjective form of an affirmation-negation contrast; it is also the subjective form of the contrast between actuality and potentiality. In fact, these two contrasts are really the same contrast under different names. Whitehead also calls this contrast the contrast between fact (i.e., the actual entities felt by the indicative feeling) and theory (i.e., the proposition) (PR 286c). He also calls it the contrast between what "is in fact" and what "might be" (PR 407a). In Whitehead's own words,

> The subjective form will only involve consciousness when the 'affirmation-negation' contrast has entered into it. In other words, consciousness enters into the subjective forms of feelings, when those feelings are components in an integral feeling whose datum is the *contrast* between a nexus which

is, and a proposition which in its own nature *negates* the decision of its truth or falsehood. The logical subjects of the proposition are the actual entities in the nexus. Consciousness is the way of feeling that particular real nexus, as in contrast with imaginative freedom about it (PR 399b).

Perhaps what Whitehead has in mind by asserting that consciousness will only emerge as (a part of) the subjective form of the affirmation-negation contrast can be expressed less technically this way. When I read a book, there are two ways I can read it. I can read it without asking questions about its content, without arguing with it, and without really thinking about it; I can read that book the way a sponge soaks up water. Or I can come to the book with certain hypotheses in mind. I can then test these hypotheses as I read, discarding them or modifying them as the text requires; in this mode of reading I am questioning, arguing with, agreeing with, or rejecting what the text is saying. Now for me personally, it is a fact that, when I read in the latter mode, I am more alert, more aware, and I get more out of the material—in short, I am more conscious. But when I read as a sponge soaks up water, usually I get sleepy, and often I can't remember what I have read right after I have read it. Even good fiction, a good before-bed-detective-tale, holds my interest by keeping me guessing about "who-done-it," and a clever adventure yarn holds my interest by projecting habits, life-styles, and ways of acting which are alternative to mine. In short, in this second mode of reading, I am more conscious than in the first. But what is this second mode of reading if not the constant confrontation of actuality with potentiality? Thus, Whitehead's claim that consciousness involves the contrast between actuality and potentiality can be well substantiated simply by paying close attention to our own experiences.[28]

V

The fifth stage of the concrescence is the satisfaction. In the satisfaction, the actual entity prehends in a perfectly determinate way every item in its

28. It may be interesting to note that Whitehead's use of the word 'speculate' is based precisely on this point. Whitehead at various times describes philosophy, physics, science, and thought as speculative. But what he means by, say, speculative physics is not a physics which makes wild guesses about the world or a physics which makes claims it cannot substantiate. Rather, what Whitehead has in mind by 'speculate' is a physics which proceeds by interrogating nature, by probing into it, and by forming hypotheses to guide the physicist's imagination. Whitehead faults Bacon for thinking that nature will yield up significant patterns and laws to mere onlookers (SMW 43b). It is this sense also that Whitehead advocates when he says that philosophy ought to be speculative. (According to Whitehead, a crook ought to fear most the speculative detective; after all, what was Sherlock Holmes if not speculative.) Whitehead writes, "I will call such demonstration "speculative demonstration," remembering Hamlet's use of the word "speculation" when he says, 'There is no speculation in those eyes'" (CN 6c).

universe—although it must be kept in mind that this determinate relation to each item will include (in the case of finite concrescences) some instances of elimination through negative prehensions. Thus the potential unity of the constituent elements in the earlier stages has been fulfilled in the actual unity of the satisfaction.

There is an apparent ambiguity in Whitehead's writings as to whether the satisfaction is ever genuinely achieved in the process of concrescence. Some passages sound as though the "achievement" of the satisfaction is equivalent to the perishing of the concrescing entity. And if the entity's reaching its satisfaction is equivalent to its perishing, then, from the standpoint of the concrescence, the satisfaction never really *is*. For example:

> The process of concrescence terminates with the attainment of a fully *determinate* 'satisfaction'; and the creativity thereby passes over into the 'given' primary phase for the concrescence of other actual entities. This transcendence is thereby established when there is attainment of *determinate* 'satisfaction' completing the antecedent entity. Completion is the perishing of immediacy: 'It never really is' (PR 130a).

> In the organic philosophy an actual entity has 'perished' when it is complete. The pragmatic use of the actual entity, constituting its static life, lies in the future. The creature perishes *and* is immortal (PR 126c).

But Whitehead also writes of the satisfaction as though it is truly attained. For example:

> This one felt contrast is the 'satisfaction', whereby the actual entity is its particular individual self; to use Descartes' phrase, 'requiring nothing but itself in order to exist'. In the conception of the actual entity in its phase of satisfaction, the entity has attained its individual separation from other things; it has absorbed the datum, and it has not yet lost itself in the swing back to the 'decision' whereby its appetition becomes an element in the data of other entities superseding it. Time has stood still—if only it could (PR 233b).

It is our opinion that these passages can be harmonized if we recognize that the satisfaction has two distinct, although coordinated, roles to play within Whitehead's system. These two roles correspond to the two sides of the rhythm of creation. On the one side there is the internal growth of an actual entity, and on the other side there is the transition from actual entity to actual entity (PR 229a, 320b).

On the side of the internal growth of an actual entity, the satisfaction is the last stage of that growth; it is the completion of the process of internal development. From this point of view the satisfaction is truly attained. This seems to be what Whitehead has in mind in the passage quoted above from PR 233b, when he writes that an actual entity in its satisfaction "has not yet lost itself in the swing back to the 'decision'." And it is in this sense that we must interpret Whitehead's statement, in his categoreal scheme, in which he *defines* the satisfaction of an actual entity as a part of that entity's act of concrescence. "The final phase in the process of concrescence, constituting an actual entity, is one complex, fully determinate feeling. This final phase is termed the 'satisfaction'" (PR 38f).

On the side of the transition from actual entity to actual entity, the satisfaction is quite beyond the process of concrescence. Here the satisfaction of an actual entity *is* the character of that entity insofar as it is a datum for prehension by future entities. But, as a datum, the internal process of concrescence has ceased, and the immediacy, which is the correlative of that process, has dissipated. The actual entity has perished! In other words, as the final determinate identity of the concrescing entity, the satisfaction also represents the identity which is prehended by the future entities (with the assumption that the finite future entities will negatively prehend some aspects of that satisfaction). But as prehended by future entities, the satisfaction is clearly beyond the process of concrescence; its existence is limited by its status as a mere datum. As Whitehead writes of the satisfaction of an actual entity, "It never really is" (PR 130a). In the following passage, Whitehead has in mind the role of the satisfaction in embodying "what the actual entity is beyond itself" (PR 335e).

> The notion of 'satisfaction' is the notion of the 'entity as concrete' abstracted from the 'process of concrescence'; it is the outcome separated from the process, thereby losing the actuality of the atomic entity which is both process and outcome. . . . But the 'satisfaction' is the 'superject' rather than the 'substance' or the 'subject' (PR 129b).

The following comment is somewhat speculative in its interpretation and cannot point to any single passage in the Whiteheadian text for its conformation, but it does seem to be the logical outcome of the case that we have been building: namely, that (A) as the last stage of concrescence, the satisfaction participates in the immediacy of the *act* of concrescing, but that (B) as the content or character of the entity in its *objective* existence, the satisfaction of an actual entity is that entity beyond the immediacy of concrescence, where, as a functioning subject, the entity has perished.

It should be noted that these two roles of the satisfaction are not at odds with each other. It is a metaphysical necessity—at least according to Whitehead's scheme—that any one actual entity be superseded by other actual entities. (This even applies to God, where God in his superjective nature is prehended by other entities.) Therefore, because the anticipation of its role in the future is necessarily a factor in an entity's present concrescence (PR 41c-d), it is only to be expected that an actual entity must aim at climaxing its concrescence by achieving that satisfaction which will also serve as its identity in the transcendent future after its subjective immediacy has evaporated and, consequently, after it has perished (cf. AI 249d-50a).

In light of our discussion thus far about the satisfaction, it should not be surprising that Whitehead provides a specific mechanism whereby an actual entity, in its satisfaction, can anticipate its future role. In *Adventures of Ideas* he leaves the impression that, in its satisfaction, every concrescing entity entertains propositions about the future: specifically, propositions about those future entities which will prehend the concrescing entity and, even more specifically, about its own role in those future entities (AI 248b-49a).[29] (The nature of these propositions, presumably, would be in accordance with our earlier discussion about propositions concerning the future [Section III.D, pp. 20-25].) By means of these propositions, the concrescing entity in the present anticipates its future role. Thus these propositions are a part of the mechanism whereby there is a transition from (A) the satisfaction as an element in the concrescence to (B) the satisfaction as the transcendent identity of the perished entity.

These propositions about the future, however, are a part of the mechanism of transition in still another way. Consider concrescing entity X, and consider entity Y which is in X's immediate future. In the satisfaction of X there will be a proposition concerning X's anticipated role in Y. It is a metaphysical necessity that as Y begins its concrescence it must incorporate some portion of X into its own identity. Moreover, Y must incorporate X in terms of X's satisfaction. A dominant element in X's satisfaction will be that proposition about Y in which X anticipates its role in Y. Y must come to terms with that proposition in X's satisfaction, and, of course, Y must also come to terms with the subjective form with which X prehended that proposition. That is, it is metaphysically impossible for Y to eliminate completely, through its own negative prehensions, X's feeling of this anticipatory proposition.[30] Rather Y must positively prehend

29. Of course, while these propositions about the future are entertained in the satisfaction, it is also true that they were created (and first entertained) at the earlier stages of concrescence. Thus these propositions have *survived into* the satisfaction.

30. Let us consider an objection to our claim that Y may not completely eliminate X's feeling of the anticipatory proposition about Y. The objector notes that in starting its process of concrescence, Y is given a 'subjective aim' by God. This subjective aim draws upon God's limitless conceptual resources. At this point, the objector asks the following question. Why are God's resources not sufficient for God to give Y a subjective aim which would allow Y to eliminate X's prehension of the proposition about Y?

After noting that we will discuss the notion of the subjective aim in Chapter Two of this Part One as well as in Part Four, we may respond to the objector as follows. First, it is metaphysically incumbent upon Y to prehend positively some portion of X's satisfaction. Now X's satisfaction is an integral unit, an aesthetic whole. Every aspect of X's satisfaction will reflect the fact that X has anticipated this-and-not-that future role. Thus, even if Y could eliminate X's specific prehension of its role in Y, Y could not totally eliminate every other aspect of X's satisfaction, where each of these other aspects would reflect X's anticipation of this-and-not-that future role. Second, while it is true that God does, in fact, give Y its subjec-

X's feeling of the proposition about its role in Y (or at least incorporate some portion of X's satisfaction which will reflect X's anticipated future role). Thus X's anticipation of its role in Y becomes a part of the very identity of Y, of what Y is. In this way, the present concrescence (say X) can affect the nature and identity of the future (say Y). Of course, Y retains its own freedom (to a greater or lesser extent) to react to X's anticipation of the future. Nevertheless, Y must react to *that* anticipation, within X's satisfaction, of *that* future role. And so, from still another angle we may see the mechanism by which the satisfaction of an actual entity provides a bridge from the role of that entity as a private concrescence to its role as a datum in, and shaper of, the transcendent future.

As mentioned above, Whitehead leaves the impression in *Adventures of Ideas* that, in its satisfaction, every actual entity entertains propositions about its role in the transcendent future. As we saw earlier in this chapter, however, in *Process and Reality* Whitehead holds that most entities are not well enough endowed to create and entertain propositions of any kind.[31] But in *Process and Reality* Whitehead does hold that all actual entities can produce physical purposes. Moreover, to a certain extent, his discussion in *Process and Reality* about physical purposes parallels his discussion of propositions about the future in *Adventures of Ideas*. That is, according to *Process and Reality*, physical purposes in the satisfaction of the concrescing entity will promote adversion or aversion in the transcendent future, and this is parallel to the role of propositions, according to *Adventures of Ideas*, in influencing the transcendent future (AI 248c-50a). In *Process and Reality*, he writes:

> This valuation accorded to the physical feeling endows the transcendent creativity with the character of adversion or of aversion. The character of adversion secures the reproduction of the physical feeling, as one element in the objectification of the subject beyond itself. . . . But a physical feeling, whose valuation produces adversion, is thereby an element with some force of persistence into the future beyond its own subject. . . . When there is aversion, instead of adversion, the transcendent creativity assumes the

---

tive aim, it is also true that God must give Y a subjective aim which is based on the assumption that Y must prehend some portion of X's satisfaction. This in turn means that God provides Y's subjective aim on the further assumption that Y must come to grips, directly or indirectly, with X's anticipated role in Y. In short, not even God can violate the metaphysical requirement that the future incorporate the past into itself. Thus Y, even with God's help, cannot eliminate all aspects of X's anticipation of its role in Y.

31. It may be well to note that, since the subjective aim is a propositional prehension, and since all entities have one, it follows that the subjective aim is the exception to the claim that most entities do not entertain any propositions. Nevertheless, it must also be remembered that the subjective aim is created by God out of *his* resources and that it is merely "appropriated" by the new entity. Thus while the new entity must of course *entertain* its subjective aim, it does not *create* that subjective aim. And in that sense, it remains true that most actual entities do not have the resources to create propositions.

character that it inhibits, or attenuates, the objectification of that subject in the guise of that feeling. Thus aversion tends to eliminate one possibility by which the subject may itself be objectified in the future (PR 422b-c; cf. PR 470c).

In *Process and Reality,* whenever Whitehead explicitly considers the actual entities in the nexus of a physical purpose (where these actual entities are the correlate of the logical subjects of a proposition), he seems to assume that they are in the past of the concrescing subject. In the passage just quoted, therefore, Whitehead's meaning could be glossed as follows: the future entities must incorporate some portion of the present entity; and when they incorporate a physical purpose, then those future entities must react to *that* physical purpose. Thus, the presence of such physical purposes in the satisfaction could explain how that present concrescence influences its future.

It remains worth asking, however, if it is possible for physical purposes to be *about* the future. Physical purposes *about* the future would be useful to Whitehead's philosophy in several ways. First, it would close the gap between *Process and Reality* and *Adventures of Ideas.* Physical purposes about the future would be very similar to the propositions about the future which are mentioned in *Adventures in Ideas.* Second, physical purposes would help explain how there could be a teleological orientation to the future, not only at the conscious level, where it is plausible to talk about the production of propositions about the future, but also throughout all reality. In this regard it is worth noting that according to Whitehead's categoreal scheme, each entity must aim at intensity of feeling in its future (PR 41c); and Whitehead, in explicating this demand, speaks of an "anticipatory feeling" of the future, which is an element "affecting the immediate complex of feeling" (PR 41d). Third, if we are correct in our explication of the satisfaction as that factor in the actual entity which provides for the transition from the actual entity as concrescence to the actual entity as objective datum, then it would seem that this anticipatory feeling must somehow be present in that satisfaction.[32] It would seem, therefore, that Whitehead's metaphysics points to the presence in the satisfaction of some feeling which is *about* the future. Furthermore, in *Adventures of Ideas* Whitehead seems to assert that this feeling about the future in the satisfaction is a propositional feeling. But in *Process and Reality* the nature of this anticipatory feeling in the satisfaction is not established, the physical purposes in the satisfaction not being truly *anticipatory* feelings.

32. This conclusion may be derived in another way also. Since there can be no elimination of feelings within the process of concrescence (PR 233b, 368a), it follows that Whitehead's "anticipatory feeling" (which is introduced as a part of the subjective aim at the initial stage of concrescence [PR 41c-d]) will necessarily be present at the satisfaction. And, it will be present in the satisfaction, quite apart from any consideration of the role of the satisfaction in the transition from entity to entity.

To build our case for physical purposes about the future, it will be helpful to remember that there is a continuity between physical purposes and propositional feelings. The primary difference between a proposition and a physical purpose is this: in a proposition the eternal object is conceived as a *potential* predicate of the logical subjects, while in a physical purpose the eternal object is construed as an *actual* quality of the felt nexus (i.e., the correlate of the logical subjects). But there need not be an absolute difference between an eternal object felt as a potential quality and that same eternal object felt as a concrete quality of a set of actual entities; this could be a matter of degree. Thus when the potentiality of the eternal object (towards a particular set of actual entities) is emphasized, we have a paradigm case of a propositional feeling; and when the concrete application of an eternal object (towards a particular set of actual entities) is emphasized, we have a paradigm case of a physical purpose. But it would also be possible to feel an eternal object as something between a purely potential and a purely concrete quality of some set of entities. Therefore a physical purpose is merely one end of a continuum of possible ways of relating an eternal object to a specific set of actual entities, with a genuine proposition as the other end of the continuum.

If we stress the continuity between a physical purpose and a propositional feeling, then we could apply our discussion of propositions about the future to physical purposes. A physical purpose *about* the future would have the following nature. The felt nexus would be some region (or group of regions) in the extensive continuum, where these regions were in the future of the prehending entity. The prehending entity would then feel an eternal object as definitely and really characterizing those regions. Thus the future would be felt as a very real and concrete presence. (This is possible because the future regions of the continuum are genuinely present in the prehending entity.) Of course, the fact that these regions *are* in the *future* of the concrescing entity would infect such a physical purpose with a degree of potentiality. Futhermore, in such physical purposes "about" the future, the eternal object characterizing the future regions could *not* be derived *from* those future regions; the eternal object could be obtained only from some past actual entity and then applied to the future regions. This also would increase the degree of potentiality of the physical purpose about the future. Thus a physical purpose "about" the future could never achieve the degree of concreteness which would be available for a physical purpose "about" the past. And yet such a physical purpose about the future may be too concrete in its attribution of the predicate to the felt nexus for that physical purpose to be considered a propositional feeling (at least as propositions are defined in *Process and Reality*).

If the above discussion is on the right track, we may assert the following. Every actual entity reaches its satisfaction with anticipatory feelings of the future. In some cases these anticipatory feelings are merely physical purposes, while in other cases they are propositional feelings. (This allows us to let stand Whitehead's statement in *Process and Reality* that all actual entities create physical purposes, while only a few of them create propositional prehensions.) But we must remember that physical purposes and propositional feelings are merely opposite ends of the same continuum. (This allows us to apply our discussion of propositional feelings about the future to physical purposes, and in particular, it allows us to apply Whitehead's discussion of anticipatory propositional feelings in *Adventures of Ideas* to physical purposes[33].)

33. Let us put this same idea slightly differently. If there is a continuity between physical purposes and propositional prehensions, and if physical purposes about the future cannot be as concrete as (is possible for) physical purposes about the past, then it follows that in AI Whitehead may have changed, according to a very natural development, the exact meaning of his vocabulary from that in PR. Specifically, in AI, Whitehead may be using the term 'propositional feeling' to include what we have called physical purposes about the future. This would be an understandable extension of terminology, since there is an ineradicable potentiality adhering to physical purposes about the future which does not adhere to physical purposes about the past; and this potentiality may be enough to incline Whitehead to call them, in AI, propositional feelings in a broad sense. If this is so, then there would be considerable harmony between AI and PR in content as far as this topic is concerned, while terminological differences would remain.

2 *The Nature of Concrescence*

IN THE FIRST CHAPTER we considered each phase in the act of concrescence separately. In this chapter we will consider the nature of the act of concrescence as a whole.

I

The act of concrescence is a drive for identity. An analogy which may not be too farfetched is this: Each new actual entity begins its concrescence with an "identity crisis," which it gradually resolves as the concrescence progresses until it is completely settled in the satisfaction.

Inherent in the first stage of concrescence is a series of possibilities of self-identity. The possibilities are gradually eliminated during the concrescence until only one possibility is left. This one remaining possibility is the actual identity achieved in the satisfaction. Thus the act of concrescence is the gradual elimination of alternative possibilities of self-identity until the actual entity has chosen one final, determinate, and concrete identity. In Whitehead's own words, "The *preceding phases* enter into their successors with *additions* which eliminate the indeterminations" (PR 225b-26a). Again we read:

> The datum is indeterminate as regards the final satisfaction. The 'process' is the addition of those elements of feeling whereby these indeterminations are dissolved into determinate linkages attaining the actual unity of an individual actual entity. The actual entity, in becoming itself, also solves the question as to *what* it is to be. Thus process is the stage in which the creative idea works towards the definition and attainment of a determinate individuality (PR 227b).

A

It is in this context that we must understand Whitehead's repeated claim that each phase in the concrescence has a propositional unity (e.g., PR

343b, 362b). The explanation runs like this. Each phase is a series of possible self-identities for the concrescing entity, where these possible self-identities are clearly eternal objects. The general potentiality of these eternal objects, however, has been focused upon the concrescing entity in question. Thus the series of possible self-identities becomes the predicate of a proposition, and the concrescing subject becomes the logical subject. In this sense, then, a phase of concrescence is (very much like) a proposition.

The one stage of concrescence which cannot be conceived to have a propositional unity is the satisfaction. This is because the satisfaction is nothing but the achievement of a concrete identity, with a determinate relation to every item in its universe. Of course, the fact that the satisfaction has a concrete and determinate unity—and not merely a propositional unity—does not eliminate the possibility that the satisfaction may include specific propositional prehensions as elements within itself. Sometimes the satisfaction of an actual entity may include propositions about its role in the future (or at least physical purposes, conceived as inchoate propositions).

B

Whitehead claims that the differences among the various phases of concrescence can be construed as the differences in the modes of ingression of eternal objects (PR 248b). A complete analysis of this claim would require a discussion of the role of eternal objects in each stage of concrescence. In part, we have already done this in Chapter One. But in part, this claim may also be elucidated by our description of the act of concrescence as a growth from a propositional unity to a concrete and determinate unity. Specifically, we will recall that an eternal object can be present at an early (i.e., pre-satisfaction) stage of concrescence as an element in a *potential* form of self-identity for that concrescence. But at the satisfaction no eternal object can function this same way; rather, in the satisfaction an eternal object is either functioning as a part of the definite and concrete self-identity of the concrescence or it is positively excluded from such a role. (If the eternal object is a part of an excluded self-identity, it does not follow that it has been somehow "thrown out," "expelled," or "eliminated" from the satisfaction; rather it is present in the satisfaction as a part of a definitely and positively rejected identity.) Thus at an early stage of concrescence an eternal object may have ingressed in the mode of a predicate of a proposition about that entity's self-identity; whereas in the satisfaction that same eternal object may have ingressed in the mode of a concrete and determinate element of that entity's self-identity, or that eternal object may have ingressed (still in satisfaction) as an element in a positively rejected self-identity. In short, in the final stage of concrescence, the mode of in-

gression is concrete—concrete in the sense of being either definitely included or definitely excluded from the final and determinate identity of
the concrescing entity.[1]

C

Along these same lines, it may be good to note that after the concrescence
has started there can be no new selection of data (PR 233b). That is, at its
first stage of concrescence, a new entity must prehend the other actual entities in its environment; and since negative prehensions are inevitable (except for God), there must be a decision concerning which aspects of each
past entity to include in positive prehensions and which to exclude in
negative prehensions. Now, given a decision to exclude some aspect of
another actual entity, that (excluded) aspect cannot be included at a later
stage of concrescence. And given a decision to include some aspect of
another actual entity, that aspect cannot be excluded at a later stage of development. What is given at the first stage can only be rearranged at the
succeeding stages; there can be no additions nor deletions. Every element
which is present at one stage of concrescence must be present at the next
stage of concrescence (and, of course, no factors can be present at the later
stage except those which are first present at the earlier stage).[2] This is what
Whitehead means when he says that there can be no negative prehensions

1. For a further development of this train of thought, consider the following. As the
concrescence progresses, there is a constant elimination of possible forms of self-identity. Thus
one way of distinguishing between an earlier and a later phase is this: the earlier stage will involve a greater range of possible self-identities than will the later phase, and the later phase will
involve a greater range of explicitly rejected self-identities than will the earlier phase.

2. It may appear that Whitehead's theory of reversion allows for additions to an actual entity at a later stage of that actual entity's concrescence. If so, then our interpretation
of Whitehead—according to which there can be no additions from outside the actual entity
after that entity's first stage of concrescence—would be incorrect.

> *The Category of Conceptual Reversion.* There is secondary origination of conceptual
> feelings with data which are partially identical with, and partially diverse from, the
> eternal objects forming the data in the first phase of the mental pole (PR 40b).

It would seem that if these later conceptual feelings have data which are partially
diverse from the eternal objects serving as data at the first phase, then these "diverse" eternal objects must have entered the concrescing entity at a later stage of development.

Whitehead himself may well have held such a view of reversion at one point in the
writing of *Process and Reality.* If so, however, he changed his mind. According to this other
view (which we take to be the normative one), the "new" eternal objects—that is, the eternal objects which are "diverse" from the "eternal objects serving as the data in the first phase
of the mental pole"—are derived from the concrescing actual entity's hybrid physical prehension of God. This prehension of God, however, also occurs at the first phase of concrescence.
Thus all eternal objects are introduced into the concrescing entity at the first phase of concrescence, and in principle the Category of Reversion is not really necessary (PR 381b-381a).

We present a further discussion of the status of reversion in note #18 of Chapter
Nineteen of this book.

within a concrescence (367d-68a). It is possible, however, for a specific prehension to survive from one stage to another with additions to, or subtractions from, its content. But even here what is deleted in one prehension must be added to another, and what is added to one prehension must first have been present in another prehension; the result is that there are no additions or deletions as we move from one phase to another, provided we consider each phase as a whole (PR 368a).

The fact that all the basic data are selected at the actual entity's first stage of concrescence should provide the context for those passages where Whitehead does, in fact, speak of "additions" within the process of concrescence. Previously in this section (p. 37), we quoted a text which may serve as an example of such a passage; we will quote it again.

> The *preceding phases* enter into their successors with *additions* which eliminate the indetermination (PR 225b-26a, Whitehead's emphases).

We will now proceed to interpret this text in the light of our claim that Whitehead's scheme rules out "additions" to a concrescence after the first stage of development. We begin by noting that in this use of the term "additions" Whitehead is referring to eternal objects and *not* to other actual entities. He makes this clear in his next sentence: ". . . the *how* of the additions, . . . [is] the *realization* of eternal objects in the constitution of the actual entity in question" (PR 226a). Now it is important to notice that these "additions" concern the *realization* of eternal objects and *not* the introduction of fundamentally new eternal objects into the concrescence. To clarify this point, let us suppose that there could be an introduction of eternal objects into the concrescence (after the first stage). In that case, either (A) the concrescing entity created those new eternal objects or (B) the new eternal objects were introduced from outside the concrescence. The first alternative (A) is impossible because, as its very name implies, an *eternal* object can be neither created nor destroyed. Whitehead himself makes this point as he continues his discussion of "additions" within a concrescence: "The definite ingression into a particular actual entity is not to be conceived as the sheer evocation of that eternal object from 'not-being' into 'being'; it is the evocation of determination out of indetermination" (PR 226a). The second alternative (B)—that is, the introduction of the new eternal objects from outside the concrescence—is also impossible. Alternative B cannot be accepted because eternal objects can exist only insofar as they are a part of some actual entity. (This is an immediate consequence of the ontological principle.) But, as we saw two paragraphs back, external actual entities can be introduced into a new concrescence only at the first stage of concrescence. Therefore, since other actual entities are the only source of new eternal objects, we may conclude that new eternal objects can be introduced (from the outside) into a concrescence only at the first stage.

Having rejected both A, the introduction of new eternal objects by creation, and B, the introduction of new eternal objects from the outside, we may assert that any sort of introduction of new eternal objects is impossible after the first stage of development. This brings us back to our previous claim that when Whitehead speaks of "additions" within a concrescence, he is referring to the "realization" of eternal objects within that concrescence. It now should be clear that such a "realization" of eternal objects does not involve the addition of any *new* eternal objects. This "realization," therefore, can involve only a change in the status of—that is, a change in the mode of ingression of—the eternal objects in the concrescence, where all of these eternal objects are to be found at the first stage of development. And so, Whitehead's talk about "additions" within an actual entity really amounts to a reminder that eternal objects change their mode of ingression as the concrescence develops. And that claim we have already discussed.

We are left with one question. If our interpretation is correct, then is not the term "additions" somewhat misleading? That is, if the process of concrescence involves a mere change in the status of eternal objects, and if this process in no sense involves the addition of new eternal objects, then why use the term "additions" at all? To answer this question, we may note the following point. At the first stage of development, each actual entity entertains a series of possible self-identities. But as the concrescence progresses, some of these possibilities are explicitly rejected and others are retained, until one final and fully determinate identity has emerged. Thus as the concrescence develops—and this is the key—we may say that the actual entity gains *additional* determination (although it is also true that as the concrescence develops, it *loses* various options for self-identity). This interpretation finds verification in passages such as the following (which we have already quoted in part):

> The definite ingression into a particular actual entity is not to be conceived as the sheer evocation of that eternal object from 'not-being' into 'being'; it is the evocation of determination out of indetermination. Potentiality becomes reality; and yet retains its message of alternatives which the actual entity has avoided (PR 226a).

Nevertheless, it must be confessed that, since no new eternal objects are involved in this "evocation of determination out of indetermination," Whitehead's use of the term "additions" is, in truth, somewhat misleading.

D

Whitehead sometimes uses the term "subject" to denote the sense of unity which an actual entity attains in its satisfaction. Therefore, just as a determinate self-identity is the capstone of the concrescence and not its foundation, so also an actual entity's status as a subject is the outcome of the process of concrescence and not its presupposition.

> Each such objectification, and each such complex of objectifications, in the datum is met with a correspondent feeling, with its determinate subjective form, until the many become one experience, the satisfaction. The philosophies of substance presuppose a subject which then encounters a datum, and then reacts to the datum. The philosophy of organism presupposes a datum which is met with feelings, and progressively attains the unity of a subject (PR 234b).

We should note, however, that it is easy to misunderstand Whitehead on this point. While Whitehead does indeed claim that an actual entity *achieves* its identity as a *determinate* subject, he is *not* thereby committed to the position that an actual entity is *totally* indeterminate when it begins its concrescence. Rather, when an actual entity begins its concrescence, it is partially determinate and partially indeterminate. We can support this claim in many ways, but we will mention only three. First, Whitehead claims that pure chaos is quite impossible in our world (PR 169c). But if the first stage of concrescence were totally indeterminate, then it would be (it seems to us) wholly chaotic. Since such chaos, however, is in principle impossible, it is surely impossible at the first stage of concrescence. The first stage of concrescence, therefore, cannot be wholly indeterminate. Second, the reader will recall that at its first stage of concrescence, a new actual entity is a collection of past actual entities. But each of these past entities has achieved its own fully determinate satisfaction. Therefore, to the extent that the new entity *is* a collection of such fully determinate entities, it follows that the first stage of the new entity is itself determinate, at least in part. Third, the fact that the new actual entity begins its concrescence as a collection of determinate past actual entities limits the range of possible self-identities which it can choose in its concrescence. In other words, given the specific nature of its first stage of concrescence, there are some self-identities which are genuine options for the new entity, while there are other self-identities which are completely unavailable to the new entity. (It should be noted that a self-identity which is completely unavailable for one actual entity might be a genuine option for another.) Now to the extent that the first stage of concrescence makes available one series of final self-identities, while ruling out another series of final self-identities, we may say that the first stage is partially determinate and partially indeterminate.

II

So far in our book we have freely discussed the stages of concrescence in terms of "first" and "last," "earlier" and "later," "prior" and "posterior."

But can Whitehead give any clear definitions of these terms? It is interesting to note that the Whiteheadian scholar William A. Christian insists that these terms are used in a unique fashion when applied to the act of concrescence. They are, in short, *sui generis*. Christian writes:

> One phase must be in some way prior to another. What sort of priority is this? Negatively, this genetic priority must be distinguished from other sorts of priority. (i) We are not to think of it as priority in physical time. We are not to think of phase A occurring at time 0100 and phase B at 0100 plus *i*, however small the increment may be. The internal process is "becoming," not "transition." (ii) Since the concrescence is a creative process in which decision occurs, it would seem that genetic priority is not the logical priority of a premise to a conclusion. (iii) For a similar reason the relation of one phase to another cannot be construed as a whole-part relation. This construction would seem to eliminate the dynamic character of the process. . . .
>
> So it seems that though genetic priority may have analogies with other sorts of priority we must accept it as something of its own kind. The categoreal explanation of concrescence is given in the categoreal scheme. For its applicability Whitehead appeals to our immediate experiences (PR 32).[3]

A

We basically agree with Christian. Nevertheless, we will develop our own interpretation in a somewhat different (though not contradictory) fashion. First, however, we wish to expand Christian's observation that genetic priority cannot be assimilated to the priority inherent in physical time. Diagram 14 will help us.

We will make the following observations about diagram 14. (A) Let rectangle R be the region occupied by some concrescing actual entity. Rectangle R will be a four-dimensional solid (that is, a four-dimensional region).[4] These four dimensions will consist of the three dimensions of ordinary space plus the dimension of time. Thus, R represents a three-dimensional solid moving through the fourth dimension of time. (B) Unfortunately, diagram 14 is two-dimensional. We are, therefore, faced with the task of representing a four-dimensional reality on a two-dimensional sheet of paper. To help us in this task, let us stipulate that the vertical axis on the paper will represent the three dimensions of space, while the horizontal axis will represent the dimension of time. The arrow T indi-

3. William A. Christian, *An Interpretation of Whitehead's Metaphysics* 80-81. Hereafter we will cite this work as *Whitehead's Metaphysics*.
4. The assumption that R is four dimensional need not hold for all eras—although it will certainly hold for this present one. We will, however, postpone any further consideration of this assumption until chapter Eight of Part Two.

cates this dimension of time. We will further stipulate that as we move from the left to the right along arrow T, we are moving from the past to the future. (C) We have (arbitrarily) divided region R into five subregions. Each subregion is a four-dimensional solid. It will be readily observed that subregion 1 is prior to subregion 2, and that subregion 2 is prior to subregion 3, and so forth. (D) The diagram also shows regions Q and S. Region Q is in the past of R, and region S in the future of R. Regions Q and S are occupied (or, in the case of S, will be occupied) by actual entities.

Before using diagram 14 to indicate the correct interpretation of the act of concrescence, we will use this diagram to illustrate a *wrong* interpretation. In Chapter One we discussed the various stages of concrescence —five phases for the more complicated entities, and four for the simpler ones. Let us consider an actual entity with five stages of development. It might seem reasonable to assume that the first stage occupies subregion 1; and *afterwards* the second stage occupies subregion 2; and *after* the second stage, the third stage occupies subregion 3; and finally subregion 5 is occupied by the satisfaction. On this scheme, when subregion 5 is occupied, the stages of concrescence which occupy the first four subregions are no longer "present"; rather, they are in the past. Likewise, when subregion 4 is being occupied, the stages of concrescence which occupy the first three subregions are no longer present, because they are in the past; and, in addition, the stage of concrescence in the fifth subregion is not present, because it is still in the future. On this interpretation, the transition from phase to phase *within* a concrescence is conceived on the analogy with physical time.

To explain Whitehead's objection to this scheme, let us note that each of R's subregions can be further divided to still smaller subregions, where these smaller subregions are in the past or the future of each other. In fact, the process of subdivision can be continued forever. Now it is precisely this possibility of endless subdivision which makes region R continuous.[5] That is, the four-dimensional "extensiveness" of region R is continuous. While the geometry of region R may be continuous, Whitehead insists that the occupation of region R (by the concrescing actual entity) is not continuous. Specifically, the occupation of region R cannot be divided into parts such that when one of these parts is "present" the other parts are either past or future (and thus not present); and *a fortiori* this process of dividing the act of occupying R cannot be continued indefinitely. Whitehead gives two primary reasons for his denial of the continuity of the act of becoming (i.e., the act of occupying R). First, it leads into Zeno's paradoxes, and these paradoxes, when properly stated, cannot be refuted (unless we give up the assumption that change is continuous) (PR 105b-

---

5. And since the extensive continuum is merely a series of regions, the fact that all regions are continuous implies that the extensive continuum is continuous.

7d). Secondly, if we examine closely our acts of experience—especially our experience of change—we will find that our experience (of change) comes in "lumps." Whitehead quotes William James as an ally.

> The authority of William James can be quoted in support of this conclusion. He writes: "Either your experience is of no content, of no change, or it is of a perceptible amount of change. Your acquaintance with reality grows literally by buds or drops of perception. Intellectually and on reflection you can divide these into components, but as immediately given, they come totally or not at all" (PR 105b-6a).

B

Let us turn now to the correct view of the act of occupying a region. In terms of diagram 14, the actual entity in region R occupies that region "all at once." Thus the initial phase of concrescence takes place in the *entire* region R. the second stage of concrescence presupposes the first stage, and, therefore, the second stage also presupposes the *entire* region R. In this sense, *every* stage in the concrescence presupposes the *entirety* of region R. In Whitehead's own words,

> Each phase in the genetic process presupposes the entire quantum. . . . The subjective unity dominating the process forbids the division of that extensive quantum which originates with the primary phase of the subjective aim. The problem dominating the concrescence is the actualization of the quantum *in solido* (PR 434b).

Again we read,

> The conclusion is that in every act of becoming [i.e., every concrescence] there is the becoming of something with temporal extension; but that the act itself is not extensive, in the sense that it is divisible into earlier and later acts of becoming which correspond to the extensive divisibility of what has become (PR 107d).

Before continuing, it may be well to make an "aside" observation. In diagram 14, regions Q, R, and S are all occupied by distinct actual entities. Region Q is prior to region R. Since, however, we are dealing with distinct actual entities (and not phases within a single actual entity), it follows that when the entity in R concresces, the entity in Q is no longer "present"; rather, the entity in Q has perished and is in the past of the entity in R. Similarly, region R is prior to region S. Therefore, the entity in R must perish before the entity in S can concresce. We should also note that each of these three entities occupies its own region "all at once." Consequently, if these three entities should happen to be elements in a conscious human being, they would be the "buds" or "drops" of experience which James discusses in the above quotation. Each such bud of experience comes after its predecessor has perished and before its successor comes into existence. But as James observes, while these buds of experience come as whole units, we can upon reflection divide them into components. Thus the entity in S, for example, can divide the entity in region R into the parts we have labeled subregions 1, 2, 3, 4, and 5; and the entity in S can divide the entity in Q in a similar manner. Further, the entity in S can "forever" divide these subregions into smaller areas. Thus S can *construct* a mathematical time which is continuous. This continuous time is composed of instants (without temporal extension) such that when any one instant is present, every other instant is either past or present (and thus not present). Also, the entity in S can connect the regions Q and R so that the transition between the two is (to use a non-mathematical term) smooth; thus S can construct a perfectly continuous extensive continuum in which there is a perfectly continuous movement of a mathematical time. In short, the entity in S has constructed Newton's absolute time. Whitehead quotes from Newton's discussion of absolute time in the *Scholium*.

> "I. Absolute, true, and mathematical time, of itself, and from its own nature, flows equably without regard to anything external, and by another name is called duration" (PR 109c).

Thus the occupation of the extensive continuum comes in distinct "chunks," where these "chunks" are anything but continuous. But *upon reflection*, we can construct a continuous "absolute, true, and mathematical" time, where this mathematical time is the fourth extensive dimension of the extensive continuum. We read,

> There is becoming of continuity, but no continuity of becoming. The actual occasions are the creatures which become, and they constitute a continuously extensive world. In other words, extensiveness becomes, but 'becoming' is not itself extensive.
>
> Thus the ultimate metaphysical truth is atomism. The creatures are atomic. In the present cosmic epoch there is a creation of continuity (PR 53a-b).

The fact that an actual entity occupies its region "all at once" will help us understand better the sense in which one stage comes "before" or "after" another.[6] As we mentioned, each phase in the concrescence

---

6. We should note that Lewis S. Ford presents a partially different interpretation of genetic succession in "Genetic and Coordinated Division Correlated." We may explain Ford's position in terms of our diagram 14. Let us assume that an actual entity concresces in region R. Now, according to Ford, a particular phase of that concrescence is associated with a particular subregion in R; for example, the first phase of concrescence is associated with subregion 1, the second phase with subregion 2, etc. (In this, Ford differs from us.) Ford also argues, however, that during the entity's concrescence, each phase is present to the other phases. Thus the phase of concrescence associated with subregion 1 is present to the phase of concrescence associated with subregion 5, and vice versa. When, however, the entity oc-

presupposes the entire region. Therefore, since each stage of concrescence is a part of the new actual entity, it follows that the first stage is present in the last stage, and it follows that all stages are present together in the new actual entity. That is, the actual entity is *not* something apart from the process of concrescence — something which first "has" the characteristics of the conformal stage and then discards them for the characteristics of the second stage, and so forth until the last stage. Rather the first stage is a series of possibilities for the self-identity of the new entity — a series conditioned, but not totally determined, by the natures of the past entities. This first stage is later modified — some possibilities of self-identity are chosen and others are rejected — but this first stage remains a part of the very identity of the new actual entity (PR 355c). That is, the new entity remains forever just *that* entity which has just *that* initial stage of concrescence. Moreover, each later stage — for example, the satisfaction — gains its identity in part from the fact that precisely *that* initial stage is present. Thus an actual entity becomes fully determinate only in its satisfaction; but the identity of the actual entity resides in the entire process of concrescence, where each stage of that concrescence is present to each later stage, and where all stages are together present in the new actual entity as a whole.

At this point, it may be wise to ask Whitehead a question. If every stage presupposes the entire region (including all of that region's temporal spread), then is it also true that a later phase of concrescence (e.g., the satisfaction) is present in an earlier stage (e.g., the conformal stage)? In some sense, the answer to this question must be: "Yes, indeed, later phases are present in the earlier stages." In part, this answer follows directly from the fact that an actual entity's occupation of an extensive region occurs "all at once." But in part, this answer seems to be implicit in many of Whitehead's comments about the process of concrescence — and especially in those comments concerning the nature of a prehension. Specifically, it will be recalled that each phase of concrescence is composed of prehensions, and it will also be recalled that each prehension must have a subject (PR 35c, 41a, 337d-38d). This subject, however, is nothing but the actual entity as a whole (PR 338c-39a, 341c-42a). Therefore, the subject — or the actual entity as a whole — must be present in each of its stages. It is in this context that we must understand Whitehead's reference to the "doctrine of the inherence of the subject in the process of production" (PR 342b). Whitehead also writes of this doctrine at greater length.

---

cupying R concresces, the entity occupying Q is already past and thus not present. And the actual entity occupying region S is still future and thus not present. (In this Ford is closer to our position.)

And so, our primary difference from Ford lies in the fact that we do not think that a particular subregion of R should be associated with a particular phase of concrescence. We give the reasons for our preference in this regard in the main text.

There is then a growth of prehensions, with integrations, eliminations, and determination of subjective forms. But the determination of successive phases of subjective forms, whereby the integrations have the characters that they do have, depends on the unity of the subject imposing a mutual sensitivity upon the prehensions. Thus a prehension, considered genetically, can never free itself from the incurable atomicity of the actual entity to which it belongs (PR 359d-60a).

We may conclude this paragraph by noting that an actual entity has no content or definition apart from that to be found in its several phases of concrescence (including the satisfaction). Therefore, Whitehead's doctrine of the immanence of an actual entity in each phase of its concrescence requires the further doctrine of the mutual immanence (within any single act of concrescence) of every stage of development in every other stage.

C

This brings us back to our original problem: the nature of "earlier" and "later" in the act of concrescence—that is, genetic priority. We have seen what genetic priority is *not:* it is not a difference in physical time. Rather, to state the positive side of this issue, there is a mutual immanence of all stages of concrescence within each other. We can also elucidate the nature of genetic priority even further. Genetic priority occurs within the context of the act of concrescence. Therefore, if we wish to state more precisely the nature of "earlier" and "later" in the concrescence, let us turn to the process of concrescence itself, as we outlined it in the previous chapter.

First, the foundation of the act of concrescence is the prehension of other actual entities. These prehensions of other actual entities constitute the first stage of the new actual entity's concrescence (as we saw previously, prehensions of other actual entities can occur *only* at the first phase of development). These prehensions of other actual entities are also the paradigmatic instances of physical prehensions (PR 35d). Thus the first stage of development is the stage of physical reality. As we progress to the second stage of development, we enter the realm of the conceptual; that is, at the second stage the actual entity has conceptual prehensions of pure eternal objects (PR 35d). And at the later phases of concrescence (i.e., third and following) the physical and the conceptual are intertwined in various ways. The point we wish to stress is this: the physical prehensions come first and the conceptual and mixed prehensions stem from those physical prehensions. Thus to the extent that, within our human experience, we have a sense of the priority of the physical to the conceptual, it follows that we have a specific experiential basis for Whitehead's discussion of genetic priority. In other words, genetic priority in Whitehead's system is the theoretical correlate of our intuitive sense of the priority of the physical to the conceptual.

The question then emerges: Do we in fact have an intuitive sense of the priority of the physical to the conceptual? Whitehead clearly assumes that we do have such an intuition, but his formal discussion of this problem is limited. (Whitehead chose instead to consider the closely related problem of perception, as we shall see in the next paragraph.) In various *obiter dicta*, however, Whitehead does delineate his own prephilosophic sense of the priority of the physical to the conceptual. For example, William Ernest Hocking team-taught a seminar in metaphysics with Whitehead. Hocking quotes Whitehead's class comments as follows:

> The simplest notion of the Real is History. And what is the prime character of History? Compulsion—symbolized by the traffic cop—no, this is still too intellectual—being tackled at Rugby, there is the Real. Nobody who hasn't been knocked down has the slightest notion of what the Real is. . . . I used to play in the middle of the scrum. They used to hack at your shins to make you surrender the ball, a compulsory element.[7]

Genetic priority is also correlated with our sense of the order of priority among the various modes of perception. Specifically, according to Whitehead, we can feel the priority of causal efficacy to presentational immediacy (as well as to symbolic reference). We will discuss the notions of causal efficacy, presentational immediacy, and symbolic reference in Part Two of this book. Since the whole of Part Two is devoted to the elaboration of these various modes of perception, we cannot even begin to do more than anticipate that discussion. Suffice it to say that causal efficacy is the theoretical name for our feelings of power and efficacy, while presentational immediacy is associated with the "images" in our sense perceptions. (Basically, presentational immediacy is sense perception as analyzed by Hume—at least in some of his moods.) It is important to note that causal efficacy is associated with the first stage of concrescence, while presentational immediacy and symbolic reference are associated with the third, fourth (if there is one), and fifth stages of concrescence. And it is also important to note that Whitehead spends large sections of *Process and Reality* (e.g., 198-217 and 255-79) trying to convince the reader that close attention to pre-philosophical experience will confirm that sense perceptions (perceptions in presentational immediacy) are derivative from feelings of power (perceptions in causal efficacy). To the extent that Whitehead succeeds, he has pointed us to another way in which genetic priority is merely the theoretical correlate of our concrete experience.

There is a third way in which our concrete experience provides a basis for our understanding of genetic priority. As we said two paragraphs above, the foundation of any actual entity's concrescence is that entity's physical prehensions of its actual world. These physical prehensions represent the

7. William Ernest Hocking, "Whitehead as I Knew Him," 13.

element of compulsion. We must conform to what is given. Once these compulsory elements have been given, however, the entity must then choose how to react to them; that is, the entity must decide what it is to be. Whitehead clearly feels that our concrete experience does confirm the fact that we must decide how to react to the compulsion of the physical world. For example, two paragraphs above we quoted (Hocking's notes on) Whitehead's class comments. The purpose of the quote was to show that Whitehead was sensitive to the priority of the element of the physical in our experience; but, if we continue the quote, it also indicates Whitehead's sensitivity to our experience of choosing how to react to these physical realities.

> Nobody who hasn't been knocked down has the slightest notion of what the Real is.... I used to play in the middle of the scrum. They used to hack at your shins to make you surrender the ball, a compulsory element—but the question was *How you took it*—your own self-creation. Freedom lies in summoning up a mentality which transforms the situation, as against letting organic reactions take their course.[8]

This experience of choosing our reaction to the given world is built into the act of concrescence. A concrescence begins with a series of possible reactions to the given—that is, it begins with a series of possible self-identities. Then, as the process of concrescence continues, the various possibilities are eliminated until only one is left. Thus an "earlier" phase of concrescence always involves more live options for self-identity than will a "later" phase of development. And so, genetic priority is the theoretical correlate of our concrete experience of choosing (within the limitations imposed by physical compulsion) our identity, of choosing our destiny, of choosing our stance toward the world; in other words, it is the correlate of our concrete experience of turning a series of alternative possibilities into one specific actual fact.

In conclusion, we may agree with Christian when he says that genetic priority is *sui generis*. Genetic priority is *sui generis* in that it is not to be assimilated to priority in physical time, nor to the logical priority of premise to conclusion, nor to any other sort of priority. Genetic priority has its own nature. At the same time, however, genetic priority can be "located" in the "map of our concrete experience." Moreover, to the extent that Whitehead's system is internally coherent, and to the extent that his system genuinely explicates our immediate experience, it follows that genetic priority can be "located" within that system, and it follows that the various interrelations among genetic priority and the other aspects of his system (including the other forms of priority) can be spelled out. In short, genetic priority may be *sui generis,* but it is not isolated either in immediate experiences or in Whitehead's theoretical system.

8. Ibid.

D

In "thematizing" the experience of choosing one's own concrete identity out of an array of possibilities, we are obviously coming close to the problem of freedom. Indeed, in the quotation on the previous page which deals with this experience, Whitehead explicitly mentions freedom.

In connection with the notion of freedom, we should mention one of the few full-scale negative critiques of Whitehead's philosophy, Edward Pols, *Whitehead's Metaphysics: A Critical Examination of Process and Reality*. Pols organizes his book around the concept of freedom, and he concludes that Whitehead's system does not give a plausible account of freedom; indeed, according to Pols, Whitehead's doctrine of freedom is, in some respects, not even self-consistent.

While we cannot analyze Pols's book in detail, we wish to note three doubtful claims in his case against Whitehead. They are: (1) Whitehead's system requires that the subjective aim (which we will discuss in the next section of this chapter) be modified during the concrescence, and yet that same system also requires that the subjective aim not be modified during the concrescence. (2) Since an actual entity becomes a genuine subject only at the *end* of the process of concrescence, it follows that there is no *thing* which can *be* free. That is, when at the end of the concrescence, the subject finally emerges—a subject which could exercise the power of freedom—there no longer is any freedom! (3) Whitehead is more of a Platonist than he himself (apparently) intended. Specifically, eternal objects have, in Whitehead's system, the traditional marks of substantiality. As a part of this claim, Pols explicates Whitehead as follows: eternal objects have both an individual essence and a relational essence, and the relational essence can "be acquired" and "grow."

It is our position that Pols has misunderstood Whitehead on all three accounts. While we cannot respond to every nuance in Pols's argument, we will discuss his first two points. Point 1 will be discussed below in Section III.D. Point 2 will be discussed in Chapter Three, Section II.D.

III

In this section we shall examine the concept of the subjective aim. Each entity must begin its concrescence with some vision of its final identity, that is, its identity in its satisfaction. This vision is its subjective aim. In our previous discussion of the satisfaction (Chapter One, Section V) we saw that the satisfaction has two roles; it is the final determinate stage of concrescence and it is the identity which later entities will prehend.[9] This

---

9. It must be remembered that finite future entities must negatively prehend some portions of each previous satisfaction.

double nature of the satisfaction is reflected back into the subjective aim. Specifically, in its subjective aim an actual entity is "aiming" at a final identity to be achieved at the end of its concrescence, and it is also aiming at its identity in the "relevant future" (PR 41c).

At the first stage of an entity's concrescence the subjective aim holds up one ideal identity as a lure for feeling. But in the very act of holding up one particular vision of itself the actual entity will also find other possible self-identities organized into a series. These other possible self-identities will be graded according to their relevance to the original identity which is at the center of the subjective aim. In short, at the first phase of concrescence, the subjective aim will involve a series of conditioned (i.e., graded) alternatives for self-identity (PR 342b).

The fact that an entity begins its development with a graded series of possible self-identities provides the explanation for several other aspects of that entity's concrescence. First, at each stage of its development an actual entity is a set of prehensions, where each of these prehensions must have a subjective form. The explanation for each of these subjective forms lies in the subjective aim. That is, an actual entity's vision of itself (i.e., subjective aim) will influence how it reacts to its given world, that is, what subjective forms it takes on (PR 29a). Second, the subjective aim explains an actual entity's choice of which aspects of its actual world to prehend negatively and which to prehend negatively.[10] That is, a new actual entity includes some aspects of its past and it excludes other aspects on the basis of its vision of its own final self-identity.

A

Whitehead defines the subjective aim as a prehension (PR 37b). But this is a special type of prehension, a propositional prehension (PR 37b). The presence of the proposition in the subjective aim allows Whitehead to describe the subjective aim as a "lure for feeling" (PR 130c, 281c). It should be pointed out, however, that on at least one occasion Whitehead speaks about a feeling *of* a subjective aim (PR 342b). In this case, the subjective aim would be the felt proposition (and not the prehension of that proposition). In any case, the context should make clear whether we are speaking of the entire propositional prehension or just the proposition itself.

10. We know of no passage where Whitehead directly states that an entity's subjective aim governs (at least in part) its production of negative prehensions. His system, however, clearly implies as much. For example, Whitehead writes, "The negative prehensions are determined by the categoreal conditions governing feelings, by the subjective form, and by the initial data" (PR 338b). Concerning this quote, we note the following two points: (A) One of these categoreal conditions (governing the creation of negative prehensions) is defined in terms of the subjective aim (PR 41c-d). (B) According to the quote, the creation of negative prehensions is governed, in part, by the subjective forms; but as we saw in the main text, such subjective forms are explained by the subjective aim.

Let us turn to the proposition per se. Our analysis in the previous chapter of future and contemporary prehensions is, once again, quite relevant. Consider first the logical subject of this proposition. Since this is a proposition about the concrescing entity, it follows that the logical subject must be the concrescing entity itself. But the logical subject cannot be the concrescing entity as a completed whole because any logical subject must be a mere 'it'. In addition, the complete entity cannot serve as the logical subject because it is impossible for the subjective aim, which is a single prehension and which is only a *part* of the whole entity, to contain the *entire* entity as one of *its* parts. Rather the logical subject may be considered to be the region in the continuum which the concrescing entity occupies, where this region *is* the concrescing entity considered as a mere 'that'.

The fact that the felt proposition in a new entity's subjective aim has such-and-such a region as its logical subject explains the choice of that particular region as the site of the new entity's concrescence. That is, the subjective aim is present at the first stage of concrescence as the guiding principle of that concrescence. The fact that this guiding principle has such-and-such a region as the site of its envisioned self-identity, therefore, explains why the other prehensions also presuppose this particular region as the site of the concrescing entity. Whitehead confirms our interpretation when he writes, "The factor of temporal endurance selected for any one actuality will depend upon its initial 'subjective aim'" (PR 195b).

The other part of the proposition felt in the subjective aim is the predicate. The basic element in the predicate is the ideal self-identity. As we saw previously, however, other self-identities must also be elements in the predicate. In fact, it would seem that all relevant self-identities must be elements in the predicate. If so, then the subjective form of the subjective aim becomes crucially important. That is, the subjective aim would be a prehension; the datum of this prehension would be a proposition; and this proposition would have a predicate composed of all the possible self-identities which are relevant to the concrescing entity. The grading among these possible self-identities would take place in the subjective form of the prehension of this proposition. One of these identities would be felt as *the* desirable option; and the others would be felt as more or less desirable options.

There is a problem, however, in our interpretation of the subjective aim as involving all the options for self-identity. At a given stage of concrescence (e.g., the first), how does the subjective aim differ from the stage as a whole? That is, a given stage of development (other than the satisfaction) has a propositional unity. Moreover, the "propositional unity" of this stage will involve (1) a logical subject consisting of the region in the continuum occupied by the concrescence and (2) a predicate consisting of all the possible self-identities which are still live options at that stage. But the proposition felt by the subjective aim involves exactly these same two elements. Thus, to repeat, why may not we simply identify the subjective aim at any given stage of concrescence with that stage itself?

At one level, the answer is easy: the subjective aim is a proposition-al prehension while a particular stage has only a propositional unity. The phase and the subjective aim will have diverse geneses, where a diversity of geneses guarantees a diversity even if all else were the same (PR 359c-60a). Thus, they would still not be identical because they would not have their origin in the same section of the actual world. Specifically, the phase of development would have its origin in the *entire* actual world—that is, every positively felt aspect of the actual world will have some role to play in bringing about that phase of concrescence. On the other hand, the sub-jective aim has its origin in one specific actual entity in that actual world: God!

B

It is not our purpose to give a complete description of Whitehead's doc-trine of God. That has been done too often and too well to be repeated here.[11] We may assume that God is a single actual entity (PR 28a). We may further assume that at the beginning of its concrescence each new finite entity prehends God, while at the conclusion of that concrescence God prehends the finite entity (PR 531c-33a).[12]

Whitehead claims that God is the source of each new entity's sub-jective aim (PR 104b, 343b, 373a, 522c). We can explain as follows. God is a part of each new entity's actual world. Therefore, given the principle that a new actual entity must positively prehend some aspect of each past en-tity in its environment, it follows that the new entity must positively prehend God also. But before the new entity ever began its concrescence, God was contemplating the emergence of that entity. That is, God prehends every past entity up to the point where the new entity will emerge. Know-

11. We will, however, discuss those aspects of the doctrine of God which impinge upon the basic topics of this book. In Part Two, we keep up a fairly steady series of comments in the footnotes dealing with God's relation to the extensive continuum. In Part Four, where our primary topic is religion and its relation to language, we have an extensive discussion of God as the source of order, etc. It should be noted, however, that the category of God and the category of religion are quite distinct in the Whiteheadian system, and, consequently, our exposition of religion is not equivalent to an exposition of God.

12. How this is possible is one of the major problems of Whiteheadian scholarship. Whitehead simply does not confront the issue in any of his writings. Cobb, in his book *A Christian Natural Theology,* abandons the notion of God as a single actual entity. Rather, in Cobb's view, God is a *series* of actual entities. Thus the "God" which a finite entity prehends is not the same "God," according to Cobb, which prehends the finite entity—because each of these "Gods" is a distinct actual entity. Lewis Ford tries to work out an interpretation of God as a single actual entity while staying completely within the structure of Whitehead's scheme. See his article "Whitehead's Concept of Divine Spatiality." Lastly, we have some scattered observations about possible solutions to this problem in Part Four.

ing that past world, God decides what kind of entity he would prefer to see emerge. Now this decision is expressed as a propositional prehension. The logical subject of the felt proposition is the region in which the new entity will concresce; and the predicate has two parts: first, the identity which God desires for that new entity, and second, all the other identities which are genuine options for the new entity. Finally, God feels this proposition with a particular subjective form: namely, (1) with the strong desire that the chosen identity be concretely attained by the new entity, and (2) with somewhat less desire that the other possible identities be concretely achieved, the amount of desire in each case corresponding to the "goodness" or "evilness" of the particular identity.[13] (In the case of positively evil identities, we may assume that this desire turns to aversion.)

Therefore, as a new finite actual entity emerges, there exists within God a propositional prehension about that entity, where this propositional prehension expresses God's hopes and fears for that new entity. The finite entity's subjective aim *is* its prehension of this propositional prehension in God. If the reader will recall the definitions given in the previous chapter, it will be evident that a subjective aim is a hybrid physical prehension (PR 343b). A hybrid physical prehension is still a physical prehension, and there are certain general characteristics of physical prehensions which are relevant here: at the first stage of concrescence, a physical prehension is essentially a repetition of what went before. In the case of the new entity's subjective aim, this means that the datum of that subjective aim will be the proposition which God felt, and the subjective form of that subjective aim will be the subjective form which God had. Thus God's desire for the new entity becomes that new entity's own desire.[14]

Concerning the relation of God to each new entity's subjective aim, there are several additional comments we might make. First, there is some sense in which, according to Whitehead, God's gift of a subjective aim marks the start of a new entity (PR 374a). Unfortunately, Whitehead never spells out the precise sense in which the subjective aim starts the concrescence.[15] At least part of the answer, however, lies in the fact that the presence of the propositional prehension within God makes God himself a lure for feeling (PR 522c). That is, the proposition in God about the prospective actual entity gives the creative force of the universe something to latch onto

13. We will discuss in Part Four how God decides which possible identities are good and which are evil. In anticipation, we will say that the best identities are those which promote intensity of experience in the concrescing actual entity, in the actual entities which are future to that concrescence, and in God.

14. This leaves the obvious problem of the freedom of the concrescing finite entity. We will discuss this problem in the next subsection of this chapter (C, pp. 56-58).

15. On page 10 of "Whitehead's Conception of Divine Spatiality" Lewis Ford tries to work out the precise way in which the subjective aim starts the concrescence. Ford's suggestion is quite in addition to the next observation we make in the text.

—(where this creative force is one of the ultimate explanations of everything else and cannot itself be explained [PR 31c-32c]). Second, the fact that
God creates the proposition which starts a new concrescence gives God
considerable control over the location of that new entity. Specifically, in
creating this proposition, God must choose a region to serve as the logical
subject. Apart from the fact that the region of the new entity must be contiguous with the regions of the past actual entities, God can choose the new
region as he wishes. The new region may be small or large, with this or
with that shape. The choice is God's. But when the creative force of the
universe latches onto that proposition, this logical subject becomes the
region which is presupposed by all of that entity's prehensions and by all
of its phases. Third, God's construction of the proposition about the new
entity must proceed on the assumption that the new entity will prehend
not only God but every other entity in its environment. This is a metaphysical requirement that not even God can circumvent. But these other past entities will become a part of the very nature of the new entity. And so, if these
other entities are evil or trivial, then God's hopes for the new entity must
be limited; but if these other entities are good, rich, and mutually com-
plementary, then God will be able to suggest a full and rich identity for the
new entity.[16] Whitehead expresses it this way:

> Thus the initial stage of the aim is rooted in the nature of God, and its com-
> pletion depends on the self-causation of the subject-superject. This func-
> tion of God is analogous to the remorseless working of things in Greek and
> Buddhist thought. The initial aim is the best for that *impasse*. But if the best
> be bad, then the ruthlessness of God can be personified as *Atè*, the goddess
> of mischief. The chaff is burnt (PR 373a).

C

The mention of the "initial aim" in the quotation brings us to our next
point: the subjective aim can change. Many of Whitehead's comments
about the subjective aim presuppose the fact that it can change. For example, Whitehead says that the subjective aim "suffers simplification"
during the concrescence (PR 342b). That is, at the first stage of development the subjective aim points to a series of possible self-identities (with
some of those identities considered more desirable than others), and as
the concrescence progresses the subjective aim points to a narrower range
of possible self-identities. Again Whitehead clearly presupposes the malleability of the subjective aim when he writes of "the development of a
subjective aim" (PR 254b).

The fact that the subjective aim can change ought to present us with
no great mysteries. The subjective aim is a prehension, and it passes

16. This theme is developed at considerable length in Chapter Eighteen of Part Four.

through stages as any other prehension does. Thus, the "initial subjective aim" is merely the subjective aim at its first stage of concrescence; it is the subjective aim as it comes directly from God. (Sometimes, as in the previous quotation, Whitehead shortens the phrase "initial subjective aim" to "initial aim.") After the initial phase the subjective aim passes from phase to phase until the satisfaction is reached. In other words our previous discussion of genetic priority applies here. To the extent that the doctrine of genetic priority is coherent, it follows that the notion of change in the subjective aim will be beyond reproach.

Whitehead needs the doctrine of the malleability of the subjective aim for a number of reasons, the most important of which is the doctrine of freedom. We explain as follows. When a new entity receives its initial aim from God, that entity will feel one possible identity as the most desirable. Moreover, given the fact that the first stage is almost totally a responsive stage, it follows that the identity which the new entity considers the most desirable at this first stage will be that identity which God previously felt was most desirable; and, likewise, the identities which the new entity finds less desirable will be those identities which God previously felt were less desirable. As the concrescence progresses beyond the first stage, however, the new entity has the option of rejecting the identity which God suggested (and which the new entity itself felt as the most desirable at its first phase), and that new entity can choose another identity as the most desirable, an identity which God considered to be less desirable. Now— and this is the main point—if the subjective aim were not malleable, then every new entity would automatically and of necessity retain God's suggested vision of its final identity. In that case, God would be responsible for every detail of the universe as we know it. Each finite entity would merely play its assigned role as a puppet in a theater. This, however, would essentially violate our concrete experience of *choosing* (within the limits of our given world) our own identity.[17] In addition, any such divine determinism through the subjective aim would make theodicy impossible. The evil of the world would be the outcome of the will of God. God would become a divine tyrant, which is morally repugnant (RM 54d-55a). Finally, we might quote a passage where Whitehead himself interrelates the various themes we have mentioned in this paragraph.

> On the contrary, the imperfection of the world is the theme of every religion which offers a way of escape, and of every sceptic who deplores the prevailing superstition. The Leibnizian theory of the 'best of possible worlds' is an audacious fudge produced in order to save the face of a Creator constructed by contemporary, and antecedent, theologians. Further, in the case of those actualities whose immediate experience is most completely open to us,

17. We discussed this experience of choosing our own identities in our analysis of genetic priority. See pages 49-50, above.

namely, human beings, the final decision of the immediate subject-superject, constituting the ultimate modification of subjective aim, is the foundation of our experience of responsibility, of approbation or of disapprobation,
of self-approval or of self-reproach, of freedom, of emphasis. This element
in experience is too large to be put aside merely as misconstruction. It
governs the whole tone of human life (PR 74b).

D

Before proceeding to the next chapter, we will discuss briefly Edward
Pols's criticisms of Whitehead's notion of the subjective aim. This brings
us to the first of the three major flaws in Pols's attempted refutation of
Whitehead's metaphysical system.

The point we will discuss here is Pols's claim that Whitehead has
worked himself into a box in regard to the subjective aim: namely,
Whitehead requires the subjective aim to be malleable, but Whitehead also
requires that the subjective aim be change*less*. As for the requirement that
the subjective aim be malleable, Pols points to the doctrine of freedom. At
this point, Pols's analysis is essentially the same as ours.

Pols never develops, however, the notion of genetic priority with
any clarity. This leads him to confuse process *within* the act of concrescence
with the kind of change involved in physical time. To understand our
criticism of Pols, it is crucial to grasp that Whitehead deals with two different types of process. The first is the process of development *within* the
actual entity. This is called concrescence. The second is the process of transition between actual entities. This is physical time. Concrescence is the
process by which the "many become one," that is, the many actual entities
of the universe which are present at the first stage of that concrescence become one new actual entity. Transition between actual entities is the
process by which the "one is added to the many," that is, the one actual
entity, after reaching its satisfaction, becomes one of the many past actual
entities which are present at the first stage of the concrescence of the new
actual entity. These two forms of process, in Whitehead's metaphysics, follow significantly different patterns, as we have seen.

The fact that an actual entity occupies its region "all at once," with
the fact that every phase of that entity presupposes the entire region,
leads Whitehead to speak of the act of concrescence as "beyond time"
or "beyond change." Of course, what Whitehead means is that, from the
standpoint of physical time where one instant of time can be present
only if all other instants are either past or future and thus no longer or
not-yet present, one cannot speak of change in the concrescence. That
is, there is no part of the concrescence such that when that part is present, the other parts are not also present. The important point is this:
when Pols points to passages which "state" that the subjective aim can-

not change, he consistently points to passages which refer to the change-lessness of the concrescence in terms of physical time. If we understand the distinction between genetic priority and physical time, then we will not find any conflict, as Pols does, between those passages which assert the malleability of the subjective aim and the concrescence (i.e., where genetic priority is at issue) and those passages which assert the im-mutability of the subjective aim and the concrescence (i.e., where physi-cal time is at stake).

Pols has a section in his book entitled, "Subjective aim: modifica-tion or indivisible unity?" In our opinion, the key to this section lies on pages 104-5, where he quotes several representative passages from *Process and Reality* about the immutability of the act of concrescence. Before con-sidering these passages about the immutability of the concrescence, however, Pols quotes a text from *Process and Reality*, 107d to remind his readers that Whitehead truly does have a doctrine of the malleability of the act of concrescence (the brackets contain Pols's addition).

> Whitehead stresses this when he says that "the act of becoming [of the crea-ture] is not extensive," although "in every act of becoming there is the be-coming of something with temporal succession" (*Whitehead's Metaphysics*, 104).

The problem here is that Pols has misquoted Whitehead. The quotation should end with the words, "with temporal extension." To say that the concrescence has "temporal succession" is to say that the act of concres-cence can be divided into parts such that when one part is present the other parts are not present. But this is precisely what Whitehead wishes to *avoid* saying! Consider the entire paragraph in *Process and Reality* which Pols has misquoted:

> The conclusion is that in every act of becoming there is the becoming of something with temporal extension; but that the act itself is not extensive, in the sense that it is divisible into earlier and later acts of becoming which correspond to the extensive divisibility of what has become (PR 107d).

It is clear that Pols has made Whitehead say the exact opposite of what Whitehead explicitly said.

After attempting to show that, according to Whitehead, the act of concrescence involves change (and, in the process, confusing physical time with genetic priority), Pols then produces other quotations to show that Whitehead does *not* allow change in the concrescence.

> But this is not all Whitehead means, as he makes clear when he says that "subjective aim does not share in this (genetic) divisibility. . . . the mental pole determines the subjective forms and . . . is inseparable from the total *res vera*" (*Whitehead's Metaphysics*, 105).

The problem with this passage is that Pols has added the parenthetical term "(genetic)" which does not occur in *Process and Reality*. It is our contention that in this passage Whitehead is speaking of the divisibility of physical time. Thus Whitehead is *not* denying that the subjective aim participates in genetic process, as Pols intimates; rather Whitehead *is* denying that the subjective aim *as a prehension in the concrescence* participates in the divisibility of physical time. In support of this interpretation we would observe that the passage occurs in a chapter called "The Extensive Continuum," where the extensive continuum has to do primarily with physical time and not with genetic process. Moreover, in the paragraph from which the quotation is taken Whitehead is saying that we can "intellectually and upon reflection" (to use James's words) divide the satisfaction of an actual entity into parts such that when one part is present the others are not present; but Whitehead is also asserting that the subjective aim does not participate in this physical divisibility. We quote from the paragraph in question.

> The *res vera*, in its character of concrete satisfaction, is divisible into prehensions which concern its first temporal half and into prehensions which concern its second temporal half. This divisibility is what constitutes its extensiveness. But this concern with a temporal and spatial sub-region means that the datum of the prehension in question is the actual world, objectified with the perspective due to that sub-region. A prehension, however, acquires subjective form, and this subjective form is only rendered fully determinate by integration with conceptual prehensions belonging to the mental pole of the *res vera*. The concrescence is dominated by a subjective aim which essentially concerns the creature as a final superject. This subjective aim is this subject itself determining its own self-creation as one creature. Thus the subjective aim does not share in this divisibility. If we confine attention to prehensions concerned with the earlier half, their subjective forms have arisen from nothing. For the subjective form which belongs to the whole is now excluded (PR 108b).

We turn now to the second passage which Pols quotes in order to show that Whitehead does *not* allow change in the concrescence. The passage is from *Process and Reality*, 380b.

> "Every actual entity is 'in time' so far as its physical pole is concerned, and is 'out of time' so far as its mental pole is concerned. It is the union of two worlds, namely, the temporal world and the world of autonomous valuation" (PR 380). Plainly he means not only that the growth of the pattern is in a duration rather than in time, but also that the subjective aim, or mental pole, in that it controls the development of that pattern, does not itself belong to the development (*Whitehead's Metaphysics*, 105).

It is our contention that, in this passage, by "time" Whitehead means "physical time." At several points in *Process and Reality* Whitehead speaks of "time in terms of those physical relations which define 'physical time'" (e.g., PR 108d, 208a, 364a). Once again Whitehead is merely pointing out that the act of concrescence does not belong to the change inherent in physical time. Whitehead is certainly *not* stating that the subjective aim is beyond the development which is inherent in the genetic process.

We turn now to the final passage which Pols quotes in order to show that Whitehead does not allow mutability in the concrescence.

> We have not merely the problem that there is no time within the development of an actual entity; we must also deal with the source of the claim that "the genetic growth . . . is undivided" (PR 435), because we are concerned with what makes an actual entity atomic (*Whitehead's Metaphysics*, 105).

Once again Whitehead has been misquoted. Whitehead does *not* say that the genetic growth is undivided! What he actually says is that in the genetic growth of an actual entity, the *region* is undivided. In his own words,

> The concrescence presupposes its basic region, and not the region its concrescence. Thus the subjective unity of the concrescence is irrelevant to the divisibility of the region. In dividing the region we are ignoring the subjective unity which is inconsistent with such division. But the region is, after all, divisible, although in the genetic growth it is undivided (PR 434d-35a).

Here again Whitehead is merely saying that the concrescence occupies its region "all at once" and that the act of concrescence cannot be divided into parts such that, when one part is present, the other parts are not present. But *that* claim does *not* entail the immutability of the subjective aim in terms of genetic growth. Whitehead himself says as much.

> Physical time makes its appearance in the 'coordinate' analysis of the 'satisfaction.' The actual entity is the enjoyment of a certain quantum of physical time. But the genetic process is not the temporal succession: such a view is exactly what is denied by the epochal theory of time. Each phase in the genetic process presupposes the entire quantum, and so does each feeling in each phase. The subjective unity dominating the process forbids the division of that extensive quantum which originates with the primary phase of the subjective aim. The problem dominating the concrescence is the actualization of the quantum *in solido*. The quantum is that standpoint in the extensive continuum which is consonant with the subjective aim in its original derivation from God (PR 434b).

We may conclude that Pols has not made his case that Whitehead is inconsistent—or even befuddled—in his treatment of the subjective aim. Specifically, to the extent that Whitehead does simultaneously affirm the mutability and the immutability of the subjective aim, he is using these words in two different senses: the subjective aim is mutable in terms of genetic growth, but it is not divisible in terms of physical time.

3 Objectification and Actuality: Whitehead's Protest against the Bifurcation of Nature

O N PAGE 10 WE QUOTED A PASSAGE in which Whitehead divides a positive prehension into five parts. It is worth quoting again.

> A feeling—that is, a positive prehension—is essentially a transition effecting a concrescence. Its complex constitution is analysable into five factors which express what that transition consists of, and effects. The factors are: (i) the 'subject' which feels, (ii) the 'initial data' which are to be felt, (iii) the 'elimination' in virtue of negative prehensions, (iv) the 'objective datum' which is felt, (v) the 'subjective form' which is *how* that subject feels that objective datum (PR 337d-38a).

The reader is also referred to diagram 4.

I

The initial datum is an actual entity as it exists in its fullness. That is, when a concrescing actual entity has achieved its satisfaction and has stopped its process of internal growth, then that actual entity has achieved a specific and determinate character. The completed actual entity now stands as a fact, and to this fact all future concrescences must conform. The completed actual entity, having *that* precise character, is an initial datum for future actual entities.

The completed actual entity must now be included in future actual entities. The very natures of future actual entities will be constituted, in part, by their inclusion of this completed, satisfied actual entity.[1] This in-

---

1. The word 'inclusion' seems basic in this context. The Whiteheadian expositor William A. Christian, however, argues that in Whitehead's metaphysics 'inclusion' is just a metaphor, and that, in fact, one actual entity 'includes' a past actual entity by repeating or reenacting in itself the eternal objects which characterized the past entity.

clusion of one actual entity into another actual entity is at the heart of Whitehead's protest against the bifurcation of nature. Whitehead, from his earliest days in the philosophy of science, felt that the division of nature into two parts, the one being the object of scientific study and the other being the world of sights and sounds in which we really live, is wholly unacceptable. For him science is not a myth. In his own words,

> What I am essentially protesting against is the bifurcation of nature into two systems of reality, which, insofar as they are real, are real in different senses. One reality would be the entities such as electrons which are the study of speculative physics. This would be the reality which is there for knowledge; although on this theory it is never known. For what is known is the other sort of reality, which is the byplay of the mind. Thus there would be two natures, one is the conjecture and the other is the dream (CN 30b).

In his polemic against the bifurcation of nature, Whitehead has some specific philosophers in mind. Descartes, in Whitehead's opinion, introduced into modern philosophy the first of these bifurcations of nature, with his realm of extended physical substances and his realm of non-extended spiritual substances. Locke, with his doctrine of primary and secondary qualities, also contributed to the bifurcation of nature. This was especially true of his doctrine of secondary qualities, which appeared one way to the perceiver (one of the two halves of nature) but which was caused by something wholly different, something which exists "out-there" independently of the mind. Such a position was easy prey for Berkeley. But the clearest example of such bifurcation is to be found in Kant, with his distinction between the world of noumena and phenomena (PR 111a). Whitehead lived before the existentialist and phenomenological movements were well known in the Anglo-Saxon lands. It is a safe guess, however, that Whitehead would feel uncomfortable with any divorce between the objective world of science, which must be abandoned to determinism, and the lived world of human beings, where freedom reigns. If—and this is a gross generalization—the existentialists would save our human integrity by systematically separating us from nature, Whitehead would save our integrity by humanizing nature.

Ultimately, however, one of the primary sources of the bifurcation of nature lies in the acceptance by most of the Western tradition of the subject-predicate form of propositions as metaphysically ultimate. The doctrine that the ultimate metaphysical situation is a quality modifying a

---

Despite the eminence of Christian as a Whiteheadian scholar, he is probably wrong on this issue, but to argue the point in terms of all the major issues involved would expand this Part One in directions which are not germane to its central topic, the theory of propositions. The remainder of Chapter Three does outline, however, one of several possible responses to Christian. For a full statement of Christian's position see chapters 7 and 8 of *Whitehead's Metaphysics*.

substance follows nicely from the correlative doctrine that the most basic type of proposition is that in which a subject is modified by a predicate (PR 218a-19a). Whitehead even relates the acceptance of the subject-predicate type of proposition as final to Hume's inability to discover his own mind through introspection (PR 210c). Hume's problem stemmed from his acceptance of the dogma that if there were a mind, it would necessarily be a substance (read "subject") with certain qualities (read "predicates"). The qualities Hume had in mind were ones like "having a sensation" or "having an idea." It is no secret, of course, that Hume found the sensations but missed the mind. Hume was indeed an apt student of Berkeley's.

Contrary to Descartes, Locke, Berkeley, Hume, and Kant, however, Whitehead held that subject-predicate propositions can have reference only to high-level abstractions (PR 45c). For example, the simple proposition, "The horse is black," involves tremendous feats of abstraction. First, the millions of actual entities must be transmuted into a feeling of the one horse. Second, the eternal object 'being black' must be pried loose and then applied to the transmuted feeling of the horse. The added steps, such as reducing the transmuted feeling of the horse to the status of an 'it' and the focusing of the predicate on that logical subject, need not be rehearsed here. Clearly, then, such seemingly basic propositions as "The horse is black," "The cat is on the mat," or "The baby is crying" do not describe genuinely metaphysical situations, and it leads only to mischief if we pretend that they do. Thus, in summary, the acceptance of the subject-predicate proposition as basic leads naturally to the characterization of the fundamental metaphysical situation as that of a substance modified by qualities, which in turn leads to the bifurcation of nature.

What then are the ultimate metaphysical actualities? Whitehead calls them actual entities. And the basic metaphysical situation is that in which one actual entity achieves its own identity by incorporating into itself past actual entities, in a coordinated symphony of becoming.

> The principle of universal relativity directly traverses Aristotle's dictum, 'A substance is not present in a subject.' On the contrary, according to this principle an actual entity *is* present in other actual entities.... The philosophy of organism is mainly devoted to the task of making clear the notion of 'being present in another entity.' ... The Aristotelian phrase suggests the crude notion that one actual entity is added to another *simpliciter*. This is not what is meant. One rôle of the eternal objects is that they are those elements which express how any one actual entity is constituted by its synthesis of other actual entities, and how that actual entity develops from the primary dative phase into its own individual actual existence, involving its individual enjoyments and appetitions. An actual entity is concrete because it is such a particular concrescence of the universe (PR 79c-80a).

The actual entities which are about to be absorbed into the new concrescing actual entity are called the initial data. An initial datum cannot, however, be incorporated into the new actual entity without some adjustments. These adjustments are basically of two sorts. First, the internal subjectivity which marked these past actual entities, when they were concrescing, is lost. When the satisfaction has been achieved, and when the final feeling no longer feels, then the actual entity has become a 'superject', and now it is ready for incorporation into other entities (PR 130a-b).[2] Second, any one past actual entity will have more component feelings than the new actual entity can use. This is because the new concrescence must integrate into itself all the past actual entities, and all these entities cannot be incorporated without conflict. A part of each actual entity must therefore be eliminated.[3] The act whereby this elimination is effected is called a negative prehension. What remains of the initial datum after having lost its immediacy and after having its unwanted portions eliminated is called the objective datum. (Compare diagram 4 and the related discussion on pages 10-11, above.)

II

The objective datum then is literally incorporated into the concrescing actual entity, but Whitehead warns us not to understand this act of incorporation "crudely." Perhaps the crudest way to understand the act of incorporation is to think of the past actual entity as having one separate and distinct identity, and the concrescing actual entity having another distinct identity, prior to and independently of the identity of the past actual entity; in that

---

2. One could argue that God's prehension of an actual entity in the world is an exception. Thus Whitehead sometimes speaks as though in the case of God's prehension of an actual entity, the (divinely prehended finite) entity is translated into God without the loss of immediacy. Compare: "In [God's] everlastingness, immediacy is reconciled with objective immortality" (PR 532b). The explanation is that God's breadth of vision is so large that what in any other situation would mean incompatibility is viewed by God as an intense contrast. Compare: "The perfection of God's subjective aim, derived from the completeness of his primordial nature, issues into the character of his consequent nature. In it there is no loss, no obstruction. The world is felt in a unison of immediacy" (PR 524e).

We need to face an exegetical problem. Does Whitehead consider subjective immediacy to be the only form of immediacy, or does he make a distinction between subjective immediacy and other forms of immediacy? No matter how wide and how perfect God's subjective aim, it is difficult to see how the finite entity's subjective immediacy could survive into God. The continuation in God of the finite entity's subjective immediacy would imply the continuation of the finite entity's concrescence in God. The continuation of the finite entity's process of concrescence would mean that it never completes its concrescence. This, however, runs counter, at a very deep level, to Whitehead's descriptions of the process of concrescence in finite entities. So it seems difficult to assert that the subjective immediacy of a finite entity continues in God. Perhaps Whitehead has some other form of immediacy in mind when he asserts that the finite entity in its "immediacy" survives into God.

3. God is an exception. In prehending a finite entity, God need not eliminate any portion of that entity. See Part Four, Chapter Nineteen, Section I.

case, the act whereby the concrescing actual entity "includes" the past actual entity would be parallel to the act whereby a glass "includes" the water which is poured into it. Clearly this is wrong. Rather, the concrescing actual entity has no identity apart from the fact that it is the integration of the past actual entities. (Although it is also true that the new actual entity is *more* than simply an integration of past entities—even so, however, the new concrescence has no identity *apart from* its role as integrator of the past.)

A

The act of incorporation, though, is more complicated than our discussion so far would indicate. The additional complication stems from the fact that this incorporation takes place by means of eternal objects playing a two-way role. In one sense, the eternal object characterizes the objective datum; in another sense, it characterizes the subjective form of the prehension of that datum. So much at least is clear when Whitehead says that simple physical feelings (which are simply acts of incorporation under a different name) conform to the past. More than this, however, is involved, as can be illustrated by the following two quotations.

> A simple physical feeling enjoys a characteristic which has been variously described as 're-enaction,' 'reproduction,' and 'conformation.' This characteristic can be more accurately explained in terms of the eternal objects involved. There are eternal objects determinant of the definiteness of the objective datum which is the 'cause,' and eternal objects determinant of the definiteness of the subjective form belonging to the 'effect.' When there is re-enaction there is one eternal object with two-way functioning, namely, as partial determinant of the objective datum, and as partial determinant of the subjective form. In this two-way rôle, the eternal object is functioning relationally between the initial data on the one hand and the concrescent subject on the other. It is playing one self-consistent role in obedience to the Category of Objective Identity (PR 364c).

> Apart from inhibitions or additions, weakenings or intensifications, due to the history of its production, the subjective form of a physical feeling is re-enaction of the subjective form of the feeling felt. Thus the cause passes on its feeling to be reproduced by the new subject as its own, and yet as inseparable from the cause. There is flow of feeling. But the re-enaction is not perfect. . . . The cause is objectively in the constitution of the effect, in virtue of being the feeler of the feeling reproduced in the effect with partial equivalence of subjective form (PR 362c-63a).

The only really clear message to come out of these passages is that Whitehead is quite difficult to understand on this point. We will try, nevertheless, to explicate the passages as follows. Let 'a' be one of the eternal objects which characterize an objective datum; further, let 'a' be that eternal object which also characterizes the subjective form of the prehension of that objective datum. Thus 'a' is the eternal object with a two-way role: 'a' is (part of) *what* the prehension feels, and 'a' is (part of) *how* the prehension feels.

B

At this point in our discussion, it is time to ask a question and to consider an objection. The question is about Whitehead's doctrine of objectification, and the objection is against our interpretation of that doctrine. The question is this. If the objective datum is a set of actual entities which are characterized by a set of eternal objects—and there is no more to be said about the nature of that objective datum—then how does a physical prehension of *that* objective datum as characterized by *those* eternal objects differ from a conceptual prehension of *those* eternal objects? In short, is an actual entity nothing more than a collection of eternal objects? And if so, then how would one distinguish between an *actual* entity which is a part of the world of process, of fact, and a collection of eternal objects which are mere potentialities?

The objection can be stated as follows. In our previous discussion, says the objector, we have intimated that the process of objectification is *more* than *merely* a repetition of eternal objects—for example, we have used the metaphor of "inclusion" in this connection. But why should we make this assumption? Would it not be simpler and more elegant, continues our objector, to say that the process of objectification *is* merely a matter of *repetition* of eternal objects—and *nothing* else? Thus, to say that one actual entity objectifies a past actual entity is to say (and *only* to say) that eternal object 'a' first characterizes one actual entity, the initial datum; and then eternal object 'a' characterizes a second actual entity, the concrescing actual entity. After all, observes the objector, when we explicated the passages quoted above on page 66, we spoke only of the repetition of eternal objects, and we had no need of any additional notion of "inclusion." The objector's case may be summarized as follows: since objectification amounts to no more than the repetition of eternal objects, our use of the notion of "inclusion" is not merely crude, but positively misleading.[4]

C

Before responding to the objector, we will try to answer the question. The difference between a set of eternal objects and an actual entity characterized by those eternal objects is that the actual entity is "a real fusion of the characters of eternal objects" (SMW 107c). But is not the appeal to "a real fusion" merely a reiteration that there *is* a difference between a set of eternal

4. Compare Christian's theory in his book as cited in note 1 on pp. 62-63. We have, of course, put Christian's interpretation into the mouth of the objector.

objects and an actual entity? (Molière in his play *Doctor in Spite of Himself*
caricatures such metaphysics by making one of his characters explain that
a sleeping potion works because it is a soporific with dormitive powers.)

In the final analysis, "the real fusion" of eternal objects into an actual entity is the result of "creativity." Creativity is to be compared to
Aristotle's notion of (prime) matter.

> 'Creativity' is another rendering of the Aristotelian 'matter,' and of the
> modern 'neutral stuff.' But it is divested of the notion of passive receptiv-
> ity either of 'form,' or of external relations; it is the pure notion of the ac-
> tivity conditioned by the objective immortality of the actual world — a
> world which is never the same twice, though always with the stable ele-
> ment of divine ordering. Creativity is without a character of its own in ex-
> actly the same sense in which the Aristotelian 'matter' is without a
> character of its own. It is that ultimate notion of highest generality at the
> base of actuality. It cannot be characterized, because all characters are more
> special than itself. But creativity is always found under conditions, and de-
> scribed as conditioned (PR 46b-47a).

In Aristotle's metaphysics, an actual entity (i.e., an entity which *is*
in the fullest sense) can be analyzed into two abstractions: matter and
form. Without the matter, the forms are merely universals; and without
the forms, matter cannot be characterized. Thus for Aristotle (on this interpretation) it is matter which provides the basis for distinguishing between an actual entity with such-and-such set of forms and those forms
considered as mere universals. (In the crudest—but rather helpful—terms,
it is matter which brings the Platonic forms down to earth.) In Whitehead's
metaphysics, eternal objects play the role of the forms, and creativity corresponds to Aristotle's (prime) matter. A set of eternal objects functions as
the determinants of an actual entity only when they characterize creativity; without creativity, they are merely a set of completely general
potentialities. On the other hand, without eternal objects, creativity would
be wholly formless, without character, and nonexistent.

There is another side to Whitehead's notion of creativity. On this
side, Whitehead's creativity can better be compared to Aquinas's notion
of "esse," as the "power of 'to be'," than to Aristotle's prime matter. In the
ultimate analysis, says Whitehead, we must explain the fact than any particular thing exists by referring to creativity. In other words, for any particular actual entity, "that" it exists is the result of creativity. But "what"
that particular entity is, is the result of (a) the past actual entities, (b) God,
and (c) its own decision. (Nothing can exist as a sheer "that"; it must have
some characteristics which account for "what" it is.)

> 'Creativity' is the principle of *novelty*. . . . The 'creative advance' is the ap-
> plication of this ultimate principle of creativity to each novel situation
> *which it originates* (PR 31f-32a; second emphasis added).

> The ultimate metaphysical principle is the advance from disjunction to conjunction, *creating* a novel entity other than the entities given in disjunction (PR 32b; emphasis added).

> In the abstract language here adopted for metaphysical statement, 'passing on' becomes 'creativity,' in the dictionary sense of the verb *creare*, 'to bring forth, beget, produce' (PR 324a).

As a result of creativity, a set of eternal objects which characterize an actual entity are infected by a particularity. Whitehead expresses this particularity by use of the term 'contrast', which has several distinct meanings in Whitehead's metaphysics. In one sense, a contrast is opposed to a 'relation', where a relation is a genus of contrasts (PR 348d-50a). For example, a particular shade of red may be related to a particular shade of green in a determinate manner; say the red is a three-by-two-inch rectangle located directly above the green which is a circle four inches in diameter: such would be a contrast. However, the set of all the possible contrasts between that particular shade of red and that particular shade of green would be a relation. But Whitehead also uses the term 'contrast' to mean that there is a particularity to actual entities which results from the presence of creativity.

> One use of the term 'contrast' is to mean that particularity of conjoint unity which arises from the realized togetherness of eternal objects. But there is another, and more usual sense of 'particularity.' This is the sense in which the term 'particular' is applied to an actual entity.
> One actual entity has a status among other actual entities, not expressible wholly in terms of contrasts between eternal objects. For example, the complex nexus of ancient imperial Rome to European history is not wholly expressible in terms of universals. . . . But it involves more. For it is the nexus of *that* Rome with *that* Europe. We cannot be conscious of this nexus purely by the aid of conceptual feelings. This nexus is implicit, below consciousness, in our physical feelings. In part we are conscious of such physical feelings, and of that particularity of the nexus between particular actual entities (PR 350b-c).[5]

We cannot conceive of or characterize this particularity, for that would reduce it to the status of one more universal. We can, however, feel this particularity. Indeed, in the last analysis, a physical prehension is simply a prehension of a datum which is infected by such particularity; whereas a conceptual prehension prehends characteristics (eternal objects) which are not so infected.

> This peculiar particularity of the nexus between actual entities can be put another way. Owing to the disastrous confusion, more especially by Hume,

---

5. There are, of course, other passages which state (or assume) that the presence of creativity gives an actual entity a status not wholly expressible in terms of eternal objects. For example: PR 30c, 76b, 86b, and 239b.

of conceptual feelings with perceptual feelings, the truism that we can only *conceive* in terms of universals has been stretched to mean that we can only *feel* in terms of universals. This is untrue. Our perceptual feelings feel particular existents (PR 351b).

In summary, the notion of particularity is closely tied to the notion of actuality. In referring to the particularity of an actual entity, Whitehead seems to be indicating that the actuality of an actual entity is more than the mere addition of creativity and eternal objects; and yet this "more," this "thatness," this "particularity" of an actual entity cannot be characterized conceptually since that would reduce it to one more eternal object. This particularity can only be felt.

We are now in a position to answer the question, "How does a prehension of an actual entity characterized by a specific set of eternal objects differ from a purely conceptual prehension of those same eternal objects?" The answer is that the functioning of creativity in the production of an actual entity results in the infection of that entity with a "peculiar particularity," a particularity which cannot be conceptualized or characterized, but only felt. In the prehension of an actual entity this particularity is felt; whereas it is absent in a purely conceptual prehension of the eternal objects which characterize the actual entity in question.

D

In the previous section, we reached the conclusion that in a physical prehension, the datum of that prehension is a past actual entity, where that past entity exhibits a "particularity" which cannot be conceptualized or characterized, but only felt. Such a claim, however, presupposes that the past actual entity is still "there" for the new actual entity to prehend—that is, it presupposes that the past actual entity is still actual in some sense. This presupposition is denied by Christian and Sherburne.[6] Christian claims that as an actual entity reaches its completion (i.e., completes its feeling of satisfaction), it is prehended by God and perishes. It is no longer available; it is gone; it has entirely vanished. Sherburne makes a similar claim. His reasoning is that actual entities are actual in virtue of their activity as self-creativity—that is, without activity there is no actuality. But as an actual entity concludes its feeling of satisfaction and loses its subjective immediacy, the process of creativity in it also stops and its activity ceases. Therefore, since actuality is a function of creativity and activity, it follows that with the passing of its satisfaction, an "actual" entity is no longer actual. Sherburne concludes his case that past "actual" entities are no longer

6. See Donald W. Sherburne, "The 'Whitehead without God' Debate: The Rejoinder." For Christian's views, see *Whitehead's Metaphysics*, 319-20.

actual by quoting from PR 43c: "It is fundamental to the metaphysical doctrine of the philosophy of organism, that the notion of an actual entity as the unchanging subject of change is completely abandoned."

It is reasonable to ask Sherburne and Christian how the past "actual" entities are prehended if they are no longer "there"; how does the past influence the present actual entities? Christian replies that the past exerts its influence through God. That is, God prehends into himself the perishing actual entity (and on Christian's view this simply means that the eternal objects which characterized the perishing actual entity are repeated in God). The new actual entity, in turn, prehends God, and, thereby, prehends the past actual entity as it is represented in God. (An interesting question about Christian's interpretation is this: would it not lead to monism? That is, one could argue that Christian's interpretation would result in the denial of finite relations, and it would make the relations of entities to God the only set of real relations. But this is a good definition of monism—something which Whitehead at least intended to avoid.)

We disagree with Sherburne and Christian. The past actual entities are really "there." Our response centers on four claims, each of which is outlined below. First Whitehead certainly writes as though the past "actual" entities are still actual. For example:

> To be actual must mean that all actual things are alike objects, enjoying objective immortality in fashioning creative actions; and that all actual things are subjects, each prehending the universe from which it arises (PR 89a).

> The doctrine of objectification is an endeavour to express how what is *settled in actuality* is repeated under limitations, so as to be 'given' for immediacy (PR 208a; emphasis added).

Second, Sherburne and Christian forget that an actual entity is both subject and superject. To take either away from the other is to leave an abstraction, a part torn from the whole. But in their emphasis on the functioning of the subject, they have ignored the fact that creativity as particularized in a specific actual entity involves the production of the subject-superject and not merely the subject. It will be recalled that in support of *his* position, Sherburne quoted Whitehead's rejection of the "notion of an actual entity as the unchanging subject of change." But in support of *our* interpretation, it is important to note what Whitehead says in the very next sentence.

> An actual entity is at once the subject experiencing and the superject of its experiences. It is subject-superject, and neither half of this description can for a moment be lost sight of. The term 'subject' will be mostly employed when the actual entity is considered in respect to its own real internal constitution. But 'subject' is always to be construed as an abbreviation of 'subject-superject' (PR 43c).

The following passage ties the actuality of an actual entity to its superjective nature even more closely than the previous quotation.

> An actuality is self-realizing, and whatever is self-realizing is an actuality. An actual entity is at once the subject of self-realization, and the superject which is self-realized (PR 340c).

The following quotation provides the theoretical foundation for the attribution of actuality to an actual entity construed as a unified subject-superject.

> The point to remember is that the fact that each individual occasion is transcended by the creative urge, belongs to the essential constitution of each such occasion. It is not an accident which is irrelevant to the completed constitution of any such occasion (AI 249b).

Third, the superjective nature of an actual entity does not contradict Whitehead's claim to have abandoned the category of substance—that is, "the notion of an actual entity as the unchanging subject of change." This is because what Whitehead is abandoning is the claim (as made for example by Aristototelians) that we are dealing with a metaphysically ultimate situation—an actual entity—when we describe, say, a horse as one and the same item which is "essentially" unchanging from birth to death, but also an item which sustains "accidental" changes such as modifications in location, size, temperature, hair-color, etc. Of course, the superjective nature of a Whiteheadian actual entity is nothing like that; it is not an Aristotelian substance. In fact, once an actual entity finishes its satisfaction and loses its subjective immediacy, an actual entity sustains no changes at all. Its incorporations into new concrescing actual entities constitute internal relations for the new entity, but they are merely external relations for the past actual entity (SMW 122c-23b).

This last point is worth expanding. To say that X has an internal relation to Y is to say that Y is a part of the very identity of X; any change in the identity of Y implies a change in the identity of X. To say that X has an external relation to Y is to say that Y is not a part of the identity of X, and thus Y could change without X being changed. The fact that the new concrescing entity has an internal relation to its past actual entities means that those past actual entities are a part of the very identity of the concrescing entity; and if the past entities were other than what they were, then the concrescing entity would be other than it is. In contrast, however, the relation of the past entities to the new concrescence is external for those past entities; no matter what the identity of the new concrescing entity, it will not affect the identity of those past entities.[7] The past en-

---

7. There is an exception. While the concrescing actual entity *in its immediacy, in its particularity* cannot be present in the past entities, there is a sense in which the concrescing entity may be reduced to the region it occupies. We have discussed this in relation to propositions

tities are not affected by what happens in the concrescing entity. The fact that the relation between the concrescing entity and the past actual entities is not symmetrical allows Whitehead to affirm (A) the real presence of the past world (the world "out-there") in the new entity as a part of the very identity of that new entity, and it also allows Whitehead to affirm (B) a genuine plurality of actual entities. If the relation between past entities and the concrescing entity were symmetrical, it would have to be either external for both the past and the present entities or it would have to be internal for both. On the one hand, if the relation were symmetrical and *external*, it would be easy to affirm a plurality of actual entities, as Leibniz did, but all of Leibniz's problems of relating his monads to each other would reappear (problems of how they know about each other, how they can interact with each other, etc.). On the other hand, if the relation between actual entities (past and present) were symmetrical and *internal*, it would be easy to relate the actual entities to each other, but it would also be difficult to affirm their plurality. This is exactly the problem faced by Hegel and the idealist tradition. It was also a problematic aspect of some Buddhist traditions.[8] Whitehead can affirm both the real presence of the "other" (i.e., the past actual entities) in the "subject" as well as a plurality of actual entities precisely because the relation between the past and the present is asymmetrical.

Fourth, *where* then is a past actual entity? The answer is, in the extensive continuum, where it will be forever. As new actual entities are created, the actualized portion of the extensive continuum expands, and the past actual entity, its immediacy having perished and evaporated, remains immobile and locked into its spatial-temporal position. And as new actual entities continue to succeed each other, the status of that past becomes even more remote. Thus we find Whitehead making the following sorts of comments.

---

about contemporary and future actual entities. The region is an element in the extensive continuum, and the entire set of relations and relata in the continuum are present in each actual entity. Therefore, (A) the region occupied by the concrescing entity is present in the past entities. Therefore, (B) the past actual entities have an internal relation to the region occupied by the concrescing entity. And therefore, (C) the past actual entities have an internal relation to the concrescing entity insofar as that concrescing entity has been *reduced to the region it occupies*.

8. Steve Odin has written a useful comparison of Whitehead's metaphysics with a school of Northeast Asian Buddhism known as Hua-yen (or Kegon-kyoo in Japanese), *Process Metaphysics and Hua Yen Buddhism: A Critical Study of Cumulative Penetration vs. Interpenetration*, (Albany: State University of New York Press, 1982). Hua-yen Buddhism assumed that each object was fully present in each other object, this mutual interpenetration extending both forwards and backwards in time. As a result, Hua-yen Buddhism affirmed that the entire universe, including the entire future, was present in each moment and each place. In such a scheme, the distinction between individual moments and individual places becomes vague. While certain religious interests may cause Hua-yen Buddhism to value highly this vagueness between individual entities, Whitehead's goal was to affirm a pluralism of individual entities.

When we further consider how to adjust Newton's other descriptions to
the organic theory, the surprising fact emerges that we must identify the
atomized quantum of extension correlative to an actual entity, with Newton's absolute place and absolute duration. Newton's proof that motion
does not apply to absolute place . . . also holds. Thus *an actual entity never
moves:* it is *where* it is and *what* it is (PR 113b; our emphases).

> Actual occasions are immovable, so that the doctrine of coinci-
> dence is nonsense (PR 508c).

We realize, however, that despite the above proof-texts, this fourth point
remains highly tendentious. This fourth point needs a major critique of
the notion of the 'extensive continuum.' In part, this critique is provided
in Chapter Eight of Part Two. While we will not reintroduce the consideration of this fourth point into that chapter, the interested reader may
wish to apply the material in that chapter to the issue raised in this fourth
point.

It should be further noted that we are opposed to the connection of
actuality with the process of self-creativity (which is the heart of Sherburne's
argument) *only* when this is taken to deny that past actual entities are also
actual. Of course, we hold that actuality attaches to an actual entity in virtue of its *unified* nature as a subject and as a superject. But when the subject
is isolated from the superject, then we will readily grant to Sherburne that
the actuality of an actual entity stems primarily from the self-creativity of
the subject—*as long as* this is not construed as denying that the superject is
also actual in at least a secondary sense. This secondary status of the actuality
of the superject must, however, be strong enough to sustain the position that
the past actual entities are still "there" for the new entity to prehend.

If we interpret actuality as suggested in the preceding paragraph,
then the term actuality becomes (to use Thomistic vocabulary) analogical.
This is, "actuality" is *directly* applied to an actual entity as subject-superject. But it may be applied *by analogy* to an actual entity construed as a superject. Moreover, it may be possible to "stretch" this analogy even further and consider the extensive continuum to be, in some slight sense,
actual in virtue of its exemplification in the initial stage of all finite actual
entities whatsoever. (Some scholars claim that even God exemplifies the
continuum: see Part Two, and Chapter Nineteen of Part Four.) If this is
true, then the regions in the extensive continuum may be considered, in a
very extended and analogical sense, to be actual entities. The importance
of considering regions in the continuum as actual entities is that it
provides us with a way of understanding propositions about the present
and about the future. That is, the logical subjects of propositions must be
actual entities. But the only aspects of contemporary and future actual entities which are in the concrescing entity are the regions they occupy. Thus
if we can consider these regions to be actual entities, then the future and

contemporary actual entities are in the concrescing entity and propositions about them can be constructed.

E

We may now respond to the objector. It will be recalled that the objector argued that objectification is merely a matter of repetition and that our use of the metaphor "inclusion" was both superfluous and misleading. In other words, continues the objector, if 'a' is the eternal object in question, then why not interpret Whitehead's claim that 'a' is (part of) *what* the prehension feels, and 'a' is (part of) *how* the prehension feels, as a claim that 'a', which first was present in the past actual entity, is *simply and merely* repeated in the new actual entity? Thus we could avoid the use of the misleading metaphor, "inclusion." In response, let us first grant that, clearly, a repetition does occur here. The eternal object which first characterized the past actual entity (as a part of the datum) is repeated in the new actual entity (as a part of the subjective form). That, however, cannot be the whole story. The past actual entity is infected by a peculiar particularity. The new actual entity is also infected by a peculiar particularity. And since each peculiar particularity is correlative to a distinct actual entity, then to the extent that each actual entity is a separate and distinct entity, it follows that each of these peculiar particularities must also be separate and distinct. (This remains the case even though these particularities cannot be characterized; each of them remains the particularity of a specific actual entity.) Thus 'a' will be implicated in one particularity in its role as a character of the objective datum, and it will be implicated in a different peculiarity in its role as a character of the subjective form of the prehension of that objective datum. It is this particularity for which the theory of "repetition" cannot account. Since the particularity of one actual entity cannot be the particularity of another actual entity, it follows that if objectification were merely a matter of the repetition of eternal objects, then the particularity of the past actual entity would not enter the new actual entity.[9] Therefore, if the particularity of the past actual entity is to be felt by the new actual entity, then that past actual entity must itself be present in the new actual entity—the new actual entity must include the past actual entity as the datum felt.

Of course, the entire initial datum cannot be present in the new actual entity; only a part of the initial datum is present, which is called the objective datum. (We discussed previously the need for negative prehensions and elimination.) Even though the particularity of an actual entity stems from the character of the actual entity as a whole, this particularity extends to every part of the actual entity. Therefore, the objective datum

---

9. It would also follow that if objectification were solely a matter of the repetition of eternal objects, the new entity would not really be new.

carries with it the particularity which belongs to the whole actual entity; and when the concrescing entity feels a past entity which has been reduced to an objective datum, that concrescing entity is still feeling the past physically, that is, as a concrete fact which is really "there" and which is more than a collection of eternal objects, of universals.

Whitehead himself stated this position in *Process and Reality.*

> A simple physical feeling has the dual character of being the cause's feeling re-enacted for the effect as subject. But this transference of feeling effects a partial identification of cause with effect, and not a mere representation of the cause. It is the cumulation of the universe and not a stage-play about it. In a simple feeling there is a double particularity in reference to the actual world, the particular cause and the particular effect (PR 363c).

It must be confessed, however, that when one first reads Whitehead's metaphysical writings, the most striking aspect of his doctrine of objectification is the repetition of eternal objects. It is only upon additional reflection that it becomes evident that these passages must be connected with the doctrine of objectification. For example, in Dorothy Emmet's book *Whitehead's Philosophy of Organism* she construed objectification primarily in terms of the repetition of eternal objects. Whitehead himself wrote her a letter reviewing this book, which Emmet quoted in her second edition. In the letter Whitehead stressed that objectification could not be limited to the repetition of eternal objects.

> (1) "You seem to me at various points to forget my doctrine of 'immanence' which governs the whole treatment of objectification. Thus at times you write as tho' the connection between past and present is merely that of a transfer of *character.* Then there arises [sic] all the perplexities of 'correspondence' in epistemology, of causality, and of memory. The doctrine of *immanence* is fundamental.[10]

III

Whitehead's polemic against the bifurcation of the world can also be developed in another direction. We turn to one of Whitehead's most distinguished students, Charles Malik. In later life, Malik became the chairman of the commission which drafted the Universal Declaration of Human Rights, president of the thirteenth session of the United Nations General Assembly, and a professor at the American University of Beirut, Lebanon. Malik wrote a Ph.D. dissertation at Harvard under Whitehead himself, "The Metaphysics of Time in the Philosophies of A. N. Whitehead and M. Heidegger" (1937), in which he compared Whitehead's philosophy with Martin Heidegger's.

10. Dorothy Emmet, *Whitehead's Philosophy of Organism,* xxii-xxiii. The emphases and bracketed material are in Emmet's book.

In the conclusion to Malik's dissertation are two interesting claims. First, Whitehead's metaphysical system is rooted in human experience, from which it derives its real meaning. Second, in trying to generalize this description to all reality, however, Whitehead loses precisely this concrete humanness from which his philosophy began.

We will present two illustrative quotations from Malik. The first indicates the true source of Whitehead's philosophy. "Every concept in Professor Whitehead's philosophy assumes its full unambiguous transparency of meaning only when it is finally reduced to personal terms, i.e., to terms which involve you in one of your modes of being as a total person" (p. 340). The second quotation indicates the ultimate result, in Malik's judgment, of Whitehead's method of generalizing from concrete human experience to all reality. "Therefore, to have ruthlessly dissolved man in things is to have affirmed his lostness in them (which is right), to have refused him the right to be freed of them (which is wrong), and to have in effect missed man as man altogether" (p. 345).

Malik raises a fundamental methodological question. As we noted previously in this chapter, the bifurcations between the human world and the natural world have been standard in Western culture at least since Descartes and reached their classical expression in Kant's distinction between the phenomenal world and the noumenal world. Do these bifurcations serve to protect our human integrity or do they destroy our human integrity by isolating us from the very world which provides us with our context? Western culture is profoundly ill at ease with this question.

On the one hand, there is a strong urge to reconnect the human with the natural world. Usually this is done by insisting on the "reduction" of the human world to the natural world. This takes place when it is asserted, for example, that "man is the naked ape." It is also done when it is asserted that the facts discovered by physics, biology, or economics provide the "really real" explanations or the most "objective" explanations of us and of our world. Sometimes the urge to reconnect the human with the natural world takes a less reductionist basis, as we saw two decades ago with the "flower children" of the 60s and 70s. These people delighted in nature, but in a nature which had been richly humanized and populated with witches, mythical beings, copper bracelets with magical powers, and flowers that preferred Mozart to Rock-n-Roll. At the academic level, we can point to Heidegger, the existentialist figure in Malik's dissertation, who truly wished to reintegrate humans with the primordial world of being, with the world as "ready-to-hand" and not merely with the world as an object for dispassionate scientific analysis or for commercial exploitation.

On the other hand, these attempts at reintegration have not been wholly successful nor universally applauded. For example, biological and economic research has not solved our ethical or political dilemmas but has merely added more dilemmas. Ethical discourse on these new issues, it would appear, demands more than scientific language if we humans are to discuss them intelligently, to say nothing of solving them. Another, and very curious, sign of the failure of modern culture to achieve our reunion with nature is the tendency of many natural and social scientists to resist speaking of "causes," and to prefer speaking of "statistically significant correlations" within a set of data. Since, as Whitehead shows many times, the concrete world of everyday experience is a world of power and causality, it follows that the gradual fading of "cause" from the scientific vocabulary hints at the increasing isolation of the contemporary scientist/observer from that concrete world. Another indication of doubt about some of our Western attempts to reintegrate human beings with the natural world is this: within the academy, many scholars in the humanities, as well as some scientists, have resisted the imperialist claim that the scientific method is the sole source of truth, arguing that other methods are also productive of truth and perhaps, on occasion, of wisdom. Similar doubts may be found outside the academy: for many people, the attraction of conservative Christianity lies partly in its insistence that human beings have "souls" which are the seat of our essential humanity, the implication being that we human beings can be reduced neither to our bodies nor to those roles which define human beings as merely one-of-the-many-species. Lastly, it is worth noting that the older bifurcation between the human and the natural world reappears even in Heidegger's philosophy. Heidegger argues for a sharp split between the authentic world (read "noumenal" world) where freedom reigns and the inauthentic world (read "phenomenal" world) which science observes, which commercial interests consider as merely "present-to-hand," and where determinism reigns.

As previously mentioned, Whitehead clearly opposes the bifurcation between the human and the scientific worlds, between the noumenal and the phenomenal worlds. Whitehead, however, has no interest in those schemes which "reduce" the human to the natural. Rather, Malik is correct that Whitehead takes human experience to be the key and that he interprets reality as a whole in light of the character of human experience. (In this Whitehead has a curious resemblance to the flower children of the 60s and 70s, but he wishes to take science seriously and demonstrates little interest in their magical copper bracelets.) Malik failed, however, to discuss *why* Whitehead is able to take human experience as a key to the nature of all reality.

At this point we will use Kant's terms "noumenal" and "phenomenal," although Whitehead does not himself employ them. For the sake of argument, let us correlate Kant's "noumenal reality" with Whitehead's "actuality" as described in the previous section.[11] We will let

11. "Correlate" does not mean "strictly equate." Obviously, there are significant differences between the technical use of "noumenon" in Kant's philosophy and the technical

"noumenal reality" refer to whatever it is that serves as the foundation for and makes possible our human world of perception, intellection, consciousness, experience, and the like. In Whitehead's system, there are two forms of noumenal reality: first, the concrescing actual entity, and second, the past actual entities.[12] The point is this. Whitehead's two forms of actuality or noumenal reality are intimately connected, each needing the other for its complete explication. The noumenal reality "out-there" (the past actual entities) becomes a part of the noumenal reality "in-here" (the concrescing actual entity); and the noumenal reality "in-here" will become one of the noumenal realities "out-there." In Whitehead's metaphysics, phenomenal reality (the world as it appears to us in ordinary human consciousness and in ordinary perception) is doubly connected to the noumenal world. The phenomenal world is (A) constructed by the new actual entity during its *concrescence,* which is one form of noumenal reality, and (B) it is constructed out of the *past actual entities,* which constitute the other type of noumenal reality.

Since Kant and Whitehead agree that the subject has a role in the production of the phenomenal world, it can be said that they also agree that the subject can have true knowledge of that phenomenal world. Kant does not, however, give a description of how the noumenal world "out-there" is present in the subject. The reason, it would seem, is that for Kant the noumenal world "out-there" simply is *not* present in the subject. Since the noumenal world "out-there" is not present in the subject, the subject has no way of moving from the phenomenal world to the noumenal world —that is, the subject has no way of making knowledge claims about the noumenal world. For Kant, the most we can do is to make certain practical postulates about the noumenal world. According to Kant, these postulates of practical reason (concerning, for example, God, immortality, and freedom) are the preconditions of our ethical practice; and they ought not to be construed as theoretical claims to knowledge about what is the case in the world "in itself." Kant's philosophy, in sum, affirms the possibility

---

use of "actuality" in Whitehead's. We make no claim that we are using "noumenon" in Kant's precise meaning. Rather we will exploit some of the suggestive similarities between Kant's "noumena" and Whitehead's "actuality" to help clarify another way in which Whitehead overcomes the bifurcations of previous philosophers, particularly Kant.

12. In Kantian philosophy, it would not be common to use the term "noumenal" to describe the subject's own reality. For Whitehead, however, the act of concrescence is the central meaning of actuality. Thus, to the extent that we adjust the Kantian term "noumenal" to fit with the Whiteheadian vision of 'actuality', it follows that "noumenal" will refer primarily to concrescence (and to the subject/superject as a whole) and secondarily to the past actual world.

When discussing Whitehead's attempt to overcome our bifurcations of nature, we will often use the term noumenal to refer to an entity's actual world. It should not be forgotten, however, that the act of concrescing is the foundation of actuality and thus the primary referent for 'noumenal' from a Whiteheadian perspective.

of genuine knowledge (as opposed to practical postulates) about the phenomenal world, but it will not allow such knowledge claims about the noumenal world.

What would a culture that is formed by Kant's perspective look like? Such a culture would prefer to limit truth-claims to language that describes the world as it appears to us—i.e., to "scientific" and other forms of "factual" knowledge of the phenomenal world. That culture would be profoundly skeptical towards alleged knowledge of the noumenal world — skeptical, for example, towards ethics, religion, art, and metaphysics insofar as they are understood to be making cognitive claims about that noumenal world. A Kantian culture will also encourage skepticism about science when construed as providing truth about the way things are in themselves.[13]

Since it is difficult if not impossible to avoid these disciplines (ethics, religion, science as providing us with cognitive contact with noumenal reality, etc.), a Kantian culture has several options. It can try to narrow the focus of the truth claims which such disciplines may "legitimately" make. Thus religious language, rather than telling us about what is the case in the world, expresses only what is "ultimate for me." Or ethics becomes an expression of the speaker's positive or negative feelings towards some item. Another option may be retreat into mysticism. For a Kantian culture, the most plausible interpretation of many of these areas, however, may well be this: such disciplines articulate the presuppositions of our actions. Thus ethics articulates the presuppositions which are necessary if as a culture we are going to opt for certain patterns of human interaction. Such ethical statements (e.g., we ought to strive for an equality of opportunity for all humans) are not construed as claims about the nature of reality, but only as expressions of the regulative commitments of our culture. The emphasis will be on practice (or praxis) as the ground and norm of such "truth".

In contrast to Kant, Whitehead gives us a description of how the

13. It is a most informal means of gathering data, but I have had many conversations on this and related topics with the scientists on the faculties of the colleges and universities where I have taught. Most physicists, for example, are aware of the contribution of the knower/scientist to the character of the world known. They often make reference to Heisenberg's famous uncertainty principle. Nonetheless, most of these people are also convinced that through their science they are making contact with reality as it is at its most basic level. (Thus, in their opinion, the world as it genuinely exists "at its roots" *is* the world which interfaces with the scientist, and it *is* the world which the experimenter helps to mold in the process of carrying out the experiments.) While such personal convictions are not a part of science as such, and while success in scientific research does not necessarily entail insight into the philosophic and theoretical underpinnings of science, it is my impression that such convictions are often essential in the motivation to continue doing scientific research. If this is correct, then we must add science, at least as understood by some scientists, to the list of disciplines which attempt to make cognitive descriptions about the character of the noumenal world, of the world as it is at its most basic and foundational level.

noumenal world "out there" is present in the noumenal world "in here." (That is, Whitehead describes how the past actual entities are present in the new concrescence as a part of its essential nature.) Therefore, the fact that the subject has a role in constructing the phenomenal world does not entail for Whitehead the isolation of the subject from the noumenal world "out there." It does not entail the limitation of knowledge to the world as constructed by human beings. It does not entail a bifurcation between the noumenal world "out there" and the subject "in here."

Earlier we mentioned that Malik failed to explain why Whitehead takes human experience as a key for interpreting all reality. We now have the theoretical justification for this use of human experience: the fact that the world "out-there" is present in the subject "in-here" means that human experience includes within itself noumenal reality and thus can serve as a guide to the nature of reality.

We also have presented the outlines of Whitehead's theoretical justification for claiming that language has the capacity to describe[14] noumenal reality — that is, to describe actuality. Whitehead agrees, of course, that language is a part of the phenomenal world which is constructed by the subject. But as we noted previously, Whitehead also argues that the subject (i.e., the concrescing actual entity) constructs this phenomenal world out of the actual entities present in the first stage of its concrescence. Thus language has an inherent connection with the noumenal world which it describes. Whitehead's denial of a bifurcation between noumenal and phenomenal actuality—that is, between the world "out-there" and the world "in-here" or between past actual entities and the concrescing actual entity—restores to language its capacity to provide us with genuine knowledge about the noumenal world.

Whitehead's argument for the capacity of language—and even of religious language — to give us cognitive contact with the actual or noumenal world would be enormously strengthened by providing a plausible description of *how* the concrescing actual entity produces ordinary human perception and language out of the noumenal world. It is the task of Parts II and III of this book to describe the details of the emergence of the human world of sense perception, symbolism, and language during the process of concrescence. And it is the task of Part IV of this book to apply this description of experience and language to the specific case of religious experience and language.

14. Whitehead never assumes that the only, or even the most significant, function of language is to describe reality. He is very much aware of the other, "non-cognitive" uses of language. Later we will discuss these other uses of language in some detail. Since, however, the capacity of ethical, religious, metaphysical, and similar forms of language to describe reality—that is, to give us information about what is the case—has often been denied, this is the issue on which we focus in the main text.

There are two final comments to be made before proceeding to the next section of this chapter. First, Whitehead's success in reuniting the object with the subject depends completely on his adopting a "process" perspective. (By "reunion of the object with the subject," we mean the presence in the concrescing entity of its past actual entities or, stated alternatively, the presence of the noumenal world "out-there" in the noumenal world "in-here".) The past world can be present in the new world precisely because it is the *past* world. Later in this book we will comment in detail on Whitehead's denial of the possibility of contemporary actual entities mutually prehending each other. The point is this: Kant assumed that if the noumenal world "out-there" were to be present in the subject, it would have to be the *contemporary* noumenal world which was present. Furthermore, in Kant's scheme, both the subject and the noumenal world "out-there" are substances which endure through time. Thus, for Kant, if the noumenal world were present in the subject, the noumenal world would lose its identity and become wholly subsumed under the subject's identity. This is one of the classic claims of idealism. Thus the presence of the contemporary noumenal world in the subject would alter Kant's metaphysical scheme into an idealism. It is Whitehead's genius, through the elimination of the category of substance and by stressing the category of process, to find a way of affirming the presence of the world "out-there" within the subject, and to do so without retreating into idealism and without losing the independent reality of that outside world.

The second of our final two comments is this. Whitehead does not deny the role of the subject in constructing the phenomenal world. He does not have a naïve realism. The history of philosophy from Descartes to Kant is the history of the increasing awareness of the contribution of the subject in the construction of world as it appears to us, that is, in the construction of the experienced world in which we actually live. Whitehead accepts that history and strongly affirms the capacity of the subject to create its own lived world. The process of concrescence (i.e., the process by which the objective universe as many becomes the subjective universe as one) is precisely the creation of the universe as we live in it. The following chapters will deal in detail with *how* the phenomenal world emerges in this process of concrescence. In Whitehead's metaphysics, it must be stressed again, the process of creating the phenomenal world is not isolated from the noumenal world of actuality. It is this connection of the phenomenal world with the noumenal world which allows Whitehead to use ordinary human experience as a key to the nature of reality and to cultivate a positive assessment of the capacity of human consciousness and language to place us in cognitive contact with reality in all its dimensions.

IV

We are now in a position to discuss the second of the three major flaws in Pols's criticism which we mentioned in the previous chapter on page 51. First let us fully state this second issue. Pols takes very seriously Whitehead's claim that an actual entity becomes a subject only at the end of its concrescence. Pols then asks a very simple question. If an actual entity is a subject only at the end of its concrescence, then what is it that becomes a subject? It appears to Pols that there is nothing which becomes a subject; rather the subject just appears! According to Pols, this is nonsense because actuality must have a base from which it operates. Without such a base, we cannot say that an actual entity is free or that it concresces. In other words, without such a base, there is nothing which can have that freedom or which can undergo the act of concrescence. Pols puts his own case as follows.

> The question now arises not whether self-creation in this sense is plausible, but whether it affords us any useful conception of the "self" that is said to create itself. It seems reasonable that an entity that creates itself should exhibit a coalescence of active power and order. It should actively master the received conditions that for Whitehead constitute actuality, and its creative activity should in doing this draw upon what is actual in a different sense. If we are told, on the contrary, that what in self-creation does not spring from the actuality of the objectively immortal world springs from nowhere, we may agree that this cannot be ruled out, but may also wonder why we should call what thus springs into being a *subject*.[15]

Pols makes much the same point in another passage.

> The metaphorical character of certain of the ideas in terms of which Whitehead's doctrine of freedom is developed does much to obscure this conclusion. Most prominent are such notions as 'lure' and 'persuasion,' which have the aspect of honorific metaphors in a context where freedom is a desirable characteristic. There must always be something that is to be persuaded, or something that is to be lured, if these words are to have any meaning. Indeed, the terms presuppose that there is a kind of recalcitrance of something or other as over against the efforts of God. This must appear as some kind of power, and yet, if our analysis is tolerably accurate, it would seem that, if anything is lured or persuaded, it is a pure indetermination, or prime matter.[16]

The most complete outline of this argument against Whitehead is on pages 156-57 of Pols's book. It is too long to be quoted *verbatim*. We may, however, summarize it as follows. The process of creating a new subject

---

15. *Whitehead's Metaphysics*, 131.
16. Ibid., 138-39.

may be ascribed, according to Whitehead's system, to creativity. But, because at the start of the concrescence there is no thing to be lured or persuaded, it follows that either (A) the emergence of the subject is to be
ascribed completely to God or (B) "the emergence of new togetherness is
so totally arbitrary as to be indistinguishable from chance."[17]

In our opinion, Pols has raised an excellent question. Given the
terms in which he frames the question, Pols's criticism has, for us, a very
real plausibility. Whether this plausibility stems from a shared common
sense or from a shared crypto-Aristotelianism, it does indeed seem proper
to demand that an actual entity "be there" if we are to speak of luring or
persuading that actual entity. Moreover, on some interpretations of
Whitehead's system, Pols's criticism seems to be unanswerable; specifically, if the past actual entities are no longer in any sense actual, or if objectification is merely a matter of the repetition of eternal objects, then
Pols's criticism is beyond reproach. We do not share, however, these interpretations of Whitehead. And, given our interpretation, we believe that
we can answer Pols's attack, and we believe that we can provide that
answer, to a large extent, on his own terms.

It will be recalled that at its first stage of concrescence an actual entity incorporates its past actual entities into itself. But these past actual entities are still in some sense actual. Therefore, since the first stage is a collection of (as well as a perspective upon) these past entities, it follows that
the new entity at its first stage of development has a form of actuality. In
other words, actuality attaches not only to the "overall" subject-superject,
and not only to the superject, and not only to the subject, but also it attaches to each phase in the act of concrescence. Whether the term
'actuality' is univocal or analogical throughout these various uses, we
must insist that an actual entity in each of these roles is still actual, and in
particular we must insist that an actual entity at each of its phases of development is genuinely actual.

> It is a process proceeding from phase to phase, each phase being the real
> basis from which its successor proceeds towards the completion of the
> thing in question. Each actual entity bears in its constitution the 'reasons'
> why its conditions are what they are. These 'reasons' are the other actual
> entities objectified for it (PR 327b).

In Section I.D of the last chapter, we stressed that at its first stage
of concrescence an actual entity was not totally indeterminate. We may
now make our application of that section. If an actual entity at its first stage
of concrescence were totally indeterminate, then there would be no sense
in which the actual entity at that phase of development would be a "thing"
or have actuality. It would be no-thing, and Pols's criticisms would be

17. Ibid., 157.

most appropriate. This is not the case. Rather, at its first stage of development, an actual entity is partially determinate and partially indeterminate, that is, the new entity is partially "open" and partially "closed." Moreover, at this first stage of development, a new actual entity gains this character, at least in part, from the fact that it *is* a collection of actual entities which have all retained (some form of) their actuality and which have passed that actuality (in a different form, perhaps) to that new entity. (Compare "Each creative act is the universe incarnating itself as one" [PR 375a].)

To give us an additional focus, we will select two sentences from Pols's criticism as we quoted it earlier, and give a specific response to each sentence. First, Pols claims that "there must always be something that is to be persuaded, or something that is to be lured, if these words are to have any meaning." It would seem, however, that by showing that the first stage of concrescence has actuality we have shown that for Whitehead there is something with actuality that can be persuaded or lured—something which can become a subject.

Pols also claims that an actual entity "should actively master the received conditions that for Whitehead constitute actuality, and its creative activity should in doing this draw upon what is actual in a different sense." There are, however, several different meanings which Pols might have in mind for this passage. In part, at least, Pols seems to be saying that an actual entity should have a "base of operations" which is actual; that is, it ought not to pop into existence from nowhere. But Whitehead provides such a base of operations in the first stage of concrescence. Moreover, each phase of growth serves as the "actual" base of operations for the next step until the satisfaction—and then the satisfaction will be incorporated into future actual entities and will serve as an element in the actual base of operations of each of these future entities.

However, in the sentence quoted, Pols may also be saying, in part, that there must be an interplay of different senses of actuality if an entity is to be free to master the given conditions in its environment. Specifically, the agent should be actual in one sense, and the materials which the agent masters should be actual in another sense. But we find this to be precisely the case in Whitehead's scheme—if we may assume that "actuality" is an analogical term. The given conditions in the environment are the past actual entities, and the agent is the concrescing entity. But a concrescing entity is actual in a sense different from that of the past actual entities. We explain as follows. We mentioned previously that if we construe "actuality" as a term with a series of analogous applications, then the paradigmatic application of "actuality" was to the subject-superject as a whole; and we also said that the term "actuality" could be applied in an analogous fashion to an actual entity in its more limited roles, such as (A) the actual entity as its satisfaction prior to becoming a superject, (B) the actual entity as a concrescing entity, and (C) the actual entity as a superject. Lastly, we held that application of "actuality" to a concrescing actual entity was less "extended" than the application to the superject. Now—to come back to our original point—since the given conditions in the environment are past actual entities, they are actual in a more extended, and thus different, sense than the concrescing entity which is actual in a more direct sense.

Pols might have two other meanings in mind for the second sentence. These additional meanings are, however, totally unacceptable from a Whiteheadian point of view. Consider agent A and received conditions C. Pols may be claiming that agent A must exist temporally prior to its encounter with conditions C. An example of this would be a sculptor who is making a statue. Clearly the sculptor exists prior to his meeting the clay, and the sculptor, after meeting the clay, freely models the clay into a statue of his choice. Whitehead, of course, would not accept this. The example involves a highly abstract situation, and it would be a mistake, in Whitehead's opinion, to confuse it with a metaphysically ultimate situation. In addition, Pols may also be claiming that the received conditions C must be wholly separate from agent A, so that the identity of agent A cannot in any sense include conditions C. The sculptor making the statue could serve as an example of this also. The sculptor is one thing, and the clay is another; and the clay does not in any way enter into the identity of the sculptor. Once again, however, Whitehead would insist that the sculptor making the statue does not represent a genuinely metaphysical situation. Thus Whitehead would reject both the claim that it is metaphysically necessary for the agent to exist temporally prior to its meeting with the received conditions and the claim that it is metaphysically necessary for the agent to have an identity which is wholly separate and distinct from the received conditions. We will not catalogue all the attacks which Whitehead makes on the kinds of philosophy implicit in both of these claims, that is, Whitehead's attacks on these themes in Aristotle, Descartes, etc. Rather, we will note that both of these claims entail the rejection of Whitehead's notion of concrescence and genetic priority. (Actually, according to Whitehead, in the act of concrescence, the agent [the new actual entity] does *not* exist temporally prior to the received conditions [the past actual entities].) It would be, however, simply dogmatic to use these two claims as a basis for rejecting Whitehead's theory of concrescence and genetic priority. Either Pols (if indeed he would affirm these latter two claims as valid interpretations of his position) would be required to provide independent reasons of significant force for thinking these two claims to be true, or Pols would be required to find reasons for rejecting Whitehead's theory of concrescence and genetic priority as inapplicable, incoherent, inconsistent, or implausible so that his position would become a more likely alternative. In fact, Pols follows the latter course; he rejects Whitehead's theory of concrescence and genetic priority as we saw in our discussion of the subjective aim. Pols, however, does not present adequate reasons for rejecting Whitehead's position. Indeed, in our opinion, he has not even understood the theory of genetic priority and concrescence—let alone given us any good reasons for rejecting it—as we demonstrated in the previous chapter.

V

In the remainder of Chapter Three we will discuss five closely related topics. First, we will consider the transitivity of the relation of inclusion. Second, we will discuss how the first three categorical obligations govern the concrescing actual entity's reduction of its initial data to objective data. Third, we will investigate Whitehead's claim that the existence of negative prehensions cannot destroy that identity which an actual entity attains as a subject-superject. Fourth, we will try to interpret Whitehead's claim that each new actual entity incorporates every one of the actual entities in its past by means of a *simple* physical prehension, where it will be remembered that a simple prehension can have only a single actual entity as its datum. Fifth, we will briefly draw out the implications of our discussion in this section for the status of propositions about contemporary and future actual entities.

The relationship of inclusion is transitive. That is, if concrescing actual entity A includes past actual entity B, and B in turn included actual entity C from its past, then A also includes C. From this process of inclusion, no entity in the actual world of A can escape positive inclusion in A.

> An actual entity in the actual world of a subject *must* enter into the concrescence of that subject by *some* simple causal feeling, however vague, trivial, and submerged. Negative prehensions may eliminate its distinctive importance. But in some way, by some trace of causal feeling, the remote actual entity is prehended positively (PR 366a).

The various acts of incorporation (i.e., objectifications), whereby the past is included in the present, are governed by categoreal obligations one, two, and three. The first categoreal obligation, "The Category of Subjective Unity," states that the process whereby the concrescing actual entity reduces an initial datum to an objective datum is guided by the fact that the concrescing actual entity must pull itself together into one complete and unified subject-superject. Thus the objective data which are abstracted from the initial data are all *compatible* for integration into *that* new actual entity. The second and third categoreal obligations, "The Category of Objective Identity" and "The Category of Objective Diversity" together guarantee that no actual entity, no matter how remote in the past, ever totally loses its identity as a separate and distinct actual entity. Whitehead writes,

Thus the process of integration, which lies at the very heart of the concrescence, is the urge imposed on the concrescent unity of that universe by the three Categories of Subjective Unity, of Objective Identity, and of Objective Diversity. The oneness of the universe, and the oneness of each element in the universe, repeat themselves to the crack of doom in the creative advance from creature to creature, each creature including in itself the whole of history and exemplifying the self-identity of things and their mutual diversities (PR 347d-48a).

We may summarize our progress in this section as follows. Let us suppose that concrescing entity A has a simple physical prehension of past entity B, and that B had a similar prehension of C, and that C had one of D, and so forth. D can be any past actual entity, no matter how remote. Now A prehends D through its prehension of B; B had prehended D through its prehension of C; and C had a direct non-mediated prehension of D. The three Categories of Subjective Identity, Objective Diversity, and Objective Identity function to guarantee that D, despite all the possibilities of negative prehension, will never disappear in this chain of physical prehensions.

The fact that D will never disappear does not mean that it necessarily retains its importance to later entities. An actual entity which lies in past epochs remote beyond measure from our own, while preserving its identity in every new actual entity, is relegated by these new entities to a trivial status as a part of the background. *Important* differences between actual entities extend only for a finite distance into the past (PR 313c). Whitehead points to the fact that science has rejected "action at a distance" as evidence that significant transmission of content normally takes place only between contiguous actual entities.

> Let two actual occasions be termed 'contiguous' when the regions constituting their 'standpoints' are externally connected. Then by reason of the absence of intermediate actual occasions, the objectification of the antecedent occasion in the later occasion is peculiarly complete. . . . The objectifications of the more distant past will be termed 'mediate'; the contiguous occasions will have 'immediate' objectification. The mediate objectifications will be transmitted through various routes of successive immediate objectifications. . . . Provided that physical science maintains its denial of 'action at a distance,' the safer guess is that direct objectification is practically negligible except for contiguous occasions; but that this practical negligibility is a characteristic of the present cosmic epoch without any metaphysical generality (PR 468c-69a).

Whitehead leaves open the possibility that, in rare cases or in other cosmic epochs, there can be the direct prehension of significant content in non-contiguous past actual entities. He points to hybrid physical prehensions as a possible mechanism (PR 469a). If this is so, then Whitehead would not rule out, on theoretical grounds, the possibility of ESP, psychokinesis, and similar phenomena (but neither is he required to accept such phenomena without adequate empirical evidence).

There is another passage, however, in which Whitehead not only asserts that a concrescing entity *may* have direct physical prehensions of *some* of its non-contiguous past entities but that a concrescing entity *must* have a distinct and direct physical prehension of *each* entity in its past, no matter how remote. In the following passage Whitehead uses the letters A, B, C, and D in the same way as we did above. A is the concrescing actual entity, and B, C, and D are all in its past. B has C and D in its past, and C has D in its past. This example can be made arbitrarily complex, with D as many generations remote from A as one wishes.

> Now B, as an initial datum for A's feeling, also presents C and D for A to feel through its mediation. Also C, as an initial datum for A's feeling, also presents D for A to feel through its mediation. Thus, in this artificially simplified example, A has D presented for feeling through three distinct sources: (i) directly as a crude datum, (ii) by the mediation of B, and (iii) by the mediation of C. This threefold presentation is D, in its function of an initial datum for A's feeling of it, so far as concerns the mediation of B and C. But, of course, the artificial simplification of the medium to two intermediaries is very far from any real case. The medium between D and A consists of all those actual entities which lie in the actual world of A and not in the actual world of D. . . .
>
> There are thus three sources of feeling, D direct, D in its nexus with C, and D in its nexus with B (PR 345c-46a).

It seems clear that Whitehead intends to make two claims on this issue of direct prehensions of non-contiguous past actual entities. First, as far as significant content is concerned, such content is passed on primarily through direct physical prehensions of the contiguous past actual entities; but Whitehead keeps open the possibility of direct prehensions of the content of the more remote past. Second, in relation to the mere fact that an actual entity existed—in terms, that is, of its sheer "being-there" — Whitehead asserts that the concrescing entity must have a unique prehension of every distinct entity in its past, without exception. The new entity must have one distinct, non-mediated prehension of each past actual entity.

Beyond these two assertions, Whitehead does not proceed. We may, however, make a reasonable assumption: the identity of a past actual entity is retained by the later generations of concrescing entities because each of those later concrescing entities must have its own distinct, direct, and non-mediated prehension of that past actual entity. That is, A's direct, non-mediated prehension of D allows A to feel D as a distinct entity within the chain of prehensions from A through B and C back to D.

In the first three chapters of this book, we have discussed propositions about the future and about contemporary actual entities. Such propositions, we argued, are possible because the future and contemporary actual entities may be considered to have been reduced to the regions that they occupy. (We further argued that such regions were more than merely eternal objects because of their association with the extensive continuum.) The concrescing entity's direct and non-mediated prehensions of every past actual entity, even in the most remote past, would seem to be similar. That is, it is difficult to imagine what objective content such prehensions would have other than the regions which those past entities occupied and that sense of "peculiar particularity" which attaches to all *actual* entities. In this case, there would be strong similarities between the status of the remote past actual entities, insofar as the concrescing entity prehends them directly and non-mediatedly, and the status of the logical subjects of propositions about contemporary and future actual entities. The similarities in status of these two groups of actual entities would indicate that Whitehead's metaphysics can indeed account for propositions about contemporary and future actual entities in a way which is rooted in the general structure of his system and not merely on an *ad hoc* basis. This is further evidence of the extraordinary coherence of Whitehead's metaphysical vision.

4 Intellectual Feelings: Truth and Judgment

THERE ARE TWO MAIN LOCI for Whitehead's discussion of intellectual feelings in *Process and Reality*, pages 290 to 295 and pages 406 to 420. Both their nomenclature and their conceptual content differ, however. For example, in the latter section, pages 406-20, Whitehead divides intellectual feelings into intuitive judgments and conscious perceptions, and in our discussion of intellectual feelings we followed this division. But in the former section, pages 290-95, Whitehead distinguishes between intuitive judgments and derivative judgments. In discussing the relation between these two sections, our fourth chapter will work through Whitehead's notions of truth and judgment.

I

As explained in Chapter One of this book, a conscious perception is the feeling of a contrast between a proposition, in its role as the datum of a 'perceptive feeling', and the logical subjects of that proposition, as they exist before being reduced to mere 'its'. An intuitive judgment is the feeling of a contrast between a proposition, in its role as the datum of an 'imaginative feeling', and the logical subjects of that proposition, as they exist before being reduced to mere 'its'. In both cases, there is the feeling of a contrast between actuality and potentiality. Such is the doctrine of the second passage (pages 406-20). We will first develop our interpretation of this issue in terms of Whitehead's doctrine in this second passage, and on page 98 we will compare our results with Whitehead's comments in the first passage (pages 290-95).

A

In the second passage, Whitehead continues by explaining that there are three types of intuitive judgments: those with a 'yes-form', those with a 'no-form', and those with a 'suspense-form'. In all three cases, there is a unity to the intuitive judgment because the same actual entities which function as the logical subjects in the proposition are also the actual entities to which the proposition is being compared.[1] In the 'yes-form', however, there is an additional basis for unity: the same eternal object which (A) serves as the predicate of the proposition and, thereby is focused upon the logical subjects considered as mere 'its', also (B) characterizes those logical subjects as they exist before their reduction to mere 'its' (PR 413b). In other words, in the 'yes-form', the constituent proposition is being compared with the logical subjects *as they are incorporated in the judging actual entity.* If this point is not well understood, then Whitehead's entire doctrine of intellectual feelings will appear to be mere gibberish. We may restate Whitehead's doctrine more precisely as follows. In an intuitive judgment with a 'yes-form', the eternal object which serves as the predicate of the constituent proposition also characterizes the actual entities which serve as the logical subjects of that proposition *as they are objectified in the judging actual entity.*

It may be useful to illustrate this doctrine in terms of a diagram. Therefore, for our discussion in this paragraph, we will refer back to diagram 13. I.F. is an imaginative propositional feeling; we will assume that there are many actual entities serving as logical subjects of the proposition felt by I.F. M is the indicative feeling through which the logical subjects of the proposition enter the concrescing actual entity—it being understood, of course, that these actual entities are a part of the concrescing entity only as objective data. Therefore, when we speak of those portions of the logical subjects which are the objective data incorporated into the concrescing entity at M, we are also speaking about that concrescing entity itself! The second important point to notice about M is this. Although the logical subjects are present in the concrescing actual entity at M only as objective data, nonetheless those objective data are present at M not as mere 'its' but as characterized by all the eternal objects which are appropriate. Thus the act of reducing the logical subjects to mere 'its' for the proposition occurs at the third stage of concrescence, well after their presence as "fully clothed" objective data has been established at the first stage. This is the reason why the abstractive box $\boxed{\text{M}}$ is located in the diagram in the third stage. Therefore, the concrescing actual entity, *using as resources only elements from its own "real internal constitution,"* makes available to the intuitive judgment not only the proposition but also the logical subjects in their status as fully clothed actualities (or at least such parts of the logical subjects as are included in the objective data).

Let us assume that the intuitive judgment which is illustrated in

---

1. This is also one of the bases for the unity of a conscious perception.

this diagram is one with a 'yes-form'. In that case, the eternal object which is felt by I.F. as a potentiality focused on the logical subjects at $\boxed{M}$, also characterizes those logical subjects in their status as physical actualities present at M. Thus the eternal object, which the concrescing actual entity first felt conceptually at O, is judged by that concrescing entity at I.J. to be present also at M as a character of physical actualities, where those actualities are a part of the very identity, of the "real internal constitution," of the judging actual entity itself. In summary, (continuing our assumption that I.J. has a 'yes-form'), it is possible to construe I.J. as a judgment about the *objectified actual entities:* specifically, as a judgment by the concrescing actual entity that an eternal object which was felt by I.F. as a potential characteristic of a set of actual entities, is also an actual characteristic of those actual entities. But at the same time, it is possible to construe I.J. as a judgment about *the concrescing actual entity itself:* specifically, as a judgment that an eternal object which is felt by I.F. as a potential characteristic of certain elements in the "real internal constitution" of the concrescing entity, is also an actual characteristic of those elements at M. These two ways of construing I.J. amount, for Whitehead, to differences of accent and not of content; this is because the objectified actual entities (which, on the first interpretation, the judgment is about) *are* elements in the "real internal constitution" of the concrescing actual entity.

The interpretation we have given of intuitive judgments seems presupposed in many of Whitehead's comments about intuitive judgments. For example,

> The term 'judgment' refers to three species among the comparative feelings with which we are concerned. In each of these feelings the datum is the generic contrast between an *objectified* nexus and a proposition whose logical subjects make up the nexus (PR 412c; emphasis added).

To the extent that an intuitive judgment is a judgment about the concrescing actual entity itself, Whitehead claims that we can be certain of its correctness. Whitehead expresses the reason for this certainty this way:

> It will be noted that the intuitive judgment in its subjective form conforms to what there is to feel in its datum. Thus error cannot arise from the subjective form of the integration constituting the judgment (PR 414d).

And yet, because such certainty depends upon the fact that in an intuitive judgment the concrescing entity is judging itself, it follows that this certainty cannot outlast the subjective functioning of the judging entity. Whitehead expresses his position in colorful language:

> Accordingly our attitude towards an immediate intuition must be that of the gladiators, *"morituri te salutamus"* ["We who are about to die, salute thee!"], as we pass into the limbo where we rely on the uncertain record (PR 409a; translation added).

Let us turn now to intuitive judgments with a 'no-form'. In the 'no-form', the eternal object which is the predicate of the constitutive proposition is incompatible with the eternal objects which characterize the actual entities serving as the logical subjects as they are objectified. The intuitive judgment with a 'no-form' may also be interpreted as a judgment by the concrescing actual entity about itself. That is, a judgment in the 'no-form' may be interpreted as the judgment by the concrescing entity that an eternal object which is predicated potentially of certain of its own elements, is incompatible with other eternal objects which actually do characterize those elements (PR 412c-13b).

B

There is, however, an important ambiguity lurking in intuitive judgments with the 'suspense-form'. In a 'suspense-form', the predicate is neither identical with the eternal objects characterizing the objectified logical subjects nor incompatible with them (PR 412c-13b). To help us understand this ambiguity, we will introduce another technical term. When an actual entity has attained its satisfaction, it is characterized by a specific set of eternal objects, it is infected by a "peculiar particularity," and it has a determinant relation to every item in its actual world. Such an actual entity is said to be existing 'formally'. The formal existence of an actual entity must be compared with its existence as an objective datum. The formal existence of an actual entity is unchanging, total, and complete; objectifications in later actual entities constitute only external relations for an actual entity considered in its formal existence. But an actual entity's status as an objective datum is constantly shifting, never being wholly the same for any two later actual entities. As an objective datum, the later actual entities are internally related to it.[2]

2. Our use of the term 'formal' in this context requires some justification. Sherburne connects this term strictly with the process of concrescence. He writes, "An actual entity considered *formaliter* is an actual entity considered as subjective, as enjoying its own immediacy of becoming," (*A Key to Whitehead's Process and Reality*, 225). In support of his position Sherburne quotes PR 129b:

> The 'formal' reality of the actuality in question belongs to its process of concrescence and not to its 'satisfaction'.

In our opinion, however, the term 'formal' bears a number of analogous uses. Basically the term 'formal' refers to the subject-superject as a whole, but only — and this is the key — insofar as it retains, without loss or addition, its own characteristics. In still other words, the formal nature of an actual entity is the nature of that entity insofar as it exists "in its own right" and without alteration by its future actual entities. It is in this sense that Whitehead quotes Descartes:

> Hence the idea of the sun will be the sun itself existing in the mind, not indeed formally, as it exists in the sky, but objectively, i.e., in the way in which objects are wont to exist in the mind; and this mode of being is truly much less perfect than that in

Now the ambiguity of an intuitive judgment in the 'suspense-form' is this. Although the eternal object in question does not characterize the logical subjects in their status as objective data within—and as elements

> which things exist outside the mind, but it is not on that account mere nothing, as I have already said (PR 118a).

And within the framework of his own system, Whitehead writes:

> That 'intensity' in the *formal constitution* of a subject-superject involves 'appetition' in its *objective* function as superject (PR 128c; Whitehead's emphases).

However, because the term 'formal' emphasizes the independence of an actual entity from the future entities which will objectify (and alter) it, Whitehead sometimes associates the term 'formal' with the *process* of concrescence even to the point of excluding the satisfaction. An example of such a passage is the quotation from PR 129b which we gave in the first paragraph. In other passages, however, Whitehead associates 'formal' with the *entire* process of concrescence *including* the satisfaction.

> The analysis of the formal constitution of an actual entity has given three stages in the process of feeling: (i) the responsive phase, (ii) the supplemental stage, and (iii) the satisfaction (PR 323b).

But, still again, Whitehead sometimes uses the term 'formal' in such a way that it can refer *only* to the satisfaction. For example,

> Actual occasions in their 'formal' constitutions are devoid of all indetermination. Potentiality has passed into realization. They are complete and determinate matter of fact, devoid of all indecision. They form the ground of obligation (PR 44b).

It is instructive to connect this last use of 'formal' with our previous discussion of the nature of the satisfaction. We said that the satisfaction has two functions. On the one hand, it is the last stage of concrescence; and on the other hand, it represents that entity in the transcendent future, after its immediacy has perished. Now insofar as (A) we connect the term 'formal' with the satisfaction, and insofar as (B) we connect the satisfaction with the act of concrescence, it follows that the formal nature of an actual entity is to be associated with the act of concrescence. But insofar as (A) we connect the term 'formal' with the satisfaction, and insofar as (B) we connect the satisfaction with the transcendent role of that actual entity, it follows that the formal nature of an actual entity is equivalent to that actual entity construed as an initial datum, before being reduced to an objective datum.

For our purposes in the above text, we may construe 'formal' in any of these senses so long as the satisfaction—in both its roles—is not excluded. We need the formal natures of actual entities for comparison with these same actual entities construed as objectified (and thus altered) data. That is, we need the natures of actual entities as they "really" are, apart from any alteration they may suffer in the process of being objectified by other entities; and the "real and complete" nature of an actual entity must include its satisfaction. Thus, in summary, for our purposes the formal nature of an actual entity must include its satisfaction.

Moreover, we may note that in the following passage, Whitehead uses the term 'formal' (A) in reference to the "whole and complete" actual entity and (B) in connection with the problem of alteration inherent in reducing an actual entity to an objective datum.

> This suspended judgment is our consciousness of the limitations involved in objectification. If, in the comparison of an imaginative feeling with fact, we merely knew what *is* and what *is not*, then we should have no basis for discovering the work of objectification in effecting omissions from the formal constitutions of things. . . . The judgment tells us what *may* be additional information respecting the formal constitutions of the logical subjects, information which is neither included nor excluded by our direct perception (PR 419a; Whitehead's emphases).

in the constitution of—the judging actual entity, nevertheless, that eternal object may still characterize those logical subjects as they exist *formally*. Such a claim depends on the fact that the objective datum of a past actual entity is only a part of the formal nature of that past actual entity. Let us consider any past entity A; to put it crudely, after we have subtracted what is present in this or that objective datum of A from the contents of the formal nature of A, there will be a portion of A left over. In a judgment with a 'suspense-form', the predicate does not characterize the logical subjects as they are actually present in the concrescing entity as objective data, but neither does that predicate conflict with anything in those objective data; therefore, the predicate *might* apply to the "left-over" portions of the logical subjects. Thus there are two ways of construing an intuitive judgment in a 'suspense-form'. First, we may concentrate on the logical subjects as they actually are objectified in the judging entity—and as they are elements in the very nature of that judging entity. In this case, the predicate definitely does not characterize the logical subjects as objectified, but there definitely is nothing in those objective data which conflicts with the predicate either. Here everything is settled; the judgment is about the judging entity itself. Second, we may concentrate on the logical subjects as they exist formally. In this case, the fact that the predicate neither characterizes the logical subjects as objectified nor conflicts with them, leaves open the possibility that the predicate *might* characterize the actual entities in their formal natures. Thus the judgment is about the formal natures of the logical subjects. An intuitive judgment in the 'suspense-form', construed in this second manner, is an example of an 'inferential judgment' (PR 418b-19a). Most judgments in everyday life are inferential judgments. For example, if someone says, "That horse is black," normally he is not attempting to draw attention to the objectifications of the horse in himself; rather he is trying to say something about the horse as it exists "out-there," that is, about the formal natures of the actual entities constituting the horse.

In the second discussion of intellectual feelings in *Process and Reality* (pages 406-20), Whitehead limits his discussion of inferential judgments to those having the 'suspense-form'. It seems clear, however, that intuitive judgments in the 'yes-form' and in the 'no-form' can also be interpreted in two ways. An intuitive judgment in the 'yes-form' may, of course, be interpreted as a judgment about the concrescing entity; that is, an intuitive judgment in the 'yes-form' may be construed as the judgment that the predicate of the constituent proposition does, in fact, characterize the logical subjects as they are objectified in the judging entity. On the other hand, an intuitive judgment in the 'yes-form' may also be interpreted as a judgment about the logical subjects in their formal natures; that is, an intuitive judgment in the 'yes-form' may also be interpreted as a judgment that the predicate of the proposition does, in fact, characterize the logical subjects in their formal natures.

Now it may seem that in the case of an intuitive judgment in the 'yes-form' we have created a bogus distinction. It may be argued that these two, supposedly different, ways of interpreting a 'yes-form' really amount to the same thing. A person who held that we have created a bogus distinction might argue as follows. The actual entities which are the logical subjects are present in the judging entity as objective data. But each such objective datum of an actual entity is a part of the formal nature of that actual entity. Therefore, when a concrescing entity makes an intuitive judgment in a 'yes-form' about itself—that is, about the logical subjects as they are objectified in that concrescing entity—it follows that the concrescing entity is also making a judgment about the logical subjects in their formal natures. In other words, when the concrescing entity judges that the predicate is present in the logical subjects insofar as they are objective data in the judging entity, it is also in fact judging that the predicate is present in the formal natures of the logical subjects, since the objective data are a part of those formal natures.

Our answer to this objection runs as follows. In the above argument (that the distinction between the two interpretations of intuitive judgments in the 'yes-form' is bogus), the objector forgot that new actual entities may inaccurately incorporate past actual entities—that is, the objector assumed, mistakenly, that an eternal object which characterizes the objective data must also characterize the formal natures of those past actual entities. For example, the objector has forgotten that reversion may add new eternal objects to the objective data—that is, to the past actual entities as objectified—where those eternal objects were never in the formal natures of those past actual entities. Such reversion may take place within a past actual entity and be transmitted to the concrescing entity (PR 414d-15a), as illustrated in diagram 9.[3] In addition, transmutation may lead to error. That is, in a transmutation, the eternal object may be applied to some set which *contains* the actual entities from which that eternal object was derived, where that larger set is treated as a single unity. This, of course, could lead to error, if that eternal object is irrelevant to the larger set. In addition, it is possible that an eternal object which was present *conceptually* in the past actual entities may be felt by the concrescing actual entity as though it was present physically in those entities (cf. PR 415b). In the light of these illustrations, we may assert that there is a basic difference between (a) an interpretation of an intuitive judgment in the 'yes-form' as a judgment about a certain set of actual entities as they are objectified in the judging entity itself and (b) an interpretation of that 'yes-form'

---

3. Diagram 8 shows a reversion as it enters a perceptive feeling, while an intuitive judgment, which we are here discussing, contains an imaginative feeling, not a perceptive feeling. Diagram 8, however, may be easily altered to show a similar pattern of reversion for an imaginative feeling.

judgment as a judgment about the formal natures of those actual entities. On the former interpretation we have an intuitive judgment which is essentially free from error. On the latter interpretation we have an inferential judgment which is essentially liable to error.

A similar distinction may be made for intuitive judgments in the 'no-form'. On the one hand, the judgment may be about a certain set of actual entities as objectified in the judging entity. In that case, the intuitive judgment would be asserting that the predicate of the constituent proposition is incompatible with the eternal objects which characterize the logical subjects as objectified. On the other hand, the judgment may be about the logical subjects in their formal natures. In that case, the judgment would be asserting that the predicate was incompatible with the eternal objects which characterize the formal natures of the logical subjects. These two interpretations cannot be reduced to one, because the actual entities as objectified may be clothed with characteristics that they did not have in their formal natures; and it may be that the predicate is incompatible only with these added characteristics and not with the characteristics of the formal natures of the logical subjects. Thus, as above, on the former interpretation we have an intuitive judgment which is fundamentally free from error. On the latter interpretation we have an inferential judgment which is essentially liable to error.

We may summarize our discussion in this section as follows. There are three forms of intuitive judgments: those with 'yes-forms', those with 'no-forms', and those with 'suspense-forms'. In each case, the judgment may be construed in two ways: first, as a judgment about the logical subjects as objectified, and second, as a judgment about the logical subjects in their formal natures. On the first interpretation, these three judgments are, in the strictest sense of the term, 'intuitive'. On the second interpretation, these three judgments are 'inferential'. The intuitive judgments are essentially free from error, while inferential judgments are not. Further, within Whitehead's scheme, an intuitive judgment has a certain priority over its corresponding inferential judgment. This is because it is impossible for a concrescing actual entity to make judgments about the formal natures of past actual entities except as those judgments are grounded in the concrescing actual entity's objectifications of those past actual entities. In other words, a concrescing entity can make a judgment about the nature of the objectifications of the logical subjects without making a judgment about the formal natures of those logical subjects; but that concrescing entity cannot make a judgment about the formal natures of the logical subjects without making a judgment about their objectifications in itself.

We are now in a position to make the promised comparison of the two passages in *Process and Reality* where Whitehead discusses intellectual feelings, first on pages 290 to 295 and the second on pages 406 to 420. In the first passage, Whitehead distinguishes between intuitive judgments and derivative judgments; in the second passage, he divides intellectual feelings into intuitive judgments and conscious perceptions.

We may ask how the nomenclature of the two sections should be correlated. Our answer falls into two parts. (A) The conscious perceptions of the second section simply have no correlate in the first section. (B) The distinction in the first section between intuitive judgments and derivative judgments corresponds to the distinction which we have emphasized in our discussion of the second section between intuitive judgments and inferential judgments.

The following series of quotations (all from pages 290-95) will show how closely the distinction between intuitive judgments and derivative judgments drawn in pages 290-95 parallels the distinction between intuitive judgments and inferential judgments which we constructed from materials found in pages 406-20. First Whitehead prepares the ground by making a distinction between a judgment about the logical subjects considered formally and a judgment about the logical subjects considered as objective data.

> This affirmation about the logical subjects is obviously 'affirmation' in a sense derivative from the meaning of 'affirmation' about the judging subject. Identification of the two senses will lead to error. In the former sense there is abstraction from the judging subject. The subjectivist principle has been transcended, and the judgment has shifted its emphasis from the objectified nexus to the truth-value of the proposition in question (PR 291c-92a).[4]

Next Whitehead gives his division of judgments into two types.

> . . . we note that judgments are divisible into two sorts. These are (i) intuitive judgments and (ii) derivative judgments (PR 292a).

Then Whitehead offers a definition of an intuitive judgment and some additional comments.

> In an intuitive judgment the integration of the physical datum with the proposition elicits into feeling the full complex detail of the proposition, in its comparison of identity, or diversity, in regard to the complex detail of the physical datum. The intuitive judgment is the consciousness of this complex detailed comparison involving identity and diversity. Such a judgment is in its nature correct. For it is the consciousness of *what is* (PR 292a).

He does the same for a derivative judgment.

> In a derivative judgment the integration of the physical datum with the proposition elicits into feeling the full complex detail of the proposi-

---

4. In PR, the third sentence begins, "In the latter sense. . . ." In his third list of editorial modifications Kline suggests that the word "former" should be substituted for "latter." We have followed his suggestion. See Kline, "Corrigenda for *Process and Reality*," 205. The editors of *Process and Reality: The Corrected Edition*, Griffin and Sherburne, have kept "latter."

tion, but does not elicit into feeling the full comparison of this detail with the complex detail of the physical fact. There is some comparison involving the remainder of the detail. But the subjective form embraces the totality of the proposition, instead of assuming a complex pattern which discriminates between the compared and the uncompared components. In derivative judgments there can be error. . . . Most judgments are derivative (PR 292b).[5]

The last two quotations need some explanation. The phrase "the physical datum" and the phrase "physical fact" refer to the logical subjects in their formal natures. In the last quotation, the phrase "remainder of the detail" refers to the objectifications of the logical subjects in the judging entity. When Whitehead talks about "the totality of the proposition," he seems to be assuming that the predicate of the proposition is a complex one, some aspects of which are directly exemplified in the objectified logical subjects, and other aspects of which are not present in the objective data but might be present in the formal natures of the logical subjects; and yet the proposition is affirmed (or denied or suspended) under the assumption that it is the entire predicate which characterizes (or does not characterize) the formal natures of the logical subjects.[6]

II

We shall next turn our attention to the question of truth and correctness. According to Whitehead, propositions are true or false, while judgments are correct or incorrect or suspended. Further, propositions involve a

5. The discussion in the main text must not be taken as implying that there is no difference between Whitehead's use of the term 'intuitive judgment' in each of the two passages (PR 290-95 and 406-20). As the series of quotations in the main text demonstrates, in the first passage (PR 290-95) the distinction is between intuitive judgments (about the concrescing entity itself) and derivative judgments (about the formal natures of the logical subjects), and there is no reference in the first passage to the distinction between imaginative and perceptive propositional feelings. In the second passage (PR 406-20), Whitehead seems to give two distinct meanings to intuitive judgments: namely, (A) intuitive judgments (about the concrescing entity itself) in distinction from inferential judgments (about the formal natures of logical subjects) and (B) intuitive judgments (based on imaginative propositional feelings) in distinction from conscious perceptions (based on perceptive propositional feelings).

Therefore, the meaning of "intuitive judgment" to be found in pages 290-95 of *Process and Reality* corresponds only with the first of the two meanings (the one we labeled [A]) of "intuitive judgment" to be found in pages 406-20.

6. We make the following additional — and somewhat speculative — observation about the distinction between an intuitive judgment and an inferential (or derivative) judgment. The distinction between an intuitive judgment and an inferential judgment is rooted primarily in the subjective form. Thus the content of, for example, an intuitive judgment in the 'yes-form' which is *about* the objectified logical subjects is the same as the corresponding inferential judgment which is *about* the formal natures of the logical subjects. Consequently, the element of intentionality implied by the word "about" stems from the subjective form (cf. PR 420a).

correspondence theory of truth, while there is a coherence theory of the correctness, incorrectness, or suspension of judgments (PR 290b-91a).[7] We explain as follows.

All propositions are true or false (PR 392a). A proposition is true if its predicate, the potentiality of which is focused on the logical subjects considered as mere 'its', also characterizes those logical subjects as they exist "fully clothed" prior to their reduction to mere 'its'; otherwise it is false. Now it is important to note that this is *not* a mere criterion of truth and falsity; rather we have defined the *nature* of truth and falsity. That is, the truth of proposition *consists in* the fact that the eternal object in the predicate also characterizes the logical subject; the *truth* of the proposition *is* this two-way functioning of the eternal object. Likewise, the falsity of a proposition *is* the failure of the eternal object to function this way.

In theory, this definition of truth could be applied to a proposition in two ways. First, a proposition could be true (or false) because the eternal object in the predicate is also present (or not present) in the logical subjects *as they are objectified* in the concrescing entity before their reduction to mere 'its'. Second, a proposition could be true (or false) because the eternal object in the predicate is also present (or not present) in the logical subjects *in their formal natures* before being either objectified or reduced to mere 'its'. (An interesting consequence of this dual nature of truth is that a proposition could have one truth value in terms of the objectified logical subjects and another truth value in terms of the formal natures of the logical subjects.) Nevertheless, when speaking of the logical subjects of a proposition in connection with the truth or falsity of that proposition, Whitehead seems usually to have in mind the formal natures of those logical subjects. The reason for such an emphasis on the formal nature of the logical subject is that the same proposition normally may be prehended by more than one actual entity; but the objectifications of the logical subjects will vary from prehending entity to prehending entity. To the extent, therefore, that the propositions will be the same in various actual entities, the emphasis will be on the formal natures of the logical subjects.

However, whether we concern ourselves with the formal natures of the logical subjects or their objectifications in the concrescing entity, we still have a correspondence theory of the nature (or content) of truth: namely, in a true proposition the role of the eternal object in the predicate will *correspond* with its role in the logical subjects, whereas in a false proposition the eternal object in the predicate will *not* have a *corresponding* role in the logical subjects.

We turn now to the coherence theory of the correctness, incorrectness, or suspension of judgments. Although every proposition is true or

---

7. See, however, Chapter One, Section III.D, where we discuss propositions about the present and future which are neither true nor false but merely possible.

false,[8] such truth or falsity can be established only by comparing the proposition with the logical subjects. This is the function of the judgment. The correctness or incorrectness of a judgment occurs at two levels. These two levels are linked to the distinction we drew earlier between "intuitive judgments" and "derivative" or "inferential judgments." Thus, at the intuitive level, the correctness or incorrectness or suspension of the judgment may not be questioned. The judgment is apodictic, and we need no criteria for establishing whether the intuitive judgment is accurate or is in error.

> It will be noted that the intuitive judgment in its subjective form conforms to what there is to feel in its datum. Thus error cannot arise from the subjective form of the integration constituting the judgment (PR 414d).

However, at the level of inferential judgments, reversion may cause error, and thus we need criteria for judging whether an inferential judgment made an error or not.

> But it [error] can arise because the indicative feeling, which is one of the actors integrated, may in its origin have involved reversion. Thus error arises by reason of operations which lie below consciousness, though they may emerge into consciousness and lie open for criticism (PR 414d-15a).

The criteria for judging the presence or lack of error in an inferential judgment are primarily pragmatic. That is, if an inferential judgment *coheres* with other such judgments, it must be correct. But if an inferential judgment does *not cohere* with our other judgments, then the judgment is in error (PR 275b).

We may summarize this section as follows. The content of the nature of the truth of a proposition *is* the *correspondence* of the role of the eternal object in the predicate with its role in the logical subjects before their reduction to mere 'its'. The falsity of a proposition *is* the lack of this correspondence. We are, however, still confronted with the task of *judging* whether this correspondence exists in the case of a specified proposition. If we judge that this correspondence exists (or does not exist) between the eternal object in the predicate and that eternal object in the *objectified* logical subjects, then we have an *intuitive judgment*. This intuitive judgment about the truth or falsity of the proposition is inherently correct. On the other hand, if we judge that a proposition is true or false in terms of the *formal natures* of the logical subjects, then we have an *inferential judgment*. Since, however, an inferential judgment may err in judging the truth or falsity of a proposition, we need *criteria* by which to make our judgments. When we judge *correctly*, we do so on the basis of the *coherence* among our various judgments. When we judge incorrectly, there is an *incoherence* which we have failed to notice. It is also possible to *suspend* our judgments of the truth or falsity of a specific proposition. We may suspend judgment

8. That is, every proposition about past logical subjects.

because it is not clear whether the judgment that the proposition is true (or false) would *cohere* (or *not cohere*) with our other judgments. But we may also suspend judgment because we are not interested in the truth of the proposition at hand.

III

According to Whitehead, God is the standard of truth. This is because God, unlike other actual entities, objectifies past actual entities into himself with a completeness which eliminates the gap between the formal natures of those past actual entities and their objective existence in God.[9] Therefore, the consequent nature of God (i.e., the objectifications in God of the past actual entities) becomes the *standard* of truth.

> The truth itself is nothing else than how the composite natures of the organic actualities of the world obtain adequate representation in the divine nature. Such representations compose the 'consequent nature' of God, which evolves in its relationship to the evolving world without derogation to the eternal completion of its primordial conceptual nature. In this way the 'ontological principle' is maintained—since there can be no determinate truth, correlating impartially the partial experiences of many actual entities, apart from one actual entity to which it can be referred (PR 18e-19a).

We may comment on this passage as follows. A proposition is true when the eternal object which is its predicate plays a two-way role: first, as a potential character of the logical subjects conceived as mere 'its', and second, as an actual character of the logical subjects. Truth *is* such two-way functioning of eternal objects. Since God prehends all actual entities, and since he prehends all propositions, all truth may be discovered as the two-way functioning of eternal objects in God. It is, however, most important to note that this is not to deny that these same eternal objects may also play two-way roles directly in the world. Whitehead's system is not an idealism. There really are truths—that is, such two-way functionings—in the world. Rather, the point is that while *some* possible propositions are felt in the world, and while *some* aspects of past entities are felt by the new entities, and while *some* of the eternal objects which might be functioning in a two-way role—that is, as truths—actually do so, in God, on the other hand, *all* possible propositions are felt, *all* aspects of the past actual entities are prehended, and *all* the eternal objects which might function in this two-way fashion—that is, as truths—actually do so. Thus God alone is omniscient. The point is God's omniscience and not the denial of the existence of truths in finite entities.

We believe that we have presented correctly the thrust of

9. Compare footnote number 2 on page 65.

Whitehead's system. Before defending Whitehead against a possible misinterpretation, let us briefly restate our argument. We understand Whitehead to hold that while God knows all truth, finite entities can know some truth. And the truths known by the finite entities are genuine truths which are genuinely present in the world. That is, these finite truths have an ontological status in their own right as genuine elements within the world, quite in addition to their status as elements within the consequent nature of God. Any lesser status for the truths in the world would turn Whitehead's system towards monism or idealism. Therefore, while Whitehead writes that "the truth itself *is* nothing else than how the composite natures of the organic actualities of the world obtain adequate representation in the divine nature" (PR 18e-19a, emphasis added), we nonetheless insist on glossing Whitehead's statement to mean that God serves only as the *standard* of truth and not as the definition of the nature of truth.

The possible misunderstanding of Whitehead runs as follows. Someone might object to Whitehead by claiming that he has reintroduced the very sort of bifurcation of reality which he so strongly wishes to avoid. Specifically, has not Whitehead divided reality into two spheres, one of which is available to human experience and one of which is forever beyond human experience? We can, the objector continues, present two concrete examples of such bifurcation. (A) The totality of the formal natures of all past entities is not available to the concrete experience of any finite actual entity; and thus there is a bifurcation between the ordinary human world of partial perspectives which is available to us and the totality of the formal natures which is forever beyond human experience. (B) The completeness of the divine consequent nature is equally beyond the experience of any finite entity; and thus there is a bifurcation between the ordinary human world and the completeness of the divine nature which is forever beyond our finite capacity to experience.

We respond that the basis of Whitehead's overcoming the bifurcations of past philosophers is to be found in his insistence that metaphysics can discuss only "what communicates with immediate fact." It is permissible to postulate, as a hypothesis similar to those of science, all sorts of things (entities, principles, processes, etc.) so long as they help us to account for immediate human experience. But Whitehead will always reject that which is in principle unknowable—that is, that which in principle cannot be experienced or that which in principle cannot be prehended by finite (human) actual entities—for that would introduce precisely such a bifurcation as he so strongly rejects.

> The adequacy of the scheme over every item does not mean adequacy over such items as happen to have been considered. It means that the texture of observed experience, as illustrating the philosophic scheme, is such that all related experience must exhibit the same texture. Thus the philosophic scheme should be 'necessary,' in the sense of bearing in itself its own war-

rant of universality throughout all experience, provided that we confine ourselves to that which communicates with immediate matter of fact. But what does not so communicate is unknowable, and the unknowable is unknown; and so this universality defined by 'communication' can suffice (PR 5c-6a).

The central question, therefore, is this: Has Whitehead, either with his notion of a determinate past truth or of a divine consequent nature, introduced something which is in principle unknowable? The core of our answer is this: While it is true that neither the determinate truth nor the divine consequent natures in their entireties are available to any one finite entity, it is also true that no portion of either the determinate past actual entities (in their formal natures) or the divine consequent nature is in principle beyond human experience.

We present three considerations in support of our thesis that the determinate truth (i.e., the complete truth about all past actual entities) does "communicate" with human experience. (A) No portion of the determinate past actual entities is in principle unavailable for human experience. While it may be extremely difficult to obtain knowledge about the specific content of remote past actual entities, this is a practical limitation and is not based in the very nature of those past entities or in the very nature of the process of concrescence. (B) Such portions of the past actual entities as may happen to be present in the concrescing actual entity are *genuinely* present in that actual entity. And (C) when a concrescing actual entity includes immediately past actual entities, each of those past entities will bring in (at least) slightly different aspects of the formal natures of *their* past actual entities. This provides verification, within the concrescence itself, for the claim that there is a determinate past beyond the limited objectifications of that past in the concrescing entity. A similar set of considerations may be constructed for the concrescing entities' prehension of the divine consequent nature. We may conclude, therefore, that neither the notion of a determinate past truth nor that of a divine consequent nature creates a new bifurcation of reality.[10]

---

10. In this chapter, we have not discussed "conscious perception." This is not an oversight. Conscious perceptions are closely linked to symbolic reference and may be considered in conjunction with symbolic reference. We will, therefore, discuss conscious perceptions in Part Two when we deal with symbolic reference.

5 The Indicative System, the Locus, and Patterns

I

A PROPOSITION IS A FORM OF POTENTIALITY in which that potentiality has been focused upon a set of actual entities. It thus is a matter of paramount importance to specify *how* that set of actual entities is isolated for consideration. The most straightforward way of isolating the logical subjects of a proposition is to indicate their position or place. Thus, according to Whitehead, the full form of any proposition is: "Those particulars *as thus indicated* in such-and-such a predicative pattern" (PR 295b; Whitehead's emphasis). To explain how the concrescing actual entity specifies the position of the particulars (i.e., the logical subjects), Whitehead develops the theory of indication, which may be outlined as follows.

1. The various relationships between actual entities are eternal objects. The only limitation is that the relationships in question must be genuinely present in the related actual entities; they may not involve arbitrary combinations of actual entities having no basis in these actual entities themselves.

2. Relationships involving two and only two actual entities as relata are called dual relations. Relations among three and only three relata are called triple relations, and so forth.

3. A general principle is an eternal object which is a set of other eternal objects, called the instances of that general principle. For example, 'color' is the general principle, while 'this specific shade of red' and 'that particular blue' are two of its instances. The general principle cannot characterize actual entities except through its instances. On the other hand, if any actual entities are characterized by an instance of the general principle, then those actual entities are also characterized by the general principle itself.

4. A nexus exhibits an indicative system of dual relations if and only if the following four conditions are met.

i. Each pair of actual entities in the nexus is related by one and only one relation.

ii. Any relation between two actual entities in the nexus does not in turn relate either of those actual entities to a third actual entity.

iii. The relations are all instances of a general principle.

iv. Given any three actual entities, A, B, and C, in the nexus, the relation between A and B and the relation between A and C suffice to define the relation between B and C.[1]

Unfortunately, Whitehead gives no examples of such an indicative system. Nonetheless, it does seem that the extensive continuum may well serve as (at least a part of) such an indicative system. There are two bases for this claim. First, Whitehead states that in developing his theory of indication, he was also defining Aristotle's category of position (PR 296c). In Whitehead's metaphysics, the extensive continuum is the most likely candidate for the office of the Whiteheadian correlate to the Aristotelian notion of position. Second, the extensive continuum meets the criteria which Whitehead established for an indicative system. However, to provide evidence for this last claim would require a lengthy analysis of the extensive continuum, and, therefore, we will leave this statement as an unsupported assertion until Chapter Three of Part Two, where we present a somewhat detailed (but not exhaustive) analysis of the extensive continuum.

In *Process and Reality*, Whitehead develops his theory of propositions on the assumption that the logical subjects are in the past of any concrescing actual entity which entertains that proposition. (However, we have seen in Chapter One, Section III.D and elsewhere, how his theory of propositions could be extended to propositions about contemporary and future actual entities.) In addition, some propositions place additional limitations upon the position of the actual entities which may entertain them. For example, the proposition, "That horse is black," may mean "That is an object which appears 'horsey' and 'black' to me, the observer." Obviously, the latter proposition could be entertained only by an actual entity whose position allowed it to be an observer of that horse. (It must be noted, however, that there are very similar propositions which may be entertained by a much larger group of entities. For example, "There is an item with such-and-such a position which would appear 'horsey' and 'black' to any appropriately situated observer.") Therefore, each proposition has a specific set of actual entities which are so located that they can entertain the proposition. This set of actual entities is called the locus of the proposition (PR 283d). The locus of a proposition may vary

---

1. Our development of the theory of indication is a paraphrase of Whitehead in PR 295d-96b.

in number from a few to all actual entities, and (if we assume that the logical subjects must be in the past) may be altered as time progresses. For example, consider the proposition, "Brutus stabbed Caesar," where this proposition is of such a nature that neither Brutus nor Caesar is assumed to be directly observable. It would seem that as each year progresses, the number of actual entities which might entertain that proposition continues to grow; so that the total number of actual entities which might have entertained that proposition from the time of Caesar to A.D. 1500 is considerably less than the total number of actual entities which might have entertained it between the time of Caesar and 1990.

Before leaving Section I, we make the following observations about the theory of indication and about the notion of the locus of a proposition. First, the indicative system must not only position the logical subjects of proposition, but it must relate that position of the logical subjects to any concrescing actual entity which might entertain that proposition. In short, the indicative system must relate the logical subjects of the proposition to the locus of the proposition. Without this system the proposition cannot be entertained; this is because, unless the position of the logical subjects can be coherently related to the concrescing entity, it would be impossible for that concrescing entity to identify the logical subjects upon which the predicate is to be focused.

> Every proposition presupposes some general nexus with an indicative relational system. This nexus includes its locus of judging subjects and also its logical subjects. This presupposition is part of the proposition, and the proposition cannot be entertained by any subject for which the presupposition is not valid. Thus in a proposition certain characteristics are presupposed for the judging subject and for the logical subjects (PR 297b).

Secondly, our discussion of the theory of indication and of the locus provides the basis for an examination of Whitehead's definition of a 'metaphysical proposition'. Whitehead's own definition runs as follows.

> A metaphysical proposition — in the proper sense of the term 'metaphysical'—signifies a proposition which (i) has meaning for any actual occasion, as a subject entertaining it, and (ii) is 'general,' in the sense that its predicate potentially relates any and every set of actual occasions, providing the suitable number of logical subjects for the predicative pattern, and (iii) has a 'uniform truth-value,' in the sense that, by reason of its form and scope, its truth value is identical with the truth-value of each of the singular propositions to be obtained by restricting the application of the predicate to any one set of logical subjects (PR 300b).

We will comment on each of the three conditions above. Condition (i) is virtually equivalent to saying that the locus of a metaphysical proposition includes all actual entities. Thus any actual entity which is sufficiently sophisticated to entertain a metaphysical proposition will have the necessary position to do so—that is, it will be within the locus of that proposition. Furthermore, no actual entity can ever be excluded from entertaining a metaphysical proposition solely on the basis of its position—that is, solely on the basis that it falls "outside" the locus of that metaphysical proposition.

In his second condition (ii), Whitehead has in mind the fact that every proposition requires a minimum (and perhaps a maximum) number of actual entities as logical subjects. For example, in the proposition, "One actual entity and one actual entity make two actual entities," two actual entities are required before the proposition can be coherently applied. Other propositions require just one actual entity; for example, "An actual entity concresces in accordance with its subjective aim." Thus, condition (ii) states that a metaphysical proposition will hold for any set of actual entities, providing that each such set contains an appropriate number of actual entities. As an example of such a metaphysical proposition, we might suggest, "One actual entity and one actual entity make two actual entities" (cf. PR 301b). Perhaps the most interesting aspect of this second condition is this: most of *Process and Reality* cannot be considered properly metaphysical. Consider, for example, the following proposition: "An actual entity, in reducing its initial data to objective data, negatively prehends some portions of the initial data." This proposition is not metaphysical because it does not apply to God, and thus it does not apply to *all* actual entities. Again our discussion of propositions is not properly metaphysical, since most actual entities do not entertain propositions (except perhaps in their subjective aims).[2] Whitehead's theory of propositions is elaborated in the context of his system of categories; therefore, we may call his theory of propositions "categoreal," even though it is not genuinely metaphysical.

The third condition (iii) for a metaphysical proposition concerns false propositions primarily. Whitehead's point may be illustrated by the general proposition, "Each actual entity entertains propositions about its past world." This is false; but someone might argue that this proposition, although false, is metaphysical because it speaks of each and every actual entity. Whitehead in his third condition (iii) is denying that such propositions are metaphysical. The reason is that, if we take the general proposition, "Each actual entity entertains propositions about its past world," and then apply it to each specific actual entity, we generate an infinite series of the following sort of singular propositions: "Actual entity A entertains propositions about its past world," and "Actual entity B entertains propositions about its past world," and "Actual entity C entertains propositions

2. Compare, however, our discussion of the essential continuity of physical purposes and propositional prehensions in footnote 33 on page 36 where all actual entities do have physical purposes.

about its past world ," and so forth. Since some actual entities do entertain propositions about their pasts, it follows that some of the singular propositions will be true; but since some actual entities do not entertain propositions about their pasts, it follows that some of the singular propositions will be false. The general proposition would be both false and metaphysical only if every one of the derivative singular propositions were false. Therefore, since the proposition, "Each actual entity entertains propositions about its past," does not generate a series of singular propositions, each of which is false, it follows according to the third condition (iii) that it is not a metaphysical proposition.

The distinction between general and singular propositions leads us to another observation. Whitehead distinguishes among three types of propositions according to the distribution of the logical subjects. First, a proposition might refer to a single, specified set of logical subjects, for example, "That horse is black." There are two limits here. On the one hand, the set of actual entities might have just one member, for example, "That actual entity is black."[3] On the other hand, the set of logical subjects might include all the actual entities, considered as a whole, for example, "The whole of reality has a type of unity." Second, the logical subjects might be grouped into distinct sets. Suppose that three horses are grazing in a field. Since each horse is a set of actual entities, the three horses amount to three sets of actual entities. In the second type of proposition, the logical subjects are grouped into sets, and the proposition refers to one or more of those sets individually. For example, "All the horses in that field are black" (PR 282d-83b, 393b-94a).

3. Of course, if we insist that the word "black" can refer only to the color as it is extended in space, then a single actual entity is not likely to be perceived as black. 'Black' as an extended visual datum can emerge only as the datum of a perception in presentational immediacy. And, while it is not metaphysically impossible, it is most unlikely that the perceiving entity would 'project' (to use Whitehead's term) a color sensum upon a region which is occupied by a single actual entity. In our era, at least, the visual powers of any perceiver with which we are acquainted (a man, a dog, an eagle, etc.) could not distinguish the region occupied by a single actual entity. And thus such a region is much too small to serve as the whole area upon which the sensum is projected—although it could serve as one part of that area. In other eras, however, the region occupied by a single actual entity might be vastly larger than is now typical, and/or the visual powers of the perceivers might be fundamentally more acute. Thus, in these other eras, a single actual entity might be perceived as black in the sense of "having a black color extended in space." (But such radical enlargement of the size of the entities and/or such increased powers of visual discrimination would require a fundamentally different system of physics and optics from the one presently inherent in this electromagnetic era of ours.)

Nevertheless, in any era, a color such as black is not basically an extended datum for visual perception. Rather 'black' is at its roots a kind of emotion—a way of feeling (PR 246c-48a). (The ordinary extended color of black is *constructed* out of this raw emotion—see Chapter Nine of Part Two.) And so, even in our own era, a single entity can be black. This is because, in this as in all eras, the essence of any actual entity is emotional. An actual entity *is* a way of feeling the world.

II

According to Whitehead, every proposition presupposes order in the universe.

> The point is that every proposition refers to a universe exhibiting some general systematic metaphysical character. Apart from this background, the separate entities which go to form the proposition, and the proposition as a whole, are without determinate character. Nothing has been defined, because every definite entity requires a systematic universe to supply its requisite status. Thus every proposition proposing a fact must, in its complete analysis, propose the general character of the universe required for that fact. There are no self-sustained facts, floating in nonentity (PR 16c-17a).

This passage occurs very early in *Process and Reality*, and stands as an unsupported assertion. However, as *Process and Reality* proceeds, it becomes clear that every aspect of the proposition implicates the order of the universe: the structure of the predicate, the nature of the logical subject, the nature of the indicative system, and the nature of the system used to symbolize that proposition. For example, the use of the spoken word to symbolize a proposition requires presentational immediacy, transmutation, etc.; and *that* presupposes an order of the universe. We will wait, however, until Section III of Chapter 15 to investigate the ways in which the predicate, the logical subjects, and the symbolization implicate the order of the universe. But in this section we wish to explore briefly how the *indicative system* of a proposition implicates the larger patterns of order.

We noted before that every proposition has the form, "These subjects *as thus indicated* in such-and-such pattern." The indicative system is, therefore, a part of the proposition itself, and without that indicative system, the proposition cannot be interpreted. But there can be no indicative system except in a universe with systematic order. The order in the universe must be sufficiently precise to permit a concrescing actual entity to relate itself to the logical subjects of the proposition; that is, the patterns of order in the universe must include both the logical subjects and the concrescing actual entity. Moreover, the patterns of order must also systematically relate the logical subjects of a proposition to *all* the actual entities which might entertain that proposition. In sum, the universe must sustain patterns of order which provide the basis for the relation, by means of the indicative system, of the logical subjects of a proposition to the locus of that proposition.

> Every proposition presupposes some general nexus with an indicative relational system. This nexus includes its locus of judging subjects and also its logical subjects. This presupposition is part of the proposition, and the proposition cannot be entertained by any subject for which the presupposition is not valid. Thus in a proposition certain characteristics are presupposed for the judging subject and for the logical subjects (PR 297b).

There are two types of order. In one sense, the order of the universe is nothing but the patterns which are to be found among the objectifications of the past actual entities within the new concrescing entity. This is the primary sense of order. In another sense, the order of the universe is the order to be found among the formal natures of the actual entities. This distinction is correlative to the distinction between intuitive judgments and inferential judgments.

And just as the inferential judgments about the formal natures of the logical subjects are based upon the intuitive judgments about the logical subjects as objectified, so also the order of nature among the formal natures of actual entities stem from the order of nature as objectified within concrescing actual entities. The reason for this is that the concrescing actual entities can participate in the order of nature among the formal natures of entities only insofar as that order is a datum to which they must conform. But it is a part of Whitehead's categoreal scheme that a new concrescing actual entity is required to conform to the past only as the past becomes an objective datum—that is, becomes a part of the "real internal constitution" of the concrescing entity. (Compare our discussion of the conformal stage of concrescence in Chapter One on pages 1-2.)

> It has been explained in the previous section that the notion of 'order' is primarily applicable to the objectified data for individual actual entities. . . . But there is a derivative sense of the term 'order,' which is more usually in our minds when we use that word. We speak of the 'order of nature,' meaning thereby the order reigning in that limited portion of the universe. . . . In any of these senses, the term 'order' evidently applies to the relations among themselves enjoyed by many actual entities which thereby form a society (PR 136b).

These patterns form a hierarchy. Whitehead spent a good amount of space discussing the hierarchy of order in the universe (PR 95-168). It is not our purpose to analyze that discussion. We simply note that the metaphysical patterns of order are the most basic. We may further observe that, as a part of that metaphysical order, the extensive continuum in its broadest scope seems presupposed in every age and epoch, while the specifications of the extensive continuum such as the three dimensions of space and the one of time seem fundamental only in our local epoch, and the patterns of electrons and protons are still less fundamental. In order of decreasing scope we find the biological patterns, the patterns of human life, and even the patterns of human social life in the United States of America. All propositions presuppose the metaphysical patterns of order. Most propositions, in this era, presuppose the patterns of order which stem from the particular specifications of the extensive continuum; and many of them also presuppose the world of electrons and protons. On the other hand, very few propositions presuppose the types of order which are unique to the city of Chicago or which are unique to Sears Tower. But every proposition presupposes an order of some sort.

III

Let us imagine someone objecting to such a theory for two reasons. First, it is not clear, argues the objector, just why a proposition presupposes the metaphysical order of the universe; nor is it clear why most propositions in our epoch presuppose the world of electrons and protons. The objector asks us to consider the proposition, "The horse is black." Now, continues our objector, the proposition, "The horse is black," does not seem to entail any metaphysical proposition such as "Every actual entity objectifies its past entities"; nor does the proposition, "The horse is black," seem to entail any scientific proposition such as, "Electrons and protons exist." At least the proposition about the horse does not seem to entail the other propositions in the same way as the proposition, "The horse is black," entails, "The horse is extended." Furthermore, says the objector, we can well imagine a situation in which both the speaker and the listener understood the proposition, "The horse is black," but in which neither of them had ever entertained a thought about metaphysics or about electrons or protons. Our objector concludes: since the proposition about the black horse does not logically entail any propositions about actual entities or any other metaphysical topic, and since it is an empirical fact that both the speaker and the listener can fully understand the proposition without any knowledge or beliefs about metaphysics or the world of electrons and protons, it therefore follows that such propositions as, "The horse is black," do not presuppose the systematic metaphysical order or the systematic electronic order of the universe.

In responding to such an objection, we must first agree with the objector that propositions such as "The horse is black," do not logically entail any metaphysical or scientific propositions of the sort mentioned. Nor did Whitehead ever imagine that a person must be conscious of all the presuppositions of a proposition before that person could understand the proposition. Rather, Whitehead's basis for asserting that every proposition presupposes the metaphysical order of the universe is that each proposition literally includes its indicated logical subjects. That is, on Whitehead's analysis, a proposition does not merely talk *about* certain entities; rather the proposition actually includes those entities.[4] Moreover,

---

4. We further explain as follows. In Chapter Three, we argued that when a prehending entity objectifies a past entity, the prehending entity does not merely repeat the characteristics of that past entity. Rather, the prehending entity "incorporates" or "includes" that

the proposition will include those actual entities as systematically related to the concrescing entity; that is, the proposition requires an indicative system to serve as the basis for relating the logical subjects to the concrescing entity. The patterns of order which are necessary for the establishment of the indicative system will be thus presupposed by the proposition. Consider, for example, the proposition, "The horse is black." Anyone entertaining that proposition must have a spatial and temporal relation to the horse in question. Therefore, the indicative system of this proposition presupposes the spatial and temporal characteristics of the extensive continuum. To serve its function in the proposition, however, the indicative system requires additional patterns of order beyond the spatial and temporal characteristics of the extensive continuum. The reason is as follows. The extensive continuum establishes a determinative set of relations between the regions occupied by the various actual entities, but the continuum by itself provides no information about the contents of the actual entities occupying those regions. That is, we need the continuum if we are to have any way of locating a set of actual entities, but we need more than the continuum if we are to know anything about the particular content of the actual entities occupying those regions—to know, for example, if those regions are occupied by a horse, a book, or empty space. Such information can be established only by observation, direct or indirect. Consider the simpler case of direct observation. We are standing in a field near a horse. Physics and physiology tell us that our observation of the horse actually consists of waves of light falling upon the atoms that constitute the horse; some the waves are reflected off the horse and into our eyeballs, where they stimulate electrical impulses in the retina; the electrical impulses are then carried along the optic nerve to the brain, where brain waves are set in motion; and the brain waves result in the observation of

---

past entity. The past entity becomes a part of the real internal constitution of that new entity. And we also argued that every past entity is so incorporated into the new entity.

Now the logical subjects of a proposition are actual entities. Therefore, if we confine ourselves to propositions about the past (a similar analysis could be made for propositions about the present and the future), it follows that the actual entities which serve as the logical subjects will also be incorporated into the new entity. But the proposition *is* the focusing of the potentiality of an eternal object upon those logical subjects—those actual entities. It is in this sense that the proposition is *about* those actual entities. And so we may conclude that the actual entities which the proposition is about are included in the prehending entity.

However, those logical subjects are included not merely in the prehending entity, but they are also incorporated into the proposition. That is, when the prehending entity creates the proposition, it does not merely focus the potentiality of the eternal object upon images or representations of the logical subjects. Rather, the prehending entity focuses the predicate upon the logical subjects themselves as they are incorporated in that prehending entity. Consequently, we may say that the proposition is not merely *about* a set of actual entities, but it genuinely *includes* those actual entities as a part of its own nature.

In Chapter Fourteen we develop this motif in relation to Whitehead's polemic against the "bifurcation of nature."

the horse. It is obvious from this account that the patterns of order associated with electrons, protons, photons, and the rest, are crucial in establishing the fact that a horse exists at a certain location. These patterns of order, therefore, are required by the indicative system of the proposition, "The horse is black," and thus are presupposed by the proposition itself.

We have shown how the proposition, "The horse is black," presupposes the systematic patterns inherent in the extensive continuum and the systematic patterns inherent in the world of electrons and protons. But this proposition also presupposes the genuinely metaphysical proposition such as "One plus one equals two" or "Any actual entity includes its past entities." A moment's reflection will indicate the need for such metaphysical propositions. For example, an indicative system can utilize the extensive continuum only if the rules of arithmetic are presupposed. Again, on Whitehead's analysis, the world of electrons and protons is based on the inclusion of past entities in present ones; therefore, an indicative system based on the systematic patterns of the world of electrons and protons is implicitly based on the proposition, "Any actual entity includes its past actual entities."

In summary: any proposition, such as the one about the horse, requires that the observer be allowed (A) to learn that a horse exists (which, in our cosmic era, means the patterns of electronic order), (B) at a certain location (which means the patterns of the extensive continuum); and both of these patterns presuppose the genuine presence of the "other" (the past actual entities) in the "subject" (the concrescing actual entity)—that is, the metaphysical patterns of order.

Our objector has one last argument against Whitehead's position. Suppose, says the objector, we grant Whitehead's position that "there are no self-sustained facts, floating in non-entity," that is, that every proposition presupposes its universe. Does not such a position entail an absolute idealism in which there can be no finite facts, in which the only coherent proposition is that one, infinitely complex proposition which describes the Absolute? If we may assume, our objector continues, that such an idealism is not viable, then we must reject Whitehead's position. In response, Whitehead's position is that the indicative system of a proposition requires only the patterns—or outlines—of order; it does not require the details. This is particularly true of the indicative system of any proposition which presupposes only the systematic structure of the universe between the logical subjects and itself. Since such an indicative system does not require the details of that portion of the universe, it follows that finite truth is possible.

PART TWO: SYMBOLISM

PART TWO PRESENTS A SYSTEMATIC SURVEY of Alfred North Whitehead's theory of symbolism. Whitehead considers both sense perception and language to be forms of symbolism. Part Two will, however, consider only sense perception—or, as Whitehead calls it, "symbolic reference"—our discussion of language being postponed until Part Three. We might also note that we will presuppose a detailed knowledge of Whitehead's philosophy of propositions as presented in Part One.

6 Symbolism

IN THIS CHAPTER WE WILL DISCUSS the general nature of symbolism. 'Symbolism' is the generic term which includes a number of specific types, such as language and sense perception (PR 274b-79b).[1]

I

Whitehead describes human symbolism as follows.

> The human mind is functioning symbolically when some components of its experience elicit consciousness, beliefs, emotions, and usages, respecting other components of its experience (S 7d-8a).

From a Whiteheadian perspective, this description is severely limited, since symbolism need not involve humans nor need it be associated with consciousness. Symbolism, however, does universally involve two sets of components. These two sets of components are present together within some concrescing actual entity, where that actual entity uses one set to elicit the other into greater prominence and effectiveness. Whitehead uses the term 'symbol' to designate the set of components which does the eliciting and 'meaning' to designate the set of components which is so elicited (S 8a; PR 274b). It should be noted that both the symbols and the meanings are present within a concrescence by means of perceptions.

Symbolism applies primarily to the objects of these perceptions. There is some question, however, about the application of the term "sym-

---

1. Lest the knowledgeable reader object to calling "sense perception" a type of symbolism, let us note that Whitehead uses "sense perception" in two ways — sometimes as equivalent to "presentational immediacy" and sometimes to "symbolic reference." (We have not yet explained either term. Presentational immediacy is the central topic of Chapter Nine, and symbolic reference of Chapter Eleven.) Presentational immediacy is not normally considered a form of symbolism. In classifying sense perception as a type of symbolism, therefore, we have in mind symbolic reference, in which data perceived in presentational immediacy are used to elicit data perceived in causal efficacy (and, occasionally, vice versa.)

bolism," to the perceptions themselves. It is our opinion that "symbolism" can apply to the relation between the perceptions themselves, albeit as the secondary meaning. Whitehead, it should be noted, sometimes describes symbolic reference—which is a form of symbolism—as holding between the perceptions themselves (PR 185c, 255a). In addition, from the standpoint of Whitehead's system, it would be somewhat arbitrary to argue that symbolic relations are restricted to the objects of perception and cannot encompass the perceptions themselves. We explain as follows. Within Whitehead's system, all perceptions are prehensions. And the objects which are perceived are, thus, the data of these prehensions. We have already noted (in Chapter One) that within an act of concrescence there can be no data without prehensions; and so there can be no objects of perceptions without perceptions. Consequently, the act of eliciting an object of perception will, to a greater or lesser extent, also involve eliciting the perception itself. And, similarly, the act of eliciting a perception will, to a greater or lesser extent, also involve eliciting the object of that perception. Thus, although the emphasis may be either upon the object of the perception or upon the perception itself (and usually it is on the objects of the perception), we must not make a rigid distinction between a symbolic relation between perceptions and a symbolic relation between the objects of perception.

Along these same lines, we should also note that there are only two basic modes of perception in Whitehead's scheme—causal efficacy and presentational immediacy. Therefore, symbols and meanings will enter a concrescence by means of perceptions in the mode of causal efficacy and/or by means of perceptions in the mode of presentational immediacy.[2]

II

In Whitehead's writings, the term 'symbolic reference' seems to have two distinct but related meanings, the one broad and the other narrow. In the broad sense, 'symbolic reference' is simply another name for symbolism. Thus we read,

> The organic functioning whereby there is transition from the symbol to the meaning will be called 'symbolic reference' (S 8a).

In this extended sense of symbolic reference, both the symbols and the meanings may be in the same perceptive mode; they may both be the objects of perception in the mode of causal efficacy or they may both be the objects of perception in the mode of presentational immediacy.

---

2. At this point it is crucial to recall that Whitehead, in accordance with his denial of the bifurcation of nature, asserts that the items perceived in either mode of experience are *both* "out-there" *and* components within the "real internal constitution" of the experiences. Compare Part One, Chapter Three, "Objectification and Actuality."

> The species from which the symbolic reference starts is called the 'species
> of symbols,' and the species with which it ends is called the 'species of
> meanings.' In this way there can be symbolic reference between two spe-
> cies in the same perceptive mode... (PR 274b).

Whitehead's use of the term 'symbolic reference' in this broad sense,
however, is somewhat rare.

Much more commonly, Whitehead restricts the meaning of the
term 'symbolic reference' to sense perception. According to Whitehead,
sense perception is a type of symbolism. In fact, it is the most basic form
of symbolism. In the first several pages of his book *Symbolism*, Whitehead
divides symbolism into three varieties. The first is ceremonial symbolism.
This is the type of symbolism embodied in architectural style, in the litur-
gies of religious groups, in flags and national anthems, and in the seating
arrangements at a White House banquet. This is a relatively superficial
level of symbolism. As Whitehead comments, "The very fact that [any one
specific form of this sort of symbolism] can be acquired in one epoch and
discarded in another epoch testifies to its superficial nature (S 1b).

A second, deeper type of symbolism is language. Language is a
more basic form of symbolism because, among other reasons, a specific
language cannot be as easily discarded as a specific form of ceremonial
symbolism. Thus it is not an option for a native speaker of English to
replace his language with Urdu—though in time he may acquire an ease
with Urdu as a second language. On the other hand, it is quite possible to
replace the ceremonial symbolism of a White House banquet with some
alternative. Language, however, also has a superficial element. With the
exception of a few cases of onomatopoeia, there are no obvious resemblances between the sound of a word—or its written-down shape—and
the appearance of that to which it refers. For example, when we sound out
the world "horse," there is no similarity between that sound and any of
the sounds made by a horse; nor does the shape of the written symbol
"horse" have any resemblance to the configuration of an actual horse.[3]

---

3. Of course, just as there are a few cases of onomatopoeia, so also there are a few
instances in which some of the shapes of a written symbol are similar to the shapes of the
thing signified. For example, in Chinese and Japanese, the written symbol for a horse may
have a shape which is not altogether unlike the shape of a real horse.

However, the existence of alphabets for symbolizing entire languages shows that
the parallelism (between the shape of a written symbol and the shape of the thing symbolized) is not an essential quality of a written language. Compare the Latin alphabet and the
written forms of English, French, German, Spanish, and Swedish; and compare the existence
of alphabets for Hebrew, Greek, Russian, Sanskrit, and Thai.

Indeed, the parallelism (between the shape of the symbol and the shape of the thing
symbolized) may serve to hinder the effectiveness of a written language. For example, early
Egyptian hieroglyphics became less pictorial as time progressed. Again the Hebrews, Greeks,
and Latins all opted for an alphabet despite the example of Egyptian hieroglyphics which
was present to them. And recently the Chinese (on the mainland) have simplified many of
their characters, making the connection between the pictorial shape of the character and the
shape of the signified item more abitrary.

The third, and deepest, level of symbolism is sense perception. Whitehead is normally thinking of this type of symbolism when he uses the term 'symbolic reference'. In this narrow sense of symbolic reference, the symbols and the meanings cannot be in the same mode of perception. Thus we find statements which define symbolic reference in such a way that it can only occur between symbols in one perceptive mode and meanings in the other perceptive mode.

> Of the two distinct perceptive modes, one mode 'objectifies' actual things under the guise of presentational immediacy, and the other mode, which I have not yet discussed, 'objectifies' them under the guise of causal efficacy. The synthetic activity whereby these two modes are fused into one perception is what I have called 'symbolic reference' (S 18b).

The requirement that symbols and meanings be in different modes of perception is one of the characteristics whereby symbolic reference in the narrow sense may be distinguished from symbolic reference in the broad sense. In the narrow sense of symbolic reference, the symbols and meanings must be in different modes of perception; in the broad sense, however, the symbols and the meanings may be—but are not required to be—in the same perceptive mode.

III

The central purpose of Part Two is to explicate the notion of symbolic reference in the narrow sense. To finish this chapter, however, we will make several observations that apply to all forms of symbolism.

First, in any act of symbolism, some of the characteristics and emotional history associated with one set of components may be precipitated upon the other. This precipitation is called symbolic transference (PR 274b; S 63a). Sometimes the direction of symbolic transference is from the symbols to the meanings (S 62b-63a). For example, feelings of the numinous dimension of reality may be symbolized by the words "feelings of the numinous dimension of reality" or by the odors of incense or by the clapping of hands or by the singing of hymns. In each case, the symbols are more easily manipulated than the meanings; that is, it is easier to manipulate words, odors, clapping, and singing than it is to manipulate the actual feelings of the numinous dimension. And yet, by symbolic transference from the symbols, the feelings of the numinous may themselves appear to be easily manipulated. But symbolic transference may also go the other way, that is, from the meanings to the symbols (S 66b-67a). For example, we commonly experience the symbols of the numinous as though the symbols themselves were numinous. Thus certain words or gestures which have been used to symbolize the sacred may themselves be experienced as sacred. (From the standpoint of the prophetic religion of the Hebrews, this opens up possibilities for idolatry.)

Second, symbolism is a creative act. Some agent must put the symbols and the meanings into the relation of symbolism.[4] By themselves, the symbols and the meanings are simply two sets of percepts, and the presence of these two sets of percepts within a concrescence does not guarantee that the concrescing entity will, in fact, yoke them into the relation of symbolism. Nor does the mere presence of these two sets of percepts guarantee which set will function as the symbols and which will function as the meanings. Of course, practical considerations make it unlikely that we will use the physical horse to symbolize the word "horse." (But it is not impossible; for example, if I am teaching English to a Japanese, the word "uma" may be the symbol and "horse" the meaning; or I may be in a field with that Japanese and use the physical horse to symbolize the English word "horse.") Further, the history of a symbol's use may make it exceedingly difficult to reverse the roles of symbol and meaning. The fact remains, however, that the joining of the two sets of percepts in the relation of symbolism—one set as symbols and the other as meanings—is the result of a decision in some actual entity or series of decisions in a set of actual entities (PR 276a, 277b).[5] Thus Whitehead associates symbolism with the freedom of an actual entity's subjective development, and not with the determinism of an actual entity's objective data. Symbolism is a goal to be achieved and not simply a fact which is given.

Third, it is a metaphysical requirement in Whitehead's scheme that every actual entity strive for intensity of experience in its satisfaction as well as in its relevant future (PR 41c). The purpose of all forms of symbolism is to help gain this intensity (S 63a). The symbols aid in bringing the meanings into prominence within the concrescence. Having been brought into prominence, the meanings may then function more effectively in the production of, for example, knowledge, emotion, insight, and practical action—all of which promote intensity of experience. However, the effectiveness of symbolism in promoting intensity of experience is balanced by the fact that it is also one of the ways in which error may enter the concrescence (S19b). And, although an error may at times be beneficial to the enduring object (which contains the actual entity with the er-

4. To place into context Whitehead's claim that the concrescing actual entity is the agent effecting the act of symbolism, it must be recalled that an actual entity is not an agent prior to its acting; rather an actual entity is constituted by its actions. In short, an actual entity *is* what it *does*. See Part One, Chapter Two, Section III and Chapter Three, Section III.

5. We give the alternative of "set of actual entities" because (in the human case) any one percipient actual entity in the soul thread inherits various patterns of symbolism, including the use of one set of percepta as symbols and another as meanings; and thus it inherits a tendency (which may be practically irresistible) towards maintaining those patterns. The percipient entity may inherit those patterns from previous members of its soul thread or from the actual entities constituting the brain and nervous system. In a broad sense, these patterns, and the drive towards their maintenance, may even be said to be inherited from previous users of that symbolism—for example, from the previous speakers of English in the last several centuries.

roneous symbolism), nonetheless, that error may also be disastrous for the enduring object. Given enough errors, one of them will almost certainly result in the destruction of the enduring object entertaining them. Thus enduring objects which gain intensity of experience from symbolism also lose survival power thereby (S 87b). Rocks and stars last far longer than insects and human beings.

Fourth, symbolism is not just a random association of meanings and symbols. There must be some common ground between the symbols and meanings (S 9c; PR 274b). This common ground provides the means by which the concrescing actual entity joins the symbols and the meaning into a symbolic relationship.[6] The common ground is more obvious in some cases than in others. For example, I have a picture of my daughter in college which often reminds me of her. In this case of symbolism, the picture is the symbol, and my memories of my daughter are the meanings. Here the common ground is obvious. The colors of the girl in the picture are about the same as the colors of the girl in my memories; likewise, the proportions of the features are similar in both percepts. In other cases, the common ground is less obvious. For example, the name of my daughter is Beth. Consider the word "Beth" in its spoken form. The sound "Beth" is a symbol for my daughter (as she is objectified in my prehensions of her), who is the meaning. But the characteristics of the sound "Beth" have not the slightest resemblance to the girl; there are no resemblances between, for example, the color, size, or smell of the symbol "Beth" and the color, size, or smell of this beautiful young woman. Rather, the common ground between symbol and meaning lies in their association in my previous experiences. The day she was born, my wife and I looked at her and named her Elizabeth; she was baptized as Elizabeth; I have addressed her as "Beth" many times; I have seen her respond to "Beth" on numerous occasions; and I have heard her say, "My name is Beth." It is this living context which provides the common ground between the symbol "Beth" and the girl-now-become-a-woman (whether we think of the actual entities which constitute her in their formal natures or as objectified). However, whether the common ground between the symbols and the meanings is obvious and direct or whether it is subtle and indirect, there must be a common ground of some sort. Without such a common ground, there can be no symbolism. Whitehead denies that a totally random conjunction of percepts could be properly considered an instance of symbolism. The common ground may not be evident to consciousness, but it will still exist within the concrescence as a factor which has not been made the object of consciousness.

6. It may be noted that the common ground must be present in the symbols and meanings themselves, independently of their status as elements within the concrescing entity. Thus the common ground is not something added to the symbols and meanings by the concrescing actual entity.

7 *Causal Efficacy*

THE NARROW FORM OF SYMBOLIC REFERENCE requires that the symbols and the meanings be in different modes of perception, one in the mode of causal efficacy and one in the mode of presentational immediacy. Therefore, before we can analyze Whitehead's theory of symbolic reference we must first outline his views on each of these perceptive modes. Since causal efficacy is the more primitive (presentational immediacy is derived from it), we will discuss it first.

I

In its primary sense, causal efficacy is power. It is that power whereby present process is made to conform to its given, settled past (AI 234a-36c). Expressed alternatively, causal efficacy is the inheritance in the present from the past (PR 182c).

Causal efficacy is also a form of perception. It is low level and lacks nuance, but it is perception all the same. Whitehead calls causal efficacy a mode of perception for the following reason. As we previously demonstrated (in Chapter Three), a concrescing entity incorporates its past into itself. We must not, however, understand this act of incorporation by means of a mechanical analogy, such as a vacuum cleaner sucking up a pile of dust. Rather we must understand it by an analogy drawn from experience—an experience such as our vague feeling of massive, dim presences about us during the night. Thus causal efficacy is best understood by an analogy to an act of perception; the concrescing entity feels its past. This feeling is the act of incorporating the past into the present. Whitehead describes causal efficacy this way:

> The former mode [i.e., causal efficacy] produces percepta which are vague, not to be controlled, heavy with emotion: it produces the sense of derivation from an immediate past, and of passage to an immediate fu-

ture; a sense of emotional feeling, belonging to oneself in the past, passing into oneself in the present, and passing from oneself in the present towards oneself in the future; a sense of influx of influence from other vaguer presences in the past, localized and yet evading local definition, such influence modifying, enhancing, inhibiting, diverting, the stream of feeling which we are receiving, unifying, enjoying, and transmitting. This is our general sense of existence, as one item among others, in an efficacious actual world (PR 271b).

In his late book *Modes of Thought*, Whitehead offers still another description of causal efficacy. In this passage, it is interesting to note how closely Whitehead ties causal efficacy to our bodily existence—though in no sense does he limit causal efficacy to feelings of our body.

One division [i.e., causal efficacy] is formed by the sense of qualitative experience derived from antecedent fact, enjoyed in the personal unity of present fact, and conditioning future fact. In this division of experience, there are the sense of derivation from without, the sense of immediate enjoyment within, and the sense of transmission beyond. This complex sense of enjoyment involves the past, the present, the future. It is at once complex, vague, and imperative. It is the realization of our essential connection with the world without, and also of our own individual existence, now. It carries with it the placing of our immediate experience as a fact in history, derivative, actual, and effective. It also carries with it the sense of immediate experience as the essence of an individual fact with its own qualities. The main characteristic of such experience is complexity, vagueness, and compulsive intensity. In one respect the vagueness yields a comparatively sharp cut division, namely, the differentiation of the world into the animal body which is the region of intimate, intense, mutual expression, and the rest of nature where the intimacy and intensity of feeling fails to penetrate. My brain, my heart, my bowels, my lungs, are mine, with an intimacy of mutual adjustment. The sunrise is a message from the world beyond such directness of relation. . . . The behaviour-systems of the human body and of intimate experience are closely entangled (MT 98b-99a).

While Whitehead states that we, as conscious human beings, rarely if ever have experiences in the mode of causal efficacy which are totally pure—that is, completely isolated and disconnected from presentational immediacy—nonetheless, there are times when we can come close to such pure experiences. Perhaps the clearest example of an (almost) pure experience in causal efficacy is our experience of ourselves as the outcome of what we were one tenth of a second ago. Speaking personally, I think it is fair to say that sane people who have not read philosophy—as well as philosophers in their non-professional moments when shooting pool and not "doing philosophy" — would never doubt that they are continuously "living-out" the influence of their past selves of one tenth of a second ago. And how else are we to describe this experience of "living-out" the influence of our immediately past selves except to say that each of us somehow experiences the survival of his own immediately past self into his present self. According to Whitehead,

> The immediate past as surviving to be again lived through in the present is the palmary instance of non-sensuous perception [that is, causal efficacy] (AI 234a).

In Whitehead's philosophy the doctrine of causal efficacy is more than just a name for certain aspects of some of our experiences. Rather, the doctrine of causal efficacy also has a theoretical role to play within Whitehead's system. Our experience of the survival of the past into the present is generalized into the doctrine that all actual entities whatsoever experience the survival of their pasts into their presents.[1] In Chapter One

---

1. It may be observed that, according to Whitehead, an ideal metaphysics ought to provide us with a system which (among other things) can interpret and explain every item of our experience, in the sense that "everything of which we are conscious, as enjoyed, perceived, willed, or thought, shall have the character of a particular instance of the general scheme" (PR 4b). Therefore, the real justification for accepting the doctrine of causal efficacy is that, in its generalized form, it does in fact aid in approaching this high ideal of a metaphysical scheme with universal applicability. And so, pre-philosophical descriptions (from common sense and/or science) of our experience of causal efficacy, although necessary and important, do not constitute the central evidence in the justification of the *metaphysical* doctrine of causal efficacy. After all, there may be other ways of describing our immediate experiences which do not involve causal efficacy. And in that case, the key test in deciding among them would not be, which one stays closest to our common sense and/or scientific way of speaking about our experiences; rather, the key test would be, which one, after being appropriately generalized, leads to a metaphysics with the widest applicability.

We assume, of course, that the metaphysical scheme which includes the generalized notion of causal efficacy can account, in terms of its own categories, for the existence of the common sense and scientific descriptions of our experience which do not appeal to causal efficacy. Consider, for example, Hume's description of the general features of our experience. Hume not only fails to include causal efficacy in his account of our experience but in addition he explicitly denies the existence of any such thing as an experience of causal efficacy. Now Whitehead feels that it is not enough to provide an alternative description of immediate experience, a description which does include causal efficacy and is intuitively more plausible (to me at least) than Hume's description. In fact, Whitehead feels that it is not even enough to show that a metaphysics which includes a generalized notion of causal efficacy can organize and explain our world far better than a metaphysics based on Hume's analysis of immediate experience—for example, Whitehead argues that his system is able to explain the success of induction, whereas, he observes, Hume's position leaves induction as a totally inexplicable and arbitrary phenomenon. Rather, Whitehead feels that he has enough evidence against Hume only when he is able to account for Hume's description of our experience. He explains that Hume's description is an abstraction; that is, Hume's description is perfectly true (a) when applied to a certain limited range of experiences (typically, the experiences of a scientist making highly precise and tightly controlled observations) and/or (b) when applied to a certain limited range of characteristics which are indeed present in almost all of our experiences (typically, those characteristics which stem from presentational immediacy and which tend to be the most striking aspects of our most alert, most conscious experiences). Thus Hume's description is an adequate account of some of the most striking characteristics of our conscious experiences, characteristics which tend to be emphasized in the experience of a scientist while making precise observations. In fact, Hume's analysis is wrong *only* if it is understood as an account of all the factors which apply to human experience in general.

we discussed the stages of concrescence. The first stage is the stage of causal efficacy, since it is here that the new actual entity incorporates into itself its past actual world. Moreover, at this first stage the concrescing actual entity must conform to the data in its past actual world; that is, it must reenact (at least certain portions of) that world. For further details, the reader is referred to the appropriate portions of Part One of this book, especially Chapters One and Three. The important point is that the prehensions which occur at an actual entity's first stage of concrescence constitute that entity's basic perceptions in the mode of causal efficacy. It must also be made clear, however, that we are now using the term 'causal efficacy' in its generalized, metaphysical sense, and that we are not using this term in the sense that it applies directly to the conscious experiences we have of the present conforming to the past.

Thus within the arena of human consciousness the palmary instance of a perception in the mode of causal efficacy is a person's experience of the survival of his own immediately past self into his present self. And within the arena of systematic metaphysics, the primary instance of a perception in the mode of causal efficacy is an actual entity's simple physical prehension of a past actual entity, such a simple physical prehension occurring in the first, conformal stage of the concrescing entity's development.

Within the realm of technical metaphysics, however, Whitehead often uses causal efficacy in an extended manner. This extension of the term 'causal efficacy' is exactly parallel with his extension of the term 'physical prehension'. In fact, the terms 'perception in causal efficacy' and 'physical prehension' seem almost to be different names for the same set of items in his system. Whitehead speaks of perceptions in the mode of causal efficacy as more or less primitive (PR 480a). The most primitive

---

We now have an explanation for the undoubted appeal which Hume's analysis has for us; the explanation is that Hume has isolated the most striking aspects of our experience, aspects which are not only extremely common, but which are also promoted by any effort on our part to be precise and alert in our observations.

Now, since many intelligent and serious thinkers are attracted by descriptions of our experience which ignore causal efficacy, and since one of the tests of a metaphysical system is its capacity to demonstrate how each experience of ours (including our attraction to alternative metaphysical systems) is an instance of its categories, it follows that Whitehead's metaphysics must be capable of explaining, in terms of its own categories, the attraction of alternative theories. In other words, unless Whitehead can account for the attraction of alternative descriptions of our experience which ignore causal efficacy, his system will fail in a crucial test case of its applicability. Therefore, Whitehead goes to great lengths to demonstrate that his system can and does account for the attractiveness of alternative systems such as Hume's.

Finally, to place this discussion into context, we hasten to note that applicability is not the only test for the acceptance of a generalized notion into a metaphysical scheme. According to Whitehead, there are others, such as the requirement that the generalized notion be coherent with the other metaphysical doctrines.

form of causal efficacy we have already discussed; it is a concrescing entity's simple physical prehension of a past actual entity. But physical purposes are also perceptions in the mode of causal efficacy (cf. PR 481d-82a, 493b). And since transmutations enter into the genesis of most physical purposes, we may assume that at least some transmutations may be classified as perceptions in the mode of causal efficacy (cf. PR 493b). Lastly, some passages *may* indicate that Whitehead considered a small class of propositional feelings to be properly labeled as perceptions in the mode of causal efficacy (cf. PR 477b-79a).[2]

We make the following six observations about causal efficacy. First, perception in causal efficacy occurs in all actual entities, from the very simplest to the most complex. Conscious actual entities may emphasize other forms of perception to such an extent that awareness of causal efficacy is eliminated. For example, an artist may be enraptured by a dazzling display of color images and, in this mood, may not know or care whether these images are the product of mirrors or whether they are qualities of enduring objects which are genuinely located at the spots where the images are perceived as located. However, although perceptions in causal efficacy can be inhibited from entry into consciousness, they cannot be eliminated by an act of consciousness; they will remain the foundation of the actual entity regardless of whether that actual entity consciously recognizes this fact or not (PR 271c). This is because, in Whitehead's system, it is a metaphysical requirement that all actual entities, including even God, must entertain simple physical prehensions, where these simple physical prehensions *are* perceptions in causal efficacy.

Second, perceptions in the mode of causal efficacy have a tendency to be massive but vague, heavy but dim, and gravid but blurred (PR 257b-58a, S 55b). It is difficult to locate what is felt strictly in the mode of causal efficacy. Indeed, one of the main functions of presentational immediacy is to aid in locating those massive, heavy, and gravid realities.

Within human experience, there is, however, a partial exception to

---

2. We might note that in PR 478c Whitehead mentions "feelings of 'causal efficacy.'" These feelings of causal efficacy are apparently to be correlated (identified?) with some subclass of the propositional feelings mentioned in 477b—specifically, with those propositional feelings which associate the sense datum "with the seats of the antecedent elements of the nervous strand." If so, we may conclude that Whitehead classified some propositional feelings as feelings in causal efficacy.

Given our previous argument that the distinction between physical purposes and propositional feelings is a matter of degree, then we should not be too surprised to find that some propositional feelings are classified under causal efficacy.

As a matter of purely personal speculation on the author's part, it is likely that in the quotation just mentioned, it was a focus on the *antecedent* elements as data of these prehensions which led Whitehead to classify these feelings under causal efficacy. The point is this: feelings in causal efficacy are feelings of the past as that past is present in the concrescing entity. (See the second section of this chapter.)

this vagueness of causal efficacy. This exception consists in the fact that a few perceptions in causal efficacy can more or less accurately discriminate the position of some organs in the body of the percipient, where these organs tend to be those through which we have our sense-perceptions of the exterior world—our eyes, ears, nose, finger tips, tongue, etc. (PR 258b).

We should note that it would be quite difficult to give a full illustration of this point because such an illustration would necessarily involve an analysis of human experience, where any complete example of ordinary human experience will involve perceptions in presentational immediacy and symbolic reference—perceptions which we have not yet discussed. Nevertheless, we may give a partial illustration of the gist of Whitehead's position as follows.

I will ask you, the reader, to consider your experience of looking at the page in the book which you are now reading. If you thoroughly examine your experience, you will note that you are looking at the sheet *with* your eyes. That is, you will become aware of the fact that your perception of the sheet of paper is mediated to you through your eyes. Moreover, even if you depend *only* upon the experience of seeing the paper with your eyes, it will be self-evident that your eyes are located in the front of your head and not on the bottom of your feet! This experience of feeling the eyes as *the means by which* the sense-perception of the paper has come to you, is an experience in causal efficacy. In short, it is by means of perception in causal efficacy that we become aware of the role of our eyes in the production of visual experiences; and in this perception in causal efficacy of the eyes, we are able to discriminate the position of the eyes in a somewhat accurate manner. Thus, as an element in your sense-perception of the sheet of paper, you have a perception in causal efficacy of the agency of your eyes in the production of the sense-perception.

To complete our illustration, it is important to note that you can also have a direct sense-perception of your eyes. For example, if your eyes hurt from too much reading, then you will become directly aware of the ache in your eyes.[3] In this case, the ache will become a sensum which is

---

3. One may be inclined to object that a feeling of an ache in the eyes cannot be a *sense-*perception. This objection may or may not be true. In either case, it is not really relevant. The term "sense-perception" is a pre-systematic term for Whitehead. We have used the term "sense-perception" in this discussion only for the sake of clarity since we have not yet presented the notions of 'presentational immediacy' and 'symbolic reference'. And 'presentational immediacy' and 'symbolic reference' are the technical terms in Whitehead's system which are meant to explicate "sense perception" in the ordinary, pre-philosophical sense. Now whether or not we would—intuitively and pre-philosophically—classify a direct perception of the eye-ache as a sense-perception, this perception *does* meet the criteria for being a perception in symbolic reference. (Only in the eleventh chapter on symbolic reference will we be in a position to back up this last claim.) And the point that we will make in the next few sentences of the main text does *not* depend on the fact that the reader can have direct sense-perceptions—in the pre-philosophical sense—of the eye-ache; rather, our point

felt as extended in a specific region of space. Thus, the direct perception of the ache in the eyes will disclose the exact position of the eyes with far more precision than the feeling in causal efficacy (of the agency of the eyes in the production of the perception of the sheet of paper) ever could.[4] In summary, we may say that, while some perceptions in causal efficacy can discriminate the positions of the percipient's bodily organs with more accuracy than is common for perceptions in causal efficacy, direct sense-perceptions of those organs—that is, perceptions in presentational immediacy and symbolic reference—can discriminate the position of those organs with even more precision (PR 258b).

Third, causal efficacy is the basis for our experience of the stubborn factuality of the past world (S 36b-37a). Of course, once a deed is done, it cannot be undone. But more importantly, once a deed is done, it will condition what comes after it. A completed event which conditions its future is called a fact. Thus the "practical man" demands to know the facts, the bare facts. (Of course, the practical man forgets that there are no "bare" facts — each actual entity prehending its objective data from its own perspective and processing those data in various ways during the drive towards its satisfaction.) Again the dominance of a completed deed as *the* conditioning factor diminishes as time passes, until it fades into insignificance—though it is never wholly obliterated. Thus the practical man thinks that "history is bunk" and demands that we keep our attention on the present—by which he means the immediate past insofar as it continues to make a difference for whatever project he has in mind. Thus we live in a world of stubborn facts, a world of "real causes," a world of causal efficacy.

Fourth, causal efficacy is the foundation for that sense of being in history which pervades human life. Each person not only inherits traditions and past patterns of social life, but such traditions and social patterns are the foundation of that person's drive for identity. That is, each actual entity—and thus each moment of human experience—comes into existence as a series of perceptions in causal efficacy of the past world. The existence of that past world in the new entity is the very foundation of that new entity's existence. Thus participation in the powerful streams of tradition and history is basic for the possibility of new existences, new actual entities.

---

depends on the fact that the reader can have direct perceptions of the eye-ache in the mode of symbolic reference.

4. A further nuance is this. A person's perception in causal efficacy of the agency of the eyes is actually a perception of the eyes as they were functioning in the *past*—although this functioning will have been in the very recent past, say a second or less. On the other hand, in the direct sense-perception (i.e., perception in symbolic reference), the ache will be felt as *contemporaneous* with the percipient. Once again, however, we will be able to back-up this claim only after we have finished our discussion of causal efficacy and after we have presented our technical discussion of symbolic reference.

Fifth, Whitehead's philosophy thus leads to a multiple relation between the self and the other(s). (A) The others, in the sense of past actual entities, exist both as initial data in their own formal natures and as objective data in their role as a part of the very identity of the concrescing actual entity. When we focus on the initial data in their own formal natures, they can be described as truly alien to the new actual entity. The peculiar particularity which defined the past entities as distinct entities will always be "other" than the new peculiar particularity which inheres in the new actual entity. In addition, the necessity of negative prehensions entails that the "other" will never be fully part of the new "self"—that is, the past actual entities cannot be prehended in their total fullness.[5] In human terms, it may be said that the others in my world remain irreducibly other. (B) And yet, when those alien past actual entities enter into the new concrescence as objective data, they become the foundation of the existence of that concrescing entity. This means that even while the past in its formal completion remains alien to me, yet I exist only because those alien realities have become the beginning of who (or what) I am. (C) The past entities— the others—while part of who I am, and while giving me the foundation of my identity, do not exhaust my identity. Each concrescing entity must drive at its own distinctive reaction to its past world. It must create a new identity which is more than merely the sum total of the identities of the past entities. That is, even though I begin each moment of my existence as the internalization of these other entities, yet I must find an identity which integrates all the conflicts in those past entities, conflicts which I have internalized as part of who I am and which I must, nevertheless, overcome in a new synthesis. The same tradition which gives birth to my identity can easily become the enemy of my fuller identity. In short, I begin as something other than my own potential self; this means both that I experience those others as providing the very possibility of achieving a self of any sort, and yet that their very otherness demands that I strive for a new self which is authentically me and thus different from my past. (D) The contemporary actual entities are not present in the concrescing entity except as regions in the continuum (a point which we fully discuss in the next section of this chapter). Yet the concrescing entity must be concerned for its contemporary world because future entities will be able to use that concrescing entity only insofar as they can coordinate their prehensions of that concrescing entity with their prehensions of that actual entity's contemporaries. In human terms, this means that at any moment in my existence there is a profound otherness to my contemporary world. (Kant's description of the noumenal world as a radical "other" which cannot enter into my phenomenal world makes excellent sense when applied to my

---

5. God, of course, is the exception who can prehend data without negative prehensions.

contemporary world.) And yet, I am ethically required to take account of the others in my contemporary world because both I and my contemporaries will share the identical destiny of being part of the same actual world for future actual entities.

Sixth, from the time of Descartes the fully conscious self has provided the Archimedean point from which the world can be surveyed and its reality and coherence assessed. Whitehead's view of causal efficacy (history/tradition) as the foundation of existence reverses this order. The world, in its very otherness and yet as present as objective data within the concrescence/self, provides the foundation for that self. A rational and conscious self is thus the occasional achievement of some actual entities —actual entities who begin their concrescences with an actual world, that is, with a set of objective data, which is rich and nuanced enough to support the drive after such a complex self-identity. Each self is complex and pluralistic in its origins (as a set of objective data), its unity being an achievement and not its point of departure.

II

In Whitehead's system, it is a basic principle that contemporary entities are causally independent (PR 95c; S 25a). In fact, the temporal relations among actual entities of past, present, and future may be defined in terms of their causal relations.

We proceed as follows. For any two actual entities X and Y, Y is in the past of X if and only if X has a perception in causal efficacy of Y; Y is in the future of X if and only if Y has a perception in causal efficacy of X; and Y is contemporaneous with X if and only if neither has a perception in the mode of causal efficacy of the other (PR 486c-87a; cf. MT 206b).[6]

We make the following observations about this series of definitions. First, in the definitions of past, present, and future, we assumed implicitly that a concrescing actual entity has a perception in causal efficacy of every past actual entity in its actual world.[7] Second, all the entities in the past of an actual entity are actual, at least in an analogous sense which is sufficiently strong to allow us to assert that the past actual entities are "there" to be prehended.[8] Third, Whitehead's metaphysical analysis leads one to expect that in everyday (pre-philosophical) experience, time and

---

6. This definition takes "perception in causal efficacy" as a primitive term. Given the very close relationship of "perception in causal efficacy" with "physical prehension," we could also define past, present, and future in terms of physical prehensions. (We have discussed physical prehensions in some detail in Part One of this book, mostly, but not entirely, in Chapters One and Three.)

7. Compare Part One, Chapter Three, Section IV.

8. Compare Part One, Chapter Three, Section II.

causality are tied together. It is the author's personal opinion that our pre-philosophical experience does tie time and causality together. We know the past as that which shapes us, molds us, and requires us to respond. We know the present as our opportunity to respond to our past—the opportunity to inject our own decisions into the stream of history. And we know the future as that realm upon which our actions and decisions will have consequences.

It follows, in our opinion, that if a person has no pre-philosophical grasp of the interplay of causality and time, then Whitehead's analysis will be of little use. Given some grasp of these notions, Whitehead's analysis will — according to his admirers — help us to a better understanding of them; but without some starting place, his philosophical definitions of time and causality "remain metaphors mutely appealing for an imaginative leap" (PR 6c). And so, speaking psychologically, some understanding of the nature of time and causality is required before Whitehead's metaphysical system can be understood.

There is another sense in which the definitions of time and causality presuppose each other in Whitehead's system. Ultimately these definitions are dependent upon such basic categories as 'actual entity', 'prehension', and 'The Fourth Category of Explanation'. But such fundamental ideas presuppose each other. This is partly because such fundamentals form the basis in terms of which all further definitions—such as those of time and causality—must be composed. (As a mathematician, Whitehead knew that all systems must have their undefined fundamental notions.) Moreover, the basic ideas of his system require each other in two additional ways. First, as we discussed in the paragraph immediately above, there must be a preliminary pre-philosophical grasping of certain elements in our experience to serve as the psychological ground for the interpretation of these basic ideas. Second, these terms can be explicated only in terms of each other. That is, it is only by weaving these terms together that a more precise understanding of their meanings can be obtained; in other words, the interplay among these basic concepts serves as the touchstone for ascertaining their precise meaning within the technical system.

> 'Coherence,' as here employed, means that the fundamental ideas, in terms of which the scheme is developed, presuppose each other so that in isolation they are meaningless. This requirement does not mean that they are definable in terms of each other; it means that what is indefinable in one such notion cannot be abstracted from its relevance to the other notions. It is the ideal of speculative philosophy that its fundamental notions shall not seem capable of abstraction from each other. In other words, it is presupposed that no entity can be conceived in complete abstraction from the system of the universe, and that it is the business of speculative philosophy to exhibit this truth. This character is its coherence (PR 5a).

Clearly then, there is a circularity to Whitehead's metaphysics. But whether this circularity is vicious can be determined only by examining the system and observing how well it can explain our experiences of the world. It is the purpose of this section to examine one portion of Whitehead's system, checking its self-consistency as well as its applicability and adequacy to our experience of the world.

III

On the basis of causal efficacy, each actual entity defines for itself three basic loci. All those complete actual entities which the concrescing actual entity perceives in the mode of causal efficacy constitute its past—that is, its actual world. All those actual entities which, if they should occur, would perceive that concrescing entity in the mode of causal efficacy, constitute the future. All those actual entities which are neither in the past nor the future of the concrescing entity are in the present—that is, they are contemporaneous with the concrescing actual entity (PR 188c-99a; 486c-87a). It is to be noted that contemporaneous events are defined negatively; that is, they are events which are in neither the past nor the future of the concrescing entity (PR 189b).

A

Diagram 15 may help in our discussion. Diagram 15 is a two-dimensional representation of (what is in our cosmic epoch) a four-dimensional situation. The arrow represents the flow of time from past to future. The circle labeled X is the concrescing actual entity. Area 1 is its future and area 4 is its past. Both areas 1 and 4 are, in fact, four-dimensional cones. Areas 2 and 3 are the present for actual entity X. Areas 2 and 3 are really subsections of one larger area; only the limitations of a two-dimensional diagram for a four-dimensional situation lead to the illusion that areas 2 and 3 are disconnected. Perhaps this is easier to see in a three-dimensional model. Imagine an axis through the center of X, an axis which in our two-dimensional diagram would lie on the paper and also be exactly perpendicular to the bottom of the page. Now rotate the whole of diagram 15 around that axis through a full 360°. Areas 1 and 4 will both be three-dimensional cones while areas 2 and 3 become parts of the three-dimensional area between the two cones. In a four-dimensional situation we would add an additional dimension to the three-dimensional diagram we just constructed.

Diagram 15 has a very important limitation. For the sake of clarity we have drawn straight lines to indicate the "edges" of X's past and future. Please note: X's past is, in the most direct sense, a set of actual entities—and *not* first and foremost a region. Therefore the dividing "line" between past area 4 and contemporary areas 2 and 3 is the "line" where the actual entities which are prehended by X touch the regions of the actual entities which are not prehended by X. There is no reason to suppose that in every case the shapes of the actual entities are such that a line describing their edges would be straight. The key therefore is this: The past is primarily a set of actual entities, and it is somewhat abstract to divide X's environment into "regions" of past, present, and future, especially where these regions are separated by straight lines which do not indicate the atomized character of these regions.

Now it is a metaphysical necessity that actual entity X have a contemporary area, but the "width" of that contemporary area is contingent upon the particular cosmic epoch during which actual entity X concresces. In our diagram 15 we have let angles 1 and 4 be approximately equal to angles 2 and 3. This, however, for our cosmic epoch, is quite misleading. In our electromagnetic era, the angles 2 and 3 are tied to the speed of light. So, if we let one unit along the time axis in diagram 15 be equal to one second, and if we let one unit along the space axis in diagram 15 be equal to one mile, then since light travels at 186,000 miles per second, angles 2 and 3 could hardly be detected on a diagram which, like diagram 15, occupies only a few inches on a standard piece of paper. Thus the line which separates area 1 from area 2 would go up the page one unit for every 186,000 units it moved to the left.

In Whitehead's system, the relation of contemporaneity need not be transitive (PR 487a, AI 252d-53a). That is, if actual entity X is contemporaneous with actual entity Y, and if actual entity Y is contemporaneous with actual entity Z, then entity X may or may not be contemporaneous with entity Z. Diagram 16 will aid in illustrating this point. In diagram 16, actual entities X and Y are contemporaries. Thus areas 3 and 4 constitute the future for X; areas 8 and 9 constitute the past of X; and areas 1, 2, 7, 6, and 5, as well as the area occupied by Y itself, constitute the present for X. As for Y, areas 2 and 3 constitute its future; areas 7 and 8, its past; and areas 1, 6, 4, 5, and 9, as well as the area occupied by X itself, constitute its present. We may assume that the area occupied by Y is a part of Y's present, and that the area occupied by X is a part of X's present.

Now imagine an actual entity lying in area 1, 6, or 5. Such an actual entity would be a contemporary of both X and Y. Next imagine an actual entity lying in area 2. Such an entity would be contemporary with X, but it would be in the future of Y. Again, imagine an actual entity lying in area 7. Such an entity would be contemporaneous with X, but it would be in the past of Y. Similarly, an actual entity in area 4 would be contemporary with Y, but it would be in the future of X. And lastly, an entity in area 9 would be contemporary with Y, but it would be in the past of X. Let this third actual entity be called Z. If Z lies in area 1, 6, or 5, the following relation would hold: X would be contemporaneous with Y; and Y would be contemporaneous with Z; and X would be contemporaneous with Z. If Z lies in area 9, however, then X would be contemporaneous with Y, and Y would be contemporaneous with Z, but X would be in the future of Z!

It will be also noticed in diagram 16 that the pasts of entities X and Y do not wholly coincide. While area 8 is the past which is common to both X and Y, areas 7 and 9 are in the past of only one of the actual entities, area 7 being contemporaneous with X and in the past of Y only, and area 9 being contemporaneous with Y and in the past of X only. Since the actual world of an entity is the set of all its past entities, it will be readily seen that the actual worlds of X and Y overlap, but they do not coincide. Also it will be observed that the farther the distance between X and Y, the smaller will be the area in which their actual worlds of X and Y overlap. On the other hand, it must be remembered that, in our cosmic epoch, angles a, b, c, and d are very small (on the previously-mentioned scale where one unit on the temporal axis equals one second and where one unit on the spatial axis equals one mile); therefore, X and Y would have to be a considerable number of miles apart before, say, less than 50% of the actual world, within the last ten seconds, if one entity was shared by the actual world of the other entity (AI 253a).

B

The fact that not all the entities which are contemporaneous with a specific actual entity X are necessarily contemporary with each other, suggests another definition. A 'duration' is a locus of actual entities such that (1) all members of that locus are contemporaneous with each other, and (2) all actual entities which are not members of that locus are in the past or future of one or more members of that locus (PR 487a).[9] Diagram 17 will help to illustrate this point. We stress that this diagram is for heuristic purposes only. We hope that it will *illustrate* some of Whitehead's views on the nature of the interrelations among actual entities. But it would be

---

9. We note that if it is metaphysically possible for contemporary actual entities to prehend each other in the mode of causal efficacy, then (A) our definitions of past, present, and future entities are confused, and (B) the notion of a duration would be equally confused —at least as we have explicated it. For a positive evaluation of the point of view that it is metaphysically possible for contemporary entities to prehend each other causally, see Ford, "Whitehead's Conception of Divine Spatiality." As the title of Ford's article indicates, the monkey wrench in Whitehead's metaphysical machine at this point is the problem of God.

Even if it is metaphysically possible for contemporary actual entities to prehend each other causally, we might still salvage our discussion of 'causal past', 'causal present', and 'causal future' as well as of 'duration' as follows: we would interpret each of these notions as applicable to only a subset of all possible actual entities—for example, to all actual entities except God.

For an illuminating discussion of the general problem of the relation of Whitehead's God to simultaneity, see Paul Fitzgerald, "Relativity Physics and the God of Process Philosophy."

dangerous to *argue from* the diagram to Whitehead's doctrines on this matter. We give two examples of such dangers. (A) It would be incorrect to assume on the basis of diagram 17 that some actual entities meet their pasts and futures at a one dimensional point only. (B) It would also be incorrect to assume on the basis of our diagram that there are "empty spaces" between actual entities; (for the sake of clarity, we have drawn the various actual entities with "space" between them, but in reality there are no "empty spaces" in the continuum, the region of a concrescing entity being contiguous on all sides with regions of other actual entities).

In diagram 17, the central actual entity is X. The thick unbroken lines show the extent of X's future and past. Everything inside the two thick unbroken lines which meet at the top of X is in the future of X, such as entity 23. Everything inside the two thick unbroken lines which meet at the bottom of X is in the past of X. And everything between these two sets of lines, such as entities 1 through 22, is contemporary with X. The lines of thick dashes set off the causal future and causal past of entities 18 and 5 in a similar manner. Every other entity in diagram 17 could have its past and future set off with similar lines. A careful look at diagram 17, therefore, should reveal quite clearly which entities are contemporaneous with a particular actual entity and which are in the past or future of that particular actual entity.

Diagram 17 reveals several durations which pass through X. We have labeled the most obvious duration Alpha. It consists of entities 1, 2, 3, 4, X, 5, 6, 7, and 8. Alpha continues both to the left of entity 1 and to the right of entity 8. Each of the entities in Alpha is contemporaneous with every other actual entity in Alpha. And every entity not in Alpha is either in the past of one or more members of Alpha or in the future of one or more of the members of Alpha. For example, entity 9 is in the past of 1, and entity 22 is in the past of 7; and entity 18 is in the future of 5, and entity 23 is in the future of 3, 4, and X (and perhaps others as well).

There are other durations which also pass through X. For example, there is a duration which includes entities 9, 10, 17, 16, X, 18, 19, and 20. (This duration, as well as all the others, includes actual entities to the left and right of the diagram.) Still another duration includes entities 11, 12, 10, 17, 16, X, 18, 19, and 20. And a fourth duration includes 11, 13, 14, 15, 16, X, 18, 19, and 20.

The "branches" which occur at entities 10 and 16 indicate one way in which, given a much larger diagram, the number of durations passing through X could be indefinitely increased. There is a "merging" in entity 11 which could be duplicated elsewhere. Whitehead notes that there may be an infinite number of durations through X (PR 487c-88a).[10]

---

10. We should note, however, that it is not a metaphysical necessity that there be an infinite number of durations through any one actual entity. Rather it is in the results of

Actual entities must have a finite spatial-temporal "spread." Thus it is impossible for the temporal dimension of a duration to diminish to an instant. At every actual entity in the duration, that duration will have some spatial "thickness."[11] Although Whitehead never says as much, it seems reasonable to assume that during any one cosmic epoch there is a fairly stable unit which expresses the size of the smallest actual entity. In terms of diagram 17, it may be that the region of actual entity 21 is too small, or it may be at the limit. The point is that, if we take X as a unit size, there will be a limit to how small we can draw actual entity 21.

For each duration through X, we may indicate two additional loci, the durational past and the durational future (PR 488b.) For any given duration, its durational past consists of the locus of all those actual entities which are in the past of one or more of the entities in that duration. The durational future of any given duration is the locus of all those actual entities which are in the future of one or more of the entities in that duration (PR 487b).[12] Thus, in diagram 17, the durational future of Alpha is the locus of all those actual entities whose regions are above Alpha, while the durational past of Alpha is the locus of all those actual entities whose regions are below Alpha. It will be observed, therefore, that for any one actual entity there will be as many durational futures and pasts as there are durations which pass through it—which in this epoch amounts to infinity.

Thus, for any given actual entity X, we have discussed six loci of actual entities. The first three are definable in terms of causal efficacy.

(1) The causal past of X.
(2) The causal future of X.
(3) The causal present of X (that is, the locus of X's contemporary actual entities).

The last three loci depend on the notion of a duration.

---

modern science that Whitehead finds the basis for his claim that there is in each entity of this epoch an infinity of durations (PR 191c). That is, in any given epoch it is metaphysically permissible, but not required, that an actual entity have more than one duration. (Since all actual entities must have, according to Whitehead's metaphysical categories, a region of contemporary entities, we may suppose that it is metaphysically required that any actual entity have at least one duration passing through it.)

To help visualize a situation in which only one duration passes through an actual entity, imagine, in diagram 17, that both angle a and angle b are increased to one hundred eighty degrees—that is, that there are two straight lines touching X, one at the top and one at the bottom. In such a situation, every entity within X's present would be contemporaneous with every other entity, and there would be no branching nor merging. Thus there would be only one duration passing through X.

11. See Palter, *Whitehead's Philosophy of Science*, 144.

12. Compare the interesting but incorrect definition of 'durational future' and 'durational past' in Schmidt, *Perception and Cosmology in Whitehead's Philosophy*, 144.

(4) A duration which includes X (there may be more than one).

(5) A specific durational future for each of the durations which includes X.

(6) A specific durational past for each of the durations which includes X.

According to Whitehead, these last three loci are also "defined purely in terms of notions derived from 'causal efficacy'" (PR 488c). That is, the concrete structures and forms of all six of these loci are at least partially determined for any one specific actual entity by the particular arrangement of the entities around it. In other words, these concrete structures and forms are not determined by purely mathematical considerations alone, but, quite to the contrary, they depend at least partially on the contingent patterns of organization in the environment of the specific entity in question.

8 The Extensive Continuum

IN CONTRAST TO THE SIX LOCI discussed in the previous chapter, there is a seventh locus, which *is* determined by purely mathematical considerations alone. This is the 'strain locus' or the 'presented locus'. The strain locus is not developed in all actual entities, only in those of sufficient complexity.

I

The notion of a strain locus is highly complicated in its technical development, but the broad outlines of its connection with ordinary, conscious human experience are not difficult to grasp. The fact is, as a moment's reflection will confirm, that we as human beings do not directly perceive the infinite number of durations into which our contemporary world may be divided. Rather, we are aware in each moment of our conscious life of a contemporary world in which each subordinate region is contemporaneous with every other region. Moreover, this contemporary world of which we are directly conscious is highly geometricized—especially when perceived visually. That is, when I see a red glass on my desk, that red image has a precise location in relation to my eyes, the desk, the walls, and so forth. In fact, I may apply Euclid's geometry to these various relations. Thus, in sum, as a human being I am conscious of a contemporary world which has two important characteristics. (1) This perceived contemporary world seems to have as one of its aspects a geometrical substructure, that is, an ideal space-time system in which the colors, shapes, and sounds are extended. And (2) this perceived contemporary world is so grounded in that geometrical substructure that it is almost a tautology to assert that any one subregion of that consciously perceived contemporary world is contemporary with any other subregion. This geometrical substructure of the perceived world is what Whitehead calls the 'strain locus' or the 'presented locus'.

Concerning this strain locus, two facts especially should be noted. (1) For ordinary—non-astronomical and non-subatomic—spans of space and time, regular Euclidean geometry seems to apply, at least as a very close approximation. And (2) for ordinary spans of space and time, if I actually live and work in accordance with the assumption that the actual entities which have concresced in that strain locus are contemporary with each other, then normally no practical ill consequences will follow in the workaday world in which I daily live. In other words, the denial that simultaneity is necessarily transitive stems from some highly theoretical considerations in speculative science; this denial is not, and could not be, derived from our ordinary perceptions of the world and from our direct practical actions which are based on those perceptions. To account for these two facts — but especially the latter — Whitehead argues that the strain locus is closely associated in the concrescing actual entity with some one duration. This "close association" need not equal identity, but it must be tight. By making this association between the strain locus and a particular duration, the concrescing entity guarantees that events which are *perceived* as contemporaneous among themselves (in the strain locus) will actually *be* contemporaneous (in the duration)—assuming, of course, that the perception corresponds with reality in the other respects also. That is, the entities in a duration really *are,* in fact, all contemporaneous with each other; and, therefore, the perceiver's association of the strain locus with such a duration is the foundation for the practical success of our activities of daily living, where these activities were predicated upon the assumption that what is perceived as simultaneous really is simultaneous. In order to secure these advantages, a sufficiently complex concrescing entity will associate its strain locus with one of its durations to a greater or lesser extent—usually greater.

The strain locus itself, as prescinded from the duration with which it may be associated, is a hunk of the geometer's ideal system of space-time. Several questions immediately arise. For example, from where did the concrescing entity derive the elements in this strain locus? The answer is to be found in the extensive continuum. The extensive continuum is a factor in the object of any perception in causal efficacy. Since the extensive continuum is composed of mathematical forms and relations, we should not be surprised to discover that Whitehead names the extensive continuum as the source of the constitutive elements in the strain locus. Therefore, before continuing our exposition of the nature of a strain locus (in the next chapter), we will devote the rest of this chapter to a discussion of the nature of the extensive continuum.

II

We make the following set of observations about the extensive continuum. The extensive continuum in Whitehead's thought is at times obscure, and we will not try to explain every aspect of it. Rather, we will center our explication of the extensive continuum on those aspects which are most relevant to Whitehead's theories of propositions, symbolism, and language.

A

The extensive continuum is, when considered by itself, an abstraction from actual entities (SMW 65d). This is required by the Ontological Principle, which states that actual entities are the final real things out of which the universe is constructed.

B

The extensive continuum is a system of all possible regions (which are the relata) and their connections (which are the relations). Thus for the extensive continuum the notion of a region is the basic building block, the unit of construction. However, the status of the notion of a region within Whitehead's larger metaphysical system is something of a mystery. According to Schmidt, when Whitehead composed *Process and Reality*, he considered a region to be a primitive notion in his system, having in this respect the same status as an eternal object, a prehension, or a subjective form; but, according to Schmidt, by the time Whitehead wrote *Adventures of Ideas*, he had decided that a region was a type of nexus.[1] This change in the status of a region is typified by the fact that in *Process and Reality* the notion of contiguity is defined in such a way that the notion of a region is presupposed in that definition, while in *Adventures of Ideas* the definition of a region presupposes the notion of contiguity (PR 468c: AI 260b).[2]

Probably it is impossible, from Whitehead's writings as they now stand, to establish the precise status of a region. Nonetheless, it may be enlightening to note some of the qualities that Whitehead packs into his notion of a region. First the elements which define a region are eternal objects. At one point Whitehead explicitly claims that the elements which define certain regions are eternal objects, and there is no reason why his comments could not be applied to any region.

---

1. Schmidt, *Perception and Cosmology in Whitehead's Philosophy*, 136-37.

2. It may be worth noting that Palter suggests, as an explanation of the reversal of the logical priority of 'region' and 'contiguity' in these two books, that they may, in fact, belong to two different chains of definitions. Palter's point, we take it, is that in the theory of extension the notion of region is the more primitive, while in the theory of causality the notion of contiguity is the more primitive. If Palter is correct, then the role of 'region' is not identical in these two theories, and neither is the role of 'contiguity'. Thus there remains to be produced some explanation of the connection between the notion of 'region' in the theory of extension and the notion of 'region' in the theory of causality; likewise, there remains to be produced some explanation of the connection between the 'contiguity' in the one theory and the notion of 'contiguity' in the other. See Palter, *Whitehead's Philosophy of Science*, 146, footnote 48.

> They define the 'strain' of the feeler, and they define the focal region which they thus relate to the feeler. In so far as we are merely considering an abstract pattern, we are dealing with an *abstract eternal object*. But as a determinant of a concrete feeling in a concrete percipient, we are dealing with the feeling as relating its subject (which includes the 'seat' in its volume) to a definite spatial region (the focal region) external to itself (PR 476b; emphasis added).

Again we read:

> Accordingly the spatio-temporal relationship, in terms of which the actual course of events is to be expressed, is nothing else than a selective limitation within the general systematic relationships among *eternal objects* (SMW 161b; emphasis added).

Second, once connected with the realm of actual entities, there is an insistent particularity to a region. My pen is at a specific spot on my desk. I may be able to move my pen, but I cannot move the spot where it is. There is an important element of truth to Newton's view of absolute space which asserts that a place is where it is, and that it cannot be moved or altered.[3] Whitehead, of course, stands opposed to Newton at many points. (For example, according to Whitehead, both space and time are, in fact, relations among actual entities; and, without those actual entities, space and time would have no ontological status. Again according to Whitehead, the identity of any one region in space-time is internally related to all other regions of space-time. For Newton, on the other hand, each section of space is complete and understandable by itself.[4]) However, Whitehead completely agrees with Newton that a specific place, or region, cannot be moved or altered (PR 124b). In this sense, a region is "infected" by the particularity of the realm of actual entities with which it is connected.[5] For this reason we may say that the extensive continuum (with its constituent regions) is "actual" in an extended and analogous sense. It is essential, however, to understand that the continuum is "actual"—even in this extended sense—only insofar as it has been occupied by actual entities and thus brought into the concrete world of actuality.[6]

C

Not only is each concrescing actual entity in the extensive continuum, but its past and future are in that continuum as well. This extensive continuum

3. Whitehead quotes Newton's proof of this at PR 110a.
4. At least this is Whitehead's often repeated view of Newton, especially in SMW and PR (e.g., SMW 46b-c, 48a-51c).
5. See Part One, Chapter Three, Section II.C where we discuss the role of Creativity as that "peculiar particularity" which allows us to distinguish a set of eternal objects from a concrete nexus or actual entity.
6. See Part One, Chapter One, Section III.D, p. 22 and Chapter Three, Section II.D, pp. 74.

is one relational complex in which all potential objectifications find their niche. It underlies the whole world, past, present, and future (PR 103a). Whitehead often writes, however, in a way that may lead the unwary reader to conclude that the past and future are "in" the extensive continuum just as a desk is "in" a room. This is sometimes called the "container view" of space-time. But the container theory is far from acceptable to Whitehead. We now explain why.

The extensive continuum, abstracted from the actual entities which are "in" it, is a systematically organized unit. As a general pattern of organization, it is an incredibly complicated eternal object. Each actual entity which is in the continuum prehends that scheme *as a whole unit*. It does not merely prehend the region which it occupies; it prehends the whole thing.

> The systematic scheme, in its completeness embracing the actual past and the potential future, is prehended in the positive experience of each actual entity. . . . The prehension of this scheme is one more example that actual fact involves in its own constitution real potentiality which is referent beyond itself (PR 112a-13a; cf. SMW 71a).

In this sense, then, it would be just as accurate to say that the extensive continuum is "in" the actual entity as it would be to say that the actual entity is in the continuum. In fact, to speak of the continuum as "in" the actual entity is, we think, the less misleading expression.

The eternal objects which constitute the extensive continuum, considered as a scheme of organization, are all 'objective'. Objective eternal objects can never be characteristics of the subjective form of a prehension; they can only be characteristics of the object of a prehension. However, at this point we need to remind ourselves that the concrescing actual entity *is* the unification of its past world into a new fact. That is, the concrescing entity incorporates its past world into itself so that some portion of every past actual entity becomes a part of the real internal constitution of the new entity.[7] Therefore, objective eternal objects, although they cannot become characteristics of the subjective forms of the new actual entity, can still become a part of the very constitution of that new entity. The role of objective eternal objects is to introduce one actual entity into the constitution of another actual entity. Speaking of objective eternal objects, Whitehead remarks,

> . . . by a necessity of its nature it is introducing one actual entity, or nexus, into the real internal constitution of another actual entity. It can never be an element in the definiteness of a subjective form. The solidarity of the world rests upon the incurable objectivity of this species of eternal ob-

7. See Part One, Chapter Three, Section II.

jects. . . . Eternal objects of the objective species are the mathematical Platonic forms. They concern the world as a medium (PR 445e-46a).

There is a distinction between prehending the extensive continuum and exemplifying that continuum. (If there were not such a distinction, then God, who clearly prehends objective eternal objects, would thereby exemplify them as well; but Whitehead apparently held that God is non-extensive.[8]) We may conclude, therefore, that an actual entity is "in" the extensive continuum when (A) it prehends the entire scheme of the continuum and (B) it exemplifies that scheme. And an actual entity exemplifies the extensive scheme when it occupies a specific region—that is, when it exemplifies a region—and when it also exemplifies the relations entailed by that region. For example, suppose that an entity occupied a perfect four-dimensional sphere at some specific place. The entity in question would then exemplify that particular region; but it would also exemplify the eternal objects 'being equidistant from its center', 'inclosing the most volume with the minimum surface', and 'not having a surface with ninety degree corners'.

We are now in a position to explain how Whitehead's theory of the extensive continuum differs from the container view of space-time. Whitehead's theory just about reverses the container theory. According to Whitehead, the future of a concrescing actual entity is *not* "out-there" waiting to be stuffed full with new entities. Rather, the extensive continuum is an eternal object prehended by a concrescing actual entity. And the future for that concrescing entity is that portion of the continuum whose regions will be occupied by actual entities which will have physical prehensions of that concrescing entity. In this sense, the future is in the concrescing entity.

> The future is immanent in the present by reason of the fact that the present bears in its own essence the relationships which it will have to the future. It thereby includes in its essence the necessities to which the future must conform. The future is there in the present, as a general fact belonging to the nature of things. It is also there with such general determinations as it lies in the nature of the particular present to impose on the particular future which must succeed it. *All this belongs to the essence of the present,* and constitutes the future, as thus determined, an object for prehension in the subjective immediacy of the present. . . . Thus the future is to the present as an object for a subject. It has an objective existence in the present. . . . What is objective in the present is the *necessity* of a future of actual occasions, and the *necessity* that these future occasions conform to the conditions inherent in the essence of the present occasion. *The future belongs to*

---

8. For the position that it would be contradictory to allow God to have physical prehensions of entities in the continuum and, at the same time, to allow God to be non-extensive, see Ford, "Whitehead's Conception of Divine Spatiality," 1-23. But whether it is contradictory or not, we think that Whitehead held to precisely this view.

the essence of present fact. . . . But its particular relationships to present fact are already realized in the nature of present fact (AI 250b-51a; emphases added).

When, however, we emphasize that each actual entity prehends the extensive continuum for itself, and that the entire continuum—past, present, and future—is in each entity, the question then arises, "Have we not created a series of continua?" In fact, if we may assume that the organization of the extensive continuum, even in its most abstract aspects, is not logically necessary—that other patterns of interrelations among actual entities are logically possible—then we may also ask why all these entities prehend the *same* extensive continuum?[9]

The answer to such questions lies in the fact that the concrescing entity incorporates the past entities into itself. In its original prehensions of its past actual entities, the new entity prehends *their* prehensions of the continuum. And, thereby, these past prehensions of the extensive continuum become a part of the new entity, and thus the continuum is introduced into the new concrescence. Stated alternatively, the new concrescence—if it is to be genuinely new and not merely a repetition of what went before—must have a novel perspective on its past world. However, this new perspective on the past world must be coordinated with the nature of the previous world; otherwise the new entity would be isolated from its past, and *that* would be a contradiction in terms since the new actual entity *is* the reorganization of its past. This required coordination between the new entity and its past is accomplished by means of the extensive continuum; that is, the new entity and its past entities exemplify different regions in the same continuum.

In summary, let us remember that we cannot, in fact, separate the act whereby the new entity obtains a novel perspective from the act whereby the new entity prehends and incorporates its past entities, including their prehensions of the extensive continuum. Therefore, we may assume that we now have Whitehead's explanation for the remarkable fact that there is only one extensive continuum from everlasting to everlasting: namely, the extensive continuum is a part of each past actual entity; and so, as the new entity incorporates these past entities into its own real inter-

9. As we shall see in Section II.D of this chapter, there are two meanings for the term 'extensive continuum', the one specific and the other abstract. The characteristics of the specific continuum may well vary from one epoch to another, while the characteristics of the abstract extensive continuum do not. However, as we shall argue in Section II.G of this chapter, even the most abstract characteristics of the continuum are not logically necessary in their application to this world of actual entities—other alternatives are possible. Therefore, we are still left with the need to explain the remarkable coincidence that, generation after generation, this same extensive continuum—in its most abstract features—is always prehended. The material in the text which immediately follows can be construed as giving this explanation for the fact that the most abstract features of the continuum are prehended without alteration or variation from everlasting to everlasting.

nal constitution, it will automatically discover that its own constitution has been organized according to the extensive continuum.[10] Whitehead wrote about objective eternal objects, such as those in the continuum, that it belongs to their very nature to introduce "one actual entity, or nexus, into the real internal constitution of another actual entity" (PR 445e).

D

In any particular epoch the extensive continuum will have two levels. In our epoch, the continuum is four-dimensional, and it allows us to measure some of the properties of enduring objects. The extensive continuum, however, need not have these characteristics in all epochs.

> Considered in its full generality, apart from the additional conditions proper only to the cosmic epoch of electrons, protons, molecules, and star-systems, the properties of this continuum are very few and do not include the relationships of metrical geometry.... In its full generality beyond the present epoch, it does not involve shapes, dimensions, or measurability; these are additional determinations of real potentiality arising from our epoch (PR 103a).

> When we analyse the properties of this continuum we discover that they fall into two classes, of which one—the more special—presupposes the other—the more general. The more general type of properties expresses the mere fact of 'extensive connection,' of 'whole and part,' of various types of 'geometrical elements' derivable by 'extensive abstraction'; but excluding the introduction of more special properties by which straight lines are definable and measurability thereby introduced (PR 147d-48a).

Whitehead's point can be explained this way. In ordinary Euclidean geometry there are some rules which apply only to two-dimensional geometry, while other rules apply only to three-dimensional geometry; but there are still other rules which apply to either two-dimensional or three-dimensional geometry. For example, given a line *l* and a point *p* which is not on line *l*, we may state Rule I: there exists one and only one line which passes through *p* and which does not intersect *l*—this Rule I will apply in a two-dimensional geometry but not in a three-dimensional geometry. On the other hand, given a line *l* and a point *p* which is not on

10. It is instructive to note how in PR 101-8 Whitehead discussed two metaphysical assumptions. The first is that ". . . the actual world, in so far as it is a community of entities which are settled, actual, and already become, conditions and limits the potentiality for creativeness beyond itself" (PR 101c). Then Whitehead discusses the sense in which the continuum is a factor in all concrescences. "The second metaphysical assumption is that the real potentialities relative to all standpoints are coordinated as diverse determinations of one extensive continuum" (PR 103a). Thus we may conclude that the continuum is a factor to which every concrescence must conform *because* that continuum is exemplified in the past of every concrescence.

line *l*, we may state Rule II: there exists an infinite number of lines which pass through *p* and which do not intersect *l*—this Rule II will hold in a three-dimensional geometry but not in a two-dimensional geometry. But now consider Rule III: any two non-coincident points will determine a line —Rule III will hold in either a two-dimensional or a three-dimensional geometry. Thus Rule I would hold in a two-dimensional continuum but not in a three-dimensional one; Rule II would hold in a three-dimensional continuum but not in a two-dimensional one; while Rule III would hold in either a two-dimensional or a three-dimensional continuum. Therefore Rule III is more abstract than either Rule II or Rule I; it would apply in more of the particular specifications of the continuum than either Rule II or I.

The most abstract properties of the continuum would be those which would apply to the continuum in any specific form whatsoever. But rule III is far from being a member of the continuum's most abstract set of properties. First of all, in Euclidean geometry there can be any number of dimensions from two to a billion and two, and more. And there is a set of rules which applies to any Euclidean geometry no matter what the number of dimensions. Moveover, in the last century, non-Euclidean geometries were discovered and formalized. Speaking non-technically, in Euclidean space the lines are "straight," while in a non-Euclidean geometry they are "curved"—either curved elliptically, as on the surface of a sphere, or curved hyperbolically as on the "seat" portion of a horse's saddle.[11] There is a highly abstract set of rules which will apply to any geometry, whether Euclidean or non-Euclidean, with any number of dimensions. This set of rules is much closer to the most abstract elements in the extensive continuum, but we are still not yet there. Measurability, according to Whitehead, depends on the availability of a congruence relation. But there are certain geometrical properties which will apply even to systems which lack this relation. Speaking intuitively, we can take a circle and twist it in all sorts of ways, so that it becomes an ellipse, then a cigar, after that a kidney, and finally a banana with rounded ends. In any ordinary terms, these shapes are not congruent—or even similar. Nonetheless, there exist certain geometrical systems which can make true statements about these various figures where each of them is considered an instance of a carefully defined set. The rules of such a set would apply to entities in an extensive continuum even though the continuum in that epoch lacked a congruence relation and, thus, did not allow for measure-

11. That is, the lines of the non-Euclidean geometries are "curved" from a Euclidean point of view. Each non-Euclidean geometry, however, will have an analogue to the straight lines of Euclidean geometry. These analogues will be the "straight lines" of the non-Euclidean geometries. The result is that the "straight lines" of the non-Euclidean geometries will be "curved" from the standpoint of Euclid; but, equally, the "straight lines" of Euclid (and common sense) will be "curved" from a non-Euclidean point of view.

ment. In short, we are left with the rules of a highly abstract geometrical system—a system whose rules will apply to entities in the continuum regardless of whether the continuum in that epoch is Euclidean or non-Euclidean, whether it has two dimensions or a million and two, and whether or not it has a congruence relation allowing measurement. Lastly, mathematicians have discovered still more abstract systems. These systems will apply to any geometry of any dimensionality, with or without a congruence relation; moreover, these highly abstract systems also have applications where there is no analogue to the notion of dimension. Whitehead claims that the most abstract elements of his extensive continuum can be described by such a system.

On pages 449-59 of *Process and Reality* he tries to make good that claim by providing such a system. It is this system which necessarily applies to the continuum in all epochs. The other characteristics of the continuum do not necessarily apply in all epochs—these are the characteristics which depend on the continuum having or not having dimensionality, which depend on the exact number of dimensions if there are any, which depend on the presence of a congruence relation, and which depend on the existence or the presence of a specific geometry, Euclidean, Elliptic, etc. Of course, the extensive continuum which is actually prehended by a concrescing entity cannot be characterized *solely* by this most abstract system; some of the more particular and specialized rules and theorems must also characterize the continuum. While the most abstract system will necessarily characterize the continuum as it is prehended by any entity whatsoever, there is no guarantee as to *which* of these specialized rules and theorems will characterize the continuum as it is prehended by the concrescing entities in this or that epoch.

When necessary to distinguish between them, we will label the most abstract system which characterizes the continuum prehended by every actual entity whatsoever as "the universal extensive continuum" and the features of the continuum which may change from age to age as "the specific extensive continuum."[12] Thus the extensive continuum as

---

12. Thus it would seem that Whitehead's discussion in Chapter II of Part IV of PR 449-59 applies to the universal continuum. In this chapter he tries to develop a geometrical system using only the notions of 'region' and 'extensive connection'. In the next chapter (PR 460-67) Whitehead defines 'straight lines'. But according to PR 147d-48a straight lines belong to a *specification* of the universal continuum. Thus Chapter III would deal with the specific continuum of this epoch.

However—and this confuses me personally—Whitehead writes as though his discussion of straight lines in Chapter III of Part IV was meant to apply to the universal continuum. For example,

Any further development of definitions and propositions will lead to mathematical details irrelevant to our immediate purposes. It suffices to have proved that characteristic properties of straight lines, planes, and three-dimensional flat spaces are discoverable in the extensive continuum without any recourse to measurement. The

prehended by some particular concrescing entity is composed of the universal continuum plus the specific continuum.

E

Whitehead makes two comments about the extensive continuum which at first sight may seem contradictory. They are: (A) the extensive continuum is continuous, and (B) the extensive continuum is atomized. The continuity in the extensive continuum depends on its aspect of potentiality. That is, each region in the continuum is the potential site of the concrescence of an actual entity. Concerning this network of regions one can say several things. First, there is no smallest region; (this, we assume, is implied by the claim that "every region includes other regions" [PR 452h]). Second, for any two regions, whether or not they themselves are directly connected, there is a third region which is directly connected with both the original regions (this, we assume, is implied by the claim that "... any two regions are mediately connected" [PR 451b]). The writer of this book is neither a mathematician nor a logician, but as an intuitive explication of 'continuous', it seems to him that a set of possible regions in which there is no smallest region and in which every pair of them is connected by a third region must be continuous. Nevertheless, it is clear that the element of continuity in this system stems from the fact that it is a network of possible regions connected by a set of possible relations. Continuity stems from the conceptual side of the universe as opposed to the concrete side; it stems from the side of the eternal objects as opposed to the side of the actual entities. And it must not be forgotten that the extensive continuum, abstractly considered, *is* an eternal object.

Not all of the possible regions in the continuum can be occupied by separate and distinct actual entities. For example, given the fact that actual entities do not overlap, then if there is one actual entity occupying region X and if there is another, contiguous actual entity occupying region Y, then there can be no actual entity occupying that region which is composed of the contiguous two halves of the regions occupied by X and Y. This is illustrated by diagram 18, in which actual entity X occupies a region composed of areas 1 and 2 and actual entity Y occupies a region composed of areas 3 and 4. Clearly there is a *possible* region composed of areas 2 and 3. But, since actual entities cannot overlap, it follows that the existence of

---

systematic character of a continuum depends on its possession of one or more ovate classes (PR 467d).

Now, does or does not Whitehead's discussion of straight lines apply only to a specification of the continuum? Are the "straight lines" of PR 147d-48a different from the "straight lines" of Chapter II of Part IV? Perhaps a professional geometer could clear up this confusion.

X and Y at their present positions excludes the occupation of the region composed of 2 and 3 by an additional single actual entity.

It may be instructive to investigate further the reasons why the region composed of 2 and 3 cannot be occupied by an actual entity. Considered in abstraction from the existence of all particular actual entities, the region composed of 2 and 3 is just as surely a potential candidate for occupation by an actual entity as the regions composed of 1 and 2 and of 3 and 4, respectively. So the reason why the region made up of 2 and 3 cannot be occupied by an actual entity has nothing to do with the nature of that region in itself, where the continuum is understood to be an abstract scheme. Rather, the reason why the region composed of 2 and 3 cannot be occupied has to do with the concrete course of actual events. That is, the region composed of 2 and 3 cannot be occupied by a single actual entity because actual entities X and Y have concresced in *their* regions. Thus the development of the world of actuality entails that some of the continuum's regions will be exemplified as the sites occupied by actual entities, while other regions will be excluded from exemplification. Thus the continuum is atomized by the actual entities. Each concrescing actual entity occupies a certain region; it occupies a chunk of the continuum. And as long as overlapping is excluded, it follows that the various actual entities will break up the continuum into a series of concrescence-sites, where each concrescence-site is finite in size, and where each concrescence-site contains no smaller concrescence-sites inside itself, and where each concrescence-site rules out the existence of at least some other concrescence-sites.

The above discussion constitutes our explication of such passages as the following.

> Continuity concerns what is potential; whereas actuality is incurably atomic (PR 95b).

> Actual entities atomize the extensive continuum. This continuum is in itself merely the potentiality for division; an actual entity effects this division (PR 104b).

> In the mere continuum there are contrary potentialities; in the actual world there are definite atomic actualities determining one coherent system of real divisions throughout the region of actuality (PR 104c).

> Thus, an act of experience has an objective scheme of extensive order by reason of the double fact that its own perspective standpoint has extensive content, and that the other actual entities are objectified with the retention of their extensive relationships (PR 105b).

> The potential scheme does not determine its own atomization by actual entities. It is divisible; but its real division by actual entities depends upon more particular characteristics of the actual entities constituting the antecedent environment (PR 105b).

F

Does the continuum grow? Is there a "becoming" of new regions as new actual entities concresce? In short, does the continuous concrescence of new entities effect any alterations in the continuum itself? Whitehead sometimes writes as though the answer to such questions were "yes." For example, about the continuum, Whitehead writes,

> The actual entities atomize it, and thereby make real what was antecedently merely potential (PR 112a).

In addition, we should make reference to a debate between John B. Cobb, Jr., and Donald W. Sherburne[13] in which they discuss extensively the question whether there is a coherent sense in which the regions may be said to "become." They also discuss at length the question of how the continuum represents a "real" potentiality—an issue which we raise below as Section G of this chapter.

Considered as an eternal object, as an abstract system, the continuum is not affected by any developments brought about by the concrescence of actual entities. This is true of any eternal object and is not a peculiarity limited to the continuum. All eternal objects are externally related to the actual entities which prehended them. Thus, considered as mere potentials, regions are neither generated nor annihilated by any development among the actual entities. On the other hand, the extensive continuum, like any other eternal object, can be prehended by an actual entity; and some of the elements in the continuum may be exemplified by that actual entity. Thus as new actual entities concresce, it follows that they will not only prehend that entire continuum—considered as a system of eternal objects—but these new concrescences will also exemplify certain of the continuum's regions and their relations which never before had been exemplified.

It would be misleading to say that the regions or their relations become actual when they exemplify new entities. No eternal object becomes actual. Rather the eternal object becomes a *characteristic* of an actual entity; and it is the whole entity which is actual and not any of its characteristics as such. In like manner, then, the regions and their relations do not become actual when they exemplify a new entity. Rather the regions become characteristics of an actual situation.[14] It must be further observed

---

13. John B. Cobb, Jr. and Donald W. Sherburne, "Regional Inclusion and the Extensive Continuum."

14. Thus, when we assert that the continuum and its regions are—by a remote analogy—"actual," we are always speaking of this actuality of the continuum only insofar as the continuum has been prehended by—and certain of its elements exhibited in—genuine actual entities. That is, when speaking of the "actuality" of the continuum and its regions, we are never speaking of the continuum as an eternal object in abstraction from its ingression in any actual entity.

that the phrase in the last sentence, "the regions become characteristics," does not imply that the regions—considered as eternal objects—are in any way affected by this change; the relation of the eternal objects to any actual entity in which they ingress is external, while it is the relation of the actual entity to the eternal object which is internal. In other words, the nature of a region, considered as an eternal object, is in no way affected by the fact that it characterizes or the fact that it does not characterize an actual entity; while the very identity of an actual entity depends on the fact that it is characterized by this region and not that region. For a further analysis of (A) the sense in which an eternal object is not affected by its ingressions in actual entities, while (B) an actual entity is determined by the ingressions of the eternal objects which characterize it, and for a further analysis of (C) the sense in which the actual entity—as infused by Creativity—is the locus of actuality, see the relevant portions of Part One, especially Chapter Three.

Thus we note that the continuum may be divided as follows. Consider any specific concrescing actual entity, X, with its prehension of the extensive continuum and with its prehensions of its past entities and their exemplifications of regions and relations from that continuum. (1) There is that region and its relations which characterize the concrescing actual entity X. (2) There are those regions and their relations which characterize X's past actual entities. (3) There are those regions and their relations which do not characterize X's past actual entities, but which might have if the course of history had been different. (4) There are those regions and their relations which may characterize X's contemporaries; but since contemporaries are causally independent, X has no direct experience of which of these regions and their relations do characterize actual entities and which do not. And finally, (5) there are those regions and their relations which may characterize the future entities which will come after X.

We note that all five portions of the continuum are defined from the point of view of an actual entity, and not from the point of view of the purely abstract nature of the continuum itself. Indeed, it is clear that any one region may fit into any of the five categories depending upon the actual course of history and depending upon which concrescing entity we choose as our base. For example, the region which characterizes X would have been a part of the future (of portion 5 of the continuum) from the point of view of a past actual entity. Therefore, when we talk of the past portion of the continuum, or of the present portion of the continuum, or of the future portion of the continuum, we are speaking from the point of view of the actual entities which have prehended the continuum and which have exemplified certain of its regions and relations. From the point of view of the continuum itself, there is no such thing as past, present, or future. In short, past, present, and future in the continuum reflect the relations of actual entities to the continuum—which relations are internal to those actual entities; they do not reflect the relations of the continuum to the actual entities—which relations are external to the continuum.

G

The extensive continuum represents a form of "real" possibility or potentiality. There seem to be three aspects to real potentiality. First, it is narrower than what Whitehead calls 'abstract possibility'. Second, this real possibility is a limitation placed on logical possibility by the natures of concrete, specific actual entities. And third, the continuum is the *first* or *basic* limitation placed on pure potentiality by actuality.

1

We take the following passage as our key.

> According to the philosophy of organism, the extensive space-time continuum is the fundamental aspect of the limitation laid upon abstract potentiality by the actual world (PR 123d).

First, real possibility constitutes a limitation on abstract possibility.[15] Of the three aspects of real possibility, we are the least certain of

---

15. The precise meaning of Whitehead's notion of 'abstract possibility' is quite difficult to unpack fully. This much, however, does seem clear. When Whitehead uses this term, he has in mind the kind of possibility which eternal objects possess when considered in abstraction from the actual course of history. That is, while it is the nature of eternal objects to be characteristics of actual entities, and, therefore, while any eternal object has an essential reference to actuality *in general* (SMW 159a-60a), nevertheless, we can consider any eternal object in abstraction from all the particularities of *specific* finite actual entities. And abstract possibility has to do, at least in part, with the relationships among eternal objects insofar as these eternal objects may be considered in total independence of the peculiarities of specific finite actual entities.

The relationship of abstract possibility to God, however, is somewhat more complicated. On the one side, God is an actual entity which interacts with other actual entities. This interaction with the other actual entities has its effect upon God (PR 523b-24d). Insofar as any arrangement of eternal objects within God is affected by God's interaction with the particularities of other actual entities, it follows that abstract possibility will apply to the relations of eternal objects in abstraction from their status in God. There is, however, another side of this issue of the relation of abstract possibility to God. On this other side, there is a sense in which abstract possibility can*not* apply to eternal objects *in abstraction from God*. This is because the ontological principle demands that any item whatsoever—including eternal objects—have being only insofar as that item is an element in some actual entity. Thus, according to Whitehead, the entire realm of eternal objects has being because each eternal object is an element in the nature of God (PR 73a-c). To be more specific, God has a conceptual prehension of each eternal object, where this conceptual prehension is wholly independent of the actual course of history. This set of purely conceptual prehensions of all eternal objects is God's primordial nature (PR 46a). However, God's primordial nature introduces a pattern (or patterns) of order among the various eternal objects (PR 46a, 48b, 315c, etc.). Without this order (or one of these orders) the eternal objects would not "be." That is, without some order, they would have no identity; without some order, eternal objects could not be recognized, thought about, envisioned, named, or used. In summary, we may say that, for Whitehead,

our understanding of this first point. Basically, however, Whitehead's point seems to be this. If the most general features of the extensive continuum were not a "limitation upon abstract possibility," then they would hold regardless of the nature of any specific actual entities; that is, no matter what the course of actual events, the most general characteristics of the continuum would apply. But in that case there would be no sense in which the "universal extensive continuum"—that is, the continuum in its most general aspects—would be a limitation of abstract possibility laid down by actuality, by the particular natures of the specific actual entities of history. Yet one of the clearest points in Whitehead's development of the notion of the continuum is precisely the point that the continuum is a limitation placed by the occurrence of actual entities upon the kind of possibility which dwells in the realm of eternal objects.

The second point may be considered an explication of the first point: namely, the continuum is a limitation on possibility stemming from the specific nature of the actual entities in history. Whitehead writes concerning the continuum,

> It is not a fact prior to the world; it is the first determination of order—that is, of real potentiality—arising out of the general character of the world. In its full generality beyond the present epoch, it does not involve shapes, dimensions, or measurability; these are additional determinations of real potentiality arising from our cosmic epoch.
>
> This extensive continuum is 'real,' because it expresses a fact derived from the actual world and concerning the contemporary actual world (PR 103a-b).

Although there is no logical necessity that actual entities relate to each other by means of the "universal extensive continuum," it happens to be a fact that they are so connected. The reason is that it is a metaphysical requirement that a new actual entity gather its past into itself and impose a new perspective upon that past. But as a matter of brute, blunt fact, for *any* new

---

abstract possibility is that possibility which obtains among eternal objects in complete abstraction from the particular course of history, in complete abstraction from the particular identities of specific actual entities, and in complete abstraction from God insofar as God depends on the actual course of history.

The relation, however, between abstract possibility and the primordial nature of God is more complicated. First, we should note that the exact kind (or kinds) of order which the primordial nature of God introduces among eternal objects is never spelled out in detail by Whitehead. (It is our opinion that the primordial nature contains at least two distinct levels of order among eternal objects; see Section G.2 of this chapter.) Second, once we have decided just what kind (or kinds) of order the primordial nature of God introduces, we must then confront the following question: Is abstract possibility equivalent to (some one of) the relations among the eternal objects introduced by the primordial nature of God? Or is it in some sense a specification of the order(s) introduced by the primordial nature, or is it broader than the order(s) in the primordial nature—and what would "specification" and "broader" mean in these contexts? We provide a brief outline of our answers to these questions in Section G.2 of this chapter.

entity, its past entities have prehended *this* continuum. Therefore this continuum is a hard fact, concretely exhibited in the data which are integrated into the very internal constitution of the new entity. As a result, if the concrescing entity is to be a new organization of *those* data, then its new perspective must be a region which is a coordinated element in that same continuum. This much we have already discussed in Section II.C of this chapter.

In light of that discussion, we will now advance to the third point and note two important senses in which the continuum constitutes the *first* limitation on pure potentiality—where this limitation arises form the specific natures of the actual entities in history. First, no matter how far back we go, each actual entity, as it concresced, found this same continuum—at least in its universal aspects—integrated into the structures of *its* past entities. Thus *any* concrescing actual entity whatsoever will find the extensive continuum exemplified in its past entities—where the concrescing entity must incorporate those past entities into its own real internal constitution. And, therefore, the continuum will be that fact to which *every* entity must conform.[16] This fact provides the basis for Whitehead's explication of our pre-philosophical conviction that there will be a future which has some kind of direct relation with the present.[17] That is, even if the future contains surprising novelties, those novelties will be new in comparison with *this* present and *this* past: and such a novel future will still be related to this present. The explication runs as follows. Once a concrescing entity, X, exemplifies a region and some of the relations of the continuum, then it becomes a fact to which all *future* entities must conform. Insofar as it is metaphysically incumbent upon the *future* entities to incorporate their past world into themselves, actual entity X with its illustration of the continuum will be in their pasts as an entity to which they must conform; in short they will have to occupy regions of their own in the continuum in order to have a perspective from which to incorporate that previous entity X which illustrated that continuum.

> All actual entities are related according to the determinations of this continuum; and all possible actual entities in the future must exemplify these determinations in their relations with the already actual world. The reality of the future is bound up with the reality of this continuum. It is the reality of what is potential, in its character of a real component of what is actual (PR 103b).

The second sense in which the extensive continuum is the fundamental limitation on pure potentiality stemming from actuality is this:

---

16. God seems to be the exception here. When we ask below if the continuum is a metaphysical feature in Whitehead's system, we will consider the relation of God to the continuum.

17. By "explication" of this pre-philosophical conviction, we mean the interpretation of this conviction in terms of the technical resources of Whitehead's system.

The continuum is the most general of all the patterns of organization which a concrescing entity will find in its environment, and it is presupposed by all the less general patterns. Thus the universal extensive continuum—that is, the continuum in its widest characteristics — is the condition for the specific extensive continuum—that is, the continuum as characterized as Euclidean or non-Euclidean, as having this or that number of dimensions, as having or lacking a congruence relation, etc. In this epoch, the specific continuum has the particular features of four-dimensionality, of Euclidean or almost Euclidean lines, etc. And this specific continuum is a condition for the presence of our electronic age; that is, the formulae for electrons, protons, photons, etc. all seem to presuppose a four-dimensional space-time system with a congruence relation. But, in turn, the electronic patterns of organization are prerequisite for the organic entities as we know them; we would have a hard time trying to understand a living creature which was not composed of electrons and protons. Finally, these electronic and organic patterns of organization seem prerequisite for human life as we know it. What, for example, would language be for creatures without corporeal bodies and without sound waves? There may be analogues among such creatures to our forms of language; but these analogues would not be our languages as we know them. The extensive continuum then is the first limitation on pure potentiality in the sense that it is the limitation—the pattern of organization—which is, in fact, presupposed by all the other limitations, by all the other patterns of organization.[18]

2

We conclude our discussion of the real potentiality of the extensive continuum with a question. The continuum may be the first limitation placed on abstract potentiality by actuality, but it remains the case that other first limitations were logically possible. Wherein, then, lies the explanation for the fact that the first limitation is *this* continuum and not something else? Our answer proceeds as follows. By the ontological principle, the explanation for this must lie in some actual entity. But no finite actual entity can serve as the explanation because the role of the continuum as the first limitation on abstract possibility is presupposed by every finite entity; that is, each and every finite entity finds the continuum already established as a fact to which it must conform. Therefore, we may not assign the responsibility for the establishment of the continuum as a factor in actuality to any finite entity. But neither can we assign the establishment of the continuum to any one specific decision on the part of God; the reason is that a specific

18. This discussion of the sense in which the continuum is a form of real potentiality or possibility also explains (1) the sense in which the extensive continuum ultimately underlies the indicative system of every proposition and (2) how the extensive continuum underlies the solidarity of the world. Whitehead explicitly relates the continuum to the solidarity of the world in several passages, e.g., PR 112a, 446a.

decision would be a decision felt by some actual entities but not by others, but the continuum is a factor for all actual entities. Therefore, the only place to locate the responsibility for the establishment of the continuum must be in God's unchanging nature. We suggest that the location of this responsibility is in God's subjective aim. His aim, in its most general aspects, does not vary; in this sense there is no shadow of turning in God. The subjective aim of God is presupposed in all of God's dealings with all finite creatures. Therefore, we may assert that the explanation for the fact that each finite actual entity finds the continuum already exemplified in its past entities is the will of God. Whitehead never raises the question of where to place the responsibility for the establishment of the continuum as the first limitation on pure abstract possibility, and, therefore, he does not mention this solution. However, this solution does seem to flow naturally from the categories of his system.

At this point a critic may well ask, Why do we not locate the responsibility for the "establishment of the continuum as the first limitation on pure abstract possibility" in the primordial nature of God—rather than in God's subjective aim? After all (continues our critic), the primordial nature of God is also quite eternal and beyond all shadow of change. And, in addition, Whitehead says that God's subjective aim is "wholly derivative from his all-inclusive primordial valuation" (PR 523c). Therefore, (concludes our critic) to say that God's *subjective aim* is the explanation for the choice of this continuum is merely a roundabout way of saying that God's *primordial nature* is the explanation for the choice of this continuum.

In response, we might observe that Whitehead also says that "the *perfection* of God's subjective aim" is "derived from the completeness of his primordial nature" (PR 524e; our emphasis). Now it is our interpretation that God's subjective aim is more than a reflex or by-product of his primordial nature. The exact character of God's subjective aim cannot be deduced from his primordial nature in a mechanical or a priori fashion. Rather, as Whitehead says, the *perfection* of the divine subjective aim depends on the fact that the primordial nature includes *all* possibilities. Thus, God can desire an infinite depth of satisfaction, and (as a means of obtaining this depth of satisfaction) God can desire to prehend positively the entirety of each finite actual entity. But this set of desires (i.e., this subjective aim) is realistic only because God has an infinite wealth of possibility in his primordial nature upon which he can draw to help him fulfill these desires. (This topic is considered at somewhat greater length in Chapter Nineteen of Part Four.) Therefore, we may say that without his primordial nature, God would not have the perfect subjective aim which he actually does possess. But this does not mean that the divine subjective aim is a mere reflex of the primordial nature. Consequently, it is permissible to assign functions to God's subjective aim which are not also functions of the primordial nature.

Let us allow our critic to speak once again. Suppose, he says, that it is true that there are functions which we may assign to the divine subjective aim which we cannot assign to the primordial nature. Nevertheless, why should we assign *this* function (i.e., the presence in the world of this-and-not-some-other continuum) to the subjective aim of God? Why, concludes our critic, should we not assign this function to the primordial nature of God?

A fully detailed response to our critic's second question would entail a fully detailed analysis of the kind of order among eternal objects which is established by the primordial nature of God. We are not prepared in this book to present such an analysis. Therefore, we will only outline a proper response to this question.

We proceed as follows. Since the particular continuum which is in fact present is a limitation on abstract possibility, it follows that this continuum is only one of many (abstractly) possible continua. Therefore, we must distinguish between two different levels of order among the eternal objects. On the one side, there is the most abstract order, wherein all the continua are equally possible. On the other side, there is the order which presupposes *this* continuum as the basis for inter-relating the various actual entities—that is, the order which presupposes *this* continuum as the basis for the arrangements of eternal objects which are *really* possible. In summary, we may distinguish between the level of purely abstract possibility at which many different continua are possible and the level of real possibility at which only this continuum is possible.

The question, then, is this. Does the primordial nature of God provide only the most abstract ordering of eternal objects or does that primordial nature also provide a more specific ordering of eternal objects? Now some passages suggest that God's primordial nature provides a rather specific ordering of eternal objects.

> This is the 'primordial nature' of God. By reason of this complete valuation, the objectification of God in each derivate entity results in *a graduation of the relevance of eternal objects* to the concrescent phases of *that* derivate occasion. . . . For effective relevance requires agency of comparison, and agency belongs exclusively to actual occasions. This divine ordering is *itself matter of fact*, thereby conditioning creativity. Thus possibility which transcends realized temporal matter of fact has a real relevance to the creative advance (PR 46a; our emphases).

On the other hand, there are also passages in which it would seem that only the most abstract ordering of eternal objects is provided by the primordial nature of God.

> This doctrine applies also to the primordial nature of God, which is his complete envisagement of eternal objects; he is not thereby directly related to the given course of history. The given course of history presupposes his

primordial nature, but his primordial natures does not presuppose it (PR 70b).

> The notion of 'subsistence' is merely the notion of how eternal objects can be components of the primordial nature of God. . . . But eternal objects, as in God's primordial nature, constitute the Platonic world of ideas.
>   There is not, however, one entity which is merely the *class* of all eternal objects. For if we conceive any class of eternal objects, there are additional eternal objects which presuppose that class but do not belong to it. For this reason, at the beginning of this section, the phrase 'the multiplicity of Platonic forms' was used, instead of the more natural phrase 'the class of Platonic forms.' A multiplicity is a type of complex thing which has the unity derivative from some qualification which participates in each of its components severally; but a multiplicity has no unity derivative *merely* from its various components (PR 73b-c).

The variety of opinions which Whitehead seems to be expressing in these quotations leaves it uncertain whether the primordial nature provides only the most abstract ordering of eternal objects or provides also a more specific ordering of eternal objects. We offer the following answer. God's primordial nature consists in a set of prehensions, his conceptual prehensions of all eternal objects whatsoever. Now we wish to focus on two elements which are present in any prehension: the datum of the prehension and the subjective form of that prehension. Thus we may analyze God's primordial nature from two sides: the side of the data and the side of the subjective forms. We will turn first to the side of the data. It is important to note that *all* eternal objects are prehended in God's primordial nature. In other words, in his primordial nature, God envisions all possibilities. It is this envisioning which gives these eternal objects their being—as is required by the ontological principle. To be prehended, that is, to gain their status in being, it is necessary that each eternal object have an identity. However, the mere fact that each eternal object has a specific and determinate essence will guarantee an order among these eternal objects. It is our interpretation that Whitehead's discussion of the individual and relational essence of eternal objects is, in fact, a discussion of the kind of order among eternal objects which is required (A) for any eternal object to have a determinate identity and, thus, (B) for any eternal object to be prehended by God and gain thereby a status in being. It is further our interpretation that 'abstract possibility' *is* this order among eternal objects which is established by the mere fact that each eternal object has a determinate identity.

We will turn now to the side of the subjective forms. God's primordial nature is a series of prehensions of all possibilities. However, God is not neutral towards these various possibilities. He desires that some of these possibilities be realized in the actual world more than he desires the realization of others. Whitehead usually speaks of God's positive concern (adversion) that each of these possibilities be realized. Nevertheless, he also speaks of the primordial nature in connection with "aversions" towards some of these possibilities (PR 48b). (In this passage, however, Whitehead is also speaking of the primordial nature as it is a factor in God's satisfaction.) Moreover, Whitehead also writes of "the *graduated* order of *appetitions* constituting the primordial nature of God" and of "the fundamental *graduation* of *appetitions* which lies at the base of things" (PR 315c; our emphases). Thus we may conclude that in God's primordial nature there is a strong urge towards the realization of some of the possibilities, a weaker urge toward the realization of other of these possibilities, and an aversion towards the realization of still other possibilities. These adversions and aversions towards these various possibilities stem from the subjective form in the various prehensions constituting the divine primordial nature.

The fact that God arranges, in his primordial nature, all these possibilities into a graduated order of desirability (from strong adversion to strong aversion) gives the realm of eternal objects an additional order. This additional order does not stem from the very identity of the eternal objects; rather, this additional order stems from the subjective forms with which God prehends these possibilities.

It is a general principle, however, that an actual entity's subjective forms derive from the subjective aim of that entity (see Chapter Two). God is no exception to this principle. Whitehead explicitly mentions the primordial nature of God in this respect.

> The 'primordial nature' of God is the concrescence of a unity of conceptual feelings, including among their data all eternal objects. The concrescence is directed by the subjective aim, that the subjective forms of the feelings shall be such as to constitute the eternal objects into relevant lures of feeling severally appropriate for all realizable basic conditions (PR 134d).

Thus the additional order among eternal objects, which stems from the subjective forms with which God prehends those eternal objects, is, in fact, explained by the divine subjective aim.

We may summarize our discussion so far as follows. There are two levels of order among the eternal objects to be found in the primordial nature of God. There is that order which stems from the mere fact that each eternal object has a determinate identity. This is abstract possibility at its widest. This is the kind of order which Whitehead analyzes under the rubric "the individual and relational essence of eternal objects." There is also the order among eternal objects which stems from the subjective forms with which God prehends these various possibilities. This additional order involves the adversion towards some 'abstract' possibilities and the aversion from other 'abstract' possibilities. This additional order is derived from the subjective aim of God. This subjective aim, while depending on the breadth of the primordial nature, cannot be deduced from that primordial nature. That is, the subjective aim of God cannot be deduced from the order among the eternal objects which we have called 'abstract possibility', because the subjective aim is the basis for choices among those abstract possibilities. On the other hand, the additional order among the eternal objects in the primordial nature of God does not provide a basis for explaining the divine subjective aim. Rather, as we saw, the subjective aim provides the explanation for this additional order.

We may now answer our original question, why do we assign responsibility for the presence of this-and-no-other continuum in the world to the divine subjective aim? Would it not be better to assign this responsibility to the divine primordial nature? In answer, we may point out that we cannot assign this responsibility to the abstract order of possibility (which is in the primordial nature in virtue of the mere fact that each eternal object has a determinate identity—an identity which relates that eternal object, at least hypothetically, to every other eternal object). If we assigned responsibility for the presence of this continuum to this abstract level of possibility, then this continuum would become the only continuum which is abstractly possible. But, in that case, the presence of this continuum is in no sense a *limitation* upon abstract possibility. On the other hand, if we assign responsibility for the presence of this continuum to the additional ordering of eternal objects in the primordial nature (where this additional ordering is established by the subjective forms with which God prehends all the eternal objects), then we must shift the real responsibility for this continuum to God's subjective aim. This is because Whitehead clearly states that the divine subjective forms with which God prehends the eternal objects results from the divine subjective aim. This is just a specialized application of the general principle that any actual entity's subjective aim is the explanation for the subjective forms with which that entity prehends its various data. Consequently, we discover that the only way in which we can assign the responsibility for *this* continuum to the primordial nature of God takes us back at once to the divine subjective aim. Therefore, we may conclude that the explanation for this continuum is the divine subjective aim.

H

Is Whitehead's continuum metaphysical in its generality? One can find an abundance of proof-texts to support an affirmative answer.

> Some general character of coordinate divisibility is probably an ultimate metaphysical character, persistent in every cosmic epoch of physical occasions. Thus some of the simpler characteristics of extensive connection,

as here stated, are probably such ultimate metaphysical necessities (PR 441c).

The second metaphysical assumption is that the real potentialities relative to all standpoints are coordinated as diverse determinations of one extensive continuum (PR 103a).

Whitehead's point—especially in the last quotation—seems to be that, if it is a metaphysical principle that each new actual entity incorporate all its past entities into itself, then it is also a metaphysical principle that there be some coordinating scheme which makes all these acts of incorporation possible. This coordinating scheme is the continuum.

Even if we allow these quotations to stand as Whitehead's most basic position on the question of the metaphysical character of the continuum, they are likely to be misleading unless we remember his technical definition of metaphysics. In fact, it may seem that Whitehead has simply contradicted himself by saying (A) that the application of this (universal) continuum to the world is the result of the specific character of reality and (B) that it is a metaphysical principle that this (universal) continuum applies to the world. The contradiction would arise if we assumed that a metaphysical principle is a form of logical necessity or has a necessity which is a priori to the specific character of the world. But in fact Whitehead's notion of metaphysics cannot be assimilated to any view which would make a metaphysical principle independent of the specific course of history—that is, independent of the particular nature of the actual world.

What then is Whitehead's view of a metaphysical principle? First, we note that he applies the term 'metaphysical' to propositions about the world as well as to the patterns and characteristics in the actual world. Second, we note that, while Whitehead typically uses the adjective 'metaphysical' to describe principles, patterns, characteristics, and assumptions, as well as truth and propositions, he does, on occasion, use it as a modifier of necessity.[19] Also, he uses it to describe obligation, need, and reason (SMW 178d).

Of all his uses of 'metaphysical,' Whitehead explicitly analyzed only his application of this term to propositions. In Part One, Chapter Five, Section I, we discussed his definition of a metaphysical proposition. Roughly speaking, we discovered that for Whitehead a metaphysical proposition is one which describes any and every actual entity or nexus of actual entities. The only limitation was that there must be an appropriate number of actual entities serving as subjects to guarantee that the predicate can be applied coherently to those subjects.

Thus 'metaphysical' and 'general' are closely related terms for

19. See, for example, PR 441c and Alfred North Whitehead, *Essays in Science and Philosophy*, 123e.

Whitehead. On Whitehead's analysis, a metaphysical principle must be completely universal with regard to the actual world, but there is no demand that it be universal with regard to all possible worlds. In other words, to show that a principle is not metaphysical, one must show that it does not apply to some aspect of this actual world. It is not enough to show that one can conceive of a possible world in which the metaphysical principle in question does not apply. There is nothing in Whitehead's definition of a metaphysical principle which would rule out the purely abstract possibility of the eternal objects being organized into a different order of relevance—an order which would eventuate in a different actual world which would be describable by different metaphysical principles. Thus, while Whitehead does describe metaphysical principles as necessary (PR 4f, 5c-6b), this 'necessity' cannot be assimilated to "logical" necessity or to any other form of necessity which is independent of the specific nature of this actual world. That is, the 'necessity' of a metaphysical principle merely points to the fact that *all* our experience exhibits this principle in such a way that (A) the other structures which are sometimes present in our experience and sometimes absent presuppose this principle and (B) any additional structure which we have reason to believe we might encounter in this world, will also presuppose this principle.[20] Therefore, to say that such-and-such is metaphysically necessary is to say that such-and-such is implied by those true metaphysical propositions which describe *our* world. It is *not* to say that such-and-such is implied by the metaphysical descriptions of any possible world whatsoever.[21]

20. For an ally in our interpretation that in Whitehead's view a metaphysical principle need not be logically necessary (i.e., applicable to all possible worlds), see Bernard Mac-Dougal Loomer, "The Theological Significance of the Method of Empirical Analysis in the Philosophy of A. N. Whitehead," 80-97.

21. At this point, someone might object to Whitehead's position as follows. Surely, says the critic, Whitehead would agree to the following statements. "Any possible world will have an order of some sort." "Any possible world will be describable by some set of metaphysical principles." "Any possible world will have characteristics (i.e., eternal objects) of some sort." And, "Any possible world will only be one of many possible worlds." Now, continues our critic, if Whitehead would agree to any of these statements, he would be committing himself to the position that some metaphysical propositions do, in fact, apply to all possible worlds. Given the examples, moreover, Whitehead would even be able to state some of the propositions. Therefore, concludes our critic, why does Whitehead insist on a definition of metaphysics which does not require that metaphysical propositions be applicable to all possible worlds?

We turn now to the response. It is a significant fact that Whitehead never (to our knowledge) discusses statements of the all-possible-worlds sort. This is not an oversight on his part. Rather, Whitehead's fundamental philosophical methodology simply is not conducive to a discussion of these sorts of propositions. He spells out his philosophic method with an admirable (and very rare) clarity on the first few pages of PR. The proper method of philosophy is empirical. We take some concept or principle which has an established application in some limited area of experience—such as physics, religion, language, love, emotion, mathematics, etc.; then we generalize this notion, attempting to free it from the limitations

Is the continuum metaphysical? More precisely, do all actual entities exemplify the continuum? Is the proposition which states that the continuum applies to all actual entities true? The passages we quoted at the beginning of this section do claim that the continuum is metaphysical. Once again, however, the problem is God. Apparently Whitehead thinks of God as a non-extensive actual entity.[22] But if God does not exemplify the continuum, then that continuum is not properly metaphysical, even on Whitehead's own technical definition of metaphysical. It is our opinion that Whitehead's system is inconsistent at this point.

Several commentators have observed that there is a weakness in the way Whitehead relates God to the continuum. Cobb's alternative to Whitehead was mentioned in the last footnote. Another interesting treatment of this problem is by Ford in "Whitehead's Conception of Divine

---

inherent in its original, specialized application. We may now consider the generalized principle a hypothesis, a hypothesis about the nature of *all* our experience. Thus we must test that hypothesis by interrogating our experience in as many different situations as possible. To be acceptable, this generalized principle must be instantiated in our experience sober, our experience drunk, in our experience loving, our experience hating, in our experience alert, our experience drowsy, in our experience scientific, our experience religious, etc. (This principle must also be consistent and coherent with our other principles, and it must be necessary in the sense described in the text.) Now—and this is the main point—we have only this world in which to test our hypotheses! We cannot experience any of the other possible worlds. In other words, it is Whitehead's goal to analyze and thematize the fundamental structures of our experience—both the content and the act of that experience. Thus our experience is the ultimate test of any "generalized principle;" and the very purpose of that generalized principle is to help thematize that experience.

Thus Whitehead never considers any "all-possible-worlds" statement because his method allows him no way to test such a statement. Moreover, such a statement is not germane to his basic philosophical purpose, which is to thematize the fundamental structures of *this* world which we experience and in which we live and move and have our being.

22. See Cobb, *A Christian Natural Theology*, 192-96. Here Cobb argues that, although Whitehead considered God a non-spatial entity, his categories equally allow the possibility that God is omnispatial. On Cobb's own personal view, God is a succession of actual entities, each of which is omnispatial but temporally limited to "the regions comprising the standpoints of all the contemporary occasions of the world," (p. 196). The problem with Cobb's own position is that contemporaneity is not transitive, so that it does not follow that all of the contemporaries of an entity are themselves contemporary with each other. Therefore, from the standpoint of any finite concrescing entity, X, it follows that God's standpoint —that is, the standpoint of the particular divine entity which is God at that point for X— cannot be identical to the standpoints of all of X's contemporaries considered as a set. The point is that "all of X's contemporaries" do not form a set which could be appropriately described as "all the contemporary occasions in the world." Further, suppose that to solve this problem we agree that a divine actual entity's temporal spread is, in fact, a duration where all parts of that duration are by definition contemporary. However, in this epoch at least, each spot in that duration is also a spot in other durations (for example, in diagram 17 in Chapter Seven, the spot occupied by entity X participates not only in duration Alpha but in many other durations as well). But it seems arbitrary to hold that God's "present-now" coincides with only one of these many possible durations. (See Fitzgerald, "Relativity Physics, and the God of Process Philosophy," 251-76. Although this article does not mention Cobb's view of theism, it is directly relevant.)

Spatiality." All of Whitehead's commentators agree that God does not occupy a finite region in the continuum. The reason God does not occupy a finite region is that his subjective aim is in some sense infinite and inclusive. Possessing this infinite subjective aim, God must either transcend the need to exemplify the continuum or occupy the entire continuum. The first alternative seems to be Whitehead's; Lewis Ford suggests the second. About Ford's suggestion, we may observe that, if God occupies the entire continuum, then either he occupies an infinite region or he occupies a set of regions with an infinite number of members in that set. Either way, God's occupation of the entire continuum would require (it would seem to this non-mathematically trained writer) significant change in the structure of Whitehead's description of the continuum on pages 449-59 of *Process and Reality*. Also, if God occupies the entire continuum, then each region occupied by a finite actual entity is a region which is occupied twice over—once the region would be exemplified by God as a subregion and once that region would be exemplified by the finite actual entity. (In and by itself, there would be no contradiction in this double exemplification of regions in the continuum because there is no contradiction in an eternal object ingressing twice into the actual world.) Finally, if God occupies the entire continuum, then God would be prior to, present with, and future to every finite actual entity in the most literal sense. And to the extent that Ford's position (A) makes God contemporary with each actual entity and (B) asserts that God and each finite entity mutually prehend each other, it follows that his position also requires that contemporaries prehend each other. Ford argues that there is nothing in the fundamental categories of Whitehead's system — understood in their metaphysical generality—which prevents contemporaries from mutually prehending each other. Rather, the prohibition of mutual causal prehensions by contemporaries is valid only for finite actual entities. Since, in the case of mutual prehensions between God and finite entities, one of the parties is not finite, it follows that the restriction on the mutual causal prehensions by contemporaries does not apply. For more details the reader is referred to Ford's article.

I

Whitehead writes that an actual entity is everywhere in the continuum. For example, we read the following about an actual entity:

> But in another sense it is everywhere throughout the continuum; for its constitution includes the objectifications of the actual world and thereby includes the continuum; also the potential objectifications of itself contribute to the real potentialities whose solidarity the continuum expresses. Thus the continuum is present in each actual entity, and each actual entity pervades the continuum (PR 104c-5a).

The explanation of this statement is that each region is internally related to every other region. At its most abstract, the continuum is one complex system of relata and relations among those relata. But the important point is that each of the relata *is*, in part, its relations to other relata. That is, each region is partially constituted by its relations to other regions. Insofar as a particular actual entity X exemplifies a particular region R, it will also exemplify all those elements which are constitutive of R. Consider R as defined by those elements which constitute the universal continuum. At this level R is internally related to every region in the continuum. Further, these relations to these other regions are a part of the very identity of R. Therefore, actual entity X in the act of exemplifying region R will also exemplify these relations of R to every other region in the continuum. However, the relations which are thus exemplified are highly abstract. Region R also is characterized by those elements which constitute the specific continuum. And this specified R is internally related to all similarly specified regions. Thus actual entity X in exemplifying this specified region R also exemplifies these relations of the specified R to the other similarly specified regions. Therefore, actual entity X, in the act of occupying region R, will necessarily exemplify some highly abstract relations of R which extend to every region in the continuum (X will exemplify these relations because they are a part of what R *is*). In addition, we may conclude that actual entity X, in the act of occupying region R, will necessarily exemplify some more specific relations of R which extend to every region in some localized portion of the continuum.

The relations of R to the other regions, however, are also constitutive of these other regions. Therefore, when X occupies R, it also exemplifies some of the elements which are integral to these other regions. It is in this sense that X is present throughout the continuum. (1) In occupying R, X exemplifies some highly abstract but perfectly determinate relations to every region in the continuum, and X also exemplifies some less abstract but equally determinate relations to every region in some portion of the continuum. (2) The relations to these other regions which X thus exemplified are elements not only in the very nature of X itself, but they are also elements in the very identity of these other regions as well.

> . . . space and time (if for simplicity we disjoin them) are given in their entireties. For each volume of space, or each lapse of time, includes in its essence aspects of all volumes of space, or of all lapses of time. The difficulties of philosophy in respect to space and time are founded on the error of considering them as primarily the loci of simple locations (SMW 71a).

> The parts [of a volume of space and time] form an ordered aggregate, in the sense that each part is something from the standpoint of every other part, and also from the same standpoint every other part is something in relation to it. Thus if A and B and C are volumes of space, B has an aspect

from the standpoint of A, and so has C, and so has the relationship of B and C. This aspect of B from A is of the essence of A. The volumes of space have no independent existence. They are only entities as within the totality; you cannot extract them from their environment without destruction of their very essence. . . . The shape of a volume is the formula from which the totality of its aspects can be derived. Thus the shape of a volume is more abstract than its aspects. It is evident that I can use Leibniz's language, and say that every volume mirrors in itself every other volume in space (SMW 65a).

At this point one might be inclined to object that Whitehead has packed too much into his notion of an actual entity occupying a region in the continuum. If each actual entity is present throughout the continuum in the sense of exemplifying relations to every other region—which relations are part of the very nature of those other regions—then why may we not simply say that each actual entity occupies the entire continuum? And so, all actual entities would, in fact, occupy the same area—namely, the entire continuum. This, however, is clearly wrong, for our experience shows us different objects situated, in some sense, at different regions in space and time.

Whitehead's discussion of the individual and relational essences of an eternal object is intended to provide a defense against such an objection. In the following text we will briefly summarize Whitehead's theory of the individual and relational essences of an eternal object, and we will apply the results of our summary to the question at hand: how different actual entities may be said to occupy different actual regions in the continuum, while it may also be said that each of these entities is present throughout the continuum. We proceed as follows. Every eternal object is a unity, but for purposes of intellectual analysis, we may divide the one seamless essence of an eternal object into two factors. The two factors are the individual essence and the relational essence. It cannot be stressed too strongly that this division of the essence of an eternal object is artificial, useful for analysis only. With this caveat in mind, we may say that the individual essence of an eternal object E is that aspect of E which is not shared by E with any other eternal object, which does not relate E to any other eternal object, which is unique to E, and which cannot be subtracted from E without destroying the identity of E. The relational essence of eternal object E is that aspect of E which relates E to other eternal objects, which need not be unique to E, but which, nevertheless, cannot be subtracted from E without destroying the identity of E.

Now regions in the continuum are, when abstracted from the actual entities which occupy them, eternal objects. As eternal objects, they have an individual essence and relational essence. Thus an actual entity, X, which occupies a region, R, exemplifies that region both in its individual essence and in its relational essence. However, (1) X *exemplifies* the individual essence of R only; it does not exemplify the individual essences of those other regions which it does not occupy. Thus our previous analysis of Whitehead's claim that each actual entity is present throughout the continuum does not entail that each actual entity occupies the entire continuum. Rather, each actual entity occupies only that region of the continuum whose individual essence it exemplifies. Nevertheless, (2) while X does not exemplify the individual essences of regions other than R, it does *exemplify* the *relational essences* of the *other* regions. We explain as follows. For the sake of simplicity we will consider R as defined by the characteristics of the universal continuum. As such, R is internally related to every other region; this is the relational essence of R. However, R is not thereby related to these other regions considered as particular eternal objects with their own individual essences. Rather, R is related to each other region only insofar as the other region meets some purely formal condition. Therefore, when actual entity X exemplifies region R and is thereby related to every region in the continuum, the fact is that X is really related to these other regions only insofar as they meet certain formal conditions. Therefore, the exemplification in X of R's relations to the other regions does not require X's exemplification of those other regions including their individual essences. It is enough that X exemplify the *relational essences* of those other regions. Now even though these relational essences are *part* of the real internal natures of these other regions, they do not constitute the *whole* of the internal natures of these other regions—for their own individual essences have been excluded. Therefore X may occupy a region R, which is internally related to every other region, without occupying— or exemplifying—every other region.[23]

---

23. This same analysis also holds if we define R in terms of the specific continuum. The specific continuum, like the universal continuum, is composed of eternal objects. Thus the specified region R is an eternal object with its relational essence to other similarly specified regions. But R is related to these other regions only insofar as they meet certain defined criteria; R is not related to them as particular regions with their own individual essences.

9 *Strain Loci*

O UR EXPERIENCES OF THE WORLD, particularly in sight, are highly geometricized. The corners of my study walls illustrate the intersection of planes. The globe on my desk has a spherical surface. Moreover, I am absolutely positive that beyond the walls of my room there is an indefinite volume of space. I may not be sure what exists in that space; but it is beyond all doubt that there is an extended volume on the other side of those walls, either empty or filled. Again, my globe has an interior spatial volume. I may not be certain whether that interior volume is empty or packed with Styrofoam, but I am totally certain that there is a volume of space inside the globe.

I

In this sense, then, we can abstract out the spatial elements in our visual perceptions. The result of this abstraction is a gigantic container into which are placed such items as globes and study walls. This container is an example of a strain locus. In light of our previous discussion of the extensive continuum, it is clear that such a container cannot be the most fundamental aspect of our experience of space-time. We rejected the notion that the extensive continuum is a vast container. Therefore, the strain locus, which is perceived as such a container, must be understood to be an organization by the perceiving entity of certain elements in the continuum. The emphasis in the strain locus is upon the geometrical patterns in the continuum such as lines, angles, curves, and planes. And all of these are constructs out of more basic elements in the continuum (PR 194d, 496a).

The connection of the strain locus with the extensive continuum cannot be overemphasized. Much of Whitehead's effort in describing the continuum is devoted to showing how straight lines can be constructed out of more basic elements in the continuum (e.g., PR 460-71). Further, since the continuum is the basis for the strain locus, it follows that the container aspects of the strain locus must be understood to be abstractions, derivative from the more basic continuum. In many passages Whitehead does not distinguish between the continuum and the strain locus (e.g., PR 95c-96c). He is able to do this because the strain locus *is* one aspect of the continuum.

The strain locus is four-dimensional. That is, our perceptions of the world grow drop by drop—corresponding to the development of the actual entities which constitute our enduring selves. Thus our experiences of the geometrical elements of the world endure through a brief flick of time. This flick may approach the ideal of an instant without duration, but it will never achieve it. Consequently, the strain locus is four-dimensional —it is a three-dimensional space enduring through time. The strain locus, then, is bounded on both sides of its temporal axis by a three-dimensional "surface" (that is, by an infinite volume of space at an instant), but it is otherwise unbounded (PR 257a).

In intuitive terms, then, the strain locus is a four-dimensional space-time container in which are placed all the ordinary physical objects of daily life, from electrons to galaxies, from our bodies to our houses. Given this intuitive analogy, however, it is important to distinguish between the container and the objects occupying it. The container is a pure hunk of the geometer's ideal space-time system, and it is quite distinct from the objects in it. Of course, in ordinary experience, the strain locus and the objects in it are always given together. They are, nevertheless, separable for the purposes of analysis. The container is the strain locus, and the objects in it are additions, not a part of its very nature.

In our intuitive explanation of the strain locus we have stressed the analogy between it and a container. This analogy, though, may seduce the unwary into thinking that the strain locus is ontologically prior to or independent of the subject perceiving it. In fact, the opposite is more nearly the case. The fact that the strain locus is an aspect of the continuum entails that the perceiver be the basis for the strain locus. In short, the continuum is a part of the real internal constitution of the perceiver.

II

What then is Whitehead's explanation of the origin and construction of the strain locus? There are two related answers to this question. First, Whitehead develops an axiomatic system showing how straight lines can be logically deduced from certain very elementary rules about the notion of extension—rules which Whitehead intends to be a rigorous, axiomatic explication of that concept of extension.[1] This system is a formal, mathe-

---

1. These straight lines need not, of course, be Euclidean, although in our diagrams (later in the chapter) we will always draw Euclidean lines for the sake of simplicity.

matical-logical structure and ought to be evaluated—in terms of both its structure and its applicability to metaphysics—only by a person knowledgeable in these sciences.[2] We will, therefore, bypass such a critique. Second, Whitehead also uses his theory of the concrescence of an actual entity to show the genetic development of the strain locus. We turn, therefore, to a brief analysis of the genesis of the strain locus.

The fundamental unit in the development of the strain locus is the strain feeling. Whitehead described a strain feeling as follows.

> A feeling in which the forms exemplified in the datum concern geometrical, straight, and flat loci will be called a 'strain' (PR 472a).

For the purposes of analysis, it will be convenient to follow Whitehead's lead and discuss the geometrical elements in the datum of a strain feeling apart from whatever other factors may happen to be found in that datum. Considered as a feeling of geometrical elements, the strain feeling defines four primary factors, (1) the seat, (2) the focal region, (3) the intermediate regions, and (4) the whole of a strain locus (PR 477a).[3]

(1) The seat is a group of points within that volume which defines the standpoint of the percipient actual entity (PR 472b). Each pair of these points defines a line called a projector (PR 492a). Each projector extends beyond the seat.

(2) All the projectors, taken as a group, define the strain locus. In Whitehead's language, the region penetrated by all the projectors is the strain locus (PR 492a). As we mentioned previously, this strain locus is

---

2. For such an evaluation, see Palter, *Whitehead's Philosophy of Science*, esp. 106-46. Palter points out that Whitehead's "straight lines" lack the metrical properties (pp. 125-26); and, of course, until such properties are added to these straight lines, they cannot function usefully in showing how we can observe such things as an object moving in a straight line. Palter continues by observing that ". . . there is considerable doubt as to whether the non-metrical straight lines of Whitehead's theory of extension can serve meaningfully to define what Whitehead calls the 'projective properties of sense perception'" (p. 143).

Now whether Palter's evaluation is correct, we do not know. And, if it is correct, we are unsure of the implications of that fact for Whitehead's philosophy. Could a mere reshuffling of the axioms of Whitehead's mathematical-logical system "save" the metrical properties of his straight lines? Would it be permissible to add the appropriate axioms to guarantee the existence of straight lines?

Palter seems to assume that Whitehead intends to develop his straight lines simply from the concept of extension, and, thus, straight lines would be implicated in the universal continuum. There is no doubt that Whitehead can be read this way. But in footnote 12 on page 149 we expressed our confusion over this very issue. In some passages (e.g., PR 147d-48a) Whitehead speaks of straight lines and measurability as belonging to the specifications of the continuum. If this is correct, would it not imply that metrical straight lines could be deduced from the concept of extension only with the aid of additional axioms? But, if additional axioms are required in any case to introduce measurability and straight lines, then it would seem proper to correct any defects in Whitehead's axiomatic system by simply inserting the appropriate axioms.

3. It is to be observed that the strain locus is also called the presented locus or the presented space.

four-dimensional, being bounded by three-dimensional surfaces at both ends of the time axis.

(3) However, in most strain feelings there is a specific region within the strain locus which is emphasized. This, the focal region, is distinguished from the other regions in the background of the strain locus. There is a select group of points in the seat of the percipient entity which, when joined by projectors, define the focal region (PR 492a). According to Whitehead, there is a 'dense concurrence' in the focal region of the projectors which emanate from the selected points in the seat (PR 476a). In any case, it is important to note that the focal region in a strain feeling is always given as implicated in the whole of the strain locus (PR 503c). For that matter, the focal region is given as implicated in the entire extensive continuum (PR 478b). In this latter case, however, we may speculate that the connection of the focal region with the entire continuum—as opposed to its connection with the strain locus—is not much emphasized in the vast majority of strain feelings. The reason for this conjecture stems from the ordinary, everyday experience of the writer; in short, I am aware, immediately and without much reflection, that the region occupied by the cup of coffee on my desk is a part of the vast scheme of space—as that space lasts through each fleeting moment of observation. I am not, however, directly aware in such an act of perception of the relation of the coffee cup to the extensive continuum as such — to the fundamental elements of the continuum as defined by Whitehead on, for example, PR 449-59.

(4) Lastly, each strain feeling also defines certain intermediate regions (PR 477a). Apparently Whitehead has in mind the regions between the focal region and the percipient entity. Again, some evidence for this is to be found in our ordinary human experiences. As I look at my study, I see the opposite wall with its shelves of books. Beyond the wall, the strain locus is vaguely felt as a volume of space without any particular regions being emphasized over the rest. On the other hand, the region this side of the wall is clearly felt as a (relatively) precise area; and it is filled with various objects, such as my armchair, which demarcate certain (relatively) well-defined subareas.

In any one act of perception there will be, typically, a variety of strain feelings, each with its own focal region. According to Whitehead these various focal regions "coalesce." Does this imply that the percipient entity creates its strain locus by adding together the various regions felt by the individual strain feelings, until eventually the percipient has built a compete strain locus without gaps or wholes? The answer to this question is "No!" Each strain feeling prehends its focal region as implicated in the entire strain locus. Moreover, within a percipient actual entity, each strain feeling defines exactly the same strain locus. Therefore, at a later stage of concrescence, the percipient actual entity may join these various focal regions into one complex pattern of distribution within the strain locus—where this strain locus was previously felt by the various strain feelings which originally defined each individual focal region. In this sense, the various regions may indeed "coalesce." But this coalescence does not create the strain locus; rather, such a coalescence presupposes the prior existence of the entire strain locus within each individual strain feeling. In the following quotation, note how the regions coalesce to "emphasize" the strain locus; there is no hint that this coalescence in any way "creates" or "constructs" the strain locus.

> In pursuance of this principle, the regions, geometricized by the various strains in such an organism, not only lie in the contemporary world, but they coalesce so as to emphasize one unified locus in the contemporary world. This selected locus is penetrated by the straight lines, the planes, and the three-dimensional flat loci associated with the strains. This is the 'strain-locus' belonging to an occasion in the history of an enduring object. This occasion is the immediate percipient subject under consideration. Each such occasion has its one strain-locus which serves for all its strains. The focal regions of the various strains all lie within this strain-locus and are in general distinct. But the strain-locus as a whole is common to all the strains. Each occasion lies in its own strain locus (PR 485d-86a).

In the above quotation, Whitehead notes that an emphasis upon the various regions may, in fact, serve to emphasize the strain locus as a whole. This, however, is a reciprocal relation. An emphasis upon the strain locus may also serve to emphasize the various regions in it (PR 482b). Such reciprocity should not surprise us. The strain locus is one aspect of the extensive continuum, and in our discussion of the continuum we observed that each region is internally related to every other region. Therefore the "whole" (that is, the extensive continuum) and each "part" (that is, each region in the continuum) are given together; and it is a matter of convention whether we emphasize the "whole" or the "part." Since, however, both "whole" and "part" are mutually interdependent, it follows that (A) logically, neither can be emphasized without the other, and (B) psychologically, an emphasis on one will tend to lead the thinker—or perceiver—to the other also.

III

The next matter to consider is a problem in Whitehead's theory of strain feelings. In a strain feeling, the focal region amounts to a region in the strain locus which is picked out for emphasis. Since the strain locus is perfectly continuous within its boundaries, we are left with a two-part problem. First, *how* is a region emphasized above its fellows? Second, *why* is this-and-not-that region so emphasized? Whitehead's solution for this problem runs as follows. The various regions are chosen because of their connection with the contrast of sensa (S 14b-15a; PR 496b). There is considerable corroboration for this doctrine to be found in ordinary human experience. The edges of the region occupied by my coffee cup coincide with the contrast between the sensa illustrating the coffee cup, such as white, shiny, smooth, etc. And there are certain other sensa which are exemplified by my desk top, such as gray, dull, mottled, etc. Now the loci of the contrasts between these two sets of sensa mark out, rather nicely, the limits of the region occupied by the coffee cup. Again, speaking personally, if I am required to discriminate among the regions which fall within some larger area where there is no contrast between sensa, then typically I will "paint in" extra sensa in my mind's eye to help me find the subregion in question. For example, suppose that I need to find the approximate center of a large field. Typically, I will draw diagonals, in my mind's eye, across the field, carefully observing where they cross. If this cannot be done simply, "in my head," I will hold my hand in front of me, close one eye, and then carefully move my hand across my visual field so that the contrast between the sensa in my hand and the sensa in the open field "out-there" traces the desired lines which allow me to find the center.

The contrast of sensa thus leads to an emphasis on distinct regions in the strain locus. But we are still left with the questions of how, within the concrescing entity, particular sensa first become associated with particular regions. To answer this question, we note that sensa are associated with the various regions at two different stages. (1) *After* the strain locus has been developed, the contrast of the sensa coincides with the demarcation of the various significant regions *within* that strain locus. All of our common conscious experiences presuppose this development; that is, the sensum of white in my coffee cup is experienced as extended in a certain location in the strain locus. (2) But the sensa may also be found in the concrescence *before* the origination of the strain feelings. At this level the sensa are not felt as extended images; rather they are felt as pulses of emotion. For example, the primordial nature of the eternal object 'red' is to be a form of emotion—the kind of emotion associated with the experiences of irritation, being startled, surprised, and the like. Only later in the concrescence, when integrated with the geometrical forms of the strain locus, does the eternal object 'red' produce that extended patch of color which we commonly called red. In any case, the various sensa, and thus the contrasts between them, are present very early in the concrescence. In fact, they are present in the raw materials out of which the strain feelings are developed. Therefore, the percipient's decision to utilize this-or-that set of points to define this-or-that focal region in the strain locus is guided by the presence of the relevant sensa, and their contrasts, in the origins of the strain feelings. In the next chapter, on presentational immediacy, this topic is further developed.

IV

Consider the following quotation.

> In the second type, the transmutation is more elaborate and shifts the nexus concerned from the antecedent bodily nexus (i.e., the 'seat') to the contemporary focal nexus (PR 479a).

In this passage Whitehead appears to associate the seat with "the antecedent body nexus." To exegete this passage, we offer the following suggestion. The very nature of an actual entity is to be an arrangement of the past into a new perspective. Thus a past actual entity becomes, by means of objectification, a part of the "real internal constitution" of the new actual entity. Now a strain feeling is defined as a prehension "in which the forms exemplified in the datum concern geometrical, straight, and flat loci (PR 472a)." There must be a source for these geometrical, straight, and flat loci. In one sense, these loci are elements in the extensive continuum; therefore the percipient must have derived them from its previous entities. But in another sense, the important fact about these loci (i.e., these points, lines, and planes) is that they are *exemplified* in the datum of a strain feeling, and thus these loci have been lifted into prominence. It is, however, highly unlikely that the final percipient has sufficient creativity to lift all the relevant loci out of the continuum into prominence and then imaginatively attribute those loci to various entities in its environment. We must assume that the final, conscious percipient found most of those loci already exemplified in some of the entities in its past environment.[4]

Therefore, (1) to the extent that the materials out of which the concrescing entity constructs its strain locus are elements in the *extensive continuum*, it follows that *all* of these materials are made available to that concrescing entity through their presence in past entities. And, (2) to the extent that the materials out of which the concrescing entity constructs its strain locus are *geometrical forms* which have been lifted into prominence and *exemplified* in various actual entities, it follows that *most* of these materials are made available to that concrescing entity through their presence as elements in past entities.

Let us summarize our discussion thus far. When Whitehead says that an *antecedent* nexus is associated with the seat for some actual entity X, he may be interpreted to mean that this antecedent nexus is the source

4. It should be noted, however, that we must grant the concrescing entity some originality to *exemplify new* elements in its strain locus. This is because its strain locus must differ at least a little from the strain locus of any previous entity. For example, the temporal dimension of the concrescing entity's strain locus must differ at least slightly from the temporal dimension of any strain locus entertained by its past entities. (This is true by definition.) Thus the concrescing entity's strain locus will necessarily involve the exemplification of at least a few elements which were not so exemplified in any previous entity.

of the materials out of which X constructs this seat, where this antecedent nexus has been objectified into the real internal constitution of X. This antecedent nexus is the source of all the materials if we are thinking of the fact that the seat is constructed out of elements found in the extensive continuum; while this antecedent nexus is the source of most of the materials if we are thinking of the fact that the seat is constructed out of exemplified, emphasized, and isolated elements of that continuum.

We have explained the sense in which the seat is associated with an antecedent nexus. In the passage quoted, however, Whitehead associates the seat with the antecedent *bodily* nexus. How are we to account for the connection with the bodily nexus? To answer this question, let us consider a specific case of perception. Let us suppose that I am seeing a red ball with my eyes. Scientists would tell us that in this case, there is a line of transmission from the original red ball to the final percipient. First, the light falls on the red ball, causing red light waves to be reflected. Some of these red light waves travel into my eyes where they set up electro-chemical impulses on the retina. Next these pulses of energy are transmitted along my optic nerve to the brain. And these impulses are then carried along various paths in my brain until they reach the final percipient. Let us further observe that this line of transmission forms a temporal sequence; that is, the act wherein the light falls on the red ball is temporally prior to the act wherein the resulting waves travel through the air, and the act wherein the red light travels through the air is prior to the act wherein the waves of red light stimulate electro-chemical impulses in my retina, and so forth. The last part of this temporal chain is the final percipient; and so, the final percipient comes *after* every other event in the line of transmission. Therefore, the final percipient incorporates into itself this entire route of transmission.

Now we make the following two assertions. (1) We assume that none of the actual entities in this chain of transmission which occurs outside the body has perceptions in the mode of presentational immediacy,[5] at least in any sophisticated form. That is, it seems highly unlikely to us that the actual entities in a wave of light have advanced perceptions in presentational immediacy. On the other hand, we will assume that the actual entities which occur inside the body, along the route of transmission, are involved precisely in the development of such perceptions in presentational immediacy. (2) Our other assumption is that the more advanced the perception in presentational immediacy, the more clearly the various straight lines, angles, curves, planes, and other components of the strain

5. It is necessary to use the concept of 'presentational immediacy' at this point (and again in Section VI of this chapter) even though we will not formally introduce 'presentational immediacy' until the next chapter. The sole relevance of presentational immediacy at this point is that it involves a strain locus in which various sensa (i.e., colors, sounds, tastes, tactile qualities, etc.) are "extended" throughout some area in that strain locus.

locus are emphasized. That is, a perception in presentational immediacy is the feeling of a sensum, such as red, as extended in the strain locus; but, judging from ordinary human experience, the more clear and precise the extension of the sensa in the locus, the more obvious is the presence of the various geometrical forms in the locus.

We are now in a position to explain the sense in which an antecedent *bodily* nexus may be associated with the seat. In the percipient's experience of seeing the red ball, the entire life of transmission is incorporated into the real internal constitution of that percipient. However, some parts of that route of transmission are more capable than others of providing the percipient with geometrical materials for the construction of the seat. That is, the actual entities inside the body have emphasized and developed, in their perceptions in the mode of presentational immediacy, such geometrical forms. Therefore, there is a nexus composed of the entities inside the body along the line of transmission, and this nexus provides the final percipient with many of the appropriate materials for constructing its seat and strain locus. And so we conclude that when Whitehead says that an antecedent *bodily* nexus is the seat for some actual entity X, he may be interpreted to mean that there is a nexus of entities which is a part of X's body, and which is a primary source of the material used to construct X's seat and strain locus insofar as that bodily nexus has been objectified into the real internal constitution of X.

V

As noted previously in Section III of Chapter Six, a concrescing actual entity associates one of its durations with a strain locus. Consider diagram 19, in which X is an actual entity. The thick lines indicate the causal past (at the bottom), the causal future (at the top), and the causal present (between the past and future). Alpha and Beta are potential strain loci, and are indicated with thin lines.

We wish to discuss the relation of these strain loci to durations. A duration, it will be recalled, is a set of actual entities having the following properties: (A) all the actual entities in the duration are contemporaneous with each other, and (B) any actual entity not in the duration will be in the causal past or future of one or more members of the duration. The basic difference between a strain locus and a duration is this: a strain locus is a *section of the extensive continuum* in which the "geometrical" elements have been heightened, while a duration is a *set of actual entities*. In relation to diagram 19, we will make the following assumption. Alpha more or less coincides with a duration of actual entities, and Beta more or less coincides with another duration of actual entities. We note, however, that this association may not be perfect. That is, the strain locus and its associated duration may not wholly coincide (PR 192f-96b). This follows from the fact that the strain locus has a wholly mathematical content, while the content of the duration is wholly physical—that is, the duration *is* a set of actual entities in the concrete world (PR 503c). However, according to Whitehead, in human experience the match between the strain locus and the associated duration is usually very close. It is not, therefore, possible to give an illustration from everyday human experience where the two do not match.

In diagram 19, the actual entities constituting the duration are not drawn in.[6] In diagram 19, X has two potential strain loci. These two potential strain loci cannot both become X's "real strain locus." The notion of a "real" strain locus can easily be illustrated by reference to conscious human experience. You as a percipient are aware of your world as involving *one* coordinated set of geometrical relations. In short, you are aware of only one strain locus. You would be wholly disoriented if there were two mutually exclusive strain loci present in your experience. You would be totally confused, for example, if the same object were perceived at the same time as both in your present and in your past (which would be possible if there were two different strain loci actualized in your experience, as we will shortly note). Whitehead generalizes this and claims that any one actual entity can actualize only one strain locus—that is, the concrescing entity settles upon one strain locus and associates one duration with that strain locus.

In high school algebra every student learns to draw a pair of perpendicular intersecting lines, called Cartesian coordinates. Once drawn, these coordinates—or axes—form the base lines around which the rest of the space on the student's paper is organized. The strain locus does much of the same sort of thing. That is, the strain locus provides an actual entity with its base line for organizing the extensive continuum and the entities in it—except in this case, the base "line" is actually a four-dimensional unit. To illustrate this, let us turn again to diagram 19. Let us suppose that Alpha is X's real strain locus. In that case, strain locus Beta would be potential only. It must be remembered that the strain locus is the "container" in which the images are projected in perception in the mode of presentational immediacy; and, therefore, the strain locus is also the "container" in which the world seems situated in conscious human experiences. Therefore, if the strain locus Alpha is the real one for X, then it follows that the space indicated by the dotted line B would intersect with X's perceived contemporary world. (It must be remembered that since this is a two-

6. Diagram 17 shows several durations passing through X, one of which we have labeled Alpha. It would be possible to combine diagram 17 and diagram 19 (though the resulting diagram would be rather messy). The combined diagram would show rather clearly the relation between the duration Alpha and the strain locus Alpha. Presumably another duration, Beta, could be drawn which would connect with strain locus Beta.

dimensional diagram of a four-dimensional situation, that every line in
diagram 19 represents a three-dimensional volume.) Now within X's perceived contemporary world—that is, within Alpha—the space represented by the dotted line B will be perceived as sloping away from X;
moreover, the farther we go along the temporal axis in Alpha—that is, in
the direction of the arrow in Alpha—the more distant will be the space
represented by B from the actual entity X. On the other hand, the volume
represented by the dotted line A will never enter the perceived contemporary world of X; that is, A never enters Alpha. Thus A is always in the
past of the perceived world of X.

   Let us suppose, however, that X makes Beta its real strain locus. In
that case, strain locus Alpha would be merely potential. Thus the perceived contemporary world of X would be contained in strain locus Beta.
Now the volume indicated by the dotted line B would be wholly in the
past of X's perceived contemporary world. On the other hand, the volume
indicated by the dotted line A would now intersect X's perceived contemporary world. It would be perceived as sloping away from X. In addition,
the farther we go along the temporal axis—that is, in the direction of the
arrow in Beta—the more distant will be the space represented by A.

   This is the sense, therefore, in which X's choice of a strain locus will
organize the extensive continuum—and the entities in it—for X. Thus X's
choice of a strain locus also organizes X's perceptions, in presentational
immediacy and symbolic reference, of the continuum and the entities in
it. Finally, we may note that one of the differences between the strain locus
and the extensive continuum is this. Each real strain locus is a hunk of the
continuum (A) in which certain of its features—namely, the geometrical
elements—have been emphasized and (B) which serves as the "baseline"
for the organization of that continuum by the actual entity. On the other
hand, the extensive continuum is that reality which provides the
geometrical features for construction into a strain locus and which is
capable of being organized in an infinity of various ways by the actual entities in it.

   Motion is defined in terms of strain loci (PR 486b, 488d, 489c-90a).
Different choices of strain loci as real will result in different perceptions
of the movement of objects. We will use diagram 20 to illustrate how motion and rest are defined in terms of strain loci. In particular, we wish to
illustrate how motion among enduring objects is defined in terms of the
intersection and non-intersection of parallel families of strain loci.

   1. A, B, C, D, E, F, G, H, and I are all actual entities.

   2. For each actual entity, the causal past, future, and present are indicated by means of the unbroken lines. The lines of dashes and dots indicate the strain locus for each entity. To help sort out the various strain
loci in this diagram, a bracket has been drawn from the upper boundary
of each strain locus to the lower boundary of that locus. Lastly, the time

arrow, if it were to be drawn would run from the bottom to the top of the page.

3. Each of these entities is "at rest" in its own strain locus. Motion is not defined for a single actual entity which is locked into its region of the continuum (PR 113b-14a, 119c, 124b, 508c). Rather, motion can be attributed only to groups of actual entities, and, in particular, to enduring objects.

4. A, B, and C form an enduring object. D, E, and F also form an enduring object, as do G, H, and I.

5. The strain loci for A, B, and C are all parallel to each other. The strain loci for D, E, and F are all parallel to each other. The strain loci for G, H, and I are all parallel to each other.

6. Since the strain loci for A, B, and C are also parallel to the strain loci for D, E, and F, these two enduring objects are at rest with respect to each other. That is, the actual entity A would perceive the enduring object composed of D, E, and F as being at rest. Similarly, actual entity D would perceive the enduring object composed of A, B, and C as being at rest.

7. Since the strain loci for D, E, and F intersect the loci for G, H, and I, these two enduring objects are in motion relative to each other. That is, the actual entity D would perceive the enduring object composed of G, H, and I as being in motion. In addition, an examination of diagram 20 will show that D will perceive this enduring object (composed of G, H, and I) as moving farther and farther from D; that is, as we proceed along the temporal axis from past to future, these two enduring objects will become farther apart. An actual entity G would perceive the enduring object composed of D, E, and F as being in motion.

In summary, for a single actual entity, motion is not defined; although if it has a strain locus, that single actual entity may be said to be at rest in that strain locus. For enduring objects, rest and motion are defined in terms of the intersection and non-intersection of families of parallel strain loci.

We hope that our exposition on rest and motion will help to illuminate passages such as these:

> Rest and motion are definable by reference to real strain-loci, and to potential strain-loci (PR 492b).

> But now it seems that the observed effectiveness of objects can only be explained by assuming that objects in a state of motion relatively to each other are utilising, for their endurance, meanings of space and of time which are not identical from one object to another. Every enduring object is to be conceived as at rest in its own proper space, and in motion throughout any space defined in a way which is not that inherent in its peculiar endurance. If two objects are mutually at rest, they are utilising the same meanings of space and of time for the purposes of expressing their endurance; if in rela-

tive motion, the spaces and times differ. It follows that, if we can conceive a body at one state of its life history as in motion relatively to itself at another stage, then the body at these two stages is utilising diverse meanings of space, and correlatively diverse meanings of time (SMW 120b).

VI

The previous section shows that motion cannot be defined for an actual entity which lacks a strain locus. Whitehead suggests that the actual entities in empty space are so low-grade that they never construct any strain loci (PR 486b).

The actual entities in a molecule or atom, however, have motion defined for them (PR 492b). But the strain loci are also the basis for perception in presentational immediacy: they form the containers into which the various sensa are projected in these perceptions.[7] In light of this close connection between the strain locus and presentational immediacy, we must ask if Whitehead's use of the strain locus to define motion for atoms and molecules implies that atoms and molecules have perceptions in presentational immediacy.

To us it seems highly improbable that atoms and molecules should have this sort of perception, at least in any developed form. On the other hand, if atoms and molecules have motion but no perceptions in presentational immediacy, then it must be possible for the strain locus to develop alone, without presentational immediacy. Now it may be that Whitehead intended to assert that the development of the strain locus is genetically prior to the development of presentational immediacy. In that case, it would be likely that a low-level entity, such as one in an atom, would develop a strain locus without also developing the more sophisticated, genetically later projections of sensa into that strain locus. On the other hand, there are some good reasons for believing that Whitehead's position on the relation of the strain locus to presentational immediacy is that the strain locus is an abstraction from presentational immediacy. That is, in the concrescence of an actual entity, the strain locus and the sensa projected into it are developed together, and only at a later stage of development is it possible for the concrescing entity to consider either the strain locus or the sensa in abstraction from the other. But if there are no strain loci without perceptions in presentational immediacy, then how are we to avoid the absurdity of attributing such perceptions in presentational immediacy to the actual entities in the electrons and protons in the coffee cup on my desk?

---

7. It is to be noted that in PR, Whitehead introduces the strain locus as the explanation of certain aspects of our perceptions in the mode of presentational immediacy.

In answer to this question, let us introduce the notion of "primitive" perceptions in presentational immediacy; thus, perceptions in presentational immediacy may be more or less primitive. We hasten to add that the introduction of the notion of "primitive" perceptions in presentational immediacy is somewhat speculative as an interpretation of Whitehead, and is not extensively developed in Whitehead's own writings.[8] Like any other perceptions in the mode of presentational immediacy, primitive ones also involve a strain locus. In a primitive perception in presentational immediacy, however, the regions in that locus are not well defined by the vivid contrasts of sensa. That is, in a highly developed perception, at least one of the regions in the strain locus is sharply outlined by vivid contrasts of sensa. As an example of a highly developed perception in presentational immediacy, consider the experience of seeing the coffee cup on my desk. Here the contrast of the glossy white sensa of the cup with the dull, mottled gray sensa of the desk marks out the region occupied by the cup with great precision. And so, in the perception of the coffee cup, the region occupied by that cup is lifted out of its anonymity as just another region in the infinite set of regions in the continuum—that is, the region occupied by the coffee cup is emphasized as a focal region in the strain locus. But even in human experience, not all of our perceptions in presentational immediacy are so precise. For example, if I am blindfolded in the middle of a concert stage, and if two violinists play a different note on each of their violins, I would have a hard time picking out the regions occupied by the notes or the regions which serve as the source of the notes, that is, the location of the two violinists. This is especially so if the notes are in harmony. Of course, in one sense, both notes fill the entire concert hall. Nonetheless, it is obvious that these sensa do not define their regions very precisely, and even the contrast between them is not much help in locating them. Still, my perception of the two notes is a perception in presentational immediacy, and, therefore, it involves a strain locus.

Now we may imagine that each electronic and protonic actual en-

---

8. At S 25a, however, Whitehead does speak of perceptions in presentational immediacy which are so "embryonic as to be negligible." Again, at PR 269c-70c, Whitehead discusses different grades of presentational immediacy. Of special interest are these two sentences about actual entities in electrons.

> In such occasions the data of the felt sensa, derived from the more primitive data of causal efficacy, are projected onto the contemporary 'presented locus' without any clear illustration of special regions in that locus. The past has been lifted into the present, but the vague differentiations in the past have not been transformed into any more precise differentiations within the present (PR 270a).

We should further note that such a primitive perception in presentational immediacy is virtually identical with (one interpretation of) a strain feeling. This is further discussed in the next chapter.

tity projects sensa into its strain locus. However, this perception in presentational immediacy is "primitive" in the sense that the perception of the two violin notes was more primitive than the perception of the coffee cup. That is, in their perceptions in presentational immediacy, electronic and protonic actual entities tend not to emphasize any of the individual regions in their strain loci; they tend not to discriminate precisely the location of those regions which they do happen to raise slightly from their anonymity in the locus; and they tend to project sensa whose contrasts neither require nor promote such precise discrimination. In short, we may imagine that the perceptions in presentational immediacy belonging to such electronic and protonic occasions amount to little more than a vague feeling of the spatialization of vague sensa vaguely contrasting.[9]

We may now summarize the results of our discussion in this section. We may assume that motion and rest are defined for such low-level actual entities as the electronic and protonic occasions in my desk. But this means that each such occasion must establish a real strain locus, since motion and rest are defined in terms of such strain loci. Does this imply that atoms, electrons, or protons have perceptions in presentational immediacy? We were not certain how to answer this question. We developed, however, a theory of "primitive" perceptions in presentational immediacy which would allow us to assert that the actual entities in electrons and protons have such perceptions in presentational immediacy without committing ourselves to the improbable thesis that such low-level entities have perceptions which are as well developed as my experience of seeing a coffee cup on my desk.

(

9. We may note the following passage:

Sometimes the whole extensive region indicated by the wider geometrical elements is only vaguely geometricized. In this case, there is feeble geometrical indication: the strain then takes the vague form of feeling certain qualities which are vaguely external (PR 473a).

The context makes clear that these felt "qualities" are sensa. Thus Whitehead is describing a perception in presentational immediacy—even if a very low level one.

10 *Presentational Immediacy*

PRESENTATIONAL IMMEDIACY is one of the two basic forms of perception in Whitehead's theory. The other is causal efficacy. Presentational immediacy is derived from causal efficacy and therefore has its genesis at a later stage in the concrescence of an actual entity. Comparing it with causal efficacy, Whitehead describes presentational immediacy as follows.

> The percepta in the mode of presentational immediacy have the converse characteristics. In comparison, they are distinct, definite, controllable, apt for immediate enjoyment, and with the minimum of reference to past, or to future. We are subject to our percepta in the mode of causal efficacy, we adjust our percepta in the mode of immediacy (PR 271d; cf. MT 99b-102b).

I

To facilitate our discussion of perception in presentational immediacy we furnish diagram 21. P is a percipient actual entity. G is an actual entity outside the percipient's body. G is characterized by the eternal object 'green'. In actual entity G, however, the eternal object 'green' functions as a throb of emotion, as a primitive form of feeling. Again the time arrow runs from the bottom of the diagram to the top. Therefore, P is later than B, O, E, and G. P is also later than P_1. Similarly, B_2 is later than O_2, and O_2 is later than E_2.

Let us suppose that the original 'green' actual entity G is prehended by a later actual entity, which is in turn prehended by a still later actual entity, and so forth—all of these together forming a wave of light which goes from G to the eyes of the percipient's body. E symbolizes one of the actual entities which constitute the percipient's eyes at the time the light wave from G reaches them. The fact that there is a break in the line from G to E indicates that the light wave travels for an indeterminate distance before reaching the percipient's eyes. The break in that line also separates the actual entities which are outside the percipient's body from the actual entities which are inside the body. The impulse set up by the impact of the light wave in the eye is carried along the optic nerve. O symbolizes one of the actual entities in the optic nerve involved in this transmission. From the optic nerve, the impulse is transmitted through the brain. B symbolizes one of the actual entities involved. Finally the impulse is received by P.

Throughout this entire chain of transmission, the eternal object 'green' was passed from entity to entity. The final percipient P "projects" (we explain this term below, pp. 208-9) that sensum 'green' into its strain locus. This projection of green into the strain locus occurs in a perception in presentational immediacy. The technical term for a sensum projected into the strain locus is an image (PR 98b-99c). In diagram 21, I symbolizes the image which is projected, and the thick line represents the projection.

The fact that I is in the strain locus tells us several significant facts about I. First, I is perceived as in the contemporary world of P. This is the basis for a commonplace of ordinary human perception. When we see a blade of grass, we see that green blade as in the present. Of course, if G is an actual entity in that green blade of grass, there is a time lapse between the moment the line of transmission leaves the blade of grass and the moment the line of transmission reaches the final percipient. This fact is indicated in diagram 21 by the relative positions of G, E, O, B, and P. And yet we are not conscious of seeing the greenness of that blade of grass as in the past; rather, we are conscious of seeing it as in the present. The explanation of this aspect of our experience is that the final percipient has taken the 'green' which was transmitted from the blade of grass and projected that 'green' into the strain locus; and so the green image is in the present. Second, we perceive the image of green as continuous. In fact, we perceive any sensum projected into the strain locus as continuous (PR 96c). The explanation is that the sensum—in this case green—is projected into the strain locus so that it becomes extended in some region of that locus. Since the region into which the sensum is projected is infinitely divisible, we may choose any subregion of that overall region in which the sensum is projected and we will discover that the sensum is extended in that subregion also. Of course, in ordinary human perception there is a lower limit to the size of the regions which we can discriminate. Nevertheless, we may well imagine a creature with greater visual acuity than ours which can discriminate far smaller regions than we (cf. MT 153c-54d). The image of green in the strain locus is continuous in the following sense: no matter how small the size of the regions which that creature can discriminate, it will discover that the image of green will be extended in any subregion of the overall region in which that image is extended.[1]

1. A critic might object to this conclusion as follows. In our current epoch of electrons, protons, and photons, there is a lower limit to the size of an object which may be perceived as (for example) green. Thus, a single photon may not be perceived as green because we can perceive green images only when we are stimulated by the proper kind of light (or the proper drugs or proper electrical change). But such light will always be a wave composed of many,

Let R be the region in which the sensum green is extended. In terms of diagram 21, I is located in R. Now P's strain locus is an aspect of the extensive continuum. Therefore, R has a dual role, as a region in P's strain locus and as a region in the extensive continuum. As a part of the strain locus, R is a region upon which P may project a sensum. But as a part of the extensive continuum, R is a possible site for the location of a concrescence. Let A be the actual entity which occupies R.[2] Since A occupies a region in P's strain locus, it follows that A will be a contemporary of P. Therefore, A and P will have no prehensions of each other in the mode of causal efficacy. They can still, however, enter *indirectly* into each other's "real internal constitutions." As for P, the extensive continuum per se is a part of its real internal constitution; and the strain locus is also a part of the very nature of P. Therefore, region R is a part of the real internal constitution of P. But the extensive continuum is also a part of the real internal constitution of A; therefore, the region occupied by P is also a part of the very nature of A. In this sense, the two actual entities objectify each other into their respective concrescences—even though the two are con-

---

many photons. (Or the proper drugs or electrical charge will always involve combinations of subatomic particles considerably more complex than a single photon.) It is impossible, continues our objector, to perceive objects as green which are smaller than a certain (scientifically obtainable) limit. Therefore, concludes our objector, it is not possible that a green image will be extended throughout every subregion of an area—no matter how small that subregion.

The critic's premises may all be true, but they do not support the conclusion. We are considering the extension of a green image in the percipient's strain locus. But this strain locus is a hunk of the mathematician's pure space and time. Now, (1) the actual entities in that strain locus (including those making up any electrons, protons, or photons) are not directly relevant to the constitution of that strain locus; and, (2) the act of actually extending the image in that strain locus is performed by the percipient actual entity and does not depend (in any direct way) upon the character of the entities in that strain locus. (In support of both [1] and [2], it is germane to observe that contemporary entities—at least finite ones —cannot directly prehend each other.) Therefore, the extension of an image in that strain locus will depend on the mathematical character of the strain locus and not on the character of the actual entities which are actually occupying the regions of that strain locus. Since any area in the strain locus can be subdivided without limit, it follows that the extension of the color of green in that area can be subdivided without limit. Consequently, no matter how acute the powers of perception some creature may possess, it will not be able to perceive subregions (of an area where the color green is extended) in which the color green is not also extended.

2. Of course, if R is the size of an ordinary object in our world (say, the size of an amoeba or of a chair) or very large (say, the size of a star), it will be a potential site for the location of a nexus of actual entities. If R is very small, it will have a potential as a subregion of an actual entity. Further, there is also the possibility that R will be occupied by a group of actual entities, where some of these entities—maybe all of them—will be located partially inside and partially outside R. In the body of this paper, for the sake of simplicity, we discuss the situation where R happens to correspond exactly with the position of an actual entity. In the following discussion, however, these other alternatives must be kept in mind. Therefore, the "actual entity A" which occupies R may, in fact, be a nexus of entities, or a part of an entity, or the parts of several entities, or some combination of these possibilities.

temporaries (PR 98a). However, beyond these roles as occupants of regions in the continuum, neither A nor P objectifies any aspect of the other into its own concrescence.

II

Whitehead often says that perceptions in presentational immediacy are never delusory (e.g., PR 99d, S 24a). This is why perceptions of this sort are often called "direct." But in what sense are perceptions in presentational immediacy free from the possibility of being delusive? There is one way of looking at perceptions in presentational immediacy in which they are not beyond the possibility of being delusive. In diagram 21, actual entity P projects the sensum, green, into its strain locus at I. We further stipulated that R would be the name for the region into which I was projected, and we also let A be the actual entity occupying R. Now insofar as P attributes the quality green to actual entity A, clearly there is the possibility of error. That is, the only aspect of A which is directly included in P is the fact that A occupies the region R. All other factors in the formal nature of A are excluded from objectification in P. Therefore, if P attributes any quality to A—such as the quality green—then P is going beyond the evidence. A may be green, but also A may not be green. Therefore, in the act of attributing a quality such as green to A, P may err.

But in what sense, then, is presentational immediacy free from error? Clearly, if P's perception in presentational immediacy is to be free from the possibility of delusion, then that perception must be understood as limited strictly to the real internal constitution of P—both in terms of the materials used to construct that perception and in terms of the content, or object, or intentionality of that perception.[3] Therefore, when analyzing P's perception in presentational immediacy of I, we must consider I a part of the real internal constitution of P; moreover, we must consider the region R into which I is projected a part of the real internal constitution of P. In this sense, P's perception of I as located in R necessarily involves an abstraction from the character of R as the site which is occupied by actual entity A, an actual entity which is contemporary with P. That is, for P's perception of I at R to be free from the possibility of delusion, we must construe P as attributing I to the region R insofar as R is a part of the continuum; and we must further understand that P in no way attributes I to the actual entity A which occupies R.

There is, however, one sense in which it is possible to interpret P as attributing I to the actual entity A while retaining a complete freedom from

---

3. The reader may wish to compare our discussion in Part One, Chapter Four, "Intellectual Feelings."

error for the resulting perception in presentational immediacy. If we wholly reduce A to the region which it occupies, then, of course, we may construe P as attributing I to actual entity A. In Part One, Chapter Four, Section I.B we explained the distinction between the formal nature of an actual entity and the objective nature of an actual entity. We may apply that distinction here also. Thus, in its perception in presentational immediacy, P attributes I to A considered objectively—but not to A considered formally—where the objective nature of A in P is nothing other than the region R which A occupies. Although such an interpretation may be somewhat idiosyncratic, it is still useful in that it allows us to assert that the sensa perceived in presentational immediacy illustrate the percipient's contemporary world of actual entities. Whitehead suggests this interpretation in several passages. At one point he wrote,

> In this explanation of Presentational Immediacy, I am conforming to the distinction according to which actual things are *objectively* in our experience and *formally* existing in their own completeness. I maintain that presentational immediacy is that peculiar way in which contemporary things are 'objectively' in our experience, and that among the abstract entities which constitute factors in the mode of introduction are those abstractions usually called sense-data: — for example, colours, sounds, tastes, touches, and bodily feelings (S 25b).

In the following quotation, Whitehead again speaks (within the context of a discussion of presentational immediacy) of one actual entity being objectively present in another, contemporary actual entity.

> This limitation of the way in which the contemporary actual entities are relevant to the 'formal' existence of the subject in question is the first example of the general principle, that objectification relegates into irrelevance, or into a subordinate relevance, the full constitution of the objectified entity. Some real component in the objectified entity assumes the rôle of being how that particular entity is a datum in the experience of the subject. In this case, the objectified contemporaries are only directly relevant to the subject in their character of arising from a datum which is an extensive continuum. They do, in fact, atomize this continuum; but the aboriginal potentiality, which they include and realize, is what they contribute as the relevant factor in their objectifications. They thus exhibit the community of contemporary actualities as a common world with mathematical relations—where the term 'mathematical' is used in the sense in which it would have been understood by Plato, Euclid, and Descartes, before the modern discovery of the true definition of pure mathematics (PR 96d-97a).

This second quotation shows that the extensive continuum (and thus the strain locus) does not function in perceptions in presentational immediacy as the percipient's private possession. Rather, the continuum functions as a characteristic of all the actual entities in it, as a form of real potentiality.[4] Therefore, the strain locus also is an aspect of all the actual entities which atomize it—where these atomizing entities are contemporary with the percipient (PR 188a).

Perceptions in presentational immediacy are free from delusion and error in the sense defined. But this is the case only because the sensa perceived in this mode are merely projections into the percipient's strain locus. Therefore, at this level, Hume's analysis of perception is correct. According to Hume, the perceived sensa tell us nothing of the past of that region in which they are located, and they tell us nothing of the future. Each perceived sensum is locked into the present and is essentially unrelated to other places at other times. And on Hume's view, the success of induction is an unexplainable mystery, unrelated to anything we know about the world; and causality is reduced to the mere succession of unrelated images.

Now Whitehead never doubts that Hume's analysis holds true for an important class of perceptions—namely, perceptions in presentational immediacy. But Whitehead does have an explanation for the phenomena to which Hume points: that perceptions in presentational immediacy are constructed in terms of the strain locus. The strain locus is constructed by the percipient with the express purpose of identifying a contemporary region of the continuum, where that region, by emphasis and exemplification, is isolated—more or less—from the continuum out of which it came. Further, the sensum which is projected into some part of the strain locus is derived from prehensions of (past) entities and not from the actual entities which occupy the section of the (contemporary) strain locus where the sensum is projected. Lastly, we may suppose that in the construction of the strain locus, the dominant regions of that locus —that is, those which illustrate the contrast of sensa—are emphasized in such a way that their essential connections with the other regions are lost. At least this seems to be the case in human perception. For example, there is a door to my study. Now I may contemplate the region occupied by that door without contemplating the other regions in space. In this sense, the region occupied by the door has what Whitehead calls simple location. Of course, some of the relations of the region of the door to other regions are directly perceived—such as the fact that the door-region is next to the wall-region, and so forth. There is nothing, however, in any of these perceived relations of the door-region which would lead me to think that the essence of that door-region included these relations. In that sense I perceive the door-region as simply located. Moreover, there are many other relations which I do not perceive at all, but which I can discover only

4. Compare: "The mathematical relations involved in presentational immediacy thus belong equally to the world perceived and to the nature of the percipient. They are, at the same time, public fact and private experience" (PR 498b).

through a formal study of geometry—such as the numerical relationship between the surface area of the door-region to its volume. And, yet, regardless of what we as humans consciously and directly perceive, all of these relations are part of the essence of the door-region. Therefore, the construction of the strain locus abstracts from the full nature of that portion of the continuum which it covers. In sum, we may conclude that the aspects of perception which Hume emphasized are explained by the nature of the strain locus and by the nature of the act whereby a sensum is projected into that strain locus.

III

Whitehead makes a considerable fuss over the role of the body in perception (e.g., PR 99b-101a). Returning now to diagram 21, we note that E, O, and B are all part of P's body. The importance of the body for percipient P becomes evident if we meditate upon the fact that normally P does not directly prehend the character of actual entity G — that is, P does not directly prehend G's identity beyond its role as a region in the continuum.[5] Therefore, G (as more than a region in the continuum) is primarily present in P as it is present in E; and E is present in P as it is present in O; and O is present in P as it is present in B. Now if significant reversion has taken place along the line of transmission, then G may be objectively present in P with some characteristic which is quite unlike any quality in its formal nature. For example, G, which in its formal nature is characterized by the eternal object 'green', may be objectively present in P as characterized by the eternal object 'red'. Therefore, accurate transmission along the entire line is most important.

But the crucial entities in this regard are in P's body. The reason is that the "organic" entities inside the body tend to be more complex than the "inorganic" entities outside the body, and thus are more likely to "garble" the transmission. There is, however, another reason why the entities in the body along the route of transmission are important for P's perception in presentational immediacy. It is quite unlikely that P has sufficient originality to construct an advanced, complicated perception in presentational immediacy entirely on its own. Rather, as soon as the line of transmission enters the body, the entities begin to develop perceptions in presentational immediacy of G. Of course, G will not be the only factor in the environment, so there will be other perceptions in presentational immediacy. At first, we may imagine that these perceptions are embryonic and primitive in the

5. Whitehead does, however, leave open the possibility of "extra-sensory perception" in which there is a direct prehension of the content of more remote actual entities. But such ESP is not the normal mode of perception, as the term "para-normal" testifies.

sense explained previously. But as the route of transmission continues, we may imagine that these perceptions become more sophisticated—especially in the brain. Finally, the ultimate percipient P develops its own perceptions in presentational immediacy (PR 178b, 476a, 477a).

The percipient's body may be important in another sense. If a person has been looking at a green blade of grass for some time, then there will be a series of "final" percipients—each of which has a perception in presentational immediacy which is highly similar to P's perception of I. In diagram 21 this is indicated by the series P, P_1, and P_2. Both P_1 and P_2 have derived their material for this perception from a line of transmission which is similar to the one which leads to P. These lines of transmission are indicated in the diagram by the series G_1, E_1, O_1, and B_1 and by the series G_2, E_2, O_2, and B_2. We may suppose that P's perception of I is greatly aided by its prehension of P_1's and P_2's perceptions of I_1 and I_2. This is because P_1's and P_2's perceptions are fully developed and not merely preparations for something more complicated later on, as is the case with the perceptions in presentational immediacy of B, O, and E. However, it is the body which supports the series of final percipients, P_2, P_1, and P. We conclude by noting that the phrase "the withness of the body" is Whitehead's term for the entire range of ways in which the body serves to support the final percipients' perceptions—especially those in presentational immediacy.

IV

What is to prevent presentational immediacy from becoming a mere aesthetic display, vivid but barren? Since Whitehead conceives presentational immediacy, in and of itself, to be free from the possibility of delusion, this question cannot be directly asked about this mode of perception. However, presentational immediacy does enter into more advanced forms of perception where truth and error, veridicality and delusions are significant alternatives. In Chapter Eleven of this book we will discuss symbolic reference, but at this point we must only adumbrate some of the topics to be considered there. Therefore, granting that perception in presentational immediacy is not subject to delusion, we may still ask, "What sorts of perceptions in presentational immediacy are most likely to be factors in those more advanced perceptions which are veridical and not delusory, true and not false?"

To answer this question we turn once again to diagram 21. Percipient P has projected sensum I onto region R of its strain locus. There is an actual entity A which occupies region R. As we mentioned, in its perception in presentational immediacy, P attributes I to A only insofar as A is present objectively in P, that is, insofar as A has been reduced to the region

R which it occupies. Now the kind of perception which enters directly into human consciousness is symbolic reference. In symbolic reference we are not conscious of merely seeing an aesthetic phantasmagoria; rather, we are conscious of seeing certain qualities of the real contemporary world. In terms of diagram 21, we attribute I to the real, formal nature of A. Therefore, the likelihood of P's perception in presentational immediacy becoming an ingredient in a true and veridical perception in symbolic reference will be increased if the sensum displayed in region R is also a characteristic of the formal nature of the entity A which occupies R—although the fact that the sensum also characterizes the formal nature of A is no proper business of that perception in presentational immediacy.[6]

The key to the ability of a percipient to project an image onto a region of its strain locus which corresponds with the formal natures of the actual entities occupying that region is this: both the percipient and the actual entities in the affected region have causal pasts which greatly overlap (PR 484d-85a; AI 280b-81a). (We discussed the notion of overlapping causal pasts [and futures] in connection with diagram 16.) In terms of the symbols we have used in our discussion of diagram 21, percipient P has a past which greatly coincides with the past of entity A (which occupies the region upon which P has projected image I in its perception in presentational immediacy). This allows P to extrapolate from their mutual past worlds to the likely qualities of the formal nature of A. Such extrapolation does require that there be various types of continuity in the world.

Let us return to diagram 21 to illustrate this point. There is a line from G_2 to G_1 and from G_1 to G. This line indicates that G inherits from G_1 and that G_1 inherits from G_2. Thus, if we assume that there is a dominant characteristic passed on from entity to entity in virtue of these prehensions, it follows that G, G_1, and G_2 all form an enduring object. Of course, any ordinary object of human perception, say a blade of grass, will involve millions of entities and not just three. Nevertheless, the principle remains the same. Now P objectifies into itself not just G but the entire enduring object. In light of its incorporation of the past enduring object—G_2, G_1, and G— into itself, P is able to estimate how that enduring object will continue; and in that sense, P is able to predict the formal natures of some of the actual entities which occupy regions in its strain locus. It is worth noting that P's extrapolation from its past to the formal natures of its contemporary actual entities is normally a semiautomatic operation which occurs primarily in the bodily actual entities along the route of transmission—that is, in E, O,

---

6. Similarly, if the sensum projected upon R does *not* characterize A, then the likelihood of P's perception in presentational immediacy becoming an ingredient in a *true* and *veridical* perception in symbolic reference will be *decreased* and the chances of its participation in a delusory perception in symbolic reference will be *increased*. Of course, there is also the possibility that the perception in presentational immediacy will not enter into any later, integrative perception; it may just die on the vine, so to speak.

and B (PR 273a). The body is so constructed that various inputs from the external environment—such as light waves and sound waves as they impinge upon the body at various angles—are translated into perceptions in presentational immediacy without significant guidance from a conscious source.[7] In a few cases, however, considerable conscious guidance is required. For example, when (after looking for a while) I see a pattern in a maze of dots, my conscious mind enables me to lift up the pattern for examination. But with or without the intervention of consciousness, the fact remains that there are enduring objects in that shared past which are likely to continue into specific regions in P's strain locus. And this fact is the explanation for the success which P has in projecting sensa into various regions of the strain locus, where these sensa are also characteristics of the actual entities occupying those regions.

There is, however, another reason for P's success in this regard. The fact is that advanced percipients are usually members of a long chain of percipients. In Whitehead's terms, advanced percipients are typically elements in the 'soul' of some body. In terms of diagram 21, P has a prehension of former percipient P_1, and P_1 in turn prehended P_2. Thus P_2, P_1, and P together form (a segment of) an enduring object; they constitute (a portion of) the soul in some body. The crucial point is this: the ongoing series of percipients constitutes a self-correcting mechanism for perceptions in presentational immediacy. Consider P_2's perception of I_2 at region R_2. The sensum which is projected into P_2's strain locus at R_2 is ultimately derived from G_2—at least in the happy case in which the line of transmission has succeeded in conveying G_2 to P_2 without major reversions. It will be convenient to make two additional assumptions. (1) We will assume that G, G_1, and G_2 are simply one segment of an enduring object which has a history far earlier than G_2. (2) We will assume that G, G_1, and G_2 are merely representatives of the actual entities in the enduring object so that there are other members of the enduring object which are situated in the regions where we have drawn I_2 and I_1 and I. Now let us return to P_2's perception of I_2 as located at R_2. We may assume that P_2 projected the image I_2 upon R_2 because P_2 estimated that the enduring object of which G_2 was one member would continue until some of its members were located at R_2. In that case, the sensum which illustrates the region R_2 in P_2's strain locus would also characterize the actual entity which occupies R_2. But there is no way in which P_2 can verify whether the actual entity which occupies R_2 is characterized by the sensum which P_2 had projected upon that region; and there is no way in which P_2 can verify whether the actual entity situated at R_2 is a member of the same enduring object as G_2. However, what P_2 cannot verify, P_1 can. In diagram 21 we have shown P_1 as prehend-

_____

7. God is the exception. He is conscious and gives each entity along the route of transmission its subjective aim.

ing indirectly G_1. But P_1 will also prehend indirectly the actual entity situated in R_2. In fact, P_1 prehends the actual entity situated at R_2 in two ways. First, the actual entity situated at R_2 is prehended by G_1 which is then transmitted along the line shown in diagram 21 to P_1. Second, P_1 prehends P_2's projection of I_2 upon R_2. Therefore, P_1 can compare the nature of the actual entity situated at R_2—as that actual entity is transmitted to P_1 through G_1—with the sensum which P_2 projected into R_2. Now let us suppose that the sensum projected upon R_2 is also one of the characteristics of the actual entity situated at R_2; in that case, P_1 can project the image I_1 upon region R_1 in *its* strain locus with the confidence that the actual entity occupying R_1 will not only be a member of the same enduring object as G_2 and G_1 but also that the entity occupying R_1 will in fact be characterized by the eternal object which P_1 has chosen to project upon R_1. On the other hand, if the sensum which P_2 projects upon R_2 is *not* one of the characteristics of the actual entity situated at R_2, then P_1 can alter its own perception in presentational immediacy; P_1 may alter the location of the region upon which it projects the sensum or P_1 may alter the character of the sensum itself. Once again, however, P_1 by itself cannot verify whether the quality projected upon R_1 is also a character of the actual entity occupying R_1. That verification can be made only by percipient P. Thus P has the experience of both P_1 and P_2 behind it when it projects I upon region R in *its* strain locus. P can correct the mistakes of P_1 and P_2 if necessary, or P can capitalize upon their successes.

Presentational immediacy is indifferent as to whether or not the eternal objects which are projected upon the various regions of the strain locus also characterize the formal natures of the entities occupying those regions. In symbolic reference, however, this correspondence between the sensa illustrated in the locus and the natures of the actual entities in these regions is of the essence; without it, a perception in symbolic reference becomes delusory. Now one of the functions of presentational immediacy is to help identify the chains of causality which are operative in the percipient's environment (PR 256b-57a, 273a-b). The percipient perceives these chains early in its concrescence in the mode of causal efficacy; but like all objects of perceptions in causal efficacy, their position is only dimly felt. Therefore, to overcome this fuzziness, the percipient takes the eternal objects which characterized those chains of causal efficacy and projects them onto the region of the strain locus where those chains are most likely to be continuing to function. In the perception in presentational immediacy itself there is only an aesthetic display of a sensum illustrating a region. In that aesthetic display, however, the identity and location of the region becomes a salient fact which remains vivid for all further integrations of that perception in presentational immediacy (PR 185a-b). Therefore, when the later perception in symbolic reference connects the sensum-extended-in-its-region with the chain of causal activity felt in causal

efficacy, the salient vividness of the location of the region serves to identify the position of the chain of causal activity for the percipient.

When we analyze a perception in symbolic reference, we find that
the object of that perception gains its importance from its connection with
the chains of activity felt in causal efficacy, while that object gains its vividness and precision of location from its connection with presentational immediacy. We note that this happy interplay between perceptions in causal
efficacy and perceptions in presentational immediacy stems from the fact
that the perceptions in presentational immediacy are derived from the
perceptions in causal efficacy (PR 262a, S 58b). That is, in presentational
immediacy, the object which is being perceived has two fundamental components: (A) the strain locus and (B) the sensa illustrated in that locus.
Both are derived from causal efficacy. (A) The strain locus is developed
from the extensive continuum, and the extensive continuum is present in
each concrescing actual entity's simple physical prehensions of past entities, where these simple physical prehensions of past entities are the most
basic form of perception in causal efficacy. And (B), as we illustrated in
our discussion of diagram 21, the percipient entity derives the eternal object which it projects upon some region of its locus from the past actual
entities in its environment. But the percipient's prehensions of the past entities are nothing other than perceptions in causal efficacy.[8]

V

Although Whitehead never says as much explicitly, it is our contention
that a perception in presentational immediacy is a perceptive propositional feeling.[9] Our primary interest is in its being a *propositional* prehension, and only secondarily are we concerned with its being a *perceptive*
propositional prehension.

We defend our claim that perceptions in presentational immediacy
are propositional prehensions as follows. Whitehead states that a percipient's prehension of the association of a sensum with a region in the strain
locus is a propositional feeling.

> The conceptual counterpart of these physical feelings can be analysed into
> many conceptual feelings, associating the sense-datum with various re-
> gions defined by the strain. This conceptual feeling, by its reference to de-
> finite regions, belongs to the secondary type termed 'propositional feel-

8. Even if the percipient should project an eternal object which it had obtained directly from God and not from the entities along the line of transmission, it is still the case that
the percipient first had to prehend God. And that prehension is a perception in causal efficacy.

9. We should note Schmidt's discussion of this point in *Perception and Cosmology in
Whitehead's Philosophy*, 146-47.

ings.' One subordinate propositional feeling associates the sense-datum with the 'seat' of the feeler, another with the 'focal' region of the feeler, another with the intermediary region of the feeler, another with the seats of the antecedent elements of the nervous strand, and so on (PR 477b-78a).

We will not discuss here Whitehead's last case, in which there is an association of the sensum with the seat of an antecedent entity. We simply note that each of these propositional feelings (other than the last) associates a sensum with a region in the strain locus. Therefore, we may conclude that each of these propositional feelings is a perception in presentational immediacy. We further note that the entire perception in presentational immediacy is a propositional feeling; the object perceived, therefore, is a proposition; and the prehension of that association is a propositional feeling.[10]

At this point we must make the following observation. As we demonstrated in Chapter One, by definition a proposition is the attribution of an eternal object to an actual entity (or group of them) considered as a mere 'it', as a mere 'that'. Now what actual entity (or entities) plays the role of the logical subject in the proposition which attributes a sensum to a region? It is our position that the logical subject must be the actual entity (or entities) which occupies the region into which the sensum is projected. And yet this actual entity (which occupies the region into which the sensum has been projected) can be the logical subject only in a very restricted sense. We explain as follows. Since the proposition felt in presentational immediacy is, by its very nature, true (that is, this proposition is the datum for a propositional feeling which cannot be delusory), it follows that all aspects of this proposition must also be a part of the real internal nature of the percipient! Therefore, the true logical subject of this proposi-

---

10. It may seem as though we should identify three components to such a perception: (1) the act of actually creating the association of the sensum with a region of the locus, that is, the act of actually projecting the sensum out into the locus; (2) the image which is thereby established; and (3) the act of perceiving the image. (We note the happy ambiguity of both the words 'projection' and 'association'; 'projection' may refer to the act of projecting or it may refer to the thing projected; likewise, 'association' may refer to the act of associating or it may refer to the relationship which is thereby established.) However, it seems more consistent with Whitehead's discussion of propositional feelings to collapse (1) and (3) together. Thus the act which projects the sensum out into the locus is the same as the act which perceives that sensum in the locus. Our reason is this: since propositions—that is, the actual things perceived—are the data of propositional feelings, it follows that the act of creating such an association of an image with a region (i.e., creating the proposition) would be a propositional feeling, and it follows that the act of perceiving that image in association with that region (i.e., prehending the proposition) would also be a propositional feeling. At no point would the proposition exist on its own, in independence of one of these two propositional feelings. But surely it is redundant to have two propositional feelings, where neither has a function which could not be simultaneously performed by the other.

The last section of this chapter (Section VIII) explains in detail Whitehead's notion of 'projection'.

tion must be the actual entity occupying the region insofar as that entity is objectified in the percipient. But this actual entity is objectively present in the percipient only as a region—as that region which it occupies. Thus the region is the logical subject insofar as it is the mode by which the actual entity occupying that region is objectively present in the percipient.

At this point we will make a second observation. Whitehead speaks of a variety of associations of the sensa with different regions in the locus. Thus we have a variety of perceptions in presentational immediacy and a variety of propositional feelings. In a conscious experience of the world, however, we are aware of only a single coordinated display of these sensa —at least at any one time. Therefore, we assume that these perceptions are united to form one later perception in presentational immediacy in which all the sensa are exhibited as one coordinated pattern of images in the strain locus. (We discussed this point earlier when we analyzed Whitehead's comment that the regions "coalesced.") Now if the individual associations of sensa with regions are propositions, we may then assume that this later association of the coordinated pattern of sensa with the strain locus is also a proposition. That is, this integrative association may be construed as the attribution of an eternal object (in this case, a highly complex one) to a logical subject (in this case, a complicated nexus of actual entities) as reduced to a mere 'it' (in this case, the regions which they occupy). And, of course, the prehension of this integrative proposition is a propositional feeling. In addition, we may assume that this propositional feeling is that perception in presentational immediacy which—at least in conscious cases—is united with a feeling in causal efficacy to form a perception in symbolic reference. Moreover, since the only form of perception of which we are directly conscious is symbolic reference, it follows that the only form of presentational immediacy with which we are directly acquainted is this late integrative variety.[11]

Thus far we have explained why perceptions in presentational immediacy are propositional feelings. We have not, however, indicated a reason for holding that perceptions in presentational immediacy are *perceptive* propositional feelings. Actually our reason is quite simple. Perceptions in presentational immediacy are the raw materials for conscious perceptions. Now the term 'conscious perception' has a technical meaning in Whitehead's metaphysics. As we explained in Chapter One, Section IV, a conscious perception is the prehension of the contrast between a proposition felt in a perceptive propositional feeling and the logical subjects of that proposition before they have been reduced to mere 'its'. Since we may

---

11. We are here assuming that the identity of the perception in presentational immediacy survives into the perception in symbolic reference, so that by careful conscious attention we can "pick out" those elements which belong to the perception in presentational immediacy. This is what Hume seems to have done.

assume that perceptions in presentational immediacy are the normal suppliers of the proposition to such conscious perceptions, we may conclude that these perceptions in presentational immediacy are *perceptive* propositional feelings.

VI

According to Whitehead, a perception in presentational immediacy is generated out of the integration of a strain feeling with a physical purpose.

> Presentational immediacy arises from the integration of a strain-feeling and a 'physical purpose,' so that, by the Category of Transmutation, the sensum involved in the 'physical purpose' is projected onto some external focal region defined by projectors (PR 493b).

A

We turn first to the physical purpose. The physical purpose may be classified as a perception in causal efficacy—as we discussed in Section I of Chapter Seven. It is, however, a unique form of causal efficacy in an important sense. As we demonstrated in Section III.E of Chapter One, in a physical purpose the eternal object which characterizes the logical subject(s) is torn loose from that logical subject and then held up for consideration in its own right as a pure eternal object. Later, however, that eternal object sinks back into (partial) immanence with the actual entity out of which it had been originally wrested. The importance of a physical purpose in this context is that it is a feeling in causal efficacy which has been modified by the introduction of conceptuality. This introduction of conceptuality allows the percipient to invest the physical purpose with a range of subjective forms which are not available to the more primitive forms of causal efficacy. Such subjective forms may include the urge for transformation of the physical purpose into a perception in presentational immediacy. In addition, it is important to remember that there is no absolute distinction between physical purposes and propositional prehensions; rather, there is a continuum running from physical purposes as the less developed to propositional prehensions as the more developed.[12]

The physical purpose supplies the eternal object which is projected into the strain locus. Therefore, the physical purpose serves as the physical recollection for the propositional feeling in question. The chain of reasoning runs as follows. The perception in presentational immediacy is a propositional feeling, and the object of that perception is a proposition. The sensum which is projected onto a region in the strain

---

12. See Chapter One, Sections III.B, E; and the final portions of Section V.

locus is the predicate of the proposition, while the region itself is the logical subject of the proposition. Whitehead chooses to call the source of the predicate of a proposition the 'physical recollection'. Since the physical purpose provides the eternal object which serves as the sensum, it follows that this physical purpose is the physical recollection of the propositional feeling.

B

We turn now to the strain feeling. Let us refer again to Whitehead's definition of a strain locus.

> A feeling in which the forms exemplified in the datum concern geometrical, straight, and flat loci will be called a 'strain.' In a strain qualitative elements, other than the geometrical forms, express themselves as qualities implicated in those forms (PR 472a).

What are these qualitative elements which are implicated in the geometrical forms? Whitehead may be speaking of the general characteristics of the extensive continuum. This is, however, unlikely. It would be an unusual, though not impossible, description of the characteristics of the continuum to call them "qualitative." The more likely interpretation of these "qualitative" elements is that they are the sensa projected into the strain locus defined by the strain feeling in question. This second interpretation would seem to be confirmed when Whitehead later mentions "this projection of sensa in a strain" (PR 473a). Consider the following example of a sensum which is projected into the strain locus by a strain feeling. The eternal object 'red' could be described as a "qualitative element." When this eternal object is found in a strain feeling, it would be present as extended in the locus. That is, when integrated with the geometrical elements felt in a strain feeling, the eternal object 'red' (whose fundamental nature is to be a form of emotion) becomes an ordinary patch of red with the geometrical properties of size, shape, and location. Thus, a quality such as the eternal object 'red' becomes a sensum which is "implicated" in the geometrical forms. Therefore the passage just quoted seems to be saying that, in a strain feeling, there are qualities such as 'red' which are felt as connected with the geometrical elements felt in that strain.

If our interpretation of 'strain feeling' is correct, then it would seem that a perception in presentational immediacy must be classified as a strain feeling. That is, a perception in presentational immediacy has a strain locus as a part of its objective datum, and, therefore, the "forms exemplified in the datum concern geometrical, straight, and flat loci." Moreover, the sensa which are projected (by a perception in presentational immediacy) into that strain locus "express themselves as qualities implicated in those forms." Therefore, a perception in presentational immediacy is one kind of strain feeling.

C

Our task now is to explain what Whitehead means when he says that a perception in presentational immediacy results from the integration of a strain feeling with a physical purpose. We quote again the relevant passage.

> Presentational immediacy arises from the integration of a strain-feeling and a 'physical purpose,' so that, by the Category of Transmutation, the sensum involved in the 'physical purpose' is projected onto some external focal region defined by projectors (PR 493b).

The obvious problem is this. It would seem that, in this passage, Whitehead is presupposing that the strain feeling is a distinct and separate prehension from the perception in presentational immediacy! But how can the strain feeling be a distinct prehension from the perception in presentational immediacy if that perception is itself a strain feeling?

To answer this question, we will make some observations about the two chapters in which Whitehead defines a strain feeling and considers the relation between a strain feeling and presentational immediacy (Chapters IV and V of Part IV of *Process and Reality*). In these chapters Whitehead defines a strain feeling in such a way that a perception in presentational immediacy must be construed as a strain feeling (PR 472a). But he then proceeds to discuss strain feelings as though they were distinct (and more primitive) prehensions than presentational immediacy! We offer the following solution. In Chapter Nine, Section VII, we developed the notion of a "primitive" perception in presentational immediacy. We further developed this notion in such a way that this "primitiveness" is a matter of degree. Primitive perceptions in presentational immediacy tend not to emphasize any of the individual regions in their strain loci; they tend not to discriminate precisely the locations of those regions which they do happen to raise slightly from their anonymity in the locus; and they tend to project sensa whose contrasts neither require nor promote such precise discrimination. In short, we may imagine that primitive perceptions amount to no more than a vague feeling of the spatialization of vague sensa vaguely contrasting. Developed perceptions in presentational immediacy are much more precise. It seems to us—and this is the key—that Whitehead uses the term 'strain feeling' to refer to what we have called "primitive" presentational immediacy; and he reserves the term 'presentational immediacy' for the advanced and developed forms of presentational immediacy. (It would take too long to defend this interpretation by discussing every major use of 'strain feeling' and every use of 'presentational immediacy' in these two chapters. The interested reader may wish to read these two chapters using our interpretation as a hypothesis to be either confirmed or discarded.)[13]

Assuming that we are correct in our interpretation of Whitehead's use (in these two chapters) of 'strain feeling' and 'presentational immediacy', we may now revert to our original problem: what does Whitehead mean when he says that a perception in presentational immediacy results from the integration of a strain feeling and a physical purpose? Our explanation is that Whitehead is claiming that an advanced perception in presentational immediacy develops from a strain feeling (i.e., a primitive perception in presentational immediacy), where that development is informed by the presence of the original physical purpose.

We explain as follows. In Chapter Nine, Section V, we stressed that it is most unlikely that a single actual entity would have sufficient resources to form a strain locus entirely by its own power, to isolate the significant regions in that strain locus, and then to attribute the appropriate sensa to those regions. Rather, a chain of actual entities is required for this task. (In the case of the final human percipient, the relevant portions of this chain are to be found in the percipient's body.) We may assume that the original transition from the physical purpose to the primitive perception in presentational immediacy is a rather automatic affair. Now, the regions in the strain locus of the resulting case of primitive presentational immediacy are not clearly distinguished from each other. Nevertheless, there is some slight isolation of separate regions even in this primitive presentational immediacy, because, in at least a vague way, there are sensa projected into various regions in that strain locus. Moreover, *these* sensa are associated, however vaguely, with *these* regions in the strain locus because the physical purpose had already associated these sensa with the appropriate regions in the extensive continuum.[14]

In order to achieve an advanced perception in presentational immediacy, the vagueness in the original, primitive presentational immediacy must be eliminated. An increase in clarity and precision is obtained when a succeeding actual entity (A) incorporates into itself the primitive presentational immediacy and physical purpose and (B) creates

---

13. Another worthy interpretation is this. It may be that in these two chapters Whitehead is using 'presentational immediacy' as an equivalent to (what in other contexts he calls) 'symbolic reference'. The primary passage which tends to support this alternative is at PR 482b-83b. While we do not believe that these two chapters as a whole support this alternative interpretation as well as they support the interpretation mentioned in the above text, it is nevertheless clear that Whitehead packs more into the term 'presentational immediacy' in these two chapters than he does elsewhere in PR. For an example of this "more," see footnote 15 on page 203.

14. In Section VII of this chapter we will discuss how this transition from a physical purpose to a perception in presentational immediacy occurs, that is, we will discuss the basis for the transition from the association of a sensum with a region in a physical purpose to the association of that sensum with a region in a perception in presentational immediacy.

its own new perception in presentational immediacy. In creating its new presentational immediacy, the succeeding actual entity utilizes the advances made by the previous actual entity in *its* primitive perception in presentational immediacy. The succeeding actual entity, however, also utilizes the physical purpose; the presence of the sensum in the physical purpose helps to reinforce the clarity of the projection of that sensum in the new presentational immediacy. While this new presentational immediacy represents a genuine gain in clarity over its predecessor, it is still not clear in comparison with a truly advanced perception in presentational immediacy. Therefore, this process is repeated until the final percipient is reached. This final percipient is the heir to a long process of development. It can take the advanced perceptions in presentational immediacy which it finds in its close predecessors and, using the physical purpose as an aid, create a final, sharp, and clear perception in presentational immediacy.[15]

In the case of human beings, this development takes place in the body; some portion of the nervous system (including, usually, the brain) serves as the location of this route of clarification and development. Each

---

15. The presence of the physical purpose in the genesis of presentational immediacy influences Whitehead's description of this mode of perception at PR 482b. Normally, Whitehead describes presentational immediacy in Humean terms, that is, Whitehead describes presentational immediacy as merely the experience of various sensa as they are extended in the percipient's strain locus, where this strain locus marks a clear distinction between the perceived present and the past and the future (e.g., PR 188b, 255a, 257a). And, normally, Whitehead leaves to 'symbolic reference' the task of transferring any feelings of efficacity from the physical purpose to the presentational immediacy. At PR 482b, however, Whitehead speaks of the 'symbolic transference' of the sense of efficacy from the physical purpose to the presentational immediacy, and he does not, in this passage, make any reference to symbolic reference. Whitehead's meaning seems to be that any prehension will bear in its own nature some trace of its origin. Now the origin of an advanced perception in presentational immediacy involves a physical purpose. Therefore, there must be some trace of that physical purpose in the advanced presentational immediacy; and in this passage Whitehead suggests that it is the sense of efficacy in the physical purpose which is inherited by the perception in presentational immediacy. Specifically, in the perception in presentational immediacy, the sensum which is projected into a region of the strain locus is felt, to some degree, as though it (the sensum) were emanating from that region; that is, the region in the strain locus is felt as though it were causally efficacious (which of course it is not).

As we mentioned, Whitehead normally leaves to 'perception in symbolic reference' this task of transferring any feelings of efficacy from the physical purpose to the presentational immediacy. We should mention another possibility: Whitehead may be developing another theory of presentational immediacy and symbolic reference which is an alternative to his "mainstream" interpretation. It is, however, also possible that he merely means (as we mentioned above) that a sense of efficacy cannot be ordinarily eliminated from a perception in presentational immediacy (because of the role of the physical purpose in the origin of that perception), while, at the same time, wishing to reserve for symbolic reference the major role in the transference of the sense of efficacy from the physical purpose to the presentational immediacy. In any case, in Chapter Eleven we develop what we consider his mainstream interpretation of the relation of 'physical purpose', 'presentational immediacy', 'symbolic transference', and 'symbolic reference'.

time there is an advance in clarification and development the new actual entity uses the achievement of its predecessor. Since the predecessor's perception in presentational immediacy is less advanced than the successor's perception, we may say that the predecessor's presentational immediacy is playing the role of 'strain feeling' to the successor's perception in presentational immediacy. Therefore, we may say that the final conscious percipient creates its own terminal perception in presentational immediacy through the integration of a strain feeling with a physical purpose.[16]

VII

In many passages Whitehead connects perception in presentational immediacy with transmutation. Consider the following series of quotations.

> In the first place, the primary status of the sensa as qualifications of affective tone must be kept in mind. They are primarily inherited as such qualifications and then by 'transmutation' are objectively perceived as qualifications of regions (AI 314e-15a).

> A strain is a complex integration of simpler feelings; . . . In the process of integration, these wider geometrical elements acquire implication with the qualities originated in the simpler stages. The process is an example of the Category of *Transmutation;* and is to be explained by the intervention of intermediate conceptual feelings. . . . This type of objectification is characterized by the close association of qualities and definite geometrical relations. It is the basis of the so-called 'projection' of sensa (PR 472b-73a; emphasis added).

> Thus, by the agency of the Category of *Transmutation,* there are two types of feelings, for which the objective datum is a nexus with undiscrim-

16. We had been working with this issue (the relation of presentational immediacy, physical purposes, and strain loci) for several years when Lewis Ford's work *The Emergence of Whitehead's Metaphysics: 1925-1929* appeared. Ford's work confirmed our intuition that Whitehead had developed his thoughts on the issues of presentational immediacy and strains over a period of several years. In particular, according to Ford, the theory of perception in three modes—causal efficacy, presentational immediacy, and symbolic reference—was in place before April 1927. This theory appears in *Symbolism* (*Emergence,* 181-2). Whitehead's theory of strains, on the other hand, was not completed until after the delivery of the Gifford Lectures and just before the final draft of *Process and Reality* (*Emergence,* 233-4).

The development of these two different areas, presentational immediacy and strains, at different times in Whitehead's life surely accounts for some of the variations in Whitehead's presentation of 'presentational immediacy' and its relation to physical purposes and to strain loci. Ford does not, however, directly address the question of Whitehead's position on 'presentational immediacy' in the chapters dealing with strains. Further, as Ford himself suggests (xi-xii), there is a "final" version of *Process and Reality.* Whatever the developments in Whitehead's thought, the material in the main text presents our best effort to explicate Whitehead's final position as presented in *Process and Reality,* the position which we have termed his "mainstream" point of view.

inated actual entities. The feelings of the first type are feelings of 'causal efficacy'; and those of the second type are those of 'presentational immediacy.' In the first type, the analogous elements in the various feelings of the various actualities of the bodily nexus are transmuted into a feeling ascribed to the bodily nexus as one entity. In the second type the *transmutation* is more elaborate and shifts the nexus concerned from the antecedent bodily nexus (i.e., the 'seat') to the contemporary focal nexus (PR 478c-79a; emphases added).

But these regions are not apprehended in abstraction from the general spatio-temporal continuum. The prehension of a region is always the prehension of systematic elements in the extensive relationship between the seat of the immediate feeler and the region concerned. When these valuations have been effected, the Category of *Transmutation* provides for the transmission to the succeeding subject of a feeling of these regions qualified by (i.e., contrasted with) that sense-datum (PR 478b; emphasis added).

Presentational immediacy arises from the integration of a strain-feeling and a 'physical purpose,' so that, by the Category of *Transmutation*, the sensum involved in the 'physical purpose' is projected onto some external focal region defined by projectors (PR 493b; emphasis added).

These quotations make it clear that transmutation plays several roles in the production of perceptions in presentational immediacy. The simplest of these uses can be explicated as follows. We refer again to diagram 21, in which the final percipient P has objectified G, G_1, and G_2. At some point during the concrescence of P, the eternal object which is derived individually from G, G_1, and G_2 is transmuted into a characteristic applying to the nexus as a whole, that is, to the entire nexus composed of G, G_1, and G_2, considered as a unit. We may assume that this transmutation takes place early in the concrescence, no later than the completion of the physical purpose. In fact, at several points Whitehead seems to think that such transmutations would occur before the final percipient begins to concresce. That is, in diagram 21, we have traced the line of transmission from G to P. Now starting with E—the eyes—the line of transmission passes through the percipient's body. It may be that the transmutation whereby the eternal object in question is applied to nexus G, G_1, and G_2, occurs in the entities which are in the body. In that case, the final percipient would inherit from the last entities in the line of transmission, somewhere in the brain, the transmutation ready-made.

Transmutation, however, also plays a role in the projection of the sensa into the strain locus. There seem to be two aspects of this use of transmutation. (1) Transmutation has something to do with the actual extension of the image in the strain locus. (2) Transmutation is involved in the shift of an eternal object from its role as a character of the nexus felt in the physical purpose to its role as a sensum extended in the strain locus.

Let us consider the first of these aspects. Transmutation is involved in the very possibility of an image existing as extended in the strain locus. We can state as follows the need which this invocation of transmutation is designed to meet. A sensum which is extended in space will extend over a region of a determinate size. No matter how small that region may be, it will include smaller subregions within it. Moreover, in any ordinary human perception, the image will extend over a fairly large area. That is, the area will be large in the sense that it could not possibly be occupied by a single actual entity. Rather, the region which is covered by the extended image can be occupied only by a substantial nexus of actual entities. Therefore, in attributing that sensum to a region in the locus, the percipient is attributing that sensum to a nexus of actual entities—at least, to the extent that this nexus is objectively present in the percipient by means of the regions which its members occupy. Now whenever Whitehead has need to speak of a characteristic as applying to a nexus of entities, considered as a unit, he tends to speak of transmutation. It is by means of the category of transmutation that an eternal object is applied to a nexus as a whole. Therefore Whitehead speaks of the category of transmutation when he speaks of the projection of a sensum into the locus, that is, when he speaks of the attribution of an eternal object (the sensum) to a nexus of actual entities (the region in which it is extended).

Let us now turn to the second aspect mentioned above, the relation of transmutation in the shift of an eternal object from its role as a character of the nexus felt in the physical purpose to its role as a sensum extended in the strain locus. It will be recalled that in transmutation the concrescing actual entity takes an eternal object and applies it to a nexus, that is, to a group of actual entities considered as a single unit. Now the question is this: Must the eternal object in question have been derived from the members of the nexus to which that eternal object is applied? Does transmutation, by definition, exclude the case where the eternal object is derived from one nexus and is then applied to a wholly distinct and separate nexus? In Whitehead's formal definition it seems that the eternal object in question must have been derived from at least some of the members of the nexus to which it is applied.

> When . . . one and the same conceptual feeling is derived impartially by a prehending subject from its analogous simple physical feelings of various actual entities in its actual world, then, in a subsequent phase of integration of these simple physical feelings together with the derivate conceptual feeling, the prehending subject may transmute the *datum* of this conceptual feeling into a characteristic of some *nexus* containing those prehended actual entities among its members, or of some part of that nexus. In this way the nexus (or its part), thus characterized, is the objective datum of a feeling entertained by this prehending subject (PR 40d).

In a passage dealing with presentational immediacy and strain feelings, Whitehead takes a different position. Here he states that it is possible for transmutation to "transfer" a quality from one nexus to a separate and distinct nexus.

> For this purpose, the Category of Transmutation is the master-principle. By its operation each nexus can be prehended . . . in terms of analogies among the members of *other* nexūs but yet relevant to it (PR 483c, emphasis added).

According to Whitehead such a transfer is easiest when the concrescing entity transfers that eternal object to a nexus composed of actual entities which are *contemporary* with that concrescing entity.

> When the recipient nexus is composed of entities contemporary with the percipient subject, this difficulty vanishes. For the contemporary entities do not enter into the constitution of the percipient subject by objectification through any of their own feelings. Thus their only direct connection with the subject is their implication in the same extensive scheme. Thus a nexus of actual entities, contemporary with the percipient subject, puts up no alternative characteristics to inhibit the transference to it of characteristics from antecedent nexūs (PR 484b).

This issue is important because, when a percipient actual entity projects a sensum upon a region in the locus, clearly the percipient entity did not derive that sensum from the actual entities occupying that region. Indeed, since the actual entities occupying the region upon which the percipient projects the sensum are all contemporary with that percipient, it follows that the only parts of their real internal constitutions which are objectively present in the percipient are the regions which they occupy; certainly these contemporary actual entities do not contribute the sensum.

To us there is something unsatisfying about Whitehead's *ad hoc* change of the definition of transmutation to account for the emergence of perceptions in presentational immediacy. We would like to propose the following explanation of how transmutation accounts for the projection of the sensum in the strain locus. Our explanation allows Whitehead's first, and more formal, definition to stand without qualification. That is, it is not necessary to assume that the eternal object (the sensum) can be derived from one group of actual entities and then transferred to an entirely distinct nexus of actual entities (the extended region in the strain locus). And yet the net result of our proposed explanation is that the transmutation eventually does transfer the eternal object (sensum) from one nexus to an entirely distinct nexus.

Our interpretation runs as follows. In Whitehead's formal definition of transmutation, it must be noted that an eternal object may be applied to a nexus even though that eternal object was derived from only *some* of the actual entities in that nexus. In other words, there is no requirement that every member of the nexus yield up the defining characteristic; it is enough that, among the actual entities constituting the nexus, there be at least a few which yield up that eternal object. As Whitehead says, ". . . the prehending subject may transmute the datum of this conceptual feeling into a characteristic of some nexus *containing* those prehended actual entities among its members . . ." (our emphasis). To apply this observation about the nature of transmutation, we refer again to diagram 21. In terms of diagram 21, we may assert that the physical purpose (which is the source of the perception in presentational immediacy) feels the nexus G, G_1, and G_2 as one unit characterized by the eternal object which will later serve as the sensum in the resulting perception in presentational immediacy. But G, G_1, and G_2 may be construed as simply a part of a larger nexus. This larger nexus would be situated not only in the regions occupied by G, G_1, and G_2, but also at the region upon which we have shown P projecting image I. Thus we would have a nexus which was composed partially of actual entities which were in the past of percipient G and partially of actual entities which are contemporary with percipient G. By the category of transmutation, the eternal object which was derived from G, G_1, and G_2 would then be applied to this nexus considered as a whole, *including that section of it which is contemporary with percipient P.* Finally, with the development of the strain locus, that portion of the nexus which fell into this strain locus would be "cut off" from the rest of the locus. The result would be an image extended in the strain locus.

We make no particular claims for this interpretation other than that it does offer an explanation for Whitehead's assertions that the projection of the sensum into the strain locus is accomplished by means of transmutation. Also, our explanation does not require us to create variations in the notion of transmutation.

VIII

Before we leave this chapter, it is important to comment on Whitehead's use of the notion of 'projection of a sensum into a region of the strain locus'. It is easy to misunderstand Whitehead's use of the term 'projection'. We have already hinted as much when we suggested (in footnote 10 on page 197) that the act whereby the sensum is projected onto the locus is identical with the act whereby the sensum is perceived in its location in the locus. The essential point to remember is that the term 'projection' originates in Whitehead's mathematical studies. Nathaniel Lawrence states this very well.

> We must recall that we are dealing not only with a mathematician, however, but specifically with a geometer for whom "projection" has a special significance. Whitehead's philosophy is enriched throughout by a fecund imagination which is willing to apply the instruments of mathe-

matics to unfamiliar tasks. Without other evidence it seems very likely that the author of works on projective geometry brought to the ingression of sense-objects a special meaning for projection.[17]

In projective geometry a 'projective property' is a property which belongs equally to any of a series of figures—where membership in this series is carefully defined. Thus the notion of a 'projective property' is very closely linked to the notion of a 'polyadic property'. It is this conception of a sensum as a polyadic characteristic which allows Whitehead to say:

> Thus if green be the sense-object in question, green is not simply at A where it is being perceived, nor is it simply at B where it is perceived as located; but it is present at A with the mode of location in B (SMW 70b).

Commenting on this passage, Lawrence notes that "in a sense the sense-object is both 'here' where the act of perception occurs and 'there' where it is perceived as located."[18]

We may now apply this understanding of 'projection' to the problem of the projection of sensa in the perception in presentational immediacy. When Whitehead says that a percipient 'projects' a sensum into the locus, he does not mean that the percipient tosses out an image into the locus the way that an umpire tosses out a baseball to the pitcher, or the way a slide projector projects an image onto the screen. Rather, Whitehead's basic analogy is from mathematics. When Whitehead says that a percipient projects an image into the locus in its perception in presentational immediacy, he means that the percipient in its perception has defined a multivalent relationship among the sensum, the region where it is perceived as located, and the percipient.

We may also apply this notion of projection to our explanation of how transmutation plays a role in the projection of the sensum into the strain locus. Even if the percipient creates the extended image by cutting off that portion of a nexus which falls in the strain locus, it is still possible for the percipient to "project" that sensum into the locus in the sense of defining a polyadic relation among the sensum, the region where it is perceived as located—or perhaps the actual entities occupying that region insofar as they are objectively present within the percipient—and the percipient. We may conclude by citing the following passage.

> The familiar language which I have used in speaking of the 'projection of our sensations' is very misleading. There are no bare sensations which are first experienced and then 'projected' into our feet as their feelings, or onto the opposite wall as its colour. The projection is an integral part of the situation, quite as original as the sense-data (S 14c).

17. *Whitehead's Philosophical Development* 167.
18. Ibid., 168.

11 Symbolic Reference and
Conscious Perception

WHEN WE ENTER THE REALM OF SYMBOLIC REFERENCE, we have arrived at the normal human perception of which we are conscious. What we ordinarily call sense perception is merely (one variety of) symbolic reference.[1] In one passage Whitehead announces that, in human experience, perceptions purely in causal efficacy or purely in presentational immediacy are "in practice unobtainable" (S 54a); but in another passage he claims that such pure perceptions are merely rare and that "great care is required to distinguish the two modes" (PR 186a). Symbolic reference integrates a perception in causal efficacy with a perception in presentational immediacy.

1. It should be noted that Whitehead occasionally uses the term 'sense-perception' as a synonym for 'presentational immediacy' (e.g., PR 126b, S 52a-53a). Why do we consider sense perception a form of symbolic reference? We may, if we wish, consider 'sense perception' a technical term referring to presentational immediacy. However, "sense perception" also has a pre-philosophical use (as well as an older and wider use in philosophical circles beyond Whitehead's system). In this popular use, "sense-perception" refers to our experience of the world through our senses; it refers to our total human experience as it is mediated to us by our senses. Whitehead makes clear that he intends 'symbolic reference' to refer to normal human experience. For example:

> When human experience is in question, 'perception' almost always means 'perception in the mixed mode of symbolic reference' (PR 255b-56a).

> Thus the result of symbolic reference is what the actual world is for us, as that datum in our experience productive of feelings, emotions, satisfactions, actions, and finally as the topic for conscious recognition when our mentality intervenes with its conceptual analysis (S 18b-19a).

In addition, when Whitehead discusses our ordinary human experience of seeing a gray stone, he considers that experience an example of symbolic reference (PR 272b-74a). We conclude that we have a license to consider that ordinary human experience to be an example of symbolic reference.

210

I

Since symbolic reference is a form of symbolism, there must be a common ground between the two pure modes of perception.[2] Symbolic reference has two such common grounds, the strain locus and the eternal objects (PR 255b-63a). Thus, each of these common grounds must be present in both of the pure modes (cf. PR 256b). Let us turn first to the presented locus (that is, the strain locus). The strain locus is present in any perception in presentational immediacy, as we described in Chapter Ten. But it is also present in any perception in causal efficacy, though in a less obvious manner. Each perception in causal efficacy places its object within the context of the extensive continuum; moreover, causal efficacy defines the past, present, and future for the percipient. Thus implicated in each perception in causal efficacy is that portion of the continuum which constitutes the percipient's 'present'. But the strain locus is nothing other than a set of elements in that 'present' which have been picked out from their background and lifted into prominence. Therefore, the strain locus is present in each of the percipient's perceptions in causal efficacy.

Let us turn now to the other common ground for the perception in symbolic reference, the eternal objects. What Whitehead has in mind is this. The sensum which is projected upon the strain locus in a perception in presentational immediacy is derived from the physical purpose. Thus an eternal object which characterized the datum of the physical purpose becomes the sensum extended in the strain locus which is perceived in presentational immediacy. We have discussed sufficiently the mechanics of this transfer. The point is that the same eternal object is perceived both in causal efficacy and in presentational immediacy, and thus we have another common ground between these two modes which allows the perception in symbolic reference to integrate them.

II

What, then, is the nature of this integration achieved by symbolic reference? Whitehead defined symbolic reference as follows.

> Then there is 'symbolic reference' between the two species when the perception of a member of one species evokes its correlate in the other species, and precipitates upon this correlate the fusion of feelings, emotions, and derivate actions, which belong to either of the pair of correlates, and which are also enhanced by this correlation (PR 274b).

2. See Part Two, Chapter Six, Section III.

From this passage, it will be readily observed that symbolic reference is a type of symbolism. But Whitehead is somewhat more specific than this passage indicates about the nature of this integration. Apparently it is his position that when a percipient connects an image felt in presentational immediacy with a nexus felt in causal efficacy, the image is considered the continuation of that nexus in the present.

Let us illustrate this in terms of diagram 21. By means of a physical purpose, the percipient P perceives the nexus G, G_1, and G_2 as characterized by the eternal object 'green'. Now P judges that this nexus, still characterized by the eternal object 'green', has persisted into the present and that the contemporary members of that nexus are located in a particular region in the present. (To make our discussion independent of diagram 21, we may restate our point more generally: the percipient judges that the chain of causal activity will continue with such-and-such a characteristic into a certain region within the present.) In addition, the percipient P has a perception in presentational immediacy of a green image as located at some region in its strain locus. In the perception in symbolic reference, P judges that the region upon which it has projected the green sensum is the same region where it has estimated the contemporary members of the nexus G, G_1, and G_2 to be located. And P further judges that the eternal object 'green'—which is felt as an extended sensum in the presentational immediacy—is, in fact, the eternal object which characterizes the contemporary actual entities in the nexus G, G_1, and G_2. (Stated more generally, the percipient further judges [A] that the image in the strain locus illustrates that region where the causal chain enters the present and [B] that the sensum felt in presentational immediacy is the eternal object which genuinely characterizes the chain of causal activity as it enters the present.) In short, the percipient conceives the image felt in presentational immediacy to be the adequate representation of the contemporary extension of the nexus felt in the physical purpose.[3]

In Chapter Six, Section III, we discussed symbolic transference. In perception in symbolic reference, we find such transference at work. In general terms, we may say that the vagueness of causal efficacy is made sharp by the presentational immediacy, and the shallowness of presentational immediacy is given depth by causal efficacy (PR 273b). Turning first to the fact that the shallowness of presentational immediacy is given depth by causal efficacy, we note that in ordinary human experience we do not merely experience images extended in space; rather, we experience con-

---

3. It may be noted that Whitehead does not explicitly state that a perception in symbolic reference makes precisely this connection between the object felt in causal efficacy and the object felt in presentational immediacy. However, as we will discuss below, when Whitehead explains how error enters into a perception in symbolic reference, he refers precisely to the breakdown of the kind of connection between the object in causal efficacy and the object in presentational immediacy which we have outlined.

crete objects in the real world. The difference between a mere image and a concrete object may be stated this way. A mere image lacks efficacy, while an object possesses precisely such efficacy. A mere image tells no tales of its origin or of its future, while a concrete object has a history and a destiny. A mere image makes no difference to those entities which will come after it, while a concrete object will continue to influence those entities which will come after. But if what is directly seen in presentational immediacy is a mere image,[4] how then does that mere image become a part of the concrete object which is perceived in ordinary human experience? The answer is that the perception in symbolic reference connects that image with a nexus felt in causal efficacy; and then, by the category of symbolic transference, the feeling of efficacy which is associated with that nexus is 'precipitated' upon the image. And so, since the image is in the percipient's contemporary world, the result of this symbolic transference is that the percipient feels a contemporary image as though it were itself efficacious—in short, the percipient feels a concrete object in its contemporary world. Concerning our experience of seeing a gray stone, Whitehead writes:

> The two modes are unified by a blind symbolic reference by which supplemental feelings derived from the intensive, but vague, mode of efficacity are precipitated upon the distinct regions illustrated in the mode of immediacy. The integration of the two modes in supplemental feeling makes what would have been vague to be distinct, and what would have been shallow to be intense. This is the perception of the grey stone, in the mixed mode of symbolic reference (PR 273b).

We now turn to the fact that, by symbolic transference, the vagueness of causal efficacy is made sharp by presentational immediacy. We note that the position of objects in perceptions in causal efficacy are but dimly perceived. Of course, the objects in themselves are determinately positioned, but the percipient's prehension of that position is fuzzy. (We discussed this topic in Section II of Chapter Seven.) Perceptions in presentational immediacy position their objects with a high degree of clarity. (The manifold reasons for this are discussed in Chapter Nine.) The perception in symbolic reference utilizes this high degree of precision to elucidate the position of the object felt in causal efficacy. The perception in symbolic reference can utilize the precision of the presentational immediacy in this way because it (i.e., the perception in symbolic reference) considers the image felt in presentational immediacy to be located in the region where the nexus (felt in the physical purpose) continues into the present, and because it also considers the extended image to be the eter-

---

4. However, as we pointed out in footnote 15 on page 203, even at the level of pure presentational immediacy the image is perceived with some sense of efficacity. Nevertheless, it is our position that it is only in symbolic reference that this image is *fully* invested with this sense of efficacity.

nal object which, in fact, characterizes the actual entities occupying the region where that image is projected. Thus, by symbolic transference, the sense of precision which characterizes the perception of the image in presentational immediacy is precipitated upon the nexus which is felt in causal efficacy. Sometimes Whitehead calls the nexuses felt in the physical purposes "chains of causal activity." So we may also say that the perceptions in presentational immediacy are used by the perceptions in symbolic reference to help us pick out those chains of causal activity in our environment which are so crucially important—either positively or negatively—for our life and well-being.

At this point it may be good to bring in a possible objection to Whitehead's theory of perception (at least as we have interpreted it). Is Whitehead being redundant? We may explain the charge of redundancy as follows. Let us return once more to diagram 21. It will be recalled that, in one of its physical purposes, percipient P felt the nexus G, G_1, and G_2 as a transmuted unit characterized by some eternal object. In a later propositional feeling, P projects that eternal object into its strain locus as an extended sensum; the result is the perception in presentational immediacy of the image I. As we explained previously, in order to create that perception of the image I, the percipient P first creates a nexus which includes G, G_1, and G_2 as well as the region upon which I will be projected; this entire nexus is characterized by the eternal object which was derived from G, G_1, and G_2 and which will be the sensum projected in the presentational immediacy. Lastly, the final perception in presentational immediacy cuts off that portion of this larger nexus which is in the strain locus, resulting in a sensum extended in the locus. But—and this is the important point — Whitehead seems to be saying that in symbolic reference the sensum felt in the perception in presentational immediacy as extended in the locus is reunited with that nexus felt in the physical purpose—in terms of diagram 21, the nexus composed of G, G_1, and G_2. This, however, evokes the question, "Has not Whitehead simply used symbolic reference to recreate the larger nexus which the perception in presentational immediacy split apart? And if so, then is it not redundant to split apart this larger nexus in the perception in presentational immediacy, only to have it reformed in the perception in symbolic reference? We seem to be spinning our wheels here."

Our response to this objection has two parts. First, the larger nexus before it is split apart by presentational immediacy (A) is not the object of a propositional feeling, (B) is not placed in the pure geometrical-mathematical forms of the strain locus, and, therefore (C) its position is not prehended by the percipient with any great precision. Consequently, if we want to have the precision of a perception in presentational immediacy, we must first create a pure mathematical-geometrical strain locus, and project a sensum upon some region in that locus. Therefore it is not until the percipient cuts off the portion of that larger nexus which lies in the strain locus that it has a perception of an object—namely, the extended sensum—which is (A) placed in the pure mathematical-geometrical forms of a strain locus, and (B) is the object of a propositional feeling, and, therefore, (C) has its position prehended with any genuine precision. In short, unless the percipient splits up the larger nexus, it cannot gain, in its later perception in symbolic reference, the significant advantage of precision— which is the gift of presentational immediacy.

There is another answer which we may also give to our objector. Let us grant that the perception in presentational immediacy (or a subordinate strain feeling) splits apart the larger nexus, retaining only the portion of that larger nexus which constitutes the sensum extended in the strain locus. In point of fact, however, the perception in symbolic reference does *not* re-create or re-form or re-constitute that original larger nexus! Rather, we are dealing here with a case of symbolism, and the perception in symbolic reference uses the presence of the extended sensum to *evoke* or *elicit* the nexus (originally felt in the physical purpose) into greater effectiveness in the production of intense feeling in the percipient's satisfaction. We may state this alternatively: the percipient uses the presence of the nexus felt in the physical purpose to evoke or elicit the extended sensum into greater effectiveness in the production of intensity. In fact, Whitehead seems to think that, to a certain extent at least, in its perception in symbolic reference, the percipient uses (A) the presence of the extended sensum and (B) the presence of the nexus to evoke each other into greater effectiveness in the production of intense feelings. But in no case does the percipient simply reconstitute—in its perception in symbolic reference or elsewhere—that larger nexus which the perception in presentational immediacy (or a subordinate strain feeling) had split apart. Rather, the perception in symbolic reference uses the presence of two disconnected and separated sections of that greater nexus to elicit each other into greater effectiveness within that concrescence. This is not the same as the reconstruction of that greater nexus. Therefore, Whitehead is not being redundant in having the percipient first split the "greater nexus" only to have that percipient "reconstitute" that greater nexus in a perception in symbolic reference — for, in fact, this greater nexus never is "reconstituted."

III

Symbolic reference is a particular form of symbolism. Therefore, the general characteristics of symbolism apply to perception in symbolic reference also. One of the general characteristics of symbolism—which we discussed in Section III of Chapter Six—is that the concrescing entity *chooses* to put two sets of percepts into the relation of symbol to meaning. In themselves, the percepts do not necessitate that they be put into a symbolic relation nor do they determine, if they are put into a symbolic relation, which will serve as symbol and which will serve as meaning. This is also true of symbolic reference. The presence in a percipient of a nexus felt in causal efficacy and the presence of an extended sensum do not guarantee the emergence of a perception in symbolic reference—and this remains the case no matter how closely related that extended sensum and that past nexus may be. Again, it is a general characteristic of symbolism that, if two sets of percepts are related symbolically, there is no reason intrinsic to those percepts why either set could not be the symbols or the meanings. Since symbolic reference is a species of symbolism, we should not be surprised to discover that when perception in symbolic reference does emerge, either the precept felt in causal efficacy or the percept felt in presentational immediacy can serve as the meaning and either can serve as the symbol.

It does seem to be an empirical fact, however, that in human perception we normally find the percept felt in presentational immediacy acting as the symbol which elicits the percept felt in causal efficacy which, in this case, plays the role of the meaning (PR 271a). In fact, this can be extended to a general principle. Typically, the direction of the symbolic relation is from the less primitive percept as symbol to the more primitive perception in meaning (S 10a). It must be immediately noted, however, that this general principle is not a hard and fast law; there are exceptions.[5] Moreover, it would be a rare perception in symbolic reference in which each percept did not elicit the other into greater effectiveness, at least to some degree. Therefore, in symbolic reference, the extended sensum serves as a symbol and the nexus serves as the meaning only "for the most part in most cases."

IV

In symbolic reference, the possibility of error enters the concrescence for the first time. Both perception in causal efficacy and perception in presentational immediacy are inherently free from error—which is not true for symbolic reference. If a perception in symbolic reference does happen to err, in what does that error consist? Whitehead comments on this subject as follows.

> Such perception can be erroneous, in the sense that the feeling associates regions in the presented locus [i.e., the strain locus] with inheritances

---

5. For example, in a dark room, my intuitive perception of (i.e., my perception in causal efficacy of) some center of activity may elicit some faint and shadowy form into greater prominence within my visual field. (Or my intuition may stimulate my awareness of some faint sound or odor in the darkness.)

from the past, which in fact have not been thus transmitted into the present regions. In the mixed mode, the perceptive determination is purely due to the bodily organs, and thus there is a gap in the perceptive logic—so to speak. This gap is not due to any conceptual freedom on the part of the ultimate subject. It is not a mistake due to consciousness. It is due to the fact that the body, as an instrument for synthesizing and enhancing feelings, is faulty, in the sense that it produces feelings which have but slight reference to the real state of the presented duration [the duration associated with the strain locus] (PR 274a; cf. AI 314c-23a; bracketed comments added).

We may make several observations about the nature of error in symbolic reference on the basis of this passage. We assume that the percipient projected a sensum onto some region of the strain locus because it is estimated that the actual entities in that region are the contemporary representatives of a nexus (whose past members are) felt in causal efficacy. Therefore, there are two ways in which the percipient can err in its perception in symbolic reference. First, the percipient errs when it assigns a sensum to a region, if the actual entities occupying that region are not themselves characterized by that sensum. Second, the percipient errs when it uses a sensum extended in the locus to elicit a nexus felt in causal efficacy, if the actual entities (occupying that region of the locus) are not, in fact, the contemporary representatives of that nexus felt in causal efficacy.

A percipient's perception in symbolic reference is erroneous if it makes either of these two mistakes—it is not required that the percipient make both mistakes at once. For example, a percipient's perception in symbolic reference would be wrong if (A) it was in error about the exact sensum which characterizes the actual entities occupying the region upon which that sensum had been projected, even though (B) that percipient is quite correct in its estimation that the actual entities in that region are the contemporary representatives of the nexus felt in causal efficacy. Such a situation could come about if the nexus in question had changed—say from the color green to the color yellow—between the time of the concrescence of its past members (felt in causal efficacy) and the time of the concrescence of its contemporary members (occupying the region of the strain locus upon which the sensum is projected). Such an error could also occur if there was a reversion along the line of transmission from the past members of that nexus to the final percipient. (In diagram 21, actual entities G, E, O, B, and P are members of such a line of transmission.)

On the other hand, the percipient would also have an erroneous perception in symbolic reference if it made the second type of mistake without making the first. That is, a percipient's perception in symbolic reference would be wrong if (A) it elicited a nexus felt in causal efficacy by means of a sensum extended in some region of its strain locus, where the actual entities in that region are *not* the contemporary representatives of the nexus felt in causal efficacy—and yet (B) the percipient may commit this error even though the actual entities occupying that region are, in fact, characterized by the very sensum which the percipient projected upon that region! Such a situation could come about if, between the time the past members of that nexus concresced and the time the contemporary members of the nexus concresce, there was a radical change in the percipient's environment—a change which destroyed or at least deflected the expected path of that nexus, while causing the actual entities in the region illustrated by the sensum to be characterized by that same sensum. For example, suppose that I am looking at a red glass on my desk. The past members of the nexus—of the red glass—concresced a fraction of a second before. On the basis of my perception in causal efficacy of those members of the nexus, I project a red sensum into the strain locus at approximately the region where I estimate that the contemporary members of the red glass are situated. But suppose that, during that fraction of a second between the concrescence of the past members of the red glass which I perceived in causal efficacy and the concrescence of the contemporary actual entities which are located in the section of the strain locus where I have projected that red sensum, a bomb exploded! Now the actual entities in the region upon which I have projected the red sensum may, in fact, be characterized by the eternal object 'red'. But they are no longer red *because* they are the outcome of the nexus we called the red glass; rather, they are red *because* they are the outcome of the bomb blast. Therefore, when in symbolic reference, I used that red sensum in the locus to elicit the red-glass-nexus which I had felt in causal efficacy, the result was that my perception in symbolic reference became erroneous.

Lastly, it is possible for a percipient to create a perception in symbolic reference which errs in both respects, that is, the sensum in question illustrates some region in the strain locus which is occupied by actual entities characterized by a different eternal object *and* those actual entities occupying the region upon which the sensum has been projected are not the outcome of the nexus felt in causal efficacy which the percipient elicited by the use of that extended sensum.

This discussion brings us to another point in our interpretation of symbolic reference. Whitehead claims that a pure perception in presentational immediacy (e.g., a perception of a mirror image) is itself not subject to being delusory (S 24a, AI 309b). In the section on presentational immediacy, we explained that such a perception in presentational immediacy was free from the possibility of error because the entire perception was constructed out of the materials present in the real internal nature of the percipient. That is, the presentational immediacy is free from error because it is concerned solely with the *objective natures* of the entities occupying the region where the extended sensum is perceived. The perception in symbolic reference, however, *is* subject to error; this is because in the symbolic reference, the percipient's concern is transferred to the *for-*

mal natures of (A) the entities occupying the region where the extended sensum is perceived in presentational immediacy *and* to the *formal natures* of (B) the nexus felt in causal efficacy. It is this switch in emphasis from the objective natures of these entities to their formal natures which accounts for the possibility of error entering at this point.

In the passage quoted in the beginning of this section, Whitehead attributes the development of error to the preconscious workings of the body; error is not the result of the intervention of consciousness. Whitehead's point seems to be that the elements which constitute the raw materials for the symbolic reference are formed in the antecedent bodily entities along the route of transmission. (In diagram 21, the series G, E, O, B, and P forms such a route of transmission.) In other words, the constituent perception in presentational immediacy of the extended sensum and the constituent perception in causal efficacy of the transmuted past nexus are both formed, primarily, in the antecedent bodily nexus along the chain of transmission. And error could result from the wrong types of reversion and/or transmutation in the genesis of the perceptions in causal efficacy and presentational immediacy.[6]

V

Do all perceptions in symbolic reference become elements in consciousness or are there some perceptions in symbolic reference which never meet the light of conscious day? This is a difficult question to answer. As noted in Section IV of Chapter One, Whitehead ascribes the rise of consciousness to the introduction of intellectual feelings. In this instance, the relevant intellectual feelings are conscious perceptions. Thus a perception in symbolic reference is conscious if it is a 'conscious perception'.

---

6. It is our opinion, however, that Whitehead overstates his case when he says that such error-producing reversions are *never* to be found in the final percipient.

> In the mixed mode, the perceptive determination is *purely* due to the bodily organs. . . . This gap is *not* due to *any* conceptual freedom on the part of the ultimate subject. It is *not* a mistake due to consciousness (PR 274a; emphases added).

Why may not there be some situations in which the final percipient *intends* to produce an inaccurate perception? An artist friend once told me that sometimes when he is sculpting he will concentrate so hard upon the potential forms in his clay that he begins to "see" those potential forms. And these forms strike him with just as much "reality," force, and vivacity as do the actual forms of the clay. In fact, sometimes the actual forms are blocked out; and while gazing at the clay he "sees" only the potential forms. Again, it is a well-known psychological phenomenon that "wish-fulfillment" sometimes causes a hallucination. (And, if we are to believe the analytic psychiatrists, this wish-fulfillment—which is clearly a kind of conceptuality—may be preconscious as well as conscious.) Why may we not attribute such artistic "seeing" and such hallucinations, at least partially, to the role of conceptuality on the part of the ultimate percipient?

It appears that a perception in symbolic reference is, at most, a candidate for inclusion in such 'conscious perceptions'. We can show this as follows. First, by definition, a conscious perception is the prehension of a contrast—namely, the contrast between (A) a proposition felt by a perceptive propositional feeling, where the logical subjects have been reduced to mere 'its', and (B) those same logical subjects in their status as fully clothed actual entities, before being stripped to mere 'its'. But given this technical definition of a conscious perception, we may conclude that a perception in symbolic reference is not a 'conscious perception.' This is because the proposition which enters into a perception in symbolic reference is the proposition which was previously felt in the perception in presentational immediacy—namely, the sensum as illustrating a region in the locus. In this proposition, the logical subjects are the entities which occupy the region upon which the sensum is projected. In a perception in symbolic reference, however, this proposition is not compared with the fully clothed logical subjects of that proposition. Rather, this proposition is used to elicit an entirely different group of actual entities; it is used to elicit the actual entities in the past nexus which served as the source of the eternal object/sensum in question. Therefore, a perception in symbolic reference does not meet the definition of a 'conscious perception'.

Does this mean, however, that, apart from further integrations into conscious perceptions, a perception in symbolic reference is in *no* sense conscious? Perhaps it does, but the issue is somewhat unclear. From Section IV in Chapter One, it will also be recalled that Whitehead tends to associate the rise of consciousness with the rise of intellectual feelings because the intellectual feelings include an affirmation-negation contrast. That is, an intellectual feeling will contrast the (A) logical subjects as they are *potentially* characterized with (B) the logical subjects as they are *actually* characterized. Thus the affirmation-negation contrast is really an actuality-potentiality contrast. Now there is a sense in which *every* perception in symbolic reference expresses an actuality-potentiality contrast. The object of the perception in presentational immediacy is a proposition; a proposition expresses potentiality. The object of the perception in causal efficacy is a transmuted nexus; this transmuted nexus is felt as an actual fact in the concrete world. In a perception in symbolic reference this potentiality (i.e., the proposition) is used to elicit the actuality (i.e., the transmuted nexus). Thus, in every perception in symbolic reference, we find the interplay of potentiality and actuality. Therefore, to the extent that consciousness is associated with the contrast between actuality and potentiality, we should expect that the first glimmerings of consciousness will appear in the subjective forms of any perception in symbolic reference. Of course, the contrast between actuality and potentiality is much more sharply drawn in conscious perceptions and in intuitive judgments. (After all, in conscious perceptions and intuitive judgments, the *same* actual entities are felt both as potentially characterized in the proposition and as actually characterized in their own right.) And so, consciousness is also much more sharply developed in these intellectual feelings than it is in perceptions in symbolic reference. Nevertheless, we would be wise not to eliminate entirely the possibility of finding the germ of consciousness present in all perceptions in symbolic reference.

VI

Conscious perceptions are a form of intellectual feelings. The other variety of intellectual feelings are intuitive judgments. The generic characteristics of intuitive judgments, which we discussed in Chapters One and Three, also apply to conscious perceptions. We will, thus, highlight only two of the central characteristics of conscious perception.

First, a conscious perception, like an intuitive judgment, is ambiguous between the sense in which it refers to the real internal constitution of the percipient and the sense in which that conscious perception refers to the formal natures of the dative actual entities in question. Speaking of conscious perceptions, Whitehead writes:

> It is to be observed that what is in doubt is not the immediate perception of a nexus which is a fragment of the actual world. The dubitable element is the definition of this nexus by the observed predicate (PR 411d-12a).

Second, the relation of truth to conscious perceptions and to symbolic reference is somewhat complicated. Previously in this chapter (primarily in Section IV, pp. 216-19), we discussed the nature of truth and error in relation to perceptions in symbolic reference. The possibility of error emerges because, in a symbolic perception, the percipient is concerned with the formal natures of the various actual entities.[7]

With regard to the *content* of the truth or error of the perception in symbolic reference, Whitehead has a correspondence theory of truth.

7. Whitehead seems to be interested in symbolic reference only insofar as it applies to the formal natures of the various actual entities. It is the function of a perception in symbolic reference, in Whitehead's system, to make the transition from an emphasis on the *objectified* actual entities (which is the case with both perception in causal efficacy and perception in presentational immediacy) to an emphasis on the *formal* natures of these entities.

We can also, however, analyze a perception in symbolic reference strictly in relation to the real internal nature of the percipient (in which case it would always be true). We cannot totally purge perception in symbolic reference from a connection with the objectified natures of the actual entities because perceptions in symbolic reference are sometimes integrated into 'conscious perceptions' (in Whitehead's technical definition). And, for reasons we mention in the main text, we must be able, in certain instances, to interpret conscious perceptions as dealing primarily with the real internal nature of the percipient, that is, with the actual entities as objectified. To retain this possibility for the *later* conscious perception, we must preserve this aspect of the *earlier* perception in symbolic reference.

There is a correspondence (or lack of it) between the perception in symbolic reference and the formal natures of the various actual entities. The perception itself, however, cannot judge its own truth or falsity. On this correspondence theory of truth, the perception in symbolic reference will *be* true or false; but the *criteria* for determining that truth or falsity are not part of that perception in symbolic reference. Rather, to find such criteria we must turn to conscious perceptions.

A conscious perception may be called an evaluation of the veridicality or erroneousness of the perception in symbolic reference. It evaluates whether or not there exists a correspondence between the perception in symbolic reference and the formal natures of the various actual entities. Of course, this is not to say that the only function of conscious perceptions is to provide such an evaluation—or even that the primary function of conscious perceptions is to provide such an evaluation. Their primary function is to contribute to the intensity of the percipient's final satisfaction. And for this purpose the veridicality or erroneousness of the constituent perception in symbolic reference may be irrelevant. For example, in savoring the delicate beauty of the Northern Lights as reflected in an arctic pool of still water, the question of the literal veridicality of the perception in symbolic reference is wholly beside the point. Nevertheless, conscious perceptions can provide such an evaluation of the veridicality of the constituent perception in symbolic reference. Conscious perceptions as the evaluations of the truth or falsity of symbolic reference are not themselves true or false. Conscious perceptions are better described as correct or incorrect.

This raises the question of the nature of the correctness or incorrectness of the conscious perception. To the extent that we are dealing with the formal natures of the actual entities in question, the possibility of incorrect conscious perceptions arises.

There are three levels at which we may look at the nature of this correctness or incorrectness of a conscious perception. On one level, experience has shown us that accurate and correct conscious perceptions tend to be forcefully vivid; also, they lie open to direct inspection.

> There are two immediate guarantees of the correctness of a conscious perception: one is Hume's test of 'force and vivacity,' and the other is the illumination by consciousness of the various feelings involved in the process. Thus the fact, that the physical feeling has not transmuted concept into physical bond, lies open for inspection. Neither of these tests is infallible (PR 411c).

At the second level, we may check to see how well the conscious perception coheres with other conscious perceptions. Whitehead has primarily in mind the coherence between the conscious perceptions in earlier and later members of an enduring object. This is the coherence theory of truth—or, more accurately, the coherence theory of the correctness of our conscious perceptions. (We note that the truth of a perception in symbolic reference is not created by, nor consists in, its coherence with other perceptions; that is, coherence does not provide us with the "being," with the "essence," or with the "identity" of a perception's veridicality. Rather, a true perception coheres with other perceptions because it is already a true perception, and so this coherence only provides us with a *test* for showing *that* a certain perception in symbolic reference is, or is not, true.)

> There is also the delayed test, that the future conforms to expectations derived from this assumption. This latter test can be realized only by future occasions in the life of an enduring object, the enduring percipient (PR 411c).

> In a slightly narrower sense the symbolism can be right or wrong; and rightness or wrongness is also tested pragmatically. Along the 'historic route' there is the inheritance of feelings derived from symbolic reference: now, if feelings respecting some definite element in experience be due to two sources, one source being this inheritance, and the other source being direct perception in one of the pure modes, then, if the feelings from the two sources enhance each other by synthesis, the symbolic reference is right; but, if they are at variance so as to depress each other, the symbolic reference is wrong (PR 275b).

This emphasis on the coherence of perceptions brings us to the third level, that is, to an emphasis on the real internal nature of the percipient. At some point along the line of the 'historic route' of percipients, one of these percipients must evaluate whether this coherence has been achieved. That is, some percipient must have objectified the perceptions which will serve as the test case. Then the percipient must evaluate whether these perceptions *as they exist objectively within the percipient* match as expected.

> So much of human experience is bound up with symbolic reference, that it is hardly an exaggeration to say that the very meaning of truth is pragmatic. But though this statement is *hardly* an exaggeration, still it *is* an exaggeration, for the pragmatic test can never work, unless on some occasion—in the future, or in the present—there is a definite determination of what is true on that occasion. Otherwise the poor pragmatist remains an intellectual Hamlet, perpetually adjourning decision of judgment to some later date (PR 275b).

PART THREE: LANGUAGE

PART THREE EXAMINES ALFRED NORTH WHITEHEAD'S PHILOSOPHY OF LAN-
GUAGE. The context of our discussion is his theory of propositions and
his theory of perception, as presented in Parts One and Two. In Part Four
we will discuss the implications of his philosophy of language for his
philosophy of religion.

12 *A Metaphysical Description of Language*

IN THIS CHAPTER, we will set Whitehead's theory of language within the framework of his metaphysical system.

I

Perhaps Whitehead's most basic claim about language is that language elicits propositional prehensions. This claim is basic in the sense that (A) it occurs in one of Whitehead's most technically developed passages in *Process and Reality* and (B) it provides a context in terms of which most of his other claims about language can be organized. Whitehead writes:

> Spoken language is merely a series of squeaks. Its function is (α) to arouse in the prehending subject some physical feeling indicative of the logical subjects of the proposition, (β) to arouse in the prehending subject some physical feeling which plays the part of the 'physical recognition,' (γ) to promote the sublimation of the 'physical recognition' into the conceptual 'predicative feeling,' (δ) to promote the integration of the indicative feeling and the predicative feeling into the required propositional feeling (PR 403d [403f in corrected edition]).

In this passage, Whitehead is merely rehearsing the genesis of a propositional feeling within the concrescence of an actual entity. In addition, Whitehead has carefully worded his description of the genesis of a propositional feeling so that it applies equally well to imaginative propositional feelings and to perceptive propositional feelings. Clearly, then, the function of language is to promote the production of propositional prehensions.

Language, thus, is a form of symbolism. As we saw in Chapter Six, the term "symbolism" has a variety of meanings in Whitehead's metaphysical system. In a narrow sense, it refers to sense perception (S 2-5). In a somewhat broader sense, however, language also may be said to function symbolically (S 2a-b). We may define symbolism, in this broad sense, as follows. A concrescing actual entity employs symbolism when that entity uses one component in its experience to elicit, promote, foster, identify, isolate, or enhance another component in its experience (cf. S 7d-8a).

This raises a question of terminology which we must address. As we saw in Section I of Chapter Six, Whitehead normally uses 'symbolism' to refer to a relation between the data of various prehensions. As we also argued in Chapter Six, however, it is legitimate to extend the term 'symbolism' to cover the prehensions themselves, as Whitehead himself does on occasion. In the passage quoted at the beginning of this Section, Whitehead describes the function of language as "arousing" and "promoting" a propositional feeling and not just a proposition. Moreover, we will shortly observe that language functions in connection with some form of sense perception. As we shall demonstrate in some detail in this chapter, language involves the entire sense perception and not just the object of the sense perception. The question is this: Is the use of the term 'symbolism' to be limited to the relation between the sense data and the propositions, or should its use extend to the linguistic relation between the entire sense perceptions and the entire propositional prehensions? This question applies, for example, to the quotation at the beginning of this section. Is the "arousing" and "promoting" described there a form of symbolism?

To answer this question, we observe that, in his references to language, Whitehead continues his normal pattern of using the word 'symbolism' to describe only the data of the sense perception and the felt propositions. He uses other terms, such as "integration," to describe the relation between the sense perception as such and the propositional prehension as such.

We will follow Whitehead's example. In the following description of language, we will restrict the term 'symbolism' to the relation between the sense data and the propositions, and we will use terms such as "elicits" or "integrates" to describe the relation between the entire sense perception and the entire propositional prehension. Yet it remains the case that, if one accepts the definition of symbolism offered above, it follows that the linguistic relation between the sense perceptions and the propositional prehensions is, in a broad but important sense, "symbolic." Thus the sense perception as a whole is an item in the experience of the language-user which is used to "elicit, promote, foster, identify, isolate, or arouse" the propositional prehension. This is Whitehead's very point in the quotation earlier in this section. It would be artificial, thus, to deny that the linguistic relation between the sense perception and the propositional prehension is, in some broad sense, "symbolic." If the reader were to use the term "symbolism" in reference to the relation between the entire prehensions (or perceptions) and not just in relation to the data of the prehensions (or perceptions), it would not alter, so far as we can tell, the metaphysical description of language offered in this chapter.

There are two sides in any act of symbolizing. The one side serves as the symbol, the other as the symbolized. In the case of spoken language, the sounds—the series of squeaks—form the one side, and the specified proposition forms the other. In the case of written language, some type of visual shapes constitutes the one side, while yet again, a proposition constitutes the other. While spoken and written language are the most important examples, other varieties of language do exist. For example, there is the language of Indian smoke signals; there is the hand language for the deaf; and people have even communicated linguistically by means of taps directly on skin, where a system such as Morse code was used to interpret the taps. Moreover, there are numerous borderline cases. For example, in Oriental dance, the movements may become so stylized that various positions and motions "mean" certain things; and thus there is a correct story to be inferred from the dance. Is this language? Clearly, if we should describe such a dance as a form of language, our description would be more than merely metaphorical. In any case, there remain two overwhelmingly common forms of language, spoken and written. And according to Whitehead, the spoken form is the more fundamental of the two (MT 44d-46a; MT 90c).

From our rapid survey of the types of language, we make the following inference. Language always operates in connection with some form of sense experience.[1] In spoken language, we hear sounds; in written language, we see certain shapes; in the tapping of Morse code, we feel the taps; in the hand language, we see certain hand positions and movements; and even in the Oriental dance, we see certain bodily configurations. Whitehead has observed this fact, and he often points to the presence of sensory experience in linguistic situations (PR 261a, 264b, 272b; MT 46b, 48c).

Whitehead's theory of sense perception—or sense experience or symbolic reference in the narrow sense—is extraordinarily nuanced and complicated. We have considered this theory at some length in Part Two. At this point, we will only note that normal human sense perception results from the interaction of the two simpler types of perception, perception in causal efficacy and perception in presentational immediacy. Both of these are typically components in an instance of sense perception. Therefore, both forms of primitive perception have their roles to play in the use of sense perception for linguistic purposes.

---

1. We will later consider the problem of interior language, that is, language as it operates when a person is merely thinking about something and not talking "out loud."

II

To illustrate the uses of causal efficacy and presentational immediacy in language, let us turn to a concrete situation. Suppose that I am in my study when I hear my wife say, "You really look tired." There are two sides to this situation. There is my wife who spoke the words; and there is myself, who hears the words. Let us consider the hearer's side first. On the hearer's side we must consider two related points. First, the hearer must be able to distinguish the words, "You really look tired," from all *other* possible words, such as "Beth called, and our first grandchild is a girl!" Second, the hearer must be able to recognize the *same* words, "You really look tired" on two different occasions. Both these points are necessary if language is to succeed as an instrument of communication among people. That is, on the one hand, a hearer who cannot distinguish among *different* words, will not know which *particular* words the speaker meant to utter. On the other hand, without the ability to recognize the *same* words in different contexts, the hearer would not be able to draw upon past experience in order to understand the words of the speaker—and without that ability, language as we know it would fail to communicate.

Both the diversity and the identity of the spoken forms are functions of the hearer's perceptions in presentational immediacy. Let us return to our example of my hearing the words, "You really look tired." Obviously, the aural configurations of "You really look tired" are quite unlike those of "Beth called, and our first grandchild is a girl!" But anything which I would be likely to consider as components in such aural configurations would be a part of the associated perceptions in presentational immediacy. For example, the volume of the sound in question, its pitch, its location, its smoothness and harmony, and its harshness and dissonance—these are all perceived in the mode of presentational immediacy. Thus, in one sense, what constitutes a sound as a word is the presentational immediacy. That is, the *difference* in aural configurations —say, between the sounds in "You really look tired" and those in "Beth called, and our first grandchild is a girl!"—is nothing other than a difference in the contents of the associated perceptions in presentational immediacy. But we may also say that I am able to recognize a word as the *same* word in a diversity of contexts because there is a similarity of pattern to my perceptions in presentational immediacy in each of those contexts.[2]

Presentational immediacy has another role to play in the linguistic situation from the point of view of the hearer. Images in presentational im-

---

2. Also exactly analogous conditions hold, if we imagine these two phrases to be communicated in written language rather than in spoken language.

mediacy are easily abstracted from their environment.[3] Other elements in our experience—such as perceptions in causal efficacy (or its data) or even propositional prehensions—are hard to isolate and even harder to manipulate. That is, the images of presentational immediacy are easily isolated, freely manipulated, and readily brought to the center of the percipient's attention. Thus the linguistic usefulness of images perceived in presentational immediacy becomes clear. Since such images can—in comparison with other elements—be easily isolated from their connections with the rest of the universe, and since such images can be freely manipulated into the focus of attention, it follows that as the hearer of the words, "You really look tired," I can react more quickly and assuredly to the aural images perceived in presentational immediacy than I can to other elements in my experience. (At least this is true most of the time.)[4] Thus there is a vast gain in our ability to use meanings whey they are symbolized by images in presentational immediacy. This is because we can directly isolate and manipulate the images, thereby indirectly isolating and manipulating the meanings which are the true carriers of thought and insight.

At this point, we will consider a possible objection to Whitehead's theory of language as we have developed it. The objector argues that we have one proposition symbolizing another proposition, which means that we are merely spinning our wheels. The objector notes that, according to Whitehead, whenever we use language, we use spoken or written words to elicit certain propositional prehensions (as clearly demonstrated by the first quotation in this chapter). The objector continues: According to Whitehead, presentational immediacy is an important element in our perceptions of words. But—and here is the rub—Whitehead also holds that a perception in presentational immediacy is itself a propositional prehension! Thus, in the linguistic act, one proposition (which is involved in the sense perception) symbolizes another proposition (which is the meaning). Our objector continues: If a proposition is intractable to isolation and manipulation when it serves as the meaning of a sentence, then why is a proposition not also intractable when it serves as an element in our per-

---

3. We discussed this point at length in Chapter Ten, and we will assume the results of that discussion.

4. Occasionally, however, we find ourselves in the position of knowing very well what proposition the speaker means to symbolize, while at the same time trying to figure out exactly what sounds the speaker made. For example, I know just enough Spanish to ask for directions to this-or-that location. Usually, by catching a word here or there, and by carefully observing my informant's hand motions and body motions, and by knowing in vague terms what a likely answer might be, I am able to figure out the answer given me—that is, I am able to prehend the appropriate proposition. But at the same time, Spanish has an unfamiliar lilt and uses sounds which I cannot duplicate. It sometimes happens that not only do I not catch most of the words my informant has used, but in addition I find myself in the position of not even catching the sounds which were uttered. And yet, at the same time, I have indeed grasped the intended proposition.

ceptions of the spoken or written words? In short, how can the propositions in our perceptions of spoken and written words serve to elicit and identify the "intractable" propositions which serve as meanings?

We respond as follows. There is a difference between just any proposition and the specific kind of proposition which *is* a sensum as extended in the strain locus. Presentational immediacy is an element in any propositional prehension which functions in a perception of the spoken and written words. The dominant characteristics of presentational immediacy, however, all relate to the strain locus—specifically, the predicate of the proposition felt in presentational immediacy is the image which has been projected onto a region in that strain locus; and the logical subjects of that proposition are the various subregions within that larger region upon which the sensum was projected. Thus, the strain locus gives the proposition felt in presentational immediacy its tractability and manipulability. In contrast to this, however, the propositions which are elements in the meanings of the sentences do not (on the whole) involve a strain locus. For example, it seems safe to assume that most of the propositions which are elements in the meanings of sentences have at least a few logical subjects which are in the past or future of the concrescing entity. Therefore, such propositions cannot have a predicate which is an image in a strain locus. And, consequently, such propositions must be more intractable than the propositions which do function in presentational immediacy. Moreover, even among those propositions whose logical subjects are entirely in the present, there is no reason to suppose that there is always a strain locus involved. To the extent, therefore, that the propositions which function in the meanings of our sentences do not involve a strain locus, it follows that they are more intractable and recalcitrant to manipulation than the propositions which do function in presentational immediacy, that is, than the propositions which function in our perceptions of the spoken or written words.

Sometimes language, however, does symbolize propositions which involve the projection of an image upon a region in a strain locus. This happens when language directly symbolizes the data of our sense perceptions. Thus, when language directly symbolizes our sense perceptions, one proposition using a strain locus symbolizes another proposition using a strain locus. As a result, the relation of language to sense perception will be somewhat different from the relation of language to thought — where thought involves propositions which do not use an image in a strain locus. Whereas the propositions of thought will be more or less intractable to isolation and manipulation, the propositions of sense perception will be relatively open to isolation and manipulation. This fact has some significant implications for the capacity of language to shape—as well as be shaped by—our sensory perceptions of the world. We examine some of these relations between language and sense perception in Section I of Chapter Seventeen. In the remainder of this chapter, however, we shall be primarily concerned with the relation of language to thought—that is, with the relation of language to propositions in which a strain locus is not a significant element.

III

The element of causal efficacy is also present in the hearer's perception of the sounds, "You really look tired." And this element is also important in the hearer's ability to distinguish the sounds, "You really look tired," from all other sounds as well as in the hearer's ability to recognize the same words in different contexts. In both cases, my judgment as to the source of the sounds is germane to my judgment as to what words I actually have heard. For example, if I judge that the source of the sounds is a Swede who has newly arrived in this country, I may well judge that the sound "yam" is actually the word "jam." Again, if the Swede is a professor who utters the sound "walue," I may well judge that the intended word is "value." But, my connection of a verbal sound with its source is nothing other than a connection of the image given in presentational immediacy with realities given by means of causal efficacy. Thus my judgment as to the source of the sounds I hear depends on perception in causal efficacy. And this judgment as to the source of the sounds may well affect my judgment as to what words I have actually heard.

The hearer's judgment of the source of the sounds has a more basic role to play in the linguistic context. The hearer's judgment as to the source of the sounds often—perhaps always—affects the nature of the propositional prehension associated with those sounds. For example, suppose that I hear the words "Come on!" If I judge that the source of the sounds was my wife, then I might associate those words with a propositional prehension which has to do with my moving from my chair and heading for the family car. On the other hand, if I am sitting in my study and I have just told an improbable story to a friend who is conversing with me, and if I judge that my friend is the source of the words "Come on!," then I would probably associate those words with a propositional feeling having to do with admitting that my story was not the whole truth. Thus causal efficacy enters into judgment as to the source of the sounds I hear, and it thereby has a deep role to play in the act whereby sounds — or visual shapes—symbolize propositions and elicit propositional prehensions.[5]

5. We note that all sensory perception involves causal efficacy. In the text, for the sake of simplicity, we have used cases where the "judgment" as to the source of the images was conscious. It must be observed, however, that this "judgment" associating the images given in presentational immediacy with a nexus given in causal efficacy is normally preconscious (see Chapter Eleven). Thus, usually I simply hear my wife say, "Come on!" or I sim-

Another role which causal efficacy plays in the linguistic situation from the point of view of the hearer may be stated as follows. Language in human beings is intimately connected with memory. The ability of the auditor to hear the same word in different contexts implies the ability to remember past occurrences of that word. At this point, there is no need to investigate the exact role which memory plays in this ability. Judging from a cursory examination of the author's own experiences, there is no need for this memory to be conscious. For example, when I hear my wife say, "You really look tired," I do not consciously force myself to recollect previous occurrences of those words, nor do I consciously compare those past occurrences with the current one before deciding which propositional prehension to associate with the words, "You really look tired." Rather, by invoking the use of memory in this context, we have no more in mind than the following. Typically, if I have never heard a word before, I will have a difficult — if not impossible — time understanding what it means. Occasionally, I can infer the meaning from the context. But the fact remains that normally ready and facile understanding of a word depends, among other factors, on my having previous experience with that word. Now in Whitehead's system, such memory—or dependence on previous experience—is a function of causal efficacy. The previous actual entities which constitute my past self—whether in my body or in my brain or in that thread of conscious entities which constitutes my 'soul'—are prehended by the present actual entity. But this prehension of such past actual entities is the palmary instance of perception in the mode of causal efficacy. Thus the past is incorporated into the present by means of causal efficacy. And this efficacy of the hearer's past self in the hearer's present self—call it memory or conditioning or whatever—is normally essential to the ability to understand what is heard.

We will consider one last role which causal efficacy plays in the linguistic situation from the point of view of the hearer. According to Whitehead, human experience comes drop by drop, where each drop is given as a whole and has a temporal thickness. Each of these drops corresponds to the concrescence of one of the actual entities in that dominant thread which constitutes the 'soul'. Whitehead never makes clear just how long one such concrescence can last. At one point he suggests that, for human beings, such a concrescence might commonly last from one tenth to one half of a second (AI 233a). In any case, one second is clearly beyond the outer limits of the length of time which a drop of ordinary human ex-

---

ply hear my friend say, "Come on!" I do not commonly force myself to judge consciously whether this aural image given in presentational immediacy is from my wife or from my friend. Nevertheless, while I may associate preconsciously the aural images of "Come on!" with a specific nexus—identified as my wife or my friend—it remains the case that this preconscious association often affects which propositional prehension I will connect with the words "Come on."

perience will endure. But we are now confronted with the fact that most verbal expressions take longer than one second to hear. For example, the sentence, "Would you please come here?" certainly takes longer than a second to deliver or to hear. Therefore, to assimilate this entire phrase into a coherent whole requires the passage of several actual entities in the soul thread. But the cumulative effect of grasping the whole sentence depends on the last actual entity prehending those previous actual entities in its soul thread which participated in the process of hearing the words. This process of incorporation is a prime example of perception in the mode of causal efficacy. Thus causal efficacy is a necessary factor in our grasping the unity and completeness of a whole sentence or a whole comment, whenever such sentences or phrases take more than a portion of a second to hear.[6]

IV

Let us turn now to the speaker. In our illustration, we imagined my wife had said, "You really look tired." To speak those words, my wife had to use her body to produce the appropriate sounds. Causal efficacy is an essential element in that production. We may explain this role of causal efficacy in somewhat more detail as follows. According to Whitehead, the 'soul' of my wife is a thread of actual entities, probably dwelling for the most part in the interstices of her brain (PR 163b, 166b, 167a). Further, at any one moment, only one of those actual entities in the soul thread will be in the act of concrescence. This concrescing member of the soul thread will be, at that moment, the most basic and concrete identity of my wife. The act of speaking will normally have its origin in such a concrescing member of the soul thread; in other words, this concrescing actual entity in the soul thread is the source of my wife's saying, "You really look tired." But this act of speaking cannot remain "bottled up" in this source—in this originating actual entity. All actual entities—except God—must perish and be prehended by future actual entities during *their* concrescences. Thus the originating actual entity—the source of the comment, "You real-

---

6. And, of course, this efficacy of the past in the present is also essential to the reader's ability to understand what is seen. We might add that causal efficacy is important to the hearer or the reader in less direct ways. For example, the transmission of sound waves is primarily a matter of causal efficacy; and the shapes of the letters in a book remain the same year after year because the actual entities in that book inherit from each other certain dominant characteristics which sustain the shapes of the letters, and this inheritance is a mode of causal efficacy.

Finally, we note that causal efficacy has a parallel role to play from the speaker's point of view. This is because it is also the case that the delivery of a phrase takes longer than the duration of a single member of the 'soul thread' of the speaker (as we discuss in the next section of this chapter).

ly look tired" — must also be prehended. Among those actual entities which prehended the originating actual entity are those entities which are in the brain and which are contiguous with that originating actual entity. These contiguous actual entities are in turn prehended by other actual entities in the brain. Thus a process of transmission of energy along a tract in the nervous system begins. The final result of this transmission along the nerve tract is the movement of my wife's vocal cords and mouth and lungs. The movement of her vocal cords, mouth, and lungs results in the creation of air waves. The air waves are of such a nature that a person with normal hearing can develop from them perceptions in presentational immediacy of the sounds, "You really look tired." We have at this point returned full circle to the auditor. In Chapter Ten we traced the route of transmission of information from the outside world through the body to the final percipient.[7] In the case of my wife's saying, "You really look tired," we have essentially reversed the process—from the originating actual entity, through the body, to the external environment. This route of transmission is an example of causal efficacy within the body of the speaker—as well, of course, as in the body of the hearer and in the air waves which come between the bodies of the speaker and hearer.

There is a certain fundamental nature to spoken language at this point. The fact that we speak with our vocal cords and mouths allows our hands and feet and other bodily parts to remain free. If this analysis of language is so far correct, then we could communicate by means of any of our bodily parts, provided only that the manipulation of the bodily part in question would result in routes of transmission—via light waves, sound waves, etc.—which could be "picked up" by the person with whom we wished to communicate and which that person could translate into images of presentational immediacy. Thus, as we previously noted, there could be a language of hand gestures, of dance, or even of eye winks. The problem with sign language and dance is that we cannot do much else while we are engaging in them. The problem with eye winks as a mode of communication is that the person with whom we wish to communicate must be positioned in a very limited area or else the winks will not be visible. When we use our voices, however, our other bodily parts are left free for other purposes, such as fighting, cooking, loving, sawing, and hoeing. Also, the hearer may be located in almost any position with regard to the speaker—even behind solid objects. According to Whitehead,

> It is interesting that from the alternatives, sight and sound, sound was the medium first developed. There might have been a language of gesticulation. Indeed, there is a trace of it. But the weak point of gesticulation is that one cannot do much else while indulging in it. The advantage of sound is that the limbs are left free while we produce it (MT 44d-45a).

7. See diagram 21 and the related discussion.

Causal efficacy has another role to play in the speaker's production of language. We may assume that the phrase, "You really look tired," takes a bit longer than a second to enunciate. (And in any case, most linguistic forms definitely do take longer than a second to enunciate; for example, "Our Father, Who art in heaven, hallowed be thy name.") On the other hand, very few—if any—of the actual entities in the soul thread endure for an entire second. Therefore, the enunciation of the sentence, "You really look tired," is a process which requires the passage of several of the actual entities in the soul thread.[8] And yet there is a sense of unity to my wife's act of uttering the phrase, "You really look tired." As one facet of this unity, we might cite the fact that, in almost any normal circumstance, it is hard to imagine my wife concentrating on the utterance of just one syllable at a time; rather, the phrase, "You really look tired," is spoken as a unity. According to Whitehead, the act of uttering "You . . ." leads from one syllable to the next until my wife completes that phrase by uttering ". . . tired." (AI 233b-35a). Each actual entity in the soul thread during the utterance of that phrase inherits the accomplishments of the past entities, and each entity also inherits the craving to continue the task of saying, "You really look tired"—a task which its predecessors had begun and, perhaps, partially executed. But according to Whitehead, "The immediate past as surviving to be again lived through in present is the palmary instance [of causal efficacy]" (AI 234a). And so we may conclude that there is a unity and wholeness to the act of saying, "You really look tired," because of the functioning of causal efficacy in the soul thread of the speaker as those words were uttered.

There is, however, a deeper role for causal efficacy in the speaker's production of language. As we have had occasion to observe at several points in this book, perception in the mode of causal efficacy is one of the primary sources from which a concrescing entity derives its identity and its actuality. A new actual entity begins its process of concrescence by incorporating its past actual entities into itself. These past actual entities become a part of the very identity of the new, concrescing entity. Thus the actuality and reality of the concrescing entity depend, in part, on these incorporations of past entities into itself. Such incorporations of past entities into the present, concrescing entity are the fundamental kind of perception in the mode of causal efficacy.[9] Thus our reality depends, in large measure, upon perception in causal efficacy.

---

8. Whitehead has a number of reasons for holding to this claim. One is the result of his phenomenological description of human experience (AI 233b-35a).

9. This is the fundamental kind of perception in the mode of causal efficacy in the sense that, within Whitehead's metaphysical scheme, all other forms of perception are derivative from it. This is not the most fundamental form of perception in causal efficacy in the sense that it is the most readily available for conscious human perception. See Chapter Seven, Section I.

To produce sound requires the use of the speaker's lungs, diaphragm, and throat. The exercise of these central organs may be felt by the members of the speaker's soul thread, but these feelings are vague, insistent, and gravid. From the standpoint of our conscious experience, they are peripheral overtones, sensed without (usually) being explicitly heard; in short, they are perceptions in causal efficacy. Therefore, the production of the spoken word evokes in the speaker feelings in causal efficacy—feelings of that power whereby our reality emerges and which gives us our identity. In short, the spoken word reinforces the speaker's sense of being an efficacious agent in a world of such agents. On the other hand, the use of our limbs does not usually produce these overtones of sensed-but-not-explicitly heard causal efficacy. Of course, for the soul thread to bring about movement in the arms or hands or legs does require the transmission of energy, and such transmission is the result of causal efficacy. Nevertheless, the muscular activity in these limbs does not seem to engender in the soul thread the same feelings of efficacy as does the functioning of our throat, lungs, and diaphragm. Thus a language based strictly on such movement of our limbs would tend *not* to sustain the same feeling of being a real, efficacious agent within a world of power as does spoken language (MT 44d-46a).

V

When talking aloud, the speaker is also a hearer of his own speech. Thus the speaker has a sense perception of his own speech. Like all other sense perceptions, this one also is a mixture of perception in presentational immediacy and perception in causal efficacy (barring deafness or some other impediment).

In the case of hearing oneself speak aloud, the function of causal efficacy is quite straightforward. The perception in causal efficacy allows the speaker to identify the source of the speech which he hears—the source being himself. The speaker, in short, hears *himself*; and he knows that it is himself because of the functioning of causal efficacy.

A

In Whitehead's system, however, this act of hearing oneself speak is somewhat more complicated than it may first appear. The reason is that the actual entities in the soul thread which *hear* the sounds are not the same as those actual entities which *originated* the sounds. The originating actual entities come first, while the hearing actual entities come later. Let us consider one of the originating actual entities—call it O—and one of the hearing actual entities—call it H. Both O and H are members of the speaker's soul thread; in our illustration, they are members of my wife's soul thread.

Further, O comes before H. As we saw previously, with the possible exception of the shortest, staccato phrases, the origination of a phrase is spread over several of the actual entities in the soul thread of the speaker, and likewise the hearing of that phrase is spread over several of the actual entities in the soul thread. In fact, we may assume that, in a long phrase, there are many intermediate members of the soul thread which are both originators and hearers of the sounds—although in this case, we may suppose that such an intermediate actual entity is the hearer of a syllable which was originated by a previous actual entity, while it itself is the originator of a syllable which will be heard only by a later actual entity in that soul thread. To simplify matters, we will assume that O is the first of the originating actual entities, while H is the last of the hearing actual entities. And so, to the extent that the originating and hearing of a phrase are unified acts, we may say that in an extended sense O is *the* originator and H *the* hearer of the phrase.

The dialogue with oneself—just as in the dialogue with different people—involves communication between distinct actual entities. This fact leads Whitehead to assert that, *in terms of metaphysical principle,* there is no fundamental difference between communication between two different people and communication between one's earlier and one's later self—at least to the extent that we concentrate on the case where one is speaking aloud.

> Language has two functions. It is converse with another, and it is converse with oneself. The latter function is too often overlooked, so we will consider it first. Language is expression from one's past into one's present. It is the reproduction in the present of sensa which have intimate association with the realities of the past. Thus the experience of the past is rendered distinct in the present, with a distinctness borrowed from the well-defined sensa. In this way, an articulated memory is the gift of language, considered as an expression from oneself in the past to oneself in the present (MT 46b).

B

It may be observed that we do not always speak aloud when we are thinking. We may call this process of communicating with ourselves, without the use of exterior sound waves, the "interior dialogue." In the terms established above, O can communicate with H without going outside the body. Whitehead never considers this "interior dialogue" between one's earlier self and one's later self to be any different in kind from the case in which one's earlier self communicates with one's later self aloud by means of external words. A moment's reflection will show us why. When we are thinking to ourselves, we still use words! For example, an English speaker uses English words, and a Japanese speaker uses Japanese words.

We may consider our perception of these interior words an instance of sense perception—in Whitehead's technical sense—for the following reasons. We will continue to use O and H in the senses previously defined. Part of H's perception of the interior words may be analyzed as stemming from perception in the mode of *presentational immediacy*. For example, associated with H's perception of the interior words, there are obviously aural images which are located in H's present. Further, these images have been projected into H's strain locus.[10] Again, these images have definite configurations—such as pitch, intensity, harshness, smoothness, and so forth. In this regard, it is interesting to note that my interior speech has the same accent as does my exterior, interpersonal speech. In addition, these interior images have the capacity for being isolated from the past and the future. Therefore, we may conclude that presentational immediacy does play a role in H's perception of the interior words. Perception in *causal efficacy*, however, also plays a role in H's perception of the interior words. That is, H locates the source of these interior words as somewhere in H's own body. In fact, H may judge the source of the interior words to be located within H's head. In terms of Whitehead's metaphysical scheme, we may observe that H's perception intertwines presentational immediacy and causal efficacy in such a way that this perception meets the definition of symbolic reference in the narrow form—that is, H's perception of the interior words meets the technical definition of *sense perception*.

The similarities between speaking out loud and the interior dialogue could be further developed in great detail. We will, however, confine our comments to one theme—the use of the body. The interior dialogue uses the percipient's body in much the same way as the ordinary act of speaking uses it. Consider the following illustration from the author's student years. More than once I completed a long and tense examination only to find myself with strained vocal cords! (Now I have a similar problem when completing my federal income tax forms and my daughter's financial aid form.)

Let us take a closer look at the use of the body during the interior, silent speech. We will continue to use the terms O and H in the sense previously established. In both the interior and exterior dialogues, O has a propositional prehension which it wishes to elicit. In order to elicit this propositional prehension, O inaugurates a line of transmission which, when it impinges upon percipient H, will result in H's perception of a word or phrase—where H uses that word or phrase to educe the desired

10. At this point, a question may be posed. Exactly where in that strain locus are these aural images projected? Our answer to this question is tentative and is based on introspection. It would seem that the images are projected into the strain locus at some spot within the skull of H. More precisely, the images are perceived as located within the area that H judges the contemporary representatives of the skull to be. Thus the words are literally within H's head—or at least those portions of the words which might be construed as aural images are so located.

propositional prehension. In the case of the *exterior* dialogue, the line of transmission goes from O through the brain to the nervous system. From there, the line of transmission goes to the appropriate muscles in the chest and throat. After that, the line of transmission goes to the air waves, and from the air waves it reenters the speaker's body through the ears, through the auditory canal, back to the brain, and thence to the final percipient H. In the case of the *interior* dialogue, the line of transmission goes from O to the brain—just as it does in the exterior dialogue. And, just as in the case of the exterior dialogue, the line of transmission enters H from the brain. It is not clear, however, just how much of the rest of the chain of transmission which is included in the case of the exterior dialogue is also included in the interior dialogue. Obviously, the line of transmission for the interior dialogue does not include that portion of the exterior dialogue's line of transmission which goes from the mouth to the ears by means of the air waves. On the other hand, my experience as a student of becoming hoarse from taking a "silent" exam proves that *sometimes* the line of transmission in the interior dialogue can go at least as far as the vocal cords. It is not clear, however, whether or not the interior dialogue *must* go all the way to the vocal cords. Can the interior dialogue sometimes consist entirely of a line of transmission which goes from O to the brain and from the brain back to H without ever leaving the brain? We do not know. There is, however, no reason in principle why this question could not be settled by the ordinary methods of physiology.

In summary, the interior dialogue of past self to present self is exactly like the exterior dialogue of past self to present self in this respect: in both cases, there is a chain of transmission which leaves O and goes to the brain and which returns to H from the brain. Thus in both cases H inherits from the brain a datum which allows H to project an image in presentational immediacy, and, when the perception of that image is united with a perception in causal efficacy, H has a sense perception—in Whitehead's technical sense of that term—of the word or phrase in question. Thus we have another sense in which we may observe a specific similarity between the interior dialogue and the exterior dialogue from one's past self to one's present self.

It is considerations of the sort mentioned which lead Whitehead to make the following claim.

> In this use of language for communication between two persons, there is in principle nothing which differs from its use by one person for communicating along the route of his own actual occasions (PR 278a).

C

At several points in this chapter we have had occasion to observe Whitehead's claim that spoken language is more basic than written language.

Our discussion of the interior dialogue gives us another reason to support this claim. The interior dialogue is similar to spoken language, as distinct from written language, in that the interior words and phrases are based upon aural images. Speaking personally, I do not have the ability to produce visual signs and shapes except as my eyes and optic nerves are stimulated. Note that in the interior dialogue, the aural images associated with the phantom words are projected into that portion of the strain locus which is within the skull of the percipient. In contrast, however, all the visual images are projected upon a portion of the strain locus which is outside the skull. (In fact, when I read silently, I "translate" the shapes of the letters which I see "out there" into sounds which I perceive "in here within my skull.")

There is no need to be dogmatic about this. Perhaps certain kinds of drugs would allow a percipient to perceive visual images which are projected upon the strain locus within that percipient's skull. One could image, for example, a light which emanated from some "interior" source. There may be people who can do this without drugs, perhaps having learned some type of self-hypnosis or form of meditation. But it does seem to be the case that our bodies are so constructed that most people can easily project aural images into that portion of their strain locus which lies inside their skulls, whereas it is either impossible or very difficult for them to do the same with visual images.[11] Thus the use of aural images in the interior dialogue is no accident, and so we have another basis for asserting the primacy of the spoken word over the written word.

VI

In the first pages of this chapter, we observed that language elicits propositional prehensions. We have discussed the language, that is, the words and phrases as spoken and heard or as written and read. We turn now to a discussion of the propositional prehensions. Part One of this book dealt extensively with propositional prehensions, and we may assume the results of that examination. Here we will try to relate the notions of propositions and propositional prehensions to the linguistic situation. We may divide our discussion of propositional prehensions into three parts. (A) The datum of a propositional prehension is a proposition. (B) Like all other propositions, a propositional prehension has a subjective form. And (C) the propositional prehension is constructed in accordance with the sub-

11. When we dream, do we project visual images? It is difficult to say. Could brain physiology detect traces of neural activity associated with projection of visual images during dreams? Whatever the answer, it does not alter the fact that, during ordinary consciousness, it is easier to produce and control aural than visual images. And this is the relevant issue in the case of language.

jective aim of the concrescing entity. In this section, we shall relate each of these points to the linguistic situation.

A

We turn first to the role of the proposition in the linguistic situation. We begin by noting that, for a proposition to function in a linguistic context, it is necessary that the *same proposition* be capable of being prehended by *two different actual entities.* That is, the primary use of language is for communication. But communication is always between two or more parties. If the two parties are distinct persons, then obviously there is at least one actual entity serving as the originator and one as the listener or reader. And if the two parties are simply one's past self and one's present self, it remains the case that at least two actual entities must be involved, namely, one's past self and one's present self. Therefore, if the listener (or reader) is to use language to grasp what the speaker (or writer) originates, then both the listening and the originating actual entity must be capable of prehending the same proposition. Whitehead developed a theory of propositions which allows for this possibility of the same proposition being prehended by different actual entities. (We developed this point in some detail in Chapter One, Section III.C.)

As we saw in the past paragraph, for a proposition to function in a linguistic context, it is necessary that the same proposition be capable of being prehended by two different actual entities. In addition, for a proposition to function in the linguistic context, it must also have an identity and status which is not dependent on its truth value. The reason is that, in our ordinary human acts of speaking, we sometimes try to get the person with whom we are speaking to agree with us that a certain fact is true. In other situations, truth is wholly irrelevant, as, for example, when we are telling fairy tales, making a joke, asking a question, or giving an order. Thus it is clear that Whitehead's theory must provide for the uses of language in which truth is sometimes relevant and sometimes not. Indeed, we find Whitehead elaborating precisely such a view.

> Thus the proposition is in fact true, or false. But its own truth, or its own falsity, is no business of a proposition. That question concerns only a subject entertaining a propositional feeling with that proposition for its datum. Such an actual entity is termed a 'prehending subject' of the proposition (PR 394b-95a).[12]

This brings us to our next point. Not only does Whitehead insist that propositions have an identity apart from their truth or falsity, but he is also emphatic that, of all the things humans can do with language and

---

12. For further details, see Chapter One, Section III.C.

propositions, the act of judging a proposition for its truth or falsity is neither the most common nor the most important. When expressing his concern on this topic, Whitehead writes in terms of "propositions" and not directly in terms of "language."

> Unfortunately theories, under their name of 'propositions,' have been handed over to logicians, who have countenanced the doctrine that their one function is to be judged as to their truth or falsehood. Indeed Bradley does not mention 'propositions' in his *Logic*. He writes only of 'judgments.' Other authors define propositions as a component in judgment. The doctrine here laid down is that, in the realization of propositions, 'judgment' is a very rare component, and so is 'consciousness.' The existence of imaginative literature should have warned logicians that their narrow doctrine is absurd. It is difficult to believe that all logicians as they read Hamlet's speech, "To be, or not to be: . . ." commence by judging whether the initial proposition be true or false, and keep up the task of judgment throughout the whole thirty-five lines. Surely, at some point in the reading, judgment is eclipsed by aesthetic delight. The speech, for the theater audience, is purely theoretical, a mere lure for feeling (PR 281a).
>
> The interest in logic, dominating overintellectualized philosophers, has obscured the main function of propositions in the nature of things. They are not primarily for belief, but for feeling at the physical level of unconsciousness. They constitute a source for the origination of feeling which is not tied down to mere datum (PR 283e-84a).

Of course, there will be a few occasions which do judge the truth or falsity of a proposition; but as a direct consequence of the fact that a proposition has a status which is not dependent on its truth or falsity, it follows that a proposition will retain its identity even though it is judged false by one actual entity, true by a second actual entity, and simply interesting by a third (PR 293b). And so, in the linguistic context, a proposition may be successfully communicated among actual entities despite a lack of consensus on its truth or falsity.

The fact remains, however, that, on Whitehead's analysis, very few propositions are ever judged as true, false, or uncertain in truth value. Rather, a proposition is first and foremost a 'lure for feeling' (PR 281a, 395c-96a).[13] The importance of this claim for language is self-evident. Since language, for Whitehead, elicits propositional prehensions, it follows that the fundamental goal of language is not so much to communicate factual descriptions of the world as it is to elicit feelings of the world. The elicited feelings are, of course, the propositional prehensions. Sometimes in the linguistic act the emphasis is on the *content* of the feelings (the felt proposition), and sometimes it is on the *way* the propositions are felt (the subjective forms of the propositional prehensions); but usually the

13. For further details, see Chapter One, Section III.C.

emphasis is on both the content of the feelings and the way that content is felt, that is, on the propositional prehension as such.

Consider now just a few of the many uses of language: telling jokes, giving greetings, preaching sermons, asking for a tool, and telling a lie. In each case, the speaker is using language which (when successful) will lead the hearer to consider some particular possibility with some particular attitude toward that possibility, that is, to prehend some proposition with a particular subjective form. Thus language is far more than a mechanism for communicating facts with an eye towards their truth and falsity. Moreover, even when we are engaged in such a descriptive use of language, we can still view that descriptive use of language as a special case of communicating a feeling of the world. We explain further as follows. Suppose that I say, "The cat is on the mat." Suppose further that I merely wish to inform someone of this fact. The proposition could be expressed as follows: "X being a cat and being on the mat." Thus both I and my listener prehend that proposition. Insofar as I genuinely desire to be informative, however, my communication with my partner will be accompanied by the incitement to believe, that is, my language will be such as to incite in my listener an attitude of belief (PR 408c). Thus my language leads my listener to prehend the specified proposition with a particular subjective form, namely, the subjective form of belief.

Whitehead has several interesting names for propositions. He calls them 'theories', 'lures for feeling', and 'tales which might perhaps be told about particular actualities' (PR 281a, 392a). All of these designations add something to our understanding of Whitehead's view of language. In saying that language elicits our prehensions of propositions, Whitehead is also saying that language elicits our feelings toward theories; it elicits our reactions to lures for feeling; and it elicits our appropriations of tales which might be told about particular entities. Thus we find another basis for stating that, in Whitehead's philosophy, the primary role of language is to share our feelings of the world and that only in a secondary sense does language serve to communicate facts about the world.

The question now becomes: What is there about a proposition which allows it to serve as a lure for feeling? The answer is that a proposition is a form of potentiality. We previously discussed the nature of this propositional potentiality in some detail in Section III.C of Chapter One. Therefore, we will summarize here only those portions of that earlier discussion which relate immediately to language. A proposition is not a potentiality in the abstract. Rather, as we saw previously, the potentiality of a proposition is always "focused in" upon specific actual entities in the environment. At the simplest level, a proposition is the potentiality of *that* being a blue wall, or of *this* being a table and being smooth, of *this* being my wife's red hair. Whereas the potentiality of an eternal object is completely general, the potentiality of a proposition is concrete. In Whitehead's system, the proposition is the bearer of what is sometimes called 'real-possibility'. We further note that propositions are the most important source of our liberation from conformity to fact. At every other point in its concrescence, an actual entity either lacks the kind of freedom which a proposition can provide or else that actual entity is building upon the freedom which a proposition has already introduced.

Let us now apply this discussion of propositions to the linguistic situation. Language elicits propositional prehensions (and thus symbolizes the felt propositions as well). Therefore, we may state that language also liberates from slavish conformity to fact. This liberating nature of language stems from the fact that, by symbolizing propositions, language educes, promotes, isolates, and emphasizes those propositions. In other words, language makes the symbolized propositions more available than they would otherwise be. Considered in themselves, propositions are difficult to isolate and evoke. But language, because of its uses of images in presentational immediacy, can be easily invoked and isolated. Thus language liberates us from slavery to factuality.

This theme of language as liberation can be extended. We note that, when human beings use language, they are normally conscious. Now consciousness can aid in increasing the real potentialities available to us, and it can aid in increasing our available store of possible reactions to our world. This last point may be substantiated by attending to our own experiences. We have all found ourselves in the situation of being unsatisfied with the obvious explanation of some event, or of being unsatisfied with the obvious course of action, or being unsatisfied with the obvious comment to make. In such a case, we have consciously and deliberately worked out alternatives. Thus our consciousness has aided us in the production of alternative real potentialities for our consideration. But the question now becomes, "*How* does consciousness aid in the production of these alternatives?" Consciousness is (an element in the subjective form of a feeling of) the contrast between actuality and potentiality. When we work out alternative explanations, or alternative courses of action, or alternative comments, we are in effect contrasting our actual world with some potential one. However, this potential world *is* a series of propositions. But—and this is the rub—in terms of the process of concrescence, propositions or real potentialities are *prior* to consciousness and *cannot* be produced by consciousness. Therefore, the actual entity must first evoke or isolate the relevant proposition and *then* make it available for *conscious* comparison with the actual world. This is the job of language.

Language elicits and promotes the desired proposition, making it available to consciousness. It produces the real potentiality which is a prerequisite to consciousness. While it is too strong to say that consciousness is the gift of language, it is the case that sustained consciousness as it is employed for the deliberate and considered production of alternatives does depend on language. We explain as follows. Full human consciousness requires that there be several propositions which enter into consciousness, each of which must be an element in the intellectual feelings of a long string of actual entities in the soul thread. Mature human consciousness also requires propositions whose logical subjects may not be present in the immediate environment and whose predicates may consist of eternal objects which are not actualized in the immediate environment. Such consciousness further requires that these propositions be recollected at will. Granted the general intractability of propositions to isolation and eduction, it follows that the above requirements placed on the production of propositions makes that production virtually impossible without an auxiliary mechanism. Language is that mechanism.

Thus while there may be consciousness which does not depend on language—such as we find in dogs and ducks—it is also the case that such non-linguistic consciousness is limited to an awareness of the immediate environment and those alternatives which are intimately associated with that environment. So, although a dog may be conscious of the need to run or to fight right now as the wolf approaches, no dog ever contemplates whether to run or fight tomorrow if the wolf approaches, and no dog ever debated whether he should have run instead of fighting when that wolf approached yesterday. Indeed, no dog ever weighed the consequences of running or fighting right now as the wolf approaches, that is, no dog ever weighed the probability of success in running as compared with fighting, even when such running and fighting are self-evident possibilities connected with the immediate environment. In that sense, no dog ever made a rational decision. Consequently, we may say that the ability to deliberate —that is, the sustained and conscious discovery and/or consideration of alternatives—is a gift of language.

In much the same way as a developed consciousness depends on language, so also a developed memory depends on language. Thus, in Whitehead's system, if we are to remember the past—in the sense of thinking, reminiscing, recalling, or examining our own past—we must do so by means of propositions. Of course, we can *feel* the past by means of causal efficacy. In fact, Whitehead calls this the "palmary instance" of perception in causal efficacy. Insofar as memory becomes conscious, however, it will by definition involve propositions. In addition, it would seem that, conscious or not, a nuanced reaction to a specific portion of our remoter past would require the use of propositions. Again, to maintain a specific memory through a long string of actual entities in the soul thread would seem to require the use of propositions. Lastly, to the extent that a person sits down and straightens out his thoughts on some topic, this effort will last through many members of the soul thread and will depend on the ability to recollect at will previous thoughts on the topic in question, that is, we have a case of memory depending on propositions. Thus a developed memory is impossible without propositions; and for all the reasons we have developed in this chapter, the ready use of propositions is found only in conjunction with language. Thus language would seem to be required if propositions are to be employed in the development of a nuanced memory. In this sense, then, a developed memory is created by language. As Whitehead says,

> Language is expression from one's past into one's present. It is the repro-duction in the present of sensa which have intimate association with the realities of the past. Thus the experience of the past is rendered distinct in the present, with a distinctness borrowed from the well-defined sensa. In this way, an articulated memory is the gift of language, considered as an expression of oneself in the past to oneself in the present (MT 46b).

B

So far in this section, we have emphasized the role of language as sym-bolizing propositions. At this point, we turn our attention to the fact that language also elicits the subjective forms of propositional prehensions.

The emphasis on language as eliciting the subjective forms of propositional prehensions flows naturally from Whitehead's definition of propositions as lures for feeling. If propositions are lures for feeling, then to ignore the question of *how* a certain proposition is felt is to ignore how that proposition has fulfilled the role for which it was created. This em-phasis also flows naturally from Whitehead's fundamental characteriza-tion of language as eliciting propositional prehensions; that is, language can hardly elicit, promote, or isolate an entire propositional prehension without eliciting, promoting, or isolating the subjective form of that propositional prehension. Thus, in the act of eliciting a propositional prehension, language will also elicit that prehension's subjective form. In other words, language always invites the listener or reader to take a specified attitude toward the proposition in question.

The importance of the listener or reader adopting the suggested at-titude will vary. In some cases, for a particular use of language to be suc-cessful, the listener must adopt the suggested subjective form, whereas the exact identity of the proposition may be less important to the linguis-tic situation. In other cases, however, the successful use of language may require that the listener prehend the designated proposition clearly and distinctly, whereas the listener's adoption of the suggested subjective form may be less important. In still other cases, the successful use of lan-guage requires both that the listener prehend the specified proposition clearly and distinctly and that the listener adopt the suggested subjective form in that prehension. But, whether the listener's adoption of the sug-gested subjective form be of the essence of the linguistic act or merely a peripheral matter, it will always remain the case that every linguistic act will involve the elicitation of a suggested subjective form. About written materials, Whitehead comments,

> No verbal sentence merely enunciates a proposition. It always includes some incitement for the production of an assigned psychological attitude in the prehension of the proposition indicated. In other words, it endeavours to fix the subjective form which clothes the feeling of the proposition as a datum. There may be an incitement to believe, or to doubt, or to enjoy, or to obey. This incitement is conveyed partly by the grammatical mood and tense of the verb, partly by the whole suggestion of the sentence, partly by the whole content of the book, partly by the material circumstances of the book, including its cover, partly by the names of the author and of the publisher. In the discussion of the nature of a proposition, a great deal of confusion has been introduced by confusing this psychological incitement with the proposition itself (AI 312c).

In the following quotation Whitehead interweaves three of the themes which we have emphasized in our discussion of language as eliciting propositional prehensions. The three themes are: (A) propositions as lures for feeling, that is, propositions as engines for the stimulation of interest; (B) the subjective forms of propositional prehensions as essential elements in the linguistic act, that is, subjective forms as that which corresponds to interest; and (C) the idea that the purpose of language is primarily to communicate feelings of the world and only secondarily to communicate true facts about the world.

> It is more important that a proposition be interesting than that it be true. This statement is almost a tautology. For the energy of operation of a proposition in an occasion of experience is its interest, and is its importance. But of course a true proposition is more apt to be interesting than a false one. Also action in accordance with the emotional lure of a proposition is more apt to be successful if the proposition be true. And apart from action, the contemplation of truth has an interest of its own. But, after all this explanation and qualification, it remains true that the importance of a proposition lies in its interest. Nothing illustrates better the danger of specialist sciences than the confusion due to handing over propositions for theoretical consideration by logicians, exclusively (AI 313b).

The subjective forms of propositional prehensions are the source of most of what we may call the grammar of a sentence. Thus the difference between a statement and a question, the difference between a wish and a boon, and the difference between an order and a (verbal) compliance may all be traced to the differences in the subjective forms with which a proposition is prehended. We may illustrate this claim as follows. Consider the proposition, "That being a window and being open." The following verbal forms may be said to educe that same proposition but with various subjective forms: (A) "The window is open"; (B) "The window is open?"; (C) "The window is open!"; (D) "The window is open?!"; (E) "Thank Heavens, the window is open!"; (F) "Oh no, the window is open." (For spoken language, substitute the appropriate vocal inflection in place of the punctuation.) In this series of verbal forms, we find the same proposition elicited but with the subjective forms of (A) acknowledgment, (B) doubt, (C) conviction, (D) astonishment, (E) relief, and (F) disappointment. In light of this example, we may observe that for Whitehead all of language is propositional. In other words, our entire realm of language has a propositional structure, and this propositional structure is the basis for all our questions as well as all our statements, for our commands as well as our descriptions of facts. Therefore, we may conclude that the Whiteheadian position that all language has a propositional structure does not entail that the fundamental and basic form of language is that of statements, descriptions, and factual information. This is because, as is quite clear by now, propositions are primarily lures for feeling and only secondarily may they be called descriptions of the world.

Let us add two additional forms to the list in the above paragraph: (G) "Open that window!"; and (H) "Oh, that the window might be open." The form in (G) represents an intention to make actual—at least when the command is successful — and (H) represents longing. The proposition elicited by verbal forms (G) and (H) is not likely to be the same as the one elicited by verbal forms (A) through (F). The reason for this is that the logical subjects indicated in verbal forms (A) through (F) are either in the past or the present of the speaker, whereas the logical subjects in verbal forms (G) and (H) are likely to be in the future of the speaker. And, to the extent that the logical subjects are different, the propositions are different. On the other hand—and this is where the complication enters—it might be that the speakers of (G) and (H) are prior to the speakers of (A) through (F), with the result that the logical subjects are the same in all eight cases; and thus all eight verbal forms might elicit the same proposition with a variety of subjective forms.

Thus tense is the major exception to our rule that the grammar of a sentence finds its source in the subjective forms of the prehension of the designated proposition. It is also the case, however, that a proposition per se is tenseless. That is, the same proposition might be in a sentence which is future tense for one speaker, present tense for another speaker, and past tense for a third speaker. Rather, the tense of a sentence reflects the relation of the logical subjects of a proposition to the concrescing entity which prehends that proposition. Thus, if the logical subjects are in the new entity's past, then the sentence is past tense. If the logical subjects are in the concrescing entity's present, then the sentence is present tense. A similar relation holds for the future. In summary, the propositional content of a sentence is tenseless. Most of the grammar of the sentence stems from the nature of the subjective form with which the proposition is held,

the exception being the tense of the sentence which stems from the relation of the prehending entity to the logical subjects of the proposition.

C

We next turn to a consideration of the fact that a propositional prehension
is constructed in accordance with the subjective aim of the concrescing
entity.

In Chapter Three we noted and discussed the distinction between
the initial data and the objective data for a new concrescence. There are
always more qualities and characteristics of a given world than any concrescing entity—except God—can organize. There is a need for some principle whereby the mass of available initial data is reduced to the positive-
ly-felt objective data. The subjective aim meets this need. It is the
subjective aim which determines which aspects of the initial data are to
be included in the new concrescence as objective data and which are to be
excluded.

This process is repeated as the concrescence continues its act of self-
formation. At the second stage of concrescence, a variety of eternal objects
is available to serve as the predicates of propositions. Therefore, at the
third stage, the new concrescence needs a principle for deciding which
propositions to prehend—unless we assume that the new concrescence
feels all the possible propositions, which is most unlikely. The subjective
aim meets this need also. That is, the concrescing entity feels those
propositions which accord with its subjective aim.

Lastly, of all the propositions which are, in fact, felt in the new concrescence, only a few will enter the direct spotlight of consciousness, a
greater number will emerge into the penumbra of consciousness, but most
will remain in the shadows hidden from the spotlight of consciousness.
Here also—and this is our point—we need a principle of selection, and
here also the subjective aim of the new concrescence meets the need.[14]

At this point, let us turn to the linguistic implications of this process
of selection. Our thesis may be put very simply. The effectiveness of language will depend on the subjective aim of the concrescing entity. If the
new entity is dominated by the subjective aim of grasping and understanding the language, then this language may be astonishingly successful in educing the appropriate propositional prehension. On the other
hand, if the subjective aim of the new concrescence does not include the
goal of reacting appropriately to the language, then the language may be
less successful in educing the appropriate propositional prehension.

14. In Section I.C of Chapter Two, we discussed the fact that each stage of a concrescence constitutes a selection from the possibilities found at the previous stage, and in Section III.C of the same chapter, we also discussed the progressive determination of the subjective aim as the new concrescence achieves its satisfaction.

Let us consider a concrete illustration of this point. Suppose that in my environment are the words, "Supper's ready! Come and get it." If I am concentrating on some complicated passage in *Process and Reality*— and if I am dominated by the subjective aim to understand that passage —then, in all likelihood, that verbal phrase will not be successful in symbolizing the desired proposition nor in eliciting the desired subjective form. At least, it will not be successful in eliciting the desired propositional prehension into the center of consciousness, although it may be successful in eliciting it into the penumbral area of consciousness. On the other hand, if I am hungry and if I am merely reading the evening's newspaper until supper time, then the verbal phrase will likely have the desired effect indeed. Thus we may conclude that an actual entity's subjective aim will influence the effectiveness of language. That is, the subjective aim will help determine just how well a particular instance of language will succeed in aiding the actual entity to construct and isolate the appropriate propositional prehension—where that appropriate propositional prehension is merely one of a vast number of such prehensions which the entity could have constructed.

The other side of the coin is that language can also affect the identity of an actual entity's subjective aim. The subjective aim at the first stage of a concrescing entity is actually a graded series of possibilities for that entity's satisfaction. In other words, the actual entity's initial subjective aim is a series of possibilities for choosing its own identity and its own perspective on the world. Furthermore, as the concrescence proceeds, the various possibilities are eliminated until there remains only one, fully determinate, self-identity, that is, the satisfaction. This final self-identity is thus the result of that actual entity's own choice.

When language is successful, it will elicit, at the third stage, a propositional prehension into increased significance within the concrescing entity. Moreover, in many cases, the language will also result in the prehended proposition becoming an element in a conscious intellectual feeling at the fourth stage. Thus in the third stage, and sometimes in the fourth also, the use of language will have a definite impact upon the structure, characteristics, and identity of the concrescing entity.

The concrescing entity eliminates various possible self-identities from consideration in light of its previous decisions and in light of the identity of the previous stages of its concrescence. Thus, as the concrescing entity moves from the third to the fourth stage, it will eliminate some of its possible self-identities in light of the identity and character of its third stage, *where the propositional prehension elicited by the language may be a prominent and central feature of that third stage*. Likewise, as the concrescing entity moves beyond the fourth stage and eliminates additional possibilities of self-identity, it will make that move in light of the identity and the character of its fourth stage, where the central features of that fourth

stage may be the result of the operation of language. And so the successful use of language can affect how the concrescing entity eliminates alternative self-identities and selects its own ultimate satisfaction. In short, the
presence of language will influence the concrescing entity's reduction of
the initial subjective aim to the final satisfaction.

In summary of the last two paragraphs, we may observe that the
identity of a concrescing entity's subjective aim will affect the success of
language, and that at the same time, the successful operation of language
will affect the identity of the subjective aim.

VII

In this chapter we have so far discussed the Whiteheadian thesis that language elicits propositional prehensions and, thus, symbolizes propositions. We have discussed the side of language and the side of the propositional prehensions. In the light of this exposition, we now proceed to the
following points. The relation of language to thought is an ancient topic
of discussion. There is obviously an intimate relation between the two, but
are they absolutely required for each other? Can there be nonlinguistic
thinking?

Thought, for Whitehead, is the production and use of propositional prehensions. But since thought is a common sense term to be explained
in terms of his system and not itself a technical term, we may suppose that
thought involves propositional prehensions as they enter into consciousness. (In this regard, "thought" is quite unlike 'mentality', which is a technical term and which Whitehead uses sometimes in connection with
preconscious aspects of a concrescence.) In the following passage,
Whitehead describes a thought in a way which reminds us of his earlier
description of a proposition as a lure for feeling, and his earlier description of a propositional prehension as a reaction to such a lure.

> A thought is a tremendous mode of excitement. Like a stone thrown into
> a pond it disturbs the whole surface of our being (MT 50c).

However, if we do associate thought with the propositional
prehensions which the use of language elicits, it follows that thought and
language are not identical. Rather, language, according to Whitehead, expresses thought—or to put it alternatively, thought expresses itself in language (MT 48d, 50b).

We may say that the use of language elicits thought and thus language symbolizes the contents of our thought. But it is also true that our
thoughts can sometimes symbolize our language. Since this may not be
very clear, especially the idea that thought sometimes symbolizes language, we explain as follows. As we say in Section III of Chapter Six, the

direction of a symbolic relation is always decided by the concrescing entity in which the symbolism occurs; it is not determined by the items which have been placed in that symbolic relation. Thus there is nothing in theory which would prevent the concrescing entity from using the thought to symbolize the language; in other words, there is nothing in theory which would prevent the actual entity from using the proposition to promote, elicit, or isolate the appropriate words and sentences. Thus Whitehead writes:

> Language also illustrates the doctrine that, in regard to a couple of properly correlated species of things, it depends upon the constitution of the percipient subject to assign which species is acting as 'symbol' and which as 'meaning.' The word 'forest' may suggest memories of forests; but equally the sight of a forest, or memories of forests, may suggest the word 'forest.' Sometimes we are bothered because the immediate experience has not elicited the word we want. In such a case the word with the right sort of correlation with the experience has failed to become importantly relevant in the constitution of our experience (PR 277b).

As the last two sentences of this paragraph indicate, Whitehead thinks that his theory can explain the human occurrence of searching for the right word, when we already have the idea. That is, the doctrine that propositions can symbolize words and sentences explains the fact that "some of us struggle to find words to express our ideas" (MT 49b). And in turn, the fact that we sometimes struggle to find words to express our ideas is evidence in the practical realm that Whitehead's theoretical doctrine is correct. The struggle to find the right words to express our ideas is typical of poets.

> For example, if you are a poet and wish to write a lyric on trees, you will walk into the forest in order that the trees may suggest the appropriate words. Thus for the poet in his ecstasy—or perhaps, agony—of composition the trees are the symbols and the words are the meaning. He concentrates on the trees in order to get at the words (S 12b).

Nevertheless, usually language symbolizes our thoughts. Or, as Whitehead sometimes phrases it, language is the normal expression of our thoughts. Thus, Whitehead can write:

> Each language is the civilization of expression in the social systems which use it. Language is the systematization of expression.
> Of all the ways of expressing thought, beyond question language is the most important (MT 48c-d).

Earlier in this book we stressed that a sustained consciousness and an articulated memory depend upon language. We may extend that claim to say that human thought is dependent on language. Clearly insofar as human thought requires developed consciousness and articulated memory, we have already seen that this is the case. But suppose we extend the notion of thought beyond its pre-philosophical meaning; suppose we define thought as our reaction to lures for feeling. Does thought in this sense still depend on language? At one level the answer is no! It is possible for a concrescing entity to create a proposition which is not symbolized by language. It is even possible for the concrescing entity to isolate this propositional prehension to some slight degree. However, given the general intractability of propositional prehensions to isolation and manipulation, it would follow that any further isolation and manipulation of this propositional prehension would require the use of language. Thus at a second level the answer is yes, that is, human thought beyond the most elementary sort, even where consciousness is at a bare minimum, requires language. (It is the role of language to effect precisely such an isolation and manipulation of propositional prehensions.) And so we may assert that, quite apart from consciousness and memory, any increase in the development of thought requires a corresponding increase in the use of language.

In addition, as we have already seen, to the extent that (A) thought requires that the *same* proposition be available to many actual entities (as, for example, when a proposition is increasingly isolated and brought to the center of a person's attention over a period of time), and to the extent that (B) thought requires the ability to recall a proposition easily, it follows that, to this same extent, thought requires language. According to Whitehead,

> . . . the mentality of mankind and the language of mankind created each other. If we like to assume the rise of language as a given fact, then it is not going too far to say that the souls of men are the gift from language to mankind.
>
> The account of the sixth day should be written, He gave them speech, and they became souls (MT 57b-c).

13 *Language and the Bifurcation of the World*

THIS WILL BE A SHORT CHAPTER, with an important point to make. Language is a part of the world. It is internal to the world. And it is one of the means whereby the world is presented to and introduced into the identity of the person using the language.

I

Whitehead's view of language stands in opposition to any theory which would find in language a source of the bifurcation of nature. In Chapter Three, Sections II and III, we presented Whitehead's notion of the "bifurcation of the world." We developed this motif in several ways. One way was to use somewhat extended versions of Kant's terms, "noumena" and "phenomena." We let "noumenal reality" refer to whatever it is that serves as the foundation for and makes possible our human world of perception, intellection, consciousness, experience, and the like. By "phenomenal reality" we meant the world as it appears to us in ordinary human consciousness and in ordinary perception. The bifurcation of the world results when we sharply contrast the phenomenal world with the noumenal world so that the noumenal world as such never enters into human experience. For example, the noumenal world may be said to "lie behind" our ordinary world while not "entering into" that ordinary world. We presented Whitehead's metaphysics as overcoming such a bifurcation of the world into noumenal and phenomenal dimensions.

What are the implications for language in a culture that is formed by Kant's perspective? Such a culture, we said, would prefer to limit truth claims to language that describes the world as it appears to us, that is, to "scientific" and other forms of "factual" knowledge of the phenomenal world. That culture would be profoundly skeptical towards alleged knowledge of the noumenal world — skeptical, for example, towards ethics, religion, art, and metaphysics insofar as they are understood to be making cognitive claims about that noumenal world. A Kantian culture will also encourage skepticism about science when construed as providing truth about the way things are in themselves.

We observed that, since it is difficult if not impossible to avoid these disciplines (ethics, religion, science as providing us with cognitive contact with noumenal reality, etc.), a Kantian culture has several options. It can try to narrow the focus of the truth claims which such disciplines may "legitimately" make. Thus religious language, rather than telling us about what is the case in the world, only expresses what is "ultimate for me." Or ethics becomes an expression of the speaker's positive or negative feelings toward some item. Another option may be retreat into mysticism. For a Kantian culture, the most plausible interpretation of many of these areas, however, may well be this: such disciplines articulate the presuppositions of our actions. Thus ethics articulates the presuppositions of those patterns of human interaction for which we as a culture have opted. Such ethical statements (e.g., we ought to strive for an equality of opportunity for all humans) are not construed as claims about the nature of reality, but only as expressions of the regulative commitments of our culture. The emphasis will be on practice (or praxis) as the ground and norm of such truth.

Our description of the linguistic theories of a Kantian culture is not purely hypothetical. If we take "Kantian" in a very broad sense, there are some important contemporary theories of language which understand language to be the source of the "landscape" of our lived world of human experience. On these theories there is a "noumenal" world behind the "phenomenal" world of human experience, where the phenomenal world is given its shape by language. We can, however, never directly experience —or at least we can never talk about—the noumenal world. We can only experience—or at least we can only talk about—the phenomenal world. Janik and Toulmin provide an interpretation of Ludwig Wittgenstein according to which his theories of language are (ultimately) derived from, and in some regards are the functional equivalent of, Kant's categories of the mind.[1]

George A. Lindbeck has developed a theory of religious doctrine which appeals to Kant explicitly.[2] In the process of providing his interpretation of religious doctrine, Lindbeck articulates a theory of language.

> In the account that I shall give, religions are seen as comprehensive interpretive schemes, usually embedded in myths or narratives and heavily ritualized, which structure human experience and understanding of self and world. . . .

---

1. Allan Janik and Stephen Toulmin, *Wittgenstein's Vienna* (New York: Simon & Schuster, A Touchstone Book, 1973).

2. *The Nature of Doctrine: Religion and Theology in a Postliberal Age* (Philadelphia: The Westminster Press, 1984).

Stated more technically, a religion can be viewed as a kind of cultural and/or linguistic framework or medium that shapes the entirety of life and thought. It functions somewhat like a Kantian *a priori*, although in this case the *a priori* is a set of acquired skills that could be different. It is not primarily an array of beliefs about the true and the good (though it may involve these), or a symbolism expressive of basic attitudes, feelings, or sentiments (though these will be generated). Rather, it is similar to an idiom that makes possible the description of realities, the formulation of beliefs, and the experiencing of inner attitudes, feelings, and sentiments.[3]

We agree with Lindbeck that language, and in particular religious language, can powerfully shape our lived experience. Our own book provides extensive evidence for this from a Whiteheadian perspective. We ourselves argue that a developed and nuanced memory, consciousness, and experience depend on the availability of language. Our problem with Lindbeck, however, is that he seems to use this insight to isolate us from "noumenal reality" and to downplay the propositional content of religious doctrine and experience. For example, Lindbeck denies the possibility of *any* pre-linguistic experience of the world. From a Whiteheadian perspective, Lindbeck has welded together language and experience (as well as welded together consciousness and experience), where this union of language and experience is a key element in Lindbeck's bifurcation of the world.

... the means of communication and expression are a precondition, a kind of quasi-transcendental (i.e., culturally formed) *a priori* for the possibility of experience. We cannot identify, describe, or recognize experience qua experience without the use of signs and symbols. These are necessary even for what the depth psychologist speaks of as "unconscious" or "subconscious" experiences, or what the phenomenologist describes as prereflective ones. In short, it is necessary to have the means for expressing an experience in order to have it.[4]

Again we can agree with Lindbeck in many ways. A precondition for experience is the involvement with the "other," that is, with "communication" in its broadest sense. In Whiteheadian terms, an actual entity begins its process of concrescence by incorporating other entities into itself as a part of its very identity. The problem with Lindbeck's position is that he seems to think that the involvement with the "other" is the outcome of the linguistic act; he fails to grasp that the very possibility of language is built on the prior involvement with the other. He also defines experience as something of which we are conscious; he fails to see that consciousness itself presupposes prior experience of the other. These presuppositions are clearly operating in the following passage.

3. Ibid., 32-33.
4. Ibid., 36-37.

One could also claim that an experience (viz., something of which one is prereflectively or reflectively conscious) is impossible unless it is in some fashion symbolized, and that all symbol systems have their origin in inter-personal relations and social interactions. It is conceptually confused to talk of symbolizations (and therefore of experiences) that are purely private.[5]

We conclude that some contemporary theories of language continue to reflect the traditional Western bifurcations of reality.[6] Such theories of language can acerbate the split between the noumenal and the phenomenal world. We note that Whitehead's theory of language is designed to avoid such bifurcations.

II

We will examine each of the major elements of Whitehead's theory of language and show how they contribute to the elimination of such bifurcations of reality. The view of language which Whitehead has articulated thus provides a basis for understanding the connection of language with human experience and with nature. Whitehead's view of language puts us into contact with that soil out of which, according to the account in Genesis, we humans have been made.

Whether in the originating or in the receiving actual entity, any linguistic act has two sides: (A) the specified propositional prehension and (B) the language, that is, the sense perception of the squeaks or shapes. One of these is used to elicit the other. As a result, the felt propositions and the perceived sensa are symbolically related in the linguistic act, with the direction of that relation depending on the circumstance. The point we wish to stress is that the propositional prehension and the sense perception include realities which are both (A) beyond the concrescing subject and at the same time (B) also *present within* the concrescence as a part of

---

5. Ibid., 37-38.

6. We might mention another related but somewhat different kind of bifurcation. This bifurcation results when we split reality into "mind" and "nature." In the world of mind, we have propositions *about* nature, but these propositions are not a part of nature and have no direct contact with nature. In the world of nature, we have the "objective facts" and "realities," but these facts and realities are fundamentally different kinds of things from the propositions which are in the mind. And thus on these theories also we have a bifurcated world. Western culture since Descartes has busily been trying to reconnect the mind—and its propositions—with the world of nature. In a broad sense, we may summarize this position, or range of positions, by saying that these theories see language and/or propositions as a net of statements *about* the world of nature but not as *a part of* that concrete world.

For examples of such theories, see *The Encyclopedia of Philosophy, s.v.* "Propositions, Judgments, Sentences, and Statements," by Richard M. Gale. According to Gale, the following men held such a view at some point in their careers: Franz Brentano, G. E. Moore, Bertrand Russell, Alexius Meinong, Edmund Husserl, G. F. Stout, Gottlob Frege, Alonzo Church, Rudolf Carnap, and C. I. Lewis.

the very identity of that concrescence. It is this dual status of the linguistic elements which allows language to "open up" the noumenal world for us, rather than making language into a barrier between the subject and the noumenal world.

III

Let us consider the propositional prehension first. Such a prehension has two aspects, the subjective form and the proposition. The proposition, in turn, has two aspects, the logical subjects in their indicated position and the predicate. Thus we will deal with three distinct elements: (1) the subjective form of the propositional prehension, (2) the logical subjects of the proposition in their indicated positions, and (3) the predicate of the proposition.

We turn first to (1), the subjective form. The subjective form is an eternal object. This eternal object entered the concrescence from one of two sources: one or more finite past actual entities or God. Both the finite entities and God can contribute material to a new entity only at that entity's first stage of concrescence and only insofar as they have become a part of the very identity of that new entity; and yet, according to Whitehead, the past actual entities simultaneously retain their own particularities and their own distinct identities.[7] Thus, from one point of view, the subjective form of the linguistically elicited propositional prehension is constructed out of the concrescing entity's own identity. From another point of view, however, this eternal object is constructed out of past actual entities which have retained their own distinct identities apart from their roles as elements in the concrescing entity. The key point in grasping Whitehead's view of language is this dual role of the past actual entities, namely, functioning as a part of the real internal constitution of the concrescing entity even while retaining their own distinct identities.

The predicate of the felt proposition (3) is also an eternal object. Thus, the account of its introduction into the new concrescence is identical with the account of the introduction of the eternal object serving as the subjective form. That is, this eternal object also is derived from actual entities which, without losing their own identities as distinct actual entities, are present at the first stage of concrescence as a part of the very identity of that concrescing entity.

The logical subjects (2) of the specified proposition constitute the last of the three elements. Two distinct cases are possible. The logical subjects may be in the causal past of the concrescing entity, or they may be in the causal present or future of the concrescing entity. Let us consider first

---

7. See Section II of Chapter Three for a defense of this claim.

the case in which the logical subjects are in the past of the concrescing entity. By definition, these logical subjects are actual entities which are present at the first stage of concrescence and which, at later stages, have been stripped of their characteristics, thereby becoming mere 'its'. Therefore, the logical subjects, when they are a part of the causal past, enter the new concrescence at the first stage; and without losing their own identities as distinct actual entities, they are a part of the real internal constitution of that new concrescence.

We now turn to the case in which the logical subjects of the proposition are in the present or future of the concrescing actual entity. In this case, as we saw in Parts One and Two, the logical subjects have been reduced to the regions which they occupy. These regions, however, are a part of the extensive continuum. This extensive continuum is an element in each past actual entity, and it is made available to the new entity as a part of that new entity's prehensions of its past actual entities.[8] Therefore, when the logical subjects of a proposition are in the present or future of the prehending entity, they enter the prehending entity as elements in previous actual entities where these previous actual entities, while not losing their own identities, are a part of the internal constitution of the new concrescence.

We will next discuss the other side of the linguistic act, the sense perceptions. Our claim is that these elements also are constructed out of various actual entities, where these actual entities, without losing their own particularity, are present in the new concrescence as a part of the very identity of that concrescence. Let us consider a sense perception in light of such a claim. A sense perception has two component perceptions: a perception in presentational immediacy and a perception in causal efficacy. A perception in presentational immediacy is nothing other than a special kind of propositional prehension. In light of our previous discussion, therefore, we may conclude that the perception in presentational immediacy is constructed out of actual entities which, without losing their own particularity, are present in the new concrescence as a part of the very identity of that concrescence.

The other constituent element in a sense perception is the perception in causal efficacy. The most basic form of perception in causal efficacy is a simple physical prehension, and all other forms of perception in causal efficacy are derivative from such simple physical prehensions.[9] But the first stage of any concrescing occasion is nothing other than the collection of all such simple physical prehensions. Therefore, we may conclude that the perception in causal efficacy is also derived from actual entities which,

8. See Section II.B of Chapter Eight.
9. See Section I of Chapter Seven.

while retaining their own identity, are present in the concrescence as a part of the very identity of that concrescence.[10]

To conclude this section, we will reemphasize the key point: the actual entities which contribute the linguistic materials simultaneously (A) retain their own particularity and identity as distinct actual entities and (B) are a part of the real internal constitution of the speaker or hearer. In Part One, we discussed extensively how one (past) individual can be present in another (later) individual. In this way, the "noumenal reality"—that is, the past actual entities—is present in, and thus available to, the concrescing entity. The linguistic relation presupposes precisely this presence of the noumenal world within the concrescing entity. Thus when eliciting, for example, the logical subjects of the symbolized proposition into greater effectiveness in the concrescing actual entity, language enables the concrescing entity to deal more fully and fruitfully with the noumenal world. Language makes the noumenal world more, not less, available to us.

IV

In the next chapter we will discuss the relation between language and abstraction. Someone might object, however, to Whitehead's metaphysics as follows. Whiteheadian philosophy, according to the objector, depicts the abstractive power of language in such a way that this abstractive power creates its own bifurcation of the world. That is, on the one side, Whitehead has the abstract world created by language—the world in which we live our daily lives. And on the other side, Whitehead has the world of past actual entities in their complexity which we cannot even consciously experience let alone fully describe. Therefore, as a bridge between this chapter and the next, we will consider some of the ways in which language functions as a mode of abstraction, and we will relate the results of our discussion to the problem of bifurcation.

Before providing an answer to this objection we will first develop the objection more fully. We begin by noting Whitehead's description of the abstractive power of language. There is literally an infinite number of actual entities objectively present in the conformal stage of a concrescing actual entity (PR 366a, 347d-48a). As far as we humans are concerned, we

---

10. Both in the case of the propositional prehensions and of perceptions in causal efficacy, we have ignored the possibility of reversion. In the case of reversion, however, the source of the reverted eternal object is God. But God also is positively prehended at the first stage of concrescence; and those portions of God which are thus positively prehended become a part of the very identity of the new concrescence, and it is these included portions of God which are the source of the reverted eternal objects. Therefore, despite the possibility of reversion, we maintain our claim that in the linguistic act, its elements are derived from materials which are present at the first stage of concrescence and which are a part of the very identity of the new concrescence.

must find some way of simplifying and organizing this mass of data if we are to deal with it rationally and consciously. We must concentrate on the repeated patterns and the centers of significant influence. Let us observe three places in the concrescence where this simplification takes place.

First, the master key by which this simplification is effected is transmutation. In fact, Whitehead suggests that it is almost entirely transmuted feelings which acquire consciousness—at least in human beings (PR 362a; cf. PR 262c). Now the nature of transmutation is this. In transmutation, the concrescing entity applies a quality, which is derived from (at least some of) the individual members of a set of actual entities, to that set as a whole, as a unit, as a single factor (PR 40d). But—and this is the important point—there is no reason to think that the concrescing actual entity will create every transmutation which it is possible for it to create. Rather, given all its possible transmutations, the concrescence will, in fact, bring only a selection of them into reality. Second, the logical subjects of the typical proposition will consist of such a transmuted nexus. But we may assume that the concrescing entity will employ, as logical subjects, only a portion of the transmuted nexuses which are functioning in that concrescence. Thus we have a second stage of simplification. Last, it is a mistake, according to Whitehead, to assume that all, or even most, propositions ever become elements in consciousness (PR 399b). Thus we have a third stage of simplification.

In Whitehead's metaphysical scheme, consciousness cannot exist except on a foundation of propositional feelings. In conscious human experience and thinking, therefore, a vast simplification has taken place. Further, this simplification is aided and abetted by language because language tends to promote and elicit propositional perceptions—often as elements in conscious feelings. And such propositional prehensions and conscious feelings are far down the road of simplification and abstraction which we have just mapped. Moreover, since the function of language is to elicit propositional prehensions, the more precise the language—in the sense of specifying a particular proposition and a particular subjective response to it—the more language will tend to focus attention upon a relatively small and isolated portion of the total spectrum of the concrescing entity's experience. The problem, therefore, is this. Must we not conclude, asks our objector, that Whitehead's view of language, despite his best intentions to the contrary, introduces a bifurcation—a bifurcation between the infinitely complex world of past actual entities as present at the first stage of concrescence and the various simplifications and isolated elements which language elicits at the later stages of the concrescence?

We may explain Whitehead's answer to this question as follows. We human beings, according to Whitehead, are not primarily thinking machines, nor are we primarily centers of consciousness. We human beings are experiencing creatures. We exist first, and only then do we think, speak, or become conscious. And our thinking, speaking, or being conscious cannot undo our existence. For Whitehead, existence and experience are coextensive terms. And thinking, being conscious, and speaking are merely specialized modes in which a few actual entities structure their experience and existence.

Crucial in this context is Whitehead's claim that the entire process of creating transmutations, propositional prehensions, and intellectual feelings lies open to inspection by the concrescing entity, and probably by some of the future members of the soul thread as well (PR 411c). Obviously, Whitehead cannot mean that such inspection is easy or that its results are obvious; otherwise, his metaphysical theory of the stages of concrescence would be clearly evident to all people everywhere, but nothing could be further from the truth. Rather, we must interpret him as follows. "If we attend closely to our experiences, we will note, for example, that our perceptions of extended images arise from other, deeper modes of experience, of being in the world."[11] Again, as we attend closely to our experiences, we will note how precarious consciousness really is and how it depends upon the presence of so many supporting factors.[12] In short, Whitehead does *not* bifurcate nature because *both* the abstract domain of language *and* the infinitely complex domain of the dative actual entities are present *within our experience* and thus lie open to our inspection.

To further our explanation of Whitehead's position on this issue, we will recall the following analysis of concrescence, which is somewhat speculative.[13] As we have observed repeatedly, one actual entity can be present in another. There is, however, no reason to limit this principle to the relationships among actual entities; it also applies, according to Whitehead, to the relationships among the various stages of the concrescence itself. Therefore, each stage of concrescence is a part of the new actual entity. The first stage is present in the last stage, and all stages are present together in the new actual entity. The actual entity is *not* something apart from the process of concrescence—something which first "has" the characteristics of the conformal stage and then discards them for the characteristics of the second stage, and so forth until the last stage. Rather the first stage is a series of possibilities for the self-identity of the new entity—a series conditioned, but not completely determined, by the natures

---

11. Compare Whitehead's many discussions of Hume with regard to this topic, e.g., PR 263-66.

12. Whitehead writes: "This account agrees with the plain facts of our conscious experience. Consciousness flickers; and even at its brightest, there is a small focal region of clear illumination, and a large penumbral region of experience which tells of intense experience in dim apprehension. The simplicity of clear consciousness is no measure of the complexity of complete experience. Also this character of our experience suggests that consciousness is the crown of experience, only occasionally attained, not its necessary base" (PR 408b).

13. See Section II.B of Chapter Two.

of the past entities. This first stage is later modified—some possibilities of self-identity are chosen and others rejected—but this first stage remains a part of the very identity of the new actual entity. That is, the new entity remains forever just *that* entity which has just *that* initial stage of concrescence. Moreover, each later stage—for example, the satisfaction—gains its identity in part from the fact that precisely *that* initial stage is present. Thus an actual entity becomes fully determinate only in its satisfaction; but the identity of the actual entity resides in the entire process of concrescence, where each stage of that concrescence is present to each later stage, and where all stages are together present in the new actual entity as a whole.

Let us consider a specific application of the discussion in the above paragraph. In a conscious feeling, there is a contrast between a proposition and the actual entities serving as the logical subjects of that proposition. In this comparison, the actual entities serving as the logical subjects play a double role: (A) insofar as these actual entities are the logical subjects of the proposition, they have been stripped of all their characteristics, but (B) insofar as these actual entities are being compared with the proposition, they are fully clothed in all their characteristics.[14] This comparison occurs at the fourth stage of concrescence. The essential point to note is that the conscious feeling which emerges at the fourth stage employs a proposition which emerges at the third stage, and this same conscious feeling employs the fully clothed actual entities as they emerge at the first stage. Thus, the fourth stage uses materials drawn directly from the third and directly from the first stage. We may also note that the actual entities which are fully clothed in the first stage are stripped in the third stage when they become the logical subjects of the proposition; and yet, in the fourth stage, the actual entity can create the conscious feeling by using not only the stripped logical subjects of the third stage but also the fully clothed actual entities of the first stage. In summary, the first stage must be just as much present to the fourth stage as is the third stage since the concrescence at its fourth stage can draw upon the actual entities not merely as they exist as altered and manipulated by the third stage but also as they exist in their completely clothed natures at the first stage.

We now have a better grasp of Whitehead's claim that the genesis of a conscious feeling is open for inspection. The reason for this openness is that a conscious feeling involves the simultaneous presence of the raw data of the first stage and the altered data of the third stage, that is, the unaltered actual entities of the first stage and the stripped logical subjects of the third stage. A claim could be made for a propositional prehension similar to that which we made for a conscious feeling, namely, that the process of alteration of the constituent material in the prehension does not destroy the immediate presence to the new entity of the original, unaltered

14. See diagrams 12 and 13 and the related discussion in Section IV of Chapter One.

materials. Thus Whitehead can acknowledge—indeed powerfully argue —that the abstractive capacity of language creates an important distinction between the pre-linguistic world and the world as shaped by language. This distinction, however, does not constitute a bifurcation in Whitehead's sense because both the pre-linguistic world and the world as shaped by language are present in the concrescing entity and lie open for inspection.[15]

15. It may be worth adding at this point a theme from the earlier portions of this chapter. The actual entities constituting both the pre-linguistic world and the world as shaped by language, while elements in the real internal constitution of the concrescing entity, also retain their own identities as distinct actual entities.

14 *Language and Abstraction*

ACCORDING TO WHITEHEAD, the chief function of language is to express abstractions (PR 253b-54a). The exact nature of the term 'abstraction' in this context is somewhat difficult to state succinctly. The only way to catch Whitehead's real understanding of this term is to see what role it plays in his metaphysical system. We observed part of that role in the last section of the previous chapter. In this chapter we shall continue our observations of the role of the term 'abstraction' in Whitehead's metaphysics, hoping thereby to indicate the meaning of the term as well.

I

As a preliminary guide to Whitehead's use of the term 'abstraction' we will observe some of the different meanings which this term has in his writings. Later we will consider specific cases in Whitehead's corpus of each of these different meanings.

First, abstraction sometimes means simplification. Let us use a photograph as an illustration. A photograph is, in fact, constituted by a vast number of dots. But when we look at the photograph the individual dots are indistinguishable, and we see only the shaded image of the nose or eyes of the person in the photograph. Within the process of concrescence, such a simplification takes place. This is the role of transmutation. Moreover, such typically human items as sense perception, ordinary forms of memory, most common forms of consciousness, and clear and distinct thoughts all depend upon this process of simplification.

Second, sometimes Whitehead uses the term 'abstraction' to mean "partial." Here an abstract element is a part torn from the whole. There are, however, various types of part-whole relations. We will mention two of them. One is the kind of part-whole relation which a brick has to the wall in which it is set. Here the whole (the wall) is merely the sum of the parts (the bricks); the weight of the wall is merely the sum of the weights of the bricks; the volume of the wall is simply the sum of the volumes of the bricks; and the density of the wall is merely the average of the densities of the bricks. In addition, each part of the whole (each brick) has the same identity whether it is in the wall or torn from the wall; that is, it has the same shape, weight, density, color, and texture either place.

There is also an aesthetic whole-part relation. Consider any great painting. Here the artistic balance of the painting as a whole may be far more than the mere addition of the balance of each of the parts; indeed, the balance of the whole may depend on a judicious lack of balance in some of its parts. Likewise, any of the parts of the painting may be (aesthetically) incomprehensible when torn from the whole painting. The fingernails in the hands of the Mona Lisa, for example, gain their identity —that is, can be understood artistically—only when placed into the context of the whole picture. According to Whitehead, the fundamental patterns of order are artistic (RM 101b).

Third, we may illustrate another meaning of 'abstraction' by means of the following list: (A) sweet red apple, (B) red apple, (C) apple, (D) edible fruit, (E) fruit, (F) organic substance, and (G) an item extended in space and time. As we proceed from left to right in the list, we move from the least abstract notion to the most abstract notion. We may further explicate this third form of abstraction as follows. If an item falls into one of the categories in the list, it will also fall *by definition* into every category to the right. Thus, if an item is an apple, it will also be *by definition* an edible fruit, a fruit, an organic substance, and an item extended in space and time. That is, an apple by definition also exemplifies the more abstract categories. On the other hand, if an item falls into one of the categories, it does *not* follow *as a matter of definition* that this item will also fall into the categories on the left. Thus, an apple need not also be a red apple or a sweet red apple—although, of course, it may just *happen* that a particular apple is also sweet and red. Another way of looking at our list is this. If we take the notion of a 'sweet red apple', and if we "subtract" the quality of 'sweetness', we are left with the notion of 'red apple', where the notion of 'red apple' is more abstract than the notion of 'sweet red apple'. Again, if we subtract the quality of 'redness' from the notion of 'red apple', we are left with the still more abstract notion of 'apple'. And this process may be continued as we move to the right on the list.

The meaning of abstraction in the third sense ought to be distinguished from the notion of 'generality'. To help us explicate this notion of generality, we will turn to the following situation. Imagine a very strange army of one million men. This army is strange because every man in this army has a large wart on his nose. Now consider the following list of patterns. (A) Having a large wart on the nose, (B) having a blemish on the nose, and (C) having a blemish on the body. It is, we may presume, sufficiently obvious that this list proceeds from the less to the more abstract (in the third of the above senses of abstract). As far as our army is concerned, however, all of these predicates are equally general; that is, all of these predicates apply to the same *number* of men. Thus, the *generality* of a concept refers to the *number* of items which as *a matter of fact* exemplify that concept. Thus, a highly abstract (third sense) term which happened to be instantiated only rarely in this world would be less general than a less abstract term which was repeatedly instantiated in this world. For example, the term 'regular polygon in five or more dimensions' is a more abstract term than 'equilateral triangle in exactly two dimensions'; yet because the world does not contain any regular polygons in five or more dimensions (so far as we know), and because the world contains many two-dimensional equilateral triangles, it follows that the notion of 'two-dimensional equilateral triangle' is more general than the notion of 'regular polygon in five or more dimensions'.

II

As we observed in the previous chapter, the initial stage of concrescence is infinitely complicated, and needs to be simplified before we can "make sense" of it. Language aids in this process. Thus language promotes abstraction in the first sense. And yet we live "out of" this infinitely rich world. Therefore, Whitehead insists that there is always more to our experience of—indeed, our knowledge of—reality than we can express in language. For example,

> We know more of the characters of those who are dear to us than we can express accurately in words. We may recognize the truth of some statement about them. It will be a new statement about something which we had already apprehended but had never formulated (RM 123b).

When discussing this abstractive power of language in the last chapter, we emphasized that the initial stage of concrescence is infinitely complex and needed simplification; and language both promoted such abstraction and, at the same time, depended upon it. Whitehead's point, however, need not be stated only in terms of his technical metaphysics. Even when we pass to the realm of sense experience, which according to Whitehead already represents a vast amount of simplification, we find that we can experience and even "know" more than we can ever say. What scholar, given even a lifetime, could describe verbally every detail of a small room, such as that scholar's study.

The importance of the fact that we can know and experience more than we can ever put into words is vastly important for Whitehead's philosophy of religion. We will discuss this point in greater detail later.

We will introduce the following quotation, not for the light it sheds on his theory of religion, but merely as another example of Whitehead's insistence that language always deals with abstractions.

> The importance of rational religion in the history of modern culture is that it stands or falls with its fundamental position, that we know more than can be formulated in one finite systematized scheme of abstractions, however important that scheme may be in the elucidation of some aspect of the order of things (RM 137b).

In summary, even in the clear world of sensual experience, we are aware of more than we could ever state. But, more basically, we are experientially related to every item in our universe; and, although our sense organs simplify our environment for us, we never fully lose our dim awareness of that richer fabric of experience which can be "seen but not seen," and "heard but not heard."

In addition to simplifying our actual world into more manageable units, language also tends to direct our attention towards some of these units to the exclusion of others. For example, if I ask the janitor not to disturb the papers on my desk, I am obviously ignoring much of the environment in which both of us are working. I am not directing the janitor's attention to the name of the college president; nor am I directing his attention to the political situation in the faculty senate. Nor am I even directing his attention to the condition of the hallway outside my office. And, of course, I am not pointing out to him the color of my desk nor the tactile quality of the papers in it. Even more important, my comments assume the existence of enduring objects such as the desk and the papers; and my comment ignores the peculiarities of the constituent molecules, atoms, and electrons as well as the peculiarities of the actual entities in those atoms and electrons. Therefore, in asking the janitor not to disturb the papers on my desk, I am making two kinds of abstractions. First, at the level of the ordinary world of desks, papers, requests, and college politics, my comment mentions some of them to the exclusion of others; and yet they are all part of the actual world at the time of utterance. (This is abstraction in the second sense: a part isolated from its aesthetic whole.) Second, in order to concentrate on such objects, acts, and events in the ordinary world, my comment necessarily involved the dismissal of most of the details operating at the level of the actual entities; and yet, these many details at the level of the actual entities are also a part of my environment. (This is abstraction in the first sense: simplification.)

As language progresses, there is a development in the direction of abstraction, in the sense of a growth of independence from any particular environment. (This is a variety of type two abstraction: part-whole.) Whitehead speaks of this growing abstraction of language from particular environments in terms of an evolutionary development.

Language arose with a dominating reference to an immediate situation. Whether it was signal or expression, above all things it was *this* reaction to *that* situation in *this* environment. In the origin of language the particularity of the immediate present was an outstanding element in the meaning conveyed. . . .

Language has gradually achieved the abstraction of its meanings from the presupposition of any particular environment. The fact that the French dictionary is published in Paris, at a definite date, is irrelevant to the meanings of the words as explained in the dictionary. . . .

Of course, we are much more civilized than our ancestors who could merely think of green in reference to some particular spring morning. There can be no doubt about our increased powers of thought, of analysis, of recollection, and of conjecture. We cannot congratulate ourselves too warmly on the fact that we are born among people who can talk about green in abstraction from spring-time. But at this point we must remember the warning—Nothing too much (MT 53b-54b).[1]

III

Language points to the variable—and therefore superficial—elements in our world. Thus language takes the most interest in items—things, events, attitudes, actions, and whatever—which are sometimes a part of our environment and sometimes not. Consider: a clap of thunder, the movement of a leaf, the act of baptizing, the shouting of a curse, and so forth. We have words to discuss thunder because it sometimes thunders and it sometimes does not. We have words to pronounce a man guilty or innocent because we sometimes have crimes and sometimes we do not, and because people arrested for such crimes are sometimes guilty and sometimes they are not. Consider how different our language would be if (A) people never committed crimes or (B) they never did anything except commit crimes. Again consider how different our language—as well as our legal institutions— would be, if the police caught the perpetrator of every crime and if the police never mistakenly arrested an innocent person.

Language was developed in response to the excitements of practical actions. It is concerned with the prominent facts. Such facts are those seized

---

1. We should add that Whitehead sees in written language, as distinct from spoken language, a major incentive to such abstraction of language from a particular environment (MT 54c-55a). In fact, at one point Whitehead sees written language, when inappropriately analyzed, as leading to a form of atomism. Thus in written language we are aware of single words with a specific dictionary meaning—a meaning which, in virtue of the intended use of the dictionary at many times and many places, must necessarily be highly abstract. And in written language we find complete sentences, each bounded by full stops. "Thus the problem of philosophy is apt to be conceived as the understanding of the interconnection of things, each understandable, apart from reference to anything else" (MT 90c).

upon by consciousness for detailed examination, with the view of emotional response leading to immediate purposeful action. The prominent facts are the variable facts,—the appearance of a tiger, of a clap of thunder, or a spasm of pain. They are the facts entering into our experience by the medium of our sense-organs. Hence the sensationalist doctrine concerning the data which are the origin of the experience (AI 209b).

There is a good reason why language concentrates on these variable elements in our environment. The variable elements are those which we can control. They are the "useful" elements (cf. PR 241a). The fact that there is a growling tiger two feet behind me offers some possibilities for action, namely, getting rid of the tiger. Again, the roll of thunder is a rather good sign of an approaching storm for which I must prepare by closing windows and putting the car into the garage.

Factors which are always present in the environment tend to be hard to describe. Consider, for example, the notion of space. Speaking physically, we are always in space. But, while children can talk of pillows, sheets, beds, tricycles, and chairs by the age of two or three, they must be twelve or thirteen before the notion of space becomes meaningful in the sense that they can clearly state, in their own words, the difference between "air" and "space." And even for adults who lack a formal education the distinction between "air" and "space" is often obscure. We may conclude, therefore, that language concentrates on the elements in our environment which are, on the one hand, variable, superficial, and useful but which, on the other hand, are massive enough to survive the elimination of the idiosyncrasies of their constituent actual entities and which are high up the scale of abstraction.

According to Whitehead, the elements which language tends to emphasize are either enduring objects or interwoven with enduring objects (PR 122d). Thus we talk about chairs, buildings, atoms, electrons, colleges, countries, and people, and many of our words are interwoven with such enduring objects. What, for example, is the color red, in our experience, if it is not the color of some thing, some enduring object which is red? Again, what is a smile without a face, a murder without a body, or an acquittal without a defendant? Even such terms as "of," "with," and "but" usually are involved in the relations of enduring objects; for example, the girl "of" his dreams, the fellow "with" the red hat, and "There 'but' for the grace of God go I."

In the Indo-European languages, this concern with enduring objects expresses itself in the subject-predicate form of grammar (cf. PR 116b, 219b; AI 197b). Thus, in English, when we make a declarative statement, we attribute some quality to a subject; for example, "The book is red"; "The cat is on the mat"; and, "The Southeast is suffering a drought." And even our questions, typically, presuppose a subject-predicate grammar.

For example, if we ask, "Where is the cat?" then the full reply would be, "The cat is on the mat." Therefore, the structure of grammar itself—at least in the Indo-European languages—is a form of abstraction.

Let us conclude this chapter by recalling our previous observation that ordinary language points to those elements in our environment which make a practical difference, and it overlooks those elements which do not. And, for the most part, any language with a rich history—German, Japanese, Chinese, Thai, Sanskrit, French, English, and so forth—discriminates with considerable accuracy between the factors which make a practical difference and those which do not.[2] The philosopher seeks liberation from these "practical" considerations enshrined in language. This is because the philosopher has the goal of seeing the basic structures of the *whole* of the universe and, therefore, is interested in those aspects of nature which ordinary language overlooks.

> Philosophy is an attitude of mind towards doctrines ignorantly entertained. By the phrase 'ignorantly entertained' I mean that the full meaning of the doctrine in respect to the infinitude of circumstances to which it is relevant, is not understood. The philosophic attitude is a resolute attempt to enlarge the understanding of the scope of application of every notion which enters into our current thought. The philosophic attempt takes every word, and every phrase, in the verbal expression of thought, and asks, What does it mean? It refuses to be satisfied by the conventional answer. As soon as you rest satisfied with primitive ideas, and with primitive propositions, you have ceased to be a philosopher (MT 233d-34a).

This quotation will serve as our transition to the next two chapters.

---

2. We need to add two qualifications. First, to some extent the same may be said of any language, even that of the most "primitive" tribe. Such tribes are often, so the anthropologists tell us, millennia old. If their languages did not provide them with a practical organization of the powers in their worlds, they would not have survived at all.

Second, we note that the languages of even the most "advanced" cultures are not always the best guide to all the significant centers of power in their environments. Modern science, which obviously has pointed out factors in our environment which make a practical difference, started on its progress only when a mathematically oriented attitude toward nature overcame the "practical" view of nature which was enshrined in the Greek language and which was systematized by the "practical" mind of Aristotle.

15 *The Imprecision of the Symbolic Relation between Language and Propositions*

ACCORDING TO WHITEHEAD, language—at least nonphilosophical language—is never symbolically related to only one proposition. There is always a variety of propositions which a specific sentence or phrase could symbolize; likewise, a particular proposition could be symbolized by a variety of sentences. In Whitehead's own words,

> This discussion can be illustrated by the proposition, 'Caesar crossed the Rubicon.' This form of words symbolizes an indefinite number of diverse propositions (PR 297c).

Consequently, Whitehead asserts,

> It is merely credulous to accept verbal phrases as adequate statements of propositions (PR 17b).

I

The imprecision concerning the propositions which a given verbal form may symbolize has three primary sources: (1) the logical subjects of the symbolized propositions, (2) the indication of those logical subjects, and (3) the eternal objects serving as the predicates of the constituent propositions.

A

A particular sentence symbolizes the logical subjects of a proposition with only enough precision to meet the practical requirements of the moment. If we add, subtract, or replace even one of the logical subjects of a proposition, we have a different proposition. As a result, any particular sentence or phrase is ambiguous as to exactly which proposition it symbolizes.

273

Consider the following example. Suppose I tell my wife, "Some of the apples are red." For practical purposes, this statement indicates the position of the logical subjects with sufficient accuracy. Both my wife and I know where to pick the apples. That is, we both know that apples tend to ripen at the top of a tree first, and we both know that our apple tree is old and is at least thirty feet tall. Furthermore, with this background, both my wife and I know that, when I mentioned that some of the apples were red, we would need a tall ladder to get to them. Thus, in terms of the communication between my wife and myself, this verbal phrase is sufficiently precise for the purposes of picking the apples or looking at them.

This precision is, however, still relative. There is still ambiguity as to which logical subjects are indicated by the verbal form, "Some of the apples are red." For example, suppose that there is a worm in one of the red apples. Are the actual entities in that worm included as members of the set of logical subjects of the symbolized proposition? Again, as long as the apples are on the tree, there will be a flow of sap between the tree and the apples, and there will be a transfer of oxygen and carbon dioxide between the atmosphere and the apple. When does an atom of oxygen cease to be a part of the apple and become a part of the atmosphere? When does a molecule of water cease to be a part of the tree and become a part of the apple? Clearly the linguistic phrase, "Some of the apples are red," is imprecise as to whether or not the actual entities in the worm are included in the set of logical subjects; and this phrase is also imprecise as to which of the actual entities in the atom of oxygen and which of the actual entities in the molecule of water are included in the set of logical subjects.

Is such imprecision bad, a flaw in language? There is no absolute answer here. It all depends on the practical purpose in mind. For the purposes which my wife and I had—picking the apples and collecting them —this ambiguity is completely irrelevant; it hardly constitutes a flaw. On the other hand, if our purpose was to run a chemical test on the apples to check their nutritional value, then sooner or later we would have to reduce the ambiguity in the original linguistic phrase by deciding whether to include any worms, which we may happen to find, as a part of the apple, or to exclude them. And if we were biologists studying the processes of digestion and excretion within an apple, we should be required to make our language very precise as to just which actual entities in the atom of oxygen and which actual entities in the molecule of water are to be included in the apple.

Let us summarize the outcome of our illustration using the phrase, "Some of the apples are red." We tried to show that every verbal form in ordinary language will have some ambiguity concerning which actual entities to include and which to exclude as logical subjects. We also tried to show that this ambiguity is a matter of degree. Lastly, we tried to show that such ambiguity is not bad provided that it is small enough to allow the linguistic form in question to achieve whatever practical purpose its users have in mind.

B

Every verbal form must indicate the location of the logical subjects and must provide a predicate to be ascribed to those logical subjects. Very often, however, the distinction in the verbal form between (A) the indication of the logical subjects and (B) the predicate to be ascribed to them, is not very clear. Whitehead seldom gives concrete examples in his writings of the point he is trying to make, but in this case he does. His example is, "Socrates is mortal" (PR 404b-e, 297b). In this phrase the term "Socrates" may serve to *indicate* the logical subjects. In that case, the verbal form could be rephrased as follows: "It—that is, that Socratic thing back in ancient Athens—is mortal." On the other hand, the term "Socrates" may be a part of the predicate; for example, "It is Socratic and mortal." Lastly, the term "Socrates" could serve both to indicate the location of the logical subjects and to provide a part of the predicate; for example, "It — that is, that Socratic thing back then—is both Socratic and mortal."

Each interpretation we gave of the sentence "Socrates is mortal" yields a distinct proposition. Thus we have another sense in which a single verbal form may symbolize a variety of propositions.

C

We turn now to still another sense in which the same verbal form may symbolize a variety of propositions: the portion of the verbal form which provides the predicate may not clearly distinguish among a variety of eternal objects. And each distinct eternal object, when predicated of the logical subjects, will result in a distinct proposition.

For a straightforward illustration of this, let us consider once again the verbal form "Some of the apples are red." There are, we note, many shades of red, each of them a distinct eternal object. Therefore, the sentence "Some of the apples are red" is capable of symbolizing at least as many propositions as there are shades of red which may be found among apples.

D

Eternal objects can be organized according to their various degrees of abstraction (in the third sense). This provides another source of linguistic ambiguity. Before we can demonstrate this point, however, we need to develop some background information.

Let us consider a particular actual entity in a particular apple which is hanging on my apple tree in the backyard. Consider the eternal object

'O'. Let 'O' be the set of *all* the eternal objects in *all* their specificity which have ingressed into this actual entity in the apple. Since 'O' is the complete description of this actual entity, it follows that nothing in the (causally past) environment could be changed without altering the identity of that actual entity—that is, without altering 'O'. For example, my wife and I own a barn behind our house. Since the actual entity in question prehended the barn, it follows that if the barn had not existed, then 'O' would have been altered and, thus, no longer 'O'. In short, if there were any changes of any sort in (the causally past) environment of the actual entity in which 'O' has ingressed, then 'O' could not have ingressed into that actual entity and, consequently, the identity of that actual entity would be different.

If we consider a more abstract eternal object, however, we will find that its ingression into the actual entity in the apple is compatible with a certain amount of variation in the nature of the environment. We can construct a hierarchy of eternal objects which have ingressed into that actual entity— a hierarchy which leads from the most specific to the most general and abstract. In the previous paragraph we examined the most specific and detailed of the eternal objects in this hierarchy, 'O'. But more abstract eternal objects also ingressed into that actual entity. Suppose that we took a great variety of red, ripe apples and asked in what way they were alike. We would point to certain characteristics. For example, the apples would be red, but they would not be exactly and precisely the same shade of red. Again the apples would have approximately the same shape, but with some variations in each apple. There are other qualities which we could mention. The sum total of all the eternal objects which could be said to ingress into *any* red, ripe apple, we will call 'red, ripe applehood'. Now 'red, ripe applehood' is an abstract eternal object. We could say, thus, that 'red, ripe applehood' had ingressed into all the apples; but this abstract eternal object was "fleshed out," "completed," and "made determinate" in different ways in each apple. This eternal object, 'red, ripe applehood', could ingress into a variety of situations without losing its self-identity. For example, it would make no difference whether or not there is a barn in my backyard.

Let us consider a more abstract eternal object. Sometimes apples are red, sometimes they are green, and sometimes they are yellow. We could ask what characteristics all apples have in common. Whatever our answer, the list would include some highly abstract qualities, such as 'being colored', 'having a shape', 'growing on apple trees', and so forth. We may call the set of these eternal objects 'applehood'. This 'applehood' is a more abstract eternal object than 'red, ripe applehood'.

Some of the eternal objects ingressing into the apples are still more abstract. For example, what would be the nature of an apple in a world with thirty-eight dimensions? And what would be the nature of an apple in a world where enduring objects—that is, things like apples, stones, and trees—could pass through each other like ghosts through walls? Probably none of us can imagine the nature of an apple in such a world. Nevertheless, there must be some highly abstract eternal object which would ingress *both* into (the actual entities of an apple in) our world *and* into (the actual entities of an "apple" in) a world of thirty-eight dimensions where "solid" objects pass through each other like ghosts through walls. Let us call this eternal object 'science fiction applehood'.

We have thus far discussed the most specific eternal object 'O' as well as three abstract eternal objects: 'red, ripe applehood', 'applehood', and 'science fiction applehood'.[1] The point to notice is that the most specific eternal object 'O' contains, as a part of its very nature, the other three abstract eternal objects. Moreover, the eternal object 'red, ripe applehood' will contain, as a part of its very identity, the eternal object 'applehood'. Lastly, 'applehood' will contain, as a part of its very nature, the eternal object 'science fiction applehood'.

Let us now make our application of this discussion to the problem of the source of linguistic ambiguity. Consider the word "apple" in the sentence "Look at that apple!" We may assume that the eternal object 'red, ripe applehood' has ingressed into each actual entity in the apple. In addition, the actual entities in the apple, *in virtue of* the ingression of the eternal object 'red, ripe applehood' into them, *also* exhibit the eternal objects 'applehood' and 'science fiction applehood'. Therefore, since the entities in the apple genuinely exhibit all of these eternal objects, it follows that the word "apple" as it functions in a particular instance will often be ambiguous as to which eternal object it actually signifies. Of course, in most practical situations the term "apple" will not be pointing directly at 'science fiction applehood'. The choice between 'red, ripe applehood' and 'applehood', however, will often be genuinely ambiguous. Eternal objects often form hierarchies of abstraction which are similar to the one we just considered: 'O', 'red, ripe applehood', 'applehood' and 'science fiction applehood'. The relation between a linguistic form and the eternal objects in such an abstractive hierarchy is often ambiguous.

II

Our next point leads us to a sense in which there is an arbitrariness in the relation between language and propositions. The point we wish to stress

---

1. There are innumerable eternal objects which could also fit into this list. For example, between 'O' and 'red, ripe applehood', there are many additional eternal objects, where (A) each such additional eternal object is more abstract than 'O', but less abstract than 'red, ripe applehood', and where (B) each of these additional eternal objects has its own level of abstraction vis-à-vis the other, additional eternal objects. We have chosen four eternal objects ('O', 'red, ripe applehood', 'applehood', and 'science fiction applehood') for the sake of convenience.

is that, when we single out an object (e.g., an apple) from its background (e.g., the yard), there is a certain arbitrariness as to which societies (that is, groupings of actual entities) we will consider to be a part of the foreground and which the background. In the previous section, we focused on the predicate of the proposition. In this section, we focus on the logical subjects of the proposition.

Let us consider our previous example, "Some of the apples are red." Each actual entity in the apple has prehended its past actual world into its very identity. But, as we noted in the previous section, this past world contains very much more than the previous actual entities in that apple. It also includes (the previous actual entities in) the apple tree, the backyard, and the planet earth. Therefore each actual entity in the apple exhibits, *as a part of its own nature,* the structures which identify and constitute the apple tree, the backyard, and the planet earth.

When a percipient entity prehends the actual entities in the apple, it follows that this percipient must exercise considerable creativity before the enduring object "apple" emerges, either as an object of perception or as an object of thought. That is, in the act of emphasizing the patterns which characterize the apple, the prehending entity must de-emphasize the structures which characterize the tree, the backyard, and the planet, where these structures, also, are genuine qualities of the actual entities in the apple. Finally, then, there must be a transmutation. That is, the patterns characterizing the apple per se are to be found, in the first instance, in the individual actual entities in the apple; and in the transmutation, these patterns are applied to the *set* of actual entities considered as a unit, as a whole.

We can now see the sense in which this process is arbitrary. We described the process whereby the apple was singled out as a unit, with the tree, the yard, and the planet considered as societies in the background. But surely this was an arbitrary decision. We might just as well have focused on the tree as the primary unit with the apples felt merely as parts of the tree. To emphasize the tree rather than the apple, however, the percipient entity would have to emphasize the characteristics which defined the tree and would have to de-emphasize those which defined the apple. Surely, to organize a specific set of actual entities into an apple—that is, into a specific society or enduring object—when those actual entities also exhibit the characteristics of and participate in other societies or enduring objects, is an arbitrary act. And yet, in most cases, when I tell my wife, "Some of the apples are red," I am surely leading both her and myself to emphasize the apples at the expense of the tree (and also at the expense of the seeds or cells or molecules in the apple). On the other hand, if I mention to my wife, "Look, our apple tree is on fire," then I would be emphasizing the tree at the expense of any of the red apples which may be part of it. And in still other situations, such as among researchers examining the ripening process in fruit, the mention of the apples' redness may result in bringing to mind the cellular structure of the apple skin. Thus language brings about a somewhat arbitrary emphasis on the apple, the tree, the parts of the apple, or some particular balance among them.

This section is our interpretation of such passages in Whitehead's text as the following.

> Further, the judging subject and the logical subjects refer to a universe with the general metaphysical character which represents its 'patience' for those subjects, also its 'patience' for those eternal objects. In each judgment the universe is ranged in a hierarchy of wider and wider societies, as explained above. . . . It follows that the distinction between the logical subjects, with their qualities and relations, and the universe as systematic background is not quite so sharply defined. . . . For it is a matter of convention as to which of the proximate societies are reckoned as logical subjects and which as background. Another way of stating this shading off of logical subjects into background, is to say that the patience of the universe for a real fact in a judging subject is a hierarchical patience involving systematic gradations of character (PR 292c-93a).

> The word 'Socratic' means 'realizing the Socratic predicate in Athenian society.' It does not mean 'Socratic, in any possible world'; nor does it mean 'Socratic, anywhere in this world' [although there are highly abstract eternal objects which do answer to both of these descriptions]: it means 'Socratic, in Athens.' Thus 'Socratic,' as here used, refers to a society of actual entities realizing certain general systematic properties such that the Socratic predicate is realizable in that environment. Also the 'Athenian society' requires that this actual world exemplifies a certain systematic scheme, amid which 'Athenianism' is realizable.

> Thus in the one meaning of the phrase 'Socrates is mortal,' the logical subjects are one singular *It* (Socrates) and the actual entities of this actual world, forming a society amid which mortality is realizable and including the former *'It.'* In the other meaning, there are also included among the logical subjects the actual entities forming the Athenian society. These actual entities are required for the realization of the predicative pattern 'Socratic and mortal' and are definitely indicated logical subjects. They also require that the general scheme of *this* actual world be such as to support 'Athenianism' in conjunction with 'mortality' (PR 404e-5a; bracketed material added; the last sentence follows Griffin and Sherburne's correction, Kline's emendation being quite different).

III

We may use our discussion in the previous section to explain Whitehead's claim that every proposition implicates a metaphysical pattern (PR 16c-17a). We will begin by comparing the eternal object 'applehood' with 'science fiction applehood'. By definition 'science fiction applehood' may

ingress into a world with thirty-eight dimensions in which "solid" substances pass through each other. The eternal object 'applehood', however,
could not ingress into such a world. Rather, 'applehood' *requires* the four
dimensions of this world (the three of space and one of time), and it *re-*
quires the pattern of mutual impenetrability among solid substances.
Thus, part of the very *identity* of 'applehood' *is* its relations to the pattern
of four-dimensionality and the pattern of mutual impenetrability. In other
words, the connection of 'applehood' to these patterns is a part of the essence of 'applehood'.[2]

Both the pattern of mutual impenetrability and the pattern of four-
dimensional space-time presuppose the larger patterns of the extensive
continuum at its most abstract. And the universal extensive continuum,
in turn, presupposes the genuinely ultimate patterns of metaphysics.[3]
Thus the essence of 'applehood' implicates a metaphysical system.

At this point, however, we must exercise some caution. Just as
'applehood' requires only the patterns of four-dimensionality and mutual
impenetrability, so also 'applehood' requires only the abstract *pattern* of the
extensive continuum and it requires only the abstract *pattern* of metaphysics.
Thus 'applehood' presupposes neither any particular arrangement of the
continuum nor any particular arrangement of the patterns of metaphysics.

Let us summarize this section. Any eternal object which characterizes concrete fact in this world will presuppose the extensive continuum.[4] And because the extensive continuum presupposes the patterns
of metaphysics, it follows that any eternal object which characterizes concrete fact in this world will presuppose the patterns of metaphysics.

This is our explanation of such passages in Whitehead's text as the
following.

> The point is that every proposition refers to a universe exhibiting
> some general systematic metaphysical character. Apart from this back-
> ground, the separate entities which go to form the proposition, and the

---

2. Our discussion of the essence of eternal objects is really a discussion of what
Whitehead calls the 'relational essence' of an eternal object. The topic of relational and individual essences of eternal objects takes us beyond the hermeneutical scope of this book.
Whitehead's discussion of relational essences is to be found in *Science and the Modern World,*
157-79, as well as in *Process and Reality,* 175d-76b, 251c-52a, 392a-b, 479c.

3. For a defense of these claims see Chapter Eight, especially Section II.H. The reader
may also wish to note the discussion in Chapter Five, Sections II and III.

4. We can, of course, consider eternal objects such as 'science fiction applehood'
which do not implicate the local patterns of order which are peculiar to this cosmic era. But
such eternal objects, while felt in purely conceptual feelings, do not concretely characterize
any actual entities in this epoch. The point is that the eternal objects which physically and
concretely do characterize actual entities in *this* world implicate not only the local patterns
of order but also the continuum and thus the patterns of metaphysics. We postpone until the
next chapter the question of whether we can conceive of eternal objects which do not implicate the extensive continuum at its most abstract and which do not implicate the patterns of
metaphysics.

proposition as a whole, are without determinate character. Nothing has been defined, because every definite entity requires a systematic universe to supply its requisite status. Thus every proposition proposing a fact must, in its complete analysis, propose the general character of the universe required for that fact. There are no self-sustained facts, floating in nonentity. . . . A proposition can embody partial truth because it only demands a certain type of systematic environment, which is presupposed in its meaning. It does not refer to the universe in all its detail (PR 16c-17a).[5]

Since a "precise language" would be a language in which the complete natures of the symbolized propositions are fully elucidated, we can now understand why Whitehead writes, "A precise language must await a completed metaphysical knowledge" (PR 18c).

5. As this quotation indicates, there are many ways to show how a proposition implicates the metaphysical patterns of the universe. In the text, our tactic was to concentrate on the eternal object serving as the predicate of the proposition (about some fact in the world). Our argument was that the extensive continuum is required by each eternal object which ingresses into this universe and which is exemplified in this universe. Our last step was to argue that the extensive continuum in turn requires the patterns of metaphysics. We could have achieved the same result in other ways. For example, we could have shown how the indication of the logical subjects of a proposition requires the extensive continuum and thus the patterns of metaphysics. (Would propositions about God be an exception since God is not in the continuum?)

16 Language: Ordinary and Metaphysical

IN THIS CHAPTER we compare metaphysical and ordinary language. By metaphysical language we mean language which symbolizes metaphysical propositions, that is, propositions which have all actual entities whatsoever as logical subjects. By ordinary language we mean language which symbolizes non-metaphysical propositions, that is, propositions which have some subset of actual entities as the logical subjects.

I

Is there a fundamental difference between the language of metaphysics and ordinary language? The answer is mixed. They are alike in some respects and different in others.

A

Metaphysical and ordinary language are basically alike in that, in both, the relation between the linguistic form and the symbolized proposition is commonly ambiguous; that is, a single linguistic form may symbolize a variety of propositions. The converse is also true: a single proposition may be symbolized by a variety of linguistic forms. Metaphysical language and ordinary language, however, are not totally identical in this regard. Rather, the relation of linguistic forms to metaphysical propositions seems to be more murky, unclear, and obscure than the relation of linguistic forms to ordinary propositions. (The reasons for this greater obscurity of metaphysical language will be mentioned below.) Thus we read,

> This faintness of impress of general ideas upon the human mind has another effect. It is difficult even for acute thinkers to understand the analogies between ideas expressed in diverse phraseologies and illustrated by different sorts of examples. Desperate intellectual battles have been fought by philosophers who have expressed the same idea in different ways (AI 220c).

It must be emphasized, though, that this is a difference of degree, not a difference in kind. Both ordinary language and metaphysical language have this ambiguous relation between the linguistic forms and the symbolized propositions; it is just that metaphysical language seems to have more of it.

B

When we turn, however, to the symbolized propositions themselves— as opposed to the relationships between the linguistic forms and these propositions—we find a difference between metaphysical and ordinary language, a difference in kind. We are referring to the following claim: an ordinary proposition will *presuppose* a metaphysical pattern, whereas a metaphysical proposition will itself *be* an aspect of this metaphysical pattern. We state our explanation in terms of the predicates of the symbolized propositions. In the previous chapter, we mentioned that the essence[1] of any eternal object which is concretely exemplified in this world implicates various patterns of order. These patterns form a hierarchy, which includes the metaphysical patterns. Now when any eternal object becomes an element in the predicate of a proposition, it follows that its associated hierarchy of patterns also becomes an element in that predicate; and thus this hierarchy of patterns becomes an element in the proposition itself. In light of this fact, we may draw the conclusion mentioned above: an ordinary proposition will presuppose this metaphysical pattern, whereas a metaphysical proposition will be a part of the metaphysical pattern.[2]

C

This leads us to a rather dramatic claim. When we compare the relation of ordinary language to its symbolized propositions with the relation of metaphysical language to its symbolized propositions, we may conclude

---

1. We are referring to the relational essence of the eternal object, to be exact.
2. We will make three additional observations. First, the metaphysical patterns themselves form a hierarchy, with the notions of 'the one', 'the many', and 'creativity' at *its* top. Since the metaphysical patterns are all equally general, the basis for the hierarchy among these patterns must be abstraction in the third sense (cf. PR 31c-32c). Second, since for Whitehead alternative metaphysical schemes are conceivable, it may be that some of these alternative metaphysical schemes share some common features with *this* metaphysical system. In that case, these common features would be a pattern more abstract than the metaphysical pattern (considered as a whole) which dominates this world. Third, when entertaining a metaphysical proposition, it is quite possible to bracket from consideration other aspects of the complete metaphysical pattern. Such bracketing would result in a less than full understanding of the metaphysical proposition in question, because, according to Whitehead, the fundamental notions of a metaphysics must be coherent, that is, require each other for their full explication.

that (in certain important aspects) ordinary language is analogical whereas metaphysical language is univocal. This, of course, reverses the traditional position.

Let us turn first to ordinary language. There are three cases here. The first is where, given two or more distinct uses of some linguistic form in ordinary language, the logical subjects of the symbolized proposition are meant to be different in each case. For example, if Abraham Lincoln had told his law partner one day in August of 1849, "Some of the apples are red," he would have been referring to different apples from those I would be referring to if I uttered the same phrase in August of 1999. Since the apples in each case are different, if follows that the logical subjects in each case are different. Therefore, even if the predicates of the two propositions were identical (which would be highly improbable), the proposition symbolized by Abraham Lincoln's utterance of this phrase would only be analogous to the proposition symbolized by my utterance of this phrase. The use of the same predicate makes the propositions "similar," while the use of entirely different sets of logical subjects makes the propositions "not identical." Here "analogous" is being used in the sense of "similar but not identical" and "alike but not the same."

The second case is where, given two or more distinct uses of some linguistic form in ordinary language, the symbolized propositions are meant to be the same in each use, and thus the logical subjects are meant to be the same. For example, perhaps a friend is visiting my wife and me, and, while chatting with them both, I happen to mention that "Some of the apples are red." Presumably, it is my intention to speak both to my wife and to my friend about the same apples and, thus, the same logical subjects. But it is quite certain that my wife will use one set of logical subjects, whereas my friend will use a slightly different set of logical subjects, and I will use a third set. The differences among these three overlapping sets will not be great, but the differences will exist.[3] To the extent that the logical subjects are different, it follows that each person will entertain a slightly different proposition.[4] Thus the one use of the linguistic phrase "Some of the apples are red" has elicited a series of analogous propositions.

---

3. There is no reason to think that the differences will be great enough to impede ordinary communication.

4. In fact, if we are to be extremely fussy at this point, it must be remembered that, while I am speaking about the apples, my identity will stretch over a number of conscious entities in my soul thread. Since, as we stressed in Chapter Twelve, communication between one's earlier self and one's later self is no different in principle from communication between one person and another, it follows that I will not use *exactly* the same set of logical subjects from one entity to the next during the time that I am speaking about the apples. We may also draw a similar conclusion about my wife and friend: each of them will use a variety of logical subjects during the time that they are listening to the sentence about the apples. Therefore the one sentence about the apples will symbolize a variety of propositions in the speaker, a variety within my wife, and a variety within my friend.

We turn to the third case. For the sake of argument, let us assume that my wife, my friend, and I all succeed in using the same set of logical subjects. There is still no guarantee that either my wife or my friend will organize the logical subjects into the same societies — into the same nexuses—as *I* had in mind when *I* uttered that linguistic form.[5] For example, perhaps my wife uses the sentence "Some of the apples are red" primarily to symbolize the nexus of actual entities in the red apples, with the nexus of actual entities in the tree serving as the background. On the other hand, perhaps in my friend's mind this linguistic form elicits *both* the nexus of the apples *and* the nexus of the tree. And yet, in speaking these words, I may have had still a different arrangement in mind.

What we wish to conclude from this illustration may be stated as follows. Every linguistic form of ordinary language symbolizes propositions in such a way that there is a fundamental openness as to how to organize the logical subjects of the proposition in terms of patterns of generality. Which societies are to be felt as a part of the foreground and which as part of the background? It is this system for organizing the logical subjects into societies of ascending generality which is not—and cannot—be determined (i.e., shaped or specified) with absolute precision by any linguistic form.[6] Therefore, given the linguistic form "Some of the apples are red," the propositions constructed by my wife and by my friend will only be analogous to each other; and both of them will be analogous to the proposition which I as the speaker originally constructed. The logical subjects of each of these propositions will not be organized into identical systems of foreground and background societies. Sometimes a very general pattern will be explicitly recognized, and at other times it will not be so recognized, either because it is too obvious to mention or because it is simply unknown. In this sense a linguistic form of ordinary language will symbolize propositions which are analogous, but not identical, to each other.

Let us now turn to metaphysical language. In relation to the specific issues mentioned above, metaphysical language is not analogical. It is univocal. In the first two cases, we showed that in ordinary lan-

---

5. In this paragraph, we are applying the results of our discussion in Section II of the previous chapter.

6. Of course, we can greatly enhance the precision by using many different sentences to organize the logical subjects into foreground and background patterns. Moreover, every sentence has a context not only in the whole of the language of the speaker/hearer and in their culture, but it also has a context in the particular situation. The context aids in specifying certain patterns as appropriate and others as inappropriate. Nevertheless, there is no reason to think that either additional sentences or a fuller context will "succeed" in totally specifying the exact arrangement of the logical subjects into foreground and background societies. (It is hard to think of a case where it would be to anybody's advantage to achieve complete and total precision in specifying the arrangement of the logical subjects into broader and narrower patterns.)

guage a single linguistic phrase can symbolize propositions with (either completely or partially) different sets of logical subjects in each proposition. Such ordinary language is analogical. This cannot happen with metaphysical language. Since the logical subjects of a metaphysical proposition include all actual entities whatsoever, it follows that there can be no uncertainty as to which actual entities are to be considered the logical subjects. Thus a linguistic form of metaphysical language will, when used on one occasion, elicit a proposition where that proposition has the same logical subjects as any other (metaphysical) proposition elicited by that linguistic form on any other occasion of its use. In the third case, we argued that ordinary language will be analogical because every linguistic form symbolizes propositions in such a way that there is a fundamental openness as to how to organize the logical subjects of the proposition into background and foreground societies. This, however, cannot happen with metaphysical language. Metaphysical propositions use all actual entities whatsoever as logical subjects. Thus there can be no nexus of wider generality which may serve as the background for the logical subjects of a metaphysical proposition. Therefore there is no question as to the system to be used for organizing the logical subjects of a metaphysical proposition; the only system is to include all actual entities and to exclude none. In this sense, metaphysical language is not analogical, it is univocal.

II

For Whitehead, the true method of philosophy is the method of generalization (PR 7b). Consequently, a metaphysical proposition has a predicate which applies to all actual entities. But at the same time Whitehead insists that "Philosophy is the criticism of abstractions which govern special modes of thought" (MT 67b; SMW 87b). Does this amount to a contradiction? Can one criticize abstractions by retreating to a higher level of abstraction? To answer these questions, it will be useful to recollect the various types of abstraction which we examined in Section I of Chapter Fourteen.

First, abstraction sometimes means simplification. Such typically human items as sense perception, ordinary forms of memory, common forms of consciousness, and clear and distinct thoughts are all dependent upon this process of simplification. In this sense they are abstractions. Since philosophy is interested in experience in all its concreteness and completeness, philosophy will, according to Whitehead, discover that these items are abstractions; philosophy will name them as such; philosophy will show their connection with the richer fabric of experience out of which they come; and philosophy will show how these abstractions are related to each other. In this sense, philosophy is the critic of abstractions. But is philosophy itself an abstraction in this sense? Now, although no person, including the philosopher, can keep track of all the details of any moment of experience, still the philosopher takes note of the fact that such a plethora of details exists, and the philosopher uses this knowledge to account for such things as sense perception and consciousness. Therefore, in this sense of abstraction, metaphysics both is and is not abstract. It *is* abstract in that even an ideal metaphysics cannot mention every detail of the universe; philosophy must be content with patterns which simplify. It is *not*, however, abstract in that (A) its patterns acknowledge and explain the variegated richness of our experience and (B) its patterns apply to every item of our experience so that every detail, even if not explicitly mentioned by these simplifying metaphysical patterns, will still illustrate those patterns.

Second, abstraction sometimes means a part of a whole. There are different types of part-whole relations, of which we mentioned two: (1) the relation which a brick (the part) has to a wall (the whole), and (2) an aesthetic whole-part relation. According to Whitehead, the fundamental patterns of order are artistic.

> The metaphysical doctrine, here expounded, finds the foundations of the world in the aesthetic experience, rather than—as with Kant—in the cognitive and conceptual experience. All order is therefore aesthetic order, and the moral order is merely certain aspects of aesthetic order. The actual world is the outcome of the aesthetic order and the aesthetic order is derived from the immanence of God (RM 101b).

Each actual entity is an aesthetic whole. Therefore, to take a part of that entity and isolate it, is to create an abstraction. When we turn to the broad areas of human knowledge and activity—that is, when we turn to areas such as law, physics, medicine, psychology, history, sports, family life, and carpentry—we still find these aesthetic whole-part patterns in operation. Each of these areas may be considered a part of the whole of life. Each of them draws upon certain aspects of the actual entities—that is, the occasions of experience—which are the bearers of life. Therefore, each of these areas of life is an abstraction from the whole. Philosophy is the attempt to find the patterns which apply to the whole of life. In light of these patterns, philosophy can provide the proper context for the understanding of each of these partial perspectives on life. Insofar as philosophy does, in fact, achieve its goal of seeing life as a whole, it points to that which is not abstract and, in doing so, provides the tools for properly critiquing the abstractions of life.

> There is one moral to be drawn. Apart from detail, and apart from system, a philosophic outlook is the very foundation of thought and life. The sort of ideas we attend to, and the sort of ideas which we push into

the negligible background, govern our hopes, our fears, our control of be-
havior. As we think, we live. This is why the assemblage of philosophic
ideas is more than a specialist study. It molds our type of civilization (MT
87d).

The third type of abstraction may be illustrated by the following
list: a particular dog named Thor, a German Shepherd, a dog, a canine, a
mammal, an animal, a living body, a body extended in space and time, a
creature. The list proceeds from the least abstract to the most abstract. Our
question is this: Is philosophy itself abstract in this sense? Or is there some
sense in which philosophy is not abstract but is merely the criticism of
such abstractions? Let us answer these questions as follows. Certainly,
philosophy is abstract—at least to some degree—in the sense that the
predicates of its propositions are abstract. For example, if we assert that
each actual entity prehends other entities, we may note that this proposition is abstract because there are many specific types of prehensions and,
even with a single type, every prehension has some characteristic which
distinguishes it from every other prehension.

The goal of philosophy, however, is *not* simply to create abstract
statements, and most certainly the goal of philosophy is not to find the
most abstract characteristics possible. We may illustrate this as follows. If
we start our philosophizing from the items which we find in everyday
life, we can easily and quickly create many abstract propositions. Thus we
look about us and we see apples, foxes, stones, and water. We then classify these items into groups of ever-increasing abstraction until we arrive
at the notion of "a thing extended in space and time." Not all things,
however, are extended in space and time. We also note that people think,
hate, will, desire, are responsible, innocent, guilty, proud, vengeful, and
sincere. In order to organize this mass of data, we conceive (in accordance
with our subject-predicate linguistic habits) of a mind which does all these
things. But this mind is not one of the objects which is extended in space
and time. We are then faced with a problem in our philosophy. We may
choose to stop with the two highly abstract statements: (1) there exist
bodies extended in space and time which do not think, and (2) there exist
minds not extended in space but which do think. This set of abstract
metaphysical claims does not, according to Whitehead, constitute a good
philosophy, because they are not coherent. That is, we are confronted with
a *fait accompli.* There are bodies and there are minds; but there is no reason
why either of them requires the other. We are left with two isolated facts,
neither of which throws any light on the other. Therefore, if we desire
coherence, we will try to find still more abstract categories. Perhaps we
say that both bodies and minds have existence, and thus existence is the
basic metaphysical category. Now it may be true that all things have existence, but this fact is singularly unhelpful in figuring out the relation be-

tween body and mind, or between art and science, or between causality and freedom. In short, it does not do what a metaphysics is supposed to do: help us organize our world and relate its various parts (science and religion, art and technology) to each other. Where, then, did our process of abstraction go wrong? The answer is that we were too eager to obtain an abstract (in the third sense) set of ideas. The mere fact that a set of ideas is highly abstract does not guarantee that this set will constitute an adequate metaphysics. The goal of metaphysics, it will be recalled, does not consist merely in obtaining that description of the world which is the most abstract possible.

To help us further elucidate the relationship between metaphysical language and abstraction in the third sense, let us recur to the notion of generality. Metaphysics is meant to be general in the sense that its patterns apply to all actual entities whatsoever. But the goal of philosophy is not merely to have a set of patterns which are abstract in the third sense. Rather, metaphysical predicates will have varying degrees of abstraction in the third sense. Some predicates, such as those constituting the category of the ultimate, will be highly abstract. Others, such as those involved in the notion of a simple physical prehension, will be far less abstract. It would not be too far from Whitehead's position to say that the ideal metaphysics would be as non-abstract—in the third sense—as possible, so long as it was completely general.

III

Several times we have observed that it is extremely difficult to correlate a given linguistic form with its proper metaphysical proposition, especially when compared with the relative ease with which we correlate ordinary language with its propositions. In explaining this disparity, it helps to remember that ordinary language draws attention to factors in our environment which are sometimes present and sometimes not, whereas in metaphysics we put language to the unaccustomed task of symbolizing factors which are always present. We may restate this observation in the terminology of this chapter. Ordinary language symbolizes factors which are sometimes present and sometimes not, because it symbolizes abstractions in the first and second sense. That is, ordinary language points to the simplifications of our experience such as we find in sense perception; and it points to isolated parts of the (aesthetic) whole of our experience such as we find in a science like psychology. On the other hand, metaphysical language symbolizes propositions which are completely general and which are not abstract in the first two senses. But since language is designed to symbolize abstractions (in the first two senses), it follows that the mere fact that metaphysical language does not symbolize such abstractions will result in its being more difficult to use than ordinary language.[7]

As we previously said, the notion of the generality of a proposition is not equivalent to the notion of abstraction in the third sense. Thus, in the metaphysical quest, our goal is not merely to obtain a set of the most abstract (in the third sense) propositions possible. Our goal is to obtain a set of general propositions, and these general propositions will vary among themselves in terms of their degree of abstraction. In a rough way, however, there does seem to be a correlation between generality and abstraction (third sense). Even the quickest of glances at Whitehead's own metaphysical system as outlined in the first part of *Process and Reality* will reveal its high level of abstraction. Moreover, a rapid survey of the metaphysical systems of Aristotle, Plotinus, Augustine, Aquinas, Scotus, Descartes, Spinoza, Leibniz, Hegel, and Lonergan will demonstrate that Whitehead is typical of all metaphysicians in this respect.

Nonmetaphysical, ordinary language occasionally symbolizes propositions of the most extreme abstraction (sense three); all one needs to do is study modern physics or astronomy to observe this much. Nonetheless, most ordinary language tends not be extremely abstract in this third sense (even though it may be very much abstract in the first and second senses). Thus, when metaphysical language requires the reader (or listener) to symbolize such extremely abstract propositions, most people will find their previous linguistic experience to be an inadequate background for

---

7. The traditional "substances" such as rocks, clouds, dogs, and vases are abstractions in both of these first two senses. For example, consider the dog as perceived by some concrescing actual entity. According to Whitehead, the "dog" is actually a collection of actual entities. These "doggy" actual entities, however, constitute only a small portion of the percipient's actual world—that is, a small portion of the infinite number of past actual entities which are objectively present in the percipient. In order to perceive the dog, the percipient entity must first isolate that collection of actual entities from all the other actual entities. Thus the dog is an abstraction in the second sense—that is, it is something isolated from a larger whole, from the percipient's actual world.

The percipient, however, not only isolates the "doggy" actual entities but also feels the dog as a single unit. This requires transmutation. The transmutation results in a perception in symbolic reference (the percipient having built up this perception in symbolic reference out of earlier perceptions in presentational immediacy and causal efficacy). This transmutation is a form of simplification and thus of abstraction in the first sense.

The point to note is that our Indo-European languages (and maybe others as well) are oriented to such items. Many people would consider rocks and dogs the very paradigms of concrete reality (of a "really real thing"). Thus our languages tend to center on these (very important) abstractions as if they were concrete. For most practical purposes this is acceptable and even necessary. It leads to problems, however, if we construe the preferences of our language as an adequate guide to the principles of metaphysics. It also explains why metaphysical language seems so difficult to many people. And it sheds light on why my beginning students become confused and resistant when I suggest that metaphysics deals with concrete reality while the sciences, ordinary language, and even sense experience has primarily to do with high level abstractions.

this task. It is no accident, therefore, that many of the very best meta-physicians have also been first rate logicians, mathematicians, or scientists: Aristotle, Scotus, Descartes, Leibniz, and Whitehead. And many of the rest have been at least capable observers of the logical, mathematical, or scientific scene: Plato, Aquinas, Spinoza, Bradley, and Lonergan.

When we approach such high abstraction, we will almost always find that our language is imprecise despite our best efforts to make it sharp. Whitehead often notes that there is no such thing as absolute precision in the scientific world. The scientific language is merely as precise as is needed for the purpose at hand, and there are often ambiguities in that language which are not discovered for centuries. For example, we find Whitehead writing as follows.

> It is a well-founded historical generalization, that the last thing to be discovered in any science is what the science is really about. Men go groping for centuries, guided merely by a dim instinct and a puzzled curiosity, till at last 'some great truth is loosened' (IM 166b-67a).

As an illustration of this principle, Whitehead considers the notion of an infinitely small quantity. This notion is at the heart of the science of calculus. It is fascinating to note, however, that although calculus may be considered the very paradigm of a precise science, the notion of an infinitely small quantity is itself quite obscure. When we ask what the language of calculus, which is founded upon this notion, is all about, we will discover a rich ambiguity. Or so says Whitehead. Leibniz, one of the inventors of the precise science of calculus, held that there genuinely exists— within the realm of mathematics, wherever that is — such things as infinitely small quantities. But Leibniz was wrong!

> The real explanation of the subject was first given by Weierstrass and the Berlin School of mathematics about the middle of the nineteenth century. But between Leibniz and Weierstrass a copious literature, both mathematical and philosophical, had grown up round these mysterious infinitely small quantities which mathematicians had discovered and philosophy proceeded to explain. Some philosophers, Bishop Berkeley, for instance, correctly denied the validity of the whole idea, though for reasons other than those indicated here. But the curious fact remained that, despite all criticisms of the foundations of the subject, there could be no reason to doubt but that the mathematical procedure was substantially right. In fact, the subject was right, though the explanations were wrong. It is this possibility of being right, albeit with entirely wrong explanations as to what is being done, that so often makes external criticism—that is so far as it is meant to stop the pursuit of a method—singularly barren and futile in the progress of science. The instinct of trained observers, and their sense of curiosity, due to the fact that they are obviously getting at something, are far safer guides (IM 169a).

In conclusion, the fact that metaphysical language is abstract in this third sense is an additional explanation for the inherent difficulty in using metaphysical language.

IV

In this chapter we have shown that most language is not as abstract (third sense) as metaphysical language and that no ordinary language is completely general in the sense of applying to all actual entities. From these facts Whitehead draws the conclusion that philosophy must create its own language. Either it must take old language and extend or distort its meaning, or it must create its own new language. As he puts it,

> Every science must devise its own instruments. The tool required for philosophy is language. Thus philosophy redesigns language in the same way that, in a physical science, pre-existing appliances are redesigned. It is exactly at this point that the appeal to the facts is a difficult operation. This appeal is not solely to the expression of the facts in current verbal statements. The adequacy of such sentences is the main question at issue. It is true that the general agreement of mankind as to experienced facts is best expressed in language. But the language of literature breaks down precisely at the task of expressing in explicit form the larger generalities—the very generalities which metaphysics seeks to express (PR 16b).

It must not be thought that the metaphysician is trying to replace our ordinary language with a perfect language—perfect in the sense that the symbolism between the linguistic form and the proposition is completely precise. That is, the Whiteheadian philosopher is not trying to reshape ordinary language so that one single verbal form can symbolize only one particular proposition or elicit only one particular subjective form. As long as ordinary language is precise enough to meet the task at hand, any additional precision will be at best superfluous and at worst destructive. For example, if my house is on fire, I will telephone the fire department to tell them that "My house is on fire!" Obviously, I will tell the operator the address of my house; and, if I can keep my wits about me, I will mention any difficulties the firemen may encounter in their efforts to get to the portion of the house where the fire is centered. I will not, however, indicate to the operator whether the subjective form which I am prehending in the proposition, "My house is on fire," is one of anxiety or merely one of worry. My specification of that factor would be self-defeating. When my house is burning down, I want firemen—not cognitive precision. Again, it would be irrelevant for me to specify the precise level of abstraction (in the third sense) of the eternal object to be symbolized by the word "house."

Nor should we ever expect to find the perfect philosophical—that is, metaphysical — language. Of course, we should try to make our metaphysical language as precise as possible. Unlike ordinary language, lack of precision never serves any useful function in metaphysics. Whitehead urges, however, the highest skepticism about any claim to have actually achieved such perfection in metaphysics. In part, this skepticism stems from the fact that metaphysical language is so different—in the ways stated in the previous sections of this chapter—from ordinary language, where we are most familiar and "at ease" with this ordinary language. There is, however, another reason. Whitehead is very much impressed by the limitations of the human intellect. We have witnessed Whitehead's concern for these limitations when we observed his doctrine that human consciousness is a fragile and flickering flame in human experience—a flame which is an occasional product of experience rather than its essence and foundation. Thus, Whitehead strongly doubts that humans will ever achieve any ultimate metaphysical scheme. Every scheme which we have so far examined—from Plato to Bradley—seems to have hidden limitations which were not observed by its author. Each of these schemes provides us with important insights into important aspects of human life, but none of them provides us with a scheme which is perfectly general—to say nothing of a scheme which is perfectly general *and* coherent, consistent, and adequate to all aspects of our experience. The belief that we have achieved a metaphysical system which represents the final truth, Whitehead calls the "dogmatic fallacy" (AI 208b).

A more subtle, and thus more mischievous, form of the dogmatic fallacy is the belief that humans have already entertained, consciously, all the basic ideas needed for a metaphysical system. On this view, the sole job of the metaphysician is to weave these ideas into the proper overall pattern. In addition, we sometimes encounter the associated belief that human beings already have the language with which to express these ideas. These beliefs are together termed, by Whitehead, the Fallacy of the Perfect Dictionary (MT 235d). The Fallacy of the Perfect Dictionary provides the basis for one of Whitehead's more interesting observations about contemporary philosophy.

> The Fallacy of the Perfect Dictionary divides philosophers into two schools, namely, the 'Critical School' which repudiates speculative philosophy, and the 'Speculative School' which includes it. The critical school confines itself to verbal analysis within the limits of the dictionary. The speculative school appeals to direct insight, and endeavours to indicate its meanings by further appeal to situations which promote such specific insights. It then enlarges the dictionary. The divergence between the schools is the quarrel between safety and adventure (MT 236c).

If Whitehead is even partially correct in his views (A) about the relation of verbal forms to propositions, (B) about the relation of ordinary language to metaphysical language, (C) about the limitations of the human intellect, (D) about the need, in metaphysics, to redesign language, and (E) about the goals of metaphysics, then any attempt to do metaphysics merely by analyzing our current linguistic forms is, at the least, mistaken. Likewise, any attempt to criticize or undercut metaphysics by merely analyzing our current linguistic forms is simply irrelevant.

17 Some Concluding Observations

AS THE TITLE OF THIS CHAPTER INDICATES, we will consider a variety of topics concerning the role of language within Whitehead's metaphysical scheme.

I

If our preceding discussions have been correct, then there is a deep and important connection between language and perception which we have not yet discussed. Language has the power to shape, organize, and even determine the content of our perceptions—at least to a very great degree. While Whitehead himself never develops this topic, it does seem to be implicit in his philosophy for the reasons stated below.

Language, according to Whitehead, elicits propositional prehensions. Sense perceptions, however, are a type of propositional prehension. To the extent, therefore, that language can shape the development of propositional prehensions, it can shape, *eo ipso*, our perceptions, and especially our sense perceptions.

Let us consider two ways in which language can affect our sense perceptions of the world. First, central in the development of most propositions—and all propositions which enter into sense perception—is the creation of transmutations. But the transmutations which actually do take place always represent a mere selection from the total number of possible ones. Therefore, language, in eliciting a certain propositional prehension, will also elicit a particular transmutation. And insofar as language has helped to elicit this-and-not-that transmutation, it follows that the other possible transmutations will remain in the background—unless, of course, there is a distinct reason, such as the simultaneous entertainment of another linguistic form, for eliciting these other transmutations. In summary, language will aid in producing this-and-not-that transmutation, which results in our perception of this-and-not-that world.

Second, a basic component in any sense perception is the constituent perception in presentational immediacy. In this perception, a certain eternal object is 'projected' into the strain locus. Thus, to the extent that language has influenced the choice of this-and-not-that eternal object for projection into the strain locus, it follows that language has influenced the organization and the content of our sense perceptions.

Let us give an illustration of both of the above points. During my high school years, I lived in the Panama Canal Zone. There was a particular beach where I had gone swimming and fishing many times. During my second year of high school, my biology teacher pointed out that this particular beach was inhabited by a small plant which looked very much like a silver dollar, except that it was reddish-gray. This plant was usually half buried in the sand and rocks. Before that lecture, I had never seen any of these plants, whereas, after the lecture, I saw them continually. In Whitehead's terms, I had previously transmuted the actual entities in the beach into one nexus, the beach. Further, the colors inherent in those actual entities were projected, in the perception in presentational immediacy, onto that one nexus so that the beach was "just sort of speckled with red, gray, and brown." But, after the instructor's lecture, I transmuted the actual entities in that plant into a nexus which was distinct from that of the beach. That is, the colors inherent in those actual entities in the plant were no longer suppressed and left unprojected into the strain locus, as they sometimes had been before the lecture; and the colors in the actual entities in the plant were no longer projected into the strain locus as a speck in the mottled beach, as had sometimes been the case before the lecture. Rather, those colors, after the lecture, were projected into the strain locus as the qualities inhering in that portion of the locus where the contemporary representatives of the plant were judged to be. In other words, because of the lecture, I now saw these plants in the beach, whereas before I saw merely the beach.

We can easily construct other illustrations of the power of language to shape our view of the world. A person trained in the linguistic habits of the universities of the twentieth century may see a mentally ill person in front of him, whereas a person trained in the linguistic habits of the sixteenth century may see a devil-possessed person. And where an American businessman may have dreamed that he flew to a distant land, the soul of a Mexican shaman may have flown from his body.

It would be easy to misinterpret our position here. We are *not* claiming that there is "merely" a "semantical difference" between the American with his dream and the Mexican shaman with his soul-flight—as though the "facts" were identical and only the "linguistic descriptions" were different. Rather, there is a sense in which the American and the Mexican have created different worlds for themselves—different "realities," if you please. We may recast this claim in terms of Whitehead's metaphysical system.

Each conscious actual entity in the soul thread of a human being—whether the American businessman or the Mexican shaman—must start its process of concrescence with all the multifarious detail of its actual world as objectified at the first stage. Let us give a name to the world as it is present at the first stage of concrescence, calling it Reality (with a capital R). However, before Reality can enter into the consciousness of the later stages of concrescence, it must be simplified, and various parts of it must be isolated into discrete units. (That is, abstractions in the first and second sense must be created.) Let us use the term "work-a-day world" to refer to the world insofar as it has entered into the later, conscious stages of concrescence.

We have four comments to make concerning the relation of the work-a-day world to Reality. (1) The work-a-day world is the result of the actual entity's creative manipulation of Reality. (2) Within each actual entity's Reality, there are many work-a-day worlds which are implicit as possibilities. (3) The actual entity's choice of a particular work-a-day world is often guided by the presence of language. And (4) this is because the work-a-day world consists largely of prehensions in which propositions figure prominently (e.g., perceptions in presentational immediacy as well as those prehensions which constitute ordinary human thinking),[1] and the function of language is to elicit such propositional prehensions. (We discussed in Chapter Twelve the mechanisms whereby language has this power to elicit propositional prehensions.)

Now there can be genuine differences between work-a-day worlds (e.g., between the American businessman's dream and the Mexican shaman's soul-flight). In other words, there can be a real difference in the *content* of these work-a-day worlds which is *not* merely a difference in the *descriptions* of those work-a-day worlds. Thus, when language guides the creation of a particular work-a-day world out of the Reality to be found at the first stage of concrescence, it is guiding the creation of the *content* of that work-a-day world and is not merely providing a description of that work-a-day world.[2]

The various social sciences, particularly sociology, have increasingly recognized that there is a genuine difference in (what we have called)

1. See Chapter Twelve, Section II. Also relevant is our discussion of the sense in which each stage of concrescence is a selection from the possibilities inherent in the previous stages; see Chapter Two, Section I.C. In this regard, we should also note the sense in which the subjective aim is progressively determined during the process of concrescence; see Chapter Two, Section III.C.

2. Nothing too much! Each work-a-day world bears in itself the scars of its birth in Reality. Less poetically, we may say that the later stages of concrescence do not eliminate the earlier stages of concrescence. Rather, all stages of concrescence are present to the actual entity as a whole. (See Section II.B of Chapter Two.) Thus, both the American businessman and the Mexican shaman will, if each is attentive to the *whole* of his own experience, feel that Reality which is the source of his work-a-day world. This Reality may be only vaguely and

the work-a-day worlds of various individuals. This is particularly so when we compare the work-a-day worlds of different groups of people, where each group has its own language. Consider the following passage from the well-known sociologists, Peter Berger and Thomas Luckman.

> For example, a psychological theory positing demoniacal possession is unlikely to be adequate in interpreting the identity problems of middle-class Jewish intellectuals in New York City. These people simply do not have an identity capable of producing phenomena that could be so interpreted. The demons, if such there are, seem to avoid them. On the other hand, psychoanalysis is unlikely to be adequate for the interpretation of identity problems in rural Haiti, while some sort of Voudun psychology might supply interpretive schemes with a high degree of empirical accuracy. The two psychologies demonstrate their empirical adequacy by their applicability in therapy, but neither thereby demonstrates the ontological status of its categories. Neither the Voudun gods nor libidinal energy may exist outside the world defined in the respective social contexts. But in these contexts they do exist by virtue of social definition and are internalized as realities in the course of socialization. Rural Haitians *are* possessed and New York intellectuals *are* neurotic. Possession and neurosis are thus constituents of both objective and subjective reality *in these contexts*. This reality is empirically available in everyday life. The respective psychological theories are empirically adequate in precisely the same sense.[3]

Whether from sociology or from anthropology or from our own experiences as travelers, suppose we accept, at a pre-metaphysical level, the fact that language does influence our perception of the world, as we illustrated above in the case of the plants in the beach, the insane/demon-possessed man, the dream/flight of the soul, and the libidinal energy/Voudun gods. It would then follow that we have in Whitehead's philosophy a theoretical and metaphysical system capable of explaining that fact. This is an area of Whitehead's philosophy which is relatively undeveloped. There is room for a full investigation of this topic.

II

A prerequisite for any act of linguistic symbolism is the presence of a common ground. We discussed this aspect of Whitehead's doctrine previously

---

faintly present to consciousness, but it will be persistently present. And on certain occasions (e.g., a dark night) the massiveness of Reality's presence may well be overwhelming (see Section I of Chapter Seven).

Therefore, while language may shape and create the work-a-day world, it does not thereby eliminate Reality. Even though we are linguistic beings, we still have a direct access to Reality in its pre-linguistic dimensions. This was the burden of Chapter Thirteen.

3. Peter L. Berger and Thomas Luckman, *The Social Construction of Reality*, 177. The emphases are Berger's.

in Section III of Chapter Six on Whitehead's theory of symbolism. The fact that language is so often seen as a merely arbitrary conjunction of sounds and meanings should warn us that this common ground is not at all obvious. As we mentioned in our previous discussion, the first place we should look for this common ground is in our past experiences. A child learns the meaning of "mama" when it hears this sound in conjunction with the presence of its mother. The common ground here is the common situation in which both the word and the meaning occur.

It is not a Whiteheadian doctrine that the primary purpose of language is to communicate specific bits of factual information. Thus even when sentences or phrases are used to make commands, utter prayers, baptize people, and give vent to our emotions, there still must be a common ground between the linguistic form and the symbolized propositional prehensions. Eventually, the original context which served as the common ground for symbol and meaning may be lost (cf. S 83b). In this case, the "arbitrariness" of language becomes very pronounced.

Unfortunately, Whitehead says little more about the specific nature of this common ground in the case of language. There would seem to be room for considerable development of Whitehead's theory of language at this point.

III

It is common among ordinary speakers of English — that is, speakers whose linguistic patterns are not directly shaped by philosophy or other theoretical considerations—to say that this-or-that sentence is true or false. From Whitehead's perspective, this means that the symbolized proposition is true or false.[4] Whitehead's theory of language entails several consequences for our understanding of the nature of truth or falsity.

First, since truth/falsity applies directly to the symbolized proposition, it follows that the sounds in the air and the squiggles on the page which serve as the symbols are not themselves true or false. Of course, they may be appropriate or inappropriate. As we shall see in the next section, there is a social history to any language system. Even in the case of a single speaker or writer, any significant linguistic activity is going to last through the concrescing and perishing of several actual entities in the soul thread; and, in that sense, linguistic activity even within a single person will also be social.

In light of this social embedding of language, there is something wrong with using the five letters "white" to symbolize what English

4. We discussed the nature of truth and falsity for propositions in Chapter One, Section III.C and in Chapter Four, Section II.

writers have normally meant by "black." English has room for codes, joking, irony, and exaggeration. Purposefully to make misleading connections between symbols and propositions, however, is to lie and deceive. Thus a deceitful speaker may reserve for himself an idiosyncratic connection between the symbol and a certain proposition, while letting the hearer make the socially expected connection between the symbol and some proposition. The language may well be true in that it elicited one true proposition in the speaker and another (albeit entirely different) true proposition in the hearer. And yet this true language is still deceitful because the socially expected connection between the symbol and the proposition has been exploited by the speaker to mislead the hearer.

Second, let us put entirely aside the question of deceit. We have observed repeatedly that ordinary language is always analogical. One use of a sentence will elicit a variety of propositions in the hearers. Each of these propositions has its own truth value. Because the elicited propositions are all analogous, the propositions are likely to be all true or all false. This is not, however, always the case. Because they are different propositions, it is also possible for one proposition to be true and another to be false or merely possible. Thus the same linguistic form can be true for one person and false for another because the truth value of the symbolized propositions may vary.

IV

Language is a social phenomenon. Often the history of a language is hundreds of years old. If we think of language groups, then the history of, for example, any Indo-European language or Chinese dialect is many thousands of years old. Each language expresses the historic wisdom of its culture about the significant factors in its environment. A language will tend to elicit those propositions in the concrescing actual entity which identify the most significant enduring objects in the environment. This allows the users of the language to control and, if necessary, alter that environment; and conversely, the language promotes the kinds of goals, expectations, and purposes which are functional in that environment (cf. AI 316d-17b). As Whitehead observes, a test of all symbolism is its pragmatic usefulness (PR 275b).

The values, ideals, and fears of a culture are all embedded in its language. A Japanese verb, for example, gives very little information about tense. If precise temporal relations cannot be inferred from the context, the Japanese language often requires a rather laborious circumlocution to express them. (Ask a Japanese to translate precisely, "By tomorrow afternoon, I shall have completed my lecture" or "He could have come tomorrow if he had not fallen sick yesterday.") On the other hand, a Japanese verb or pronoun will typically provide a very precise indication of the relative social status of the people involved in the conversation.

This societal history of a language allows it to perform two tasks simultaneously. On the one hand, language gives freedom and power to the individual. It does so in a variety of ways. It can give focus to our thoughts by eliciting particular prehensions of particular propositions. That is, it allows us to focus on those powers in nature, in society, and in ourselves which would otherwise remain hidden in the background, working their effects, for benefit or harm, without our control or conscious recognition of them. Thus, when we use language, we gain a greater efficacy—and thereby a greater freedom—to work our will.

> The symbolic expression of instinctive forces drags them out into the open: it differentiates them and delineates them. There is then opportunity for reason to effect, with comparative speed, what otherwise must be left to the slow operation of the centuries amid ruin and reconstruction (S 69a).

On the other hand, language also allows society to coordinate the efforts of its members. While it is obviously desirable for us as individuals to use language to sharpen our grasp of the instinctive forces, both in the environment and in ourselves, so that we can more effectively work our will, nevertheless, it is not desirable for these efforts to frustrate the similar efforts of other people. To a significant extent, the social background of language prevents this mutual frustration. Because language carries in itself the values of a culture as well as that culture's view of the external environment, people who have learned the same language will have learned similar values and similar ways of looking at the world and at themselves. People who look at the world and themselves in similar ways, and people who have shared attitudes about the purpose and meaning of life, will likely find cooperation easier, more fruitful, and more "natural." But cooperation will be more difficult, more barren, and more "artificial" for people who have different languages because this difference in languages will almost certainly entail a difference in attitudes toward the world and a difference in self-understanding. (Compare the story of the Tower of Babel in the Book of Genesis.) With regard to language, Whitehead writes:

> The imperative instinctive conformation to the influence of the environment has been modified. Something has replaced it, which by its superficial character invites criticism, and by its habitual use generally escapes it. Such symbolism makes connected thought possible by expressing it, while at the same time it automatically directs action. In the place of the force of instinct which suppresses individuality, society has gained the efficacy of symbols, at once preservative of the commonweal and of the individual standpoint. . . . This function of language depends on the way it has been used, on the proportionate familiarity of particular phrases, and on the

emotional history associated with their meanings and thence derivatively transferred to the phrases themselves. . . . But in an especial manner, language binds a nation together by the common emotions which it elicits, and is yet the instrument whereby freedom of thought and of individual criticism finds its expression (S 66a-68b).

PART FOUR: RELIGION

PART FOUR OF OUR BOOK deals with Whitehead's theory of religion. In this portion of the book, we will build upon our previous discussions of Whitehead's philosophy. Part Four is divided into three chapters. First (Chapter Eighteen) we will discuss Whitehead's theory of religious experience. Second (Chapter Nineteen) we will analyze his concept of God insofar as it explicates his theory of religious experience. Third (Chapter Twenty) we will apply his philosophy of language to his philosophy of religion. It must not be thought, however, that only the third chapter (Chapter Twenty) will presuppose the material which we developed in the previous parts. Rather, the whole of Part Four will depend upon the previous discussion.

18 Religious Experience

FOR WHITEHEAD, IT IS A BASIC METHODOLOGICAL PRINCIPLE that all philosophical construction must start with human experience. Theoretical concepts are important, but their importance lies in their ability to explicate our experience. Whitehead's discussion of religion follows this pattern. He starts with religious experience as his datum, and he introduces God primarily in the attempt to understand this experience.

I

Although experience is the datum from which we start, it is also the case that we always experience our world in the light of some theoretical structure. At first glance, Whitehead's comments on religious experience seem disorganized, ad hoc, obscure, and even contradictory. There is, however, a principle of organization which greatly clarifies these comments. Whitehead has in mind his theory of an actual entity as a concrescence. In any concrescence, there are ultimately two main factors. On the one side, there is the actual world from which the concrescence originates. The actual world is a collection of completed, determinate facts. On the other side, there is the actual process of concrescence in which the collection of completed facts is molded into a new unity. As a rough principle of distinction, we may say that science rules over the actual world out of which each new actual entity arises, whereas religion rules over the process of concrescence.

> Religion is centered upon the harmony of rational thought with the sensitive reaction to the percepta from which experience originates. Science is concerned with the harmony of rational thought with the percepta themselves. . . . Religion deals with the formation of the experiencing subject; whereas science deals with the objects, which are the data forming the primary phase in this experience. The subject originates from, and amid, given conditions; science conciliates thought with this primary matter of fact;

and religion conciliates the thought involved in the process with the sensitive reaction involved in that same process. The process is nothing else than the experiencing subject itself (PR 24a; cf. SMW 185c).

The fact that religion rules over the domain of concrescence leads us to the notion of religion as the realm of solitude. We explain as follows. Let us consider the concrescing actual entity in relation to its past, present, and future. The past world is present in the new actual entity as its first stage of development, but there is no longer any growth or development or process in that past world. Growth and development belong exclusively to the new actual entity as it creates its own individual identity. As for its present and future, we find that the concrescing actual entity is isolated from its contemporary and its future actual entities. The only relation which a concrescing entity has with its contemporaries is the fact that it shares with them, to a greater or lesser extent, the same past world. A similar situation holds for the future: the concrescing entity can experience to some degree the conditions to which the future entities will be forced to conform, but the present entity cannot literally experience the future entities in their fullness as concrescing subjects or as determinate and concrete facts. In summary, the actual process of concrescence is a private affair which cannot be shared with any other actual entity.[1]

Religion deals with the process of concrescence. Since each act of concrescence is essentially a private matter, it follows that religion in its essence is a matter of solitude.

> The great religious conceptions which haunt the imaginations of civilized mankind are scenes of solitariness: Prometheus chained to his rock, Mahomet brooding in the desert, the meditations of the Buddha, the solitary Man on the Cross. It belongs to the depth of the religious spirit to have felt forsaken, even by God (RM 19b; cf. RM 16b-c).

Although religion deals with the private process of concrescence, it perceives in that process an element which is permanent—indeed, everlasting. The religious person deals with the temporal in terms of the eternal and sees the enduring hidden in the bosom of the passing.

> Religion is the art and the theory of the internal life of man, so far as it depends on the man himself and on what is permanent in the nature of things (RM 16a; cf. RM 60a-b and PR 247a).

The recognition of the presence of the eternal in the process of concrescence gives that concrescence certain typical qualities. In the third section of this chapter, we will discuss these qualities at some length. At this

---

1. Even God is not an exception to the isolation of a concrescing actual entity; that is, the concrescing entity cannot experience God as a contemporary, functioning entity. This is because even God is present to the concrescing entity only as one of the past objective data of the first stage of concrescence.

point, it is enough to say that religious insight tends to produce in the concrescing entity the qualities of (that is, the subjective forms of) joy, refreshment, vitality, and peace (PR 47a, AI 367b). Henry Ford once defined history as "one damned thing after another." It is the permanent side of the nature of things which prevents the passage from actual entity to actual entity from sinking into the boredom of "one thing after another" (RM 77c-78a). By providing a sense of abiding worth, religion rescues life from tedium (PR 23c).

In assigning religion the domain of the subjective concrescence and science the domain of the objective data, Whitehead has not given religion the worse portion. In particular, we must not see Whitehead as reserving the realm of factuality and truth for science, while relegating religion to the realm of opinion and conjecture. Rather, for Whitehead, the actuality of an actual entity depends, in a crucial way, upon that entity's *process* of self-creation, that is, upon that entity's *act* of concrescence. Of course, an actual entity is still actual even after it has been superseded by later actual entities.[2] It is, nevertheless, the act of concrescence which provides an actual entity its fundamental claim on actuality, and every other sense in which an entity might be said to be actual is derivative. As a result, science deals with a world which is actual in a derivative and secondary sense, while religion deals with the heart and core and homeland of actuality.

There is another sense in which Whitehead has not given religion the worse portion. Religion guides the concrescence of an actual entity, but, after the concrescence has reached its satisfaction, that entity will be superseded by other actual entities; and for these later entities the original entity will be an objective datum. In short, each concrescing entity will eventually become an objective datum for later concrescences. Science, however, studies these objective data. As a result, religion presides over the creation of the world which science studies. According to Whitehead, moreover, an actual entity always enjoys some freedom to specify *how* its concrescence will occur. Since religion attempts to guide this concrescence, it follows that religious insight and belief can make a difference in the kind of world which science studies. Science studies the world which has been; religion envisions the world which might be. And since religion deals with the core of actuality, it follows that religion can, in the long run, alter the world which science studies. Therefore, science must never be allowed to circumscribe the area in which religion operates by saying that such-and-such a religious ideal is out of tune with the facts or is unrealistic; rather, religion has the power to alter reality, in the long run, to fit the ideal.

Since religion deals with the creation of the heart of actuality, it will be of overwhelming importance wherever it reaches explicit recognition. Moreover, the operation of religious principles and the existence of reli-

2. See Chapter Three, Section II.D.

gious feelings need not always involve consciousness. The importance of religion thus may well extend into the lives of people who are not overtly religious and who may even be opposed, at the conscious level, to religion.

To assert the importance of religion is not, however, to assert its necessary goodness. History does not teach that religion has always produced people whose lives have increased the opportunity for intense, nuanced, and harmonious experience with their fellow human beings, to say nothing of other creatures. Some of the worst crimes have been committed in the name of religion. Religion's importance is beyond doubt; its goodness is not.

> In considering religion, we should not be obsessed by the idea of its necessary goodness. This is a dangerous delusion. The point to notice is its transcendent importance; and the fact of this importance is abundantly made evident by the appeal to history (RM 17c; cf. PR 279a).

II

As we saw in the first section, religion is the application of the permanent side of the universe to the act of concrescence. This, however, raises a problem. For Whitehead, the process of the universe is a self-evident fact. How, then, does this "permanent side of things" find its niche in a world of endless change? How are we to verify the religious person's assertion that there exist ideals which are applicable to the concrescence of all actual entities at all times? Moreover, is there really any sense in which the accomplishments of one generation are preserved from the ravages of the next? Clearly, at one level of abstraction, the answer to the last question is "No!" We will all agree that the noblest achievements of one period of time are only partially preserved by the next period. (In technical terms, concrescing [finite] entities always objectify past actual entities with the elimination of some portion of those past entities; this is necessary if the concrescing entities are to have any significant freedom to determine their own identities.) How then are we to account for this religious intuition into the permanent side of things—the permanent principles of concrescence on the one hand, and the permanent significance of our accomplishments on the other? Is this merely wishful thinking on the part of religious people? This is the primary religious problem according to Whitehead.

> The most general formulation of the religious problem is the question whether the process of the temporal world passes into the formation of other actualities, bound together in an order in which novelty does not mean loss.
>
> The ultimate evil in the temporal world is deeper than any specific evil. It lies in the fact that the past fades, that time is a 'perpetual perishing.' Objectification involves elimination. The present fact has not the past fact with it in any full immediacy (PR 517a-b).

In part, the solution to the religious problem lies in the development of rational religion. According to Whitehead, the notion of a rational religion depends on the assumptions (A) that there exist patterns of coordination of values and (B) that these patterns apply at all times and places. In short, there are patterns of coordinated value which are metaphysical in their scope (RM 31b) and which, therefore, apply both to human conduct and to human thought. That is, these patterns are implicated in the act of concrescence, and both human action and human thought will involve these patterns of coordinated value which serve as the basis for rational religion (RM 30c).[3]

A

As the term 'rational religion' implies, the patterns of coordinated value are rational—that is, they are, at least, consistent and coherent. By consistent, Whitehead means that these patterns will neither contradict each other nor will they contradict any other pattern at the same level of generality. By coherent, Whitehead means that these patterns are not just a collection of isolated elements. Rather, each of these patterns requires the others in the sense that no one pattern "can be abstracted from its relevance to the other" patterns (PR 5a). The patterns form an aesthetic whole which cannot be broken without loss to the identity of the whole and to the identity of each element in that whole (cf. AI 336b-38a).[4]

Whitehead connects religion with the belief that the world as a whole is rational. The application of the patterns of coordinated value to *all* actuality implies that there is a coherence and an interrelatedness to actuality. The scientific quest is sustained, in part, by a belief in the rationality of the world, that is, the belief that the relevant facts in some domain can be described as instances of general principles. Thus rational religion's cultivation and articulation of the universal patterns of coordinated value will both engender and strengthen that belief in the rationality of the world which undergirds the scientific enterprise. For Whitehead, religion and rationality reinforce each other.

---

3. As matter of terminology, we note the following. So far as we can ascertain, Whitehead always uses the term "religion" in connection with human activity. Whitehead links the term 'rational religion', however, with the patterns of coordinated value. These patterns are metaphysical in scope.

Therefore, while it is only in the human context (religion) that Whitehead discusses conscious and reflective decisions to live in accordance with these patterns, the patterns themselves (in their most general form) apply to all actual entities, whether human or not, whether conscious or not, and whether members of enduring objects or not.

4. Whitehead is not arguing, it is important to note, that each pattern must be *defined* in terms of the others. This is not a doctrine of internal relations.

> That we fail to find in experience any elements intrinsically incapable of exhibition as examples of general theory is the hope of rationalism. This hope is not a metaphysical premise. It is the faith which forms the motive for the pursuit of all sciences alike, including metaphysics. . . . The preservation of such faith must depend on an ultimate moral intuition into the nature of intellectual action—that it should embody the adventure of hope. Such an intuition marks the point where metaphysics—and indeed every science— gains assurance from religion and passes over into religion (PR 67a-b).

In this quotation, Whitehead associates rationality with an idea which we mentioned only in passing. He connects rationality with the notion of a general theory, where each concrete fact is understood as an "instance" of a general principle. To say that the patterns of coordinated value are rational, therefore, is to say that these patterns are abstract principles which are "instantiated" in each act of concrescence.[5] It is the abstract character of these patterns which allows them to be permanent elements in a world of change. The details change, but the abstract ideals remain the same.

B

This brings us to a problem in Whiteheadian interpretation. Whitehead is famous for his tenacious insistence that no one ideal can serve for all people in all periods—to say nothing of all actual entities in all aeons. This is a motif which is woven into his entire book, *Adventures in Ideas*. We will quote one passage as an illustration.

> The foundation of all understanding of sociological theory—that is to say, of all understanding of human life—is that no static maintenance of perfection is possible. This axiom is rooted in the nature of things. . . . The pure conservative is fighting against the essence of the universe (AI 353h-54a).

How then are we to account for the supposed permanence of the patterns of coordinated value? Whitehead accepts religion as giving us a genuine insight into the permanent nature of things, and he says that this insight involves values, ideas, and visions of perfection. Is there a contradiction here? We do not think so. The patterns of coordinated value are highly abstract and are completely general. Thus, they allow many—in fact, an infinite number of—different ways in which they can be instantiated. The way in which one period of history will "flesh them out" will not be the same as another period of history. Thus different visions can— and must—arise in history. But these visions of perfection will be different insofar as they are concrete. At a more abstract level, they will share

---

5. By "abstract," we mean abstract in the third sense as described in Section I of Chapter Fourteen. They are also completely general in the sense described in that same section.

certain features. These shared features *are* the patterns of coordinated value of rationalized religion.

We maintain that this solution is necessary if Whitehead's metaphysics is not to sink into a slough of pointlessness. The reason is this: metaphysics aims at developing patterns which are completely general in the sense that they apply to all actual entities at all times. According to Whitehead, the heart of each actual entity is its act of concrescence, during which the actual entity chooses a satisfaction (i.e., ideal of itself) at which to aim. A concrescence thus necessarily involves the notions of an ideal and of value. Therefore, if there were not some features which all ideals and all values share in common, then we could not develop a metaphysical scheme which applied to the central notion of concrescence. In short, by denying that perfection can, in any sense, remain the same from generation to generation, Whitehead would be undercutting his entire metaphysical project—which we feel is most unlikely.

C

These patterns of coordinated value provide a counter-theme to Whitehead's association of religion with solitariness. Of course, these patterns apply to the concrescence of an actual entity, and in that sense they point to the close connection of religion with solitude. In the very act of guiding the solitary concrescence, however, these patterns reunite that concrescence with the larger world. We explain as follows. The act of concrescence "is obligated" to aim at intensity of experience. This aim at intensity of experience has two factors: first, the aim at intense experience *within* the concrescing actual entity, and, second, the aim at intense experience in the actual entities in the relevant *future* (PR 41c-d).

Whitehead analyzes in some detail the various elements which promote such intensity of experience. We will only summarize his position in the briefest possible manner.[6] An intense experience will involve (A) the feeling of a contrast among many individuals; the more individuals, the more intense will be the feeling, provided that the uniqueness of each individual is maintained and is not clouded over. Again, an intense experience will involve (B) individuals which in their own nature stand out from each other; for example, a patch of green will stand out from a patch of red in a far more striking way than a patch of light gray will stand out from a patch of cream white—all other things being equal. Last, an experience will have intensity to the extent that (C) its content is felt as an over-all aesthetic harmony and not merely as a collection of unrelated or conflicting elements (cf. AI 336b-40a). Thus we ought not to

---

6. These elements are analyzed in depth by Spencer in "The Ethics of Alfred North Whitehead."

identify this technical use of the phrase "intensity of experience" with its ordinary use where, for example, a pain may be intense but it will hardly involve aesthetic harmony. Of course, we must realize that an aesthetic harmony may require a refreshing contrast, or even a judicious amount of disharmony; thus, for example, a certain amount of pain in the proper context (say the pain felt by a well-conditioned athlete as he finishes a vigorous workout) may be a positive good.

A concrescing entity starts its drive at intense experience from its first phase. After the first stage, the concrescence can only rearrange the materials and options given to it at that first stage. Therefore, the concrescing actual entity's capacity for developing intense experiences is limited by the character and quality of the material present at its first stage. For example, consider an environment with many individuals, each with a strong sense of uniqueness, and assume that the individuals in this environment stand out from each other in a dramatic way. Further assume that these individuals have developed with reference to each other in such a way that they are compatible for integration into an aesthetic whole. A new actual entity which has objectified such an environment into its first stage of concrescence will have the possibility of deep and intense experience indeed.

We said in the first paragraph of this subsection that there are two factors in the drive toward intensity of experience in an actual entity, the first being the obligation to drive toward intensity *within* the satisfaction of the actual entity. The second factor is the actual entity's obligation to drive at intensity of experience in the actual entities of its relevant *future* (PR 41c-d). The actual entity is able to drive towards intensity of experience in the future because the concrescing entity knows something of the present factors which will survive into the future. The future entities *must* conform, to a greater or lesser extent, to *these* factors. Thus, the present actual entity knows the future by knowing the present.[7]

The concrescing actual entity must aim at intensity of experience in its transcendent future. In doing so, it thereby increases its own intensity of experience in the present.[8] The assumption which Whitehead seems to make is that the more the present actual entity is capable of aiding the

---

7. We are building upon the discussion of the immanence of the future in the present to be found in Section II.C of Chapter Eight.

8. There is a problem which is worth raising at this point. Let us grant that the concrescing entity is obligated to seek its own intensity of experience and that the anticipation of intense future experiences contributes to the intensity of the present experience. The problem: Is an actual entity's obligation to seek intense future experiences a *separate* obligation from its obligation to seek its own present intensity of experience? Or should we say that *because* the anticipation of intense future experiences increases intensity in the present, the concrescing entity is *therefore* obligated to seek future intensity as an aspect of its prior obligation to seek its *own* intensity of experience?

We are inclined to the position that sees the obligation to seek intense experiences in the future as arising out of the concrescing entity's prior obligation to seek its own intense

production of intense experiences in future actual entities, the greater will be its present anticipation of that role; and the greater its present anticipation, the more intense will be its present experience as a whole. The task then for the present actual entity is to create an identity which will aid the production of intense experiences in the future—both for the sake of the future and for its own sake. This is accomplished by surveying those present factors which will survive into the future. The point to note, however, is that the actual entities in the future will have their own freedom in deciding how to react to these factors (which are now "present" but which will be "past" to the future concrescences), and so the present actual entity can anticipate only the *outlines* of its future. Of course, the outlines of the immediate future are known in considerable detail, while the outlines which apply to the more distant future are more abstract. In either case, the present actual entity knows enough about the future to know what its own final self-identity should be in order to promote the production of intense experiences in its future. The present entity must be a strong individual which is so related to the surrounding individuals that the future actual entities can form an aesthetically balanced feeling of them—that is, of the present actual entity and its neighbors. To the extent that the present actual entity can create such an identity, the present entity will achieve depth of feeling.

The ultimate extension of the present actual entity's ability to gain intensity of experience from its anticipations of the future would result from the present entity's anticipation of its role in *all* of future actuality. To anticipate its role in all of future actuality, however, would require a

---

experiences. The reason is that the concrescence is the central form of actuality for Whitehead. The status of the future is derived from the fact that this concrescence started as an organization of many past data, achieves its own identity, and then becomes one more addition to the many data. The necessity for the future thus emerges out of the character of the past and present. It would seem plausible, therefore, to see an obligation towards the future as arising out of a prior obligation towards the present.

The reader should be aware that there is no agreement about this issue. Some Whiteheadian scholars strongly disagree with us. (For example, John B. Cobb, Jr., in a personal conversation with the author in Tokyo, 1980.) The issue becomes clearer if we state it in terms of God. Is God obligated to aim at intense experiences for the entities in his future (that is, intense experiences for creatures, such as us) *because* it increases his own intensity of satisfaction? Or does God's obligation towards creation exist quite independently of his own drive towards his own intensity of experience?

The first alternative makes God's own glory (his own intensity of satisfaction) the final cause of all his actions. This is not a very Whiteheadian motif. The second alternative makes the obligation to drive after future intensity of experience into an ultimate which is simply "there" as a moral reality to which any concrescing actual entity must conform. This second alternative coheres well with the Whiteheadian claim that there are two types of process: concrescence (thus obligation to the present) and transition (thus obligation to the future). And it coheres well with the motif that each actual entity is really a subject (present obligation) and a superject (future obligation). But this second alternative does not cohere so well, it seems to us, with the Whiteheadian claim that the here-and-now concrescence is the *foundation* of all actuality. This is the key argument in favor our position.

knowledge of the metaphysical patterns governing the concrescence of actual entities. This brings us back to rational religion's patterns of coordinated value. Each actual entity has an ideal self-identity, and the patterns of coordinated value are abstract elements which are present in each and every ideal self-identity. Thus, to the extent that a new actual entity guides its development in the light of these patterns of coordinated value, the new entity can enjoy anticipations of its positive role in all of actuality.

We have now come to the opposite pole from solitude. When an actual entity—solitary in its concrescence, to be sure—guides that concrescence in the light of rational religion's patterns of coordinated value, it has in that very act affirmed its solidarity with the world as a whole. In rational religion, solitude and world-affirmation meet.

> In its solitariness the spirit asks, What, in the way of value, is the attainment of life? And it can find no such value till it has merged its individual claim with that of the objective universe. Religion is world-loyalty.
>
> The spirit at once surrenders itself to this universal claim and appropriates it for itself. So far as it is dominated by religious experience, life is conditioned by this formative principle, equally individual and general, equally actual and beyond completed act (RM 59b-c).

In its fullness, world-loyalty has a Kantian flavor. Since the present actual entity knows only the outlines of the future—and only the metaphysical outlines of the future as a whole—it follows that the present entity will know individual future actual entities only as representatives of a type or class of entities. But to increase its own anticipation of its role in *all* of future actuality, the present entity must consider each actual entity only insofar as it is a representative of the entire class of actual entities.

Of course, the present actual entity does know the outlines of the immediate future in some detail. In the human case, this opens up a very common temptation. I am well aware that my own future well-being crucially depends on the well-being of my own body as well as my family, my home, my company, and my nation. (That is, my continuation as an enduring society depends on the continuation of certain other enduring societies in my environment.) The temptation is to abandon my concern for all actual entities and to focus instead on my role in the future insofar as it impinges upon those people who are near and dear to me and upon those objects and institutions (houses and nations) upon which my own well-being rests. To succumb to this temptation, however, is a failure at two levels. First, it is to abandon the obligation to aim at intensity of experience in the relevant future, where a knowledge of the patterns of rational religion make the entire future into the relevant future. Second, it is to limit my ability to anticipate a role in the entire transcendent future and thereby limit my present intensity of experience. The person who acts self-

ishly lacks the imagination to see his role in the entire future and thereby
deprives himself of the fuller satisfactions of action in accordance with rational religion's patterns of coordinated value.

Therefore, in addition to considering the details of its near future,
the present actual entity must also consider each and every future entity
insofar as each such future entity is a representative of the entire class of
actual entities. The present entity must do its best to contribute to all of
actuality, where this is in addition to any contribution it may make to this-
or-that specific future entity.

> Now, so far as concerns religion, the distinction of a world-conscious-
> ness as contrasted with a social consciousness is the change of emphasis in
> the concept of rightness. A social consciousness concerns people whom you
> know and love individually. Hence, rightness is mixed up with the notion of
> preservation. Conduct is right which will lead some god to protect you; and
> it is wrong if it stirs some irascible being to compass your destruction. Such
> a religion is a branch of diplomacy. But a world-consciousness is more dis-
> engaged. It rises to the conception of an essential rightness of things. The in-
> dividuals are indifferent, because unknown (RM 39c-40a).

D

In contrast to a rational religion, there is also such a thing as a barbaric
religion. What Whitehead has in mind is this. A rational religion points
to a set of general ideas which are consistent and coherent and which
promote an affirmation of all actuality. A barbaric religion points to factors which are inconsistent or incoherent or which repress the affirmation of all actuality.

According to Whitehead, some of the common points of view to be
found both in the Bible and in Western theology represent such a bar-
barism. (Other portions of the Bible and Western theology, or course, understand God in ways that are consonant with rational religion.) His
polemic against many of the traditional Western concepts of God is too
well known to be repeated here. We shall only observe why Whitehead
thinks that such a "God" is (at best, a sublimation of) a barbaric notion (AI
212c, 213c, 216c-17a). This "God" is conceived as very much transcendent.
As such he is exempted from the categories which apply to every other
entity. Whitehead describes this as paying metaphysical compliments to
God. As a result of these metaphysical compliments, this concept of God
is uncoordinated with our understanding of the rest of actuality. This lack
of coordination results not so much in a contradiction between this "God"
and our knowledge of the world as in a lack of contact in our experience
between this "God" and the world in which we live. Consequently, while
we may not be able to prove the non-existence of this "God," we also lack
any positive reason for thinking that he does exist (RM 68b-c). In sum-

mary, we lack any way of systematically connecting this "God" with our ordinary human world; none of the alleged proofs seems to work, and any alleged experience of this "God" will be adventitious, ad hoc, and susceptible to explanation as "merely" the result of wish fulfillment, neurosis, or a bit of rancid cheese.[9] A system of actuality which includes such a "God" is incoherent, inharmonious, and unaesthetic. It is barbaric.

E

In this section, we have stressed that the patterns of coordinated value are highly abstract. In Whitehead's opinion, this abstraction is closely connected with the permanence, universality, and rationality of these patterns. These patterns, however, can serve as a guide to the new concrescence only insofar as they have been "fleshed out" in detail. The reason for this is simple: there is no such thing as value in the abstract (RM 100a). Each individual actual entity strives for a specific goal—a specific self-identity. Thus the patterns of coordinated value will be found in an individual concrescence only as abstract elements in the very specific ideal which guides that concrescence.

The task for religion, then, is to express these abstract patterns in specific terms. In part, this is automatically done.[10] Since these patterns are metaphysical in their generality, it follows that they are exemplified in every actual entity. The more explicit these patterns become in an actual entity, the more effective they will be in guiding the concrescence. Thus the function of religion is to make these patterns explicit and, thereby, to make them more effective in guiding the development of the actual entity.

> Religion should connect the rational generality of philosophy with the emotions and purposes springing out of existence in a particular society, in a particular epoch, and conditioned by particular antecedents. Religion is the translation of general ideas into particular thoughts, particular emotions, and particular purposes. . . . Religion is an ultimate craving to infuse into the insistent particularity of emotion that non-temporal generality which primarily belongs to conceptual thought alone (PR 23c).

9. Langdon Gilkey makes a similar observation on the origin of the Death of God movement. He claims that Karl Barth and other neo-orthodox thinkers made God so utterly transcendent that the relationship of God to our everyday life was lost. At best, God broke into our lived-experience like a "bolt out of the blue." The result was that God became so detached that the Death of God thinkers found it convenient (for this among other reasons) to declare him dead. Barth unwittingly had helped to sharpen the guillotine blade that the Death of God advocates used to chop "God" off from the body of Christology, ecclesiology, and ethics. (Curiously, these thinkers did not declare the decapitated body to be dead—only the head!) See Gilkey, *Naming the Whirlwind*, 73-146.

10. As we observed in Section III of Chapter Two of Part One, God is the source of each entity's subjective aim. God, therefore, is the source of the "automatic" relevance of the abstract patterns of coordinated value to the particular nature of each actual entity.

    Creaturely freedom enters into our discussion of the patterns of rational religion at two levels. At the first level, each pattern allows for many different instantiations where each instantiation is legitimate and good. Thus creaturely freedom is a positive good insofar as (A) it chooses among equally valid ways of fleshing out the patterns or (B) it creates or discovers a valid concretization of the patterns. Such choosing, creating, and discovering of particular instantiations of the patterns is necessary before these abstract ideals can be made concrete and, thus, real.

    There is, however, a second and more somber form of creaturely freedom. We have the capacity to distort the ideals themselves. We turn now to some comments on evil and the patterns of coordinated value. Implicit in our discussion of rational religion's patterns of coordinated value has been the claim that these patterns can be exemplified to a greater or lesser extent. In this regard, the patterns of coordinated value have a status unlike that of other metaphysical patterns. For example, consider the metaphysical proposition, "Each actual entity prehends its past actual entities." Either the predicate of this proposition is exemplified in each actual entity or it is not so exemplified. This is not the case, however, with the patterns of coordinated value, which may be partially realized and partially discarded. For Whitehead, the existence of evil is proof positive that the patterns of rational religion are not completely exemplified in reality (RM 49b, 74c).

    In this regard, let us note two aspects of his doctrine of evil. First, an actual entity is evil to the extent that it creates a self-identity which later entities cannot integrate into a harmonious relation with its surrounding entities (RM 93b). In short, it has blocked the production of intense—and aesthetically balanced—feelings in some area of the future where it *could* have helped produce intense and well-balanced feelings instead. In this sense, evil is a failure of rationality. That is, an evil actual entity has the capacity of considering its role in the production of intense feelings within some large section of the future—perhaps even future actuality as a whole —but has chosen instead to consider its role only within some very limited portion of future actuality. In another sense, the essence of evil is bad timing. The same actual entity which in one context blocks the production of deep feelings in the future might have, in another context, provided needed relief or aesthetic contrast.

    The second aspect of evil is that, in its own nature, evil is positive (RM 93b). That is, an evil actual entity might thwart the production of intense experience in the future; nevertheless, the identity which that entity has achieved constitutes a positive act of self-affirmation *for that entity.*

    Since the presence of evil in the world shows that rational religion's patterns of coordinated value are not completely exemplified in actuality, we must conclude that these patterns of coordinated value are present to each actual entity only as ideals. While these patterns are metaphysical and thus do apply to each actual entity (as ideals), they do *not* apply to each actual entity in the sense that they are fully realized in the final identity achieved by each entity. Rather, these patterns apply to each entity only in the sense that they are abstract elements in each actual entity's ideal self-identity. The following passage sums up many of the themes which we have discussed in this section.

> But there is a large consensus, on the part of those who have rationalized their outlook, in favour of the concept of a rightness in things, partially conformed to and partially disregarded. So far as there is conscious determination of actions, the attainment of this conformity is an ultimate premise by reference to which our choice of immediate ends is criticised and swayed. The rational satisfaction or dissatisfaction in respect to any particular happening depends upon an intuition which is capable of being universalized. This universalization of what is discerned in a particular instance is the appeal to a general character inherent in the nature of things (RM 65b).

III

In this section, we will discuss Whitehead's description of the patterns of coordinated value. We have already considered some of their characteristics. They are permanent, universal, rational, abstract, ideal, and express a quality of potential rightness inherent in things. What else did Whitehead have to say about these patterns?

A

Whitehead makes two sorts of additional comments on the patterns of coordinated value. On the one hand, he sometimes attempts to give a pre-systematic description of these patterns. The assumption seems to be that these patterns are data which are to be explained by his metaphysical system. From this point of view, the patterns are not directly a part of his system—although Whitehead would be the first to admit that his system has entered into and at least partially structured his description of the data (PR 21b-22a). On the other hand, he sometimes equates the "true" content of the (rationalized) religious insight directly with some aspect of his metaphysical system.

As an example of a passage where Whitehead directly equates the true content of religious insight with his metaphysics, consider the following passage.

> Religion is founded on the concurrence of three allied concepts in one moment of self-consciousness, concepts whose separate relationships to fact and whose mutual relations to each other are only to be settled jointly by some direct intuition into the ultimate character of the universe.

These concepts are:

1. That of the value of an individual for itself.
2. That of the value of the diverse individuals of the world for each other.
3. That of the value of the objective world which is a community derivative from the interrelations of its component individuals, and also necessary for the existence of each of these individuals (RM 58b-f).

The first of these concepts is simply an alternative formulation of a principle which we have much discussed, that the act of valuing a self-identity is the very heart of actuality. The second of these concepts is that, in its drive for intensity of experience, an actual entity must anticipate its role in other actual entities. The third concept is that the past actual world has value for the concrescing entity. Thus Whitehead sees religion as pointing directly toward his metaphysics—which is, of course, what we should expect, since Whitehead desires his metaphysics to be applicable to all our human experiences.

Most of Whitehead's descriptions of the patterns of rational religion are not, however, expressed directly in terms of his metaphysical scheme—although, as we observed above, he has used his metaphysics to organize and interpret his data. One of the more dominant motifs in Whitehead's pre-systematic description of rational religion is that religion, at its finest, points to the element of persuasion in the world (AI 213c, 218b). Compulsion may seem to dominate everything, but, in fact, there is the element of persuasion luring us to new types of experience. The patterns of coordinated value express the ideal side of the universe. The ideal, however, is ultimately characterized by harmony (AI 350c-51a). That is, the patterns of coordinated value are persuasive because they express the ideal of harmony. In short, rational religion points to the tenderness of love as the divine element of the universe (PR 520d-21a).

Closely related to Whitehead's motif of religion as persuasion is his admiration of the "interim" ethics of the New Testament. Believing that the world was about to end, the early Christians were free to speculate on the nature of an ideal life—a life in which one could love one's enemies, forgive a man seven times seventy times, and give the robber one's undershirt as well as one's outer shirt. Of course, if these precepts were literally followed at the present, society would instantly collapse (AI 18b), but, as we mentioned in the first section of this chapter, religion ultimately has the power to transform the world. The patient operation of the lure of religious ideals can alter the very structures of the universe.

The progress of humanity can be defined as the process of transforming society so as to make the original Christian ideals increasingly practicable for its individual members (AI 18b).

No description of the patterns of coordinated value would be complete without introducing the notion of peace. Whitehead's basic discussion of peace occurs at the end of *Adventures of Ideas*, where it is linked with truth, beauty, art, and adventure. Peace provides the context for these other four factors and is thus the most basic of the group (AI 367a). We shall therefore confine our discussion to peace. Whitehead does not explicitly connect peace with religion nor with religion's patterns of coordinated value; but the connection is there implicitly. Peace is the result of living a life in which the ideals of religion are expressed concretely—that is, a life in which each actual entity in the soul has allowed the patterns of coordinated value to mold the act of concrescence. At least, that is how we would interpret passages such as the following, in which Whitehead gives his description of peace.

> It has a positive feeling which crowns the 'life and motion' of the soul. It is hard to define and difficult to speak of. It is not a hope for the future, nor is it an interest in present details. It is a broadening of feeling due to the emergence of some deep metaphysical insight, unverbalized and yet momentous in its coordination of values (AI 367b).

In the next passage, peace is said to promote intensity of experience in the present by forcing the concrescing entity to consider its role in all of actuality. This is, of course, very similar to Whitehead's description of rational religion's patterns of coordinated value.

> Thus Peace is the removal of inhibition and not its introduction. It results in a wider sweep of conscious interest. It enlarges the field of attention. Thus Peace is self-control at its widest,—at the width where the 'self' has been lost, and interest has been transferred to coordinations wider than personality. Here the real motive interests of the spirit are meant, and not the superficial play of discursive ideas. Peace is helped by such superficial width, and also promotes it. In fact it is largely for this reason that Peace is so essential for civilization. It is the barrier against narrowness. One of its fruits is that passion whose existence Hume denied, the love of mankind as such (AI 368b).

Finally, we must note a theme which will be a major consideration in Chapter Twenty, that peace—and the patterns of coordinated value—are distinct from the verbal phrases which describe and promote them. Therefore, the concrete *realization* of peace and rational religion is far more important than their proper *description*. The following paragraph occurs near the end of Whitehead's chapter on peace. Although it is part of a larger section pointing to the need for God, it also illustrates the theme that peace is not primarily a matter of words.

> *Non in dialectica complacuit Deo salvum facere populum suum.* [It did not please God to save his people by means of dialectic.] This saying, quoted by Cardinal Newman, should be the motto of every metaphysician. He is seeking, amid the dim recesses of his ape-like consciousness and beyond

the reach of dictionary language, for the premises implicit in all reasoning. The speculative methods of metaphysics are dangerous, easily perverted. So is all Adventure; but Adventure belongs to the essence of civilization (AI 38b; translation of Latin added).[11]

B

Before leaving this section, we must ask the following questions. How adequate is Whitehead's description of religion? Does Whitehead really connect his metaphysics with religion as it exists in the concrete world? Or has he created merely an empty theory of religion with no genuine application? According to Whitehead, the chief danger in doing philosophy is the narrowness of evidence (PR 512a). Moreover, "this narrowness arises from the idiosyncrasies and timidities of particular authors, of particular social groups, of particular schools of thought, or particular epochs in the history of civilization" (PR 512a). Whitehead writes about religion as a latitudinarian Anglican. Has this fact biased his description of religion?

One of the characteristics most notably lacking in Whitehead's description of rational religion is what Rudolf Otto calls the numinous.[12] The object of a genuinely numinous experience is the *mysterium tremendum*.[13] The mysterium tremendum will be felt as awesome, overwhelming, and urgent. It is also felt as "wholly other." According to Otto,

> Taken in the religious sense, that which is 'mysterious' is—to give it perhaps the most striking expression—the 'wholly other' . . . that which is quite beyond the sphere of the usual, the intelligible, and the familiar, which therefore falls quite outside the limits of the 'canny', and is contrasted with it, filling the mind with blank wonder and astonishment.[14]

In another passage, Otto writes,

> The truly 'mysterious' object is beyond our apprehension and comprehension, not only because our knowledge has certain irremovable limits, but because in it we come upon something inherently 'wholly other', whose kind and character are incommensurable with our own, and before which we therefore recoil in a wonder that strikes us chill and dumb.[15]

In his book *The Sacred and the Profane*, Mircea Eliade begins by summarizing Otto's work, which he considers accurate but incomplete. According to Eliade, the manifestations of the sacred are characterized by their discontinuity with the profane world, that is, the natural world, the

---

11. As this quotation indicates, our emphasis on rational religion as promoting peace should not be taken to exclude the qualities of adventure or zest from religion.
12. Otto, *The Idea of the Holy*, 5-11.
13. Ibid., 12.
14. Ibid., 26.
15. Ibid., 28.

everyday world, the ordinary world. In this sense, Eliade's work continues Otto's interpretation of the numinous as the wholly other. In his own words,

> Man becomes aware of the sacred because it manifests itself, shows itself, as something wholly different from the profane. . . . It could be said that the history of religions—from the most primitive to the most highly developed—is constituted by a great number of hierophanies, by manifestations of the sacred realities. From the most elementary hierophany—e.g., a manifestation of the sacred in some ordinary object, a stone or a tree—to the supreme hierophany (which, for a Christian, is the incarnation of God in Jesus Christ) there is no solution of continuity. In each case we are confronted by the same mysterious act—the manifestation of something of a wholly different order, a reality that does not belong to our world, in objects that are an integral part of our natural "profane" world.[16]

According to Eliade, the sense of the sacred as wholly other and as discontinuous is typical of all religion whatsoever. This claim has been challenged, however. For example, Ninian Smart, in discussing Otto's theory of the numinous as the wholly other, denies that such an emphasis on discontinuity is appropriate for such figures as the Buddha and Shankara. But even Smart willingly admits that Otto's description does hold for much of the religious world: for Isaiah's vision in the temple, for Paul's vision on the Damascus Road, for the call of Muhammad, and for the theophany in the Bhagavad-Gita.[17] He writes,

> Otto makes much of the separation between the Other and the creature, between God and man. In this he is right, for it is indeed characteristic of numinous, prophetic experiences that there is a sense of the gulf fixed between the experiencer and the Other, just as in worship, which expresses awe, there is a sense of the gulf fixed between the worshiper and the Object of worship—a gulf to be bridged, if at all, by the gracious condescension of the Other. All this characterizes one aspect of the religious life well.[18]

We return now to Whitehead. It is, I think, fair to say that Whitehead does not take this sense of the numinous as his key to the essence of rational religion. Whitehead is not unaware of this aspect of religion, but he considers it a primitive or barbaric feature of religions, claiming that it results from the sublimation of the sense of power. With simplicity and clarity, Whitehead writes,

> The collection of Psalms is not properly a reflective book. . . . There is joy in the creative energy of a supreme ruler who is also a tribal champion. There is the glorification of power, magnificent and barbaric:

16. Eliade, *The Sacred and the Profane,* 11.
17. Smart, *The Philosophy of Religion,* 13.
18. Ibid., 13-14.

> The earth is the Lord's, and the fullness thereof; the world, and they
> that dwell therein.
>
> Who is this king of glory? The Lord of hosts, he is the king of
> glory. (Psalms xxiv.)

Magnificent literature! But there is no solution here of the difficulties which
haunted Job. This worship of glory arising from power is not only dangerous: it arises from a barbaric conception of God. I suppose that even the
world itself could not contain the bones of those slaughtered because of
men intoxicated by its attraction. This view of the universe, in the guise of
an Eastern empire ruled by a glorious tyrant, may have served its purpose. . . . [But] The glorification of power has broken more hearts than it
has healed (RM 54b-55a; bracketed word added).

Again Whitehead writes,

> On the whole, the Gospel of love was turned into a Gospel of fear.
> The Christian world was composed of terrified populations.
>
> "The fear of the Lord is the beginning of knowledge," said the Prov-
> erb (i. 7). Yet this is an odd saying, if it be true that "God is love."
>
> In flaming fire taking vengeance on them that know not God
> and that obey not the gospel of our Lord Jesus Christ; says Paul.
>
> Who shall be punished with everlasting destruction from the
> presence of the Lord, and from the glory of his power. (II Thes-
> salonians i. 8, 9.)
>
> The populations did well to be terrified at such ambiguous good
> tidings, which lost no emphasis in their promulgation (RM 72c-73d).

A number of issues arise from Whitehead's comments on the role
of "glory" or the "wholly other" in religion. When Whitehead speaks of
the "sublimation of power," he is speaking of the sublimation of coercive
power. God becomes the ultimate tyrant. If someone's fascination with
the numinous becomes intoxication with coercive power resulting in a
greater willingness to break bones and murder hostages, then we also
must join Whitehead in rejecting the numinous as a guide to the deeper
character of religion.

It may, however, be worth trying to develop an interpretation of the
numinous (or God as "wholly other") which is consistent with Whitehead's
metaphysical scheme but which does not appeal to the "sublimation" of
coercive power. John B. Cobb, Jr., has offered an interpretation according
to which (his Whiteheadian based concept of) God is "wholly other." According to Cobb, to say that God is wholly other is to say that (A) God is
numerically other than human beings, (B) God is not an object of sense perception, (C) God does not occupy a particular region in the continuum,
and, therefore, (D) God is also absolutely present with me.[19]

---

19. *A Christian Natural Theology*, 238-46.

Cobb's comments are helpful, but in our opinion they do not go far enough. Whitehead's original insight remains correct: many religious visions are connected with the sublimation of power. There is, however, in Whitehead's own system another type of power, namely, creativity. It seems to us that it is possible to construe much of the traditional Christian, Jewish, Islamic, and even Hindu discussion of "the Wholly Other" as a description of the human encounter with creativity. Creativity gives each actual entity its being. Creativity is prior to each actual entity. Creativity is not the object of any prehension, and it is neither an actual entity, nor an eternal object, nor an enduring object, nor an enduring society. Given this description, it seems to us that creativity satisfies Cobbs' criteria for being the Wholly Other: creativity is numerically other than us human beings, not an object of any sort of prehension, not located at any particular region, and yet always and totally present with me. The numinous thus may be interpreted as resulting from our human encounter with creativity.

In Western religion, the numinous has been traditionally identified with God. This is not possible on Whitehead's scheme because he clearly distinguishes between creativity and God. Is it, however, essential to retain Whitehead's distinction between God and creativity? Many Whiteheadian scholars defend the distinction because they see his clear separation between God and creativity as essential for human freedom. Lewis Ford writes,

> If God creates the occasion by bringing it into being, then God determines what that occasion will be. All the activity and freedom of the concrescence is thereby by-passed.[20]

The reunion of creativity and God, however, would certainly support the classical Western view of God as the Wholly Other and the numinious. Whether this reunion could be accomplished without cutting the nerve of Whitehead's whole enterprise, and especially of his extraordinary description of creaturely freedom, is the open question.

The question is very important. The union of Whitehead's God with creativity would open up his process vision for a much larger number of traditional Christians (and perhaps Jews and Muslims as well), and it would allow Whitehead to appropriate much more of the Western heritage of religious affirmation of God as the numinous and as the source of being. The danger, of course, is the loss of his powerful description of human freedom and of his description of the divine as persuasive rather than coercive.[21]

20. Personal letter from Lewis S. Ford to the author, January 3, 1984.
21. Cobb has discussed a similar issue from the point of view of the relation between Christianity and Buddhism in *Beyond Dialogue*. By retaining the clear distinction between God and creativity, Cobb is able to affirm two ultimates. The one ultimate is God, the other

IV

Whitehead discerns three stages in the development of Western religion: first, the expression of a general idea; second, the exemplification of that idea; third, the metaphysical elaboration of that idea. Plato expressed the idea, Jesus exemplified it, and the theologians of Alexandria and Antioch elaborated it. Whitehead says that these are the three phases of a "revelation" (AI 213b).

A

Plato's intuition, which was the first step, was that the divine element in the world was to be conceived as a persuasive agency and not as a force of compulsion (AI 213c). In short, Plato had grasped the essential nature of rational religion. Before discussing the second stage, let us skip to the third. The question before the early Christian theologians was: How are we to conceive the world so that we can rationally understand God as a persuasive agent? Of course, the early theologians saw themselves as primarily answering questions about the nature(s) of the Christ and about the nature of God. But in solving these special problems, they worked out various theories of the direct immanence of God in the world (the two natures of Christ and pneumatology) and the direct immanence of God within himself (the Trinity). This doctrine of immanence is the key, in Whitehead's opinion, to understanding how God can be ultimately persuasive and yet effective in changing the world. Speaking of these theologians, Whitehead says,

> My point is that in the place of Plato's solution of secondary images and imitations, they demanded a direct doctrine of immanence. It is in this respect that they made a metaphysical discovery. They pointed out the way in which Platonic metaphysics should develop, if it was to give a rational account of the rôle of the persuasive agency of God (AI 216b).

Emptiness. To do this, Cobb distinguishes "reality" from "actuality." Emptiness is the ultimate reality, while God is the ultimate actuality. Neither ultimate is above or behind the other. Consider the following quotation from Cobb.

> If for the Christian there is no such religious subordination, then there is no subordination at all. If God is the one, cosmic, everlasting actualization of ultimate reality on whom all ephemeral actualizations depend, God's non-identity with ultimate reality in no way subordinates God to it, for God is the ultimate *actuality*. God as the ultimate actuality is just as ultimate as is Emptiness as ultimate *reality*. Emptiness is different from God, and there is no God apart from Emptiness. But it is equally true to say that there is no Emptiness apart from God. Emptiness is not "above" or "beyond" God (pp. 112-13).

The point to note is that Cobb's position on the existence of two ultimates would be undermined if God were reunited with Creativity.

We turn to a discussion of the second of the three steps. Rational religion has a core of ideas which have been exemplified at various points in history (RM 34b). In the Western case, the insight of Plato was exemplified in the life of Christ. Christ embodied the ideal of an effective, persuasive love. Christ's life is the supreme ideal (RM 56d-57a). The power of Christianity is the power of a historical embodiment of this ideal.

> I need not elaborate. Can there be any doubt that the power of Christianity lies in its revelation in act, of that which Plato divined in theory? (AI 214c).

Even Christ's teachings are not primarily statements about the ideal so much as they are concrete examples of it. That is, the parables and beatitudes of Jesus are not philosophic lectures about the essence of religion; they are not even dialogues between the master and his students. Rather, they are concrete and specific illustrations of the essence of religion. Just as Jesus often illustrated the patterns of rational religion in his actual life, so he also illustrated them in fictional situations and in maxims and proverbs which even the simplest child could grasp. Jesus' life and teachings are the immediate expression of a direct insight into the essence of religion. Thus, Jesus bypasses explicit statements about the abstract principles of religion—such as we find in Plato's intuition and the theologian's elaboration. Rather, it is for us to discern the general principles which are embodied in his life and in his teachings.

> The reported sayings of Christ are not formularized thought. They are descriptions of direct insight. The ideas are in his mind as immediate pictures, and not as analyzed in terms of abstract concepts. He sees intuitively the relations between good men and bad men; his expressions are not cast into the form of an analysis of the goodness and badness of man. His sayings are actions and not adjustments of concepts. He speaks in the lowest abstractions that language is capable of, if it is to be language at all and not the fact itself.
>
> In the Sermon on the Mount, and in the Parables, there is no reasoning about the facts. They are seen with immeasurable innocence. Christ represents rationalism derived from direct intuition and divorced from dialectics (RM 56b-c).

B

Whitehead's comments about the three stages of this revelation raise a question about his view of history and its relation to theology. We should note first that it would be unfair to Whitehead to interpret his comments as an attempt to give a scientific analysis of a chain of cause and effect which leads from Plato to Jesus. From a scientific point of view, the main source of Jesus' ideas was the Palestinian Judaism into which he was born.[22] We can, however, interpret Whitehead as follows. Philosophy normally begins by reflecting on our recurring and ordinary experiences. Christian theology, on the other hand, begins with the reality of Jesus in which it finds a summit of attainment beyond any immediate clarity. Whitehead attempts to put this summit of attainment into a context of general ideas in order to provide us with some insight and, perhaps, clarity. When Whitehead puts Jesus into the context of these Platonic ideas, he discovers that the picture/life/teachings of Jesus *cohere* with the Platonic ideals and with the insights of rational religion.

For Whitehead, the concrete birth, life, and death of Jesus of Nazareth has importance for metaphysics and religion because it embodies certain universal themes and motifs. For the orthodox and traditional Christian interpretation of Jesus, however, this is not enough. Western theology has wanted to give a still greater significance to the events themselves. Especially in connection with soteriology, the church has always insisted on the historical man Jesus and a cross made of wood, set on a real hill outside an actual city at a specific time. Most of the orthodox have also insisted that Jesus' death and sufferings (and resurrection) are more than mere historical facts, but the orthodox have agreed that they were at least facts. To illustrate this, let us turn to Augustus Hopkins Strong's book, *Systematic Theology*. This work was meant to be a guide to orthodox Protestant thought, and several generations of the better-educated American clergy learned their theology from it. Strong, in discussing the atonement, confesses that the Fathers were right in emphasizing the historical facts surrounding the passion and the resurrection.

> To our fathers the atonement was a mere historical fact, a sacrifice offered in a few hours upon the Cross. It was a literal substitution of Christ's suffering for ours, the payment of our debt by another, and upon the ground of that payment we are permitted to go free. Those sufferings were soon over, and the hymn, "Love's Redeeming Work is Done," expressed the believer's joy in a finished redemption. And all this is true. But it is only a part of the truth.[23]

22. It is wise not to be overly dogmatic at this point. Jesus' Palestine and Plato's Greece were both part of the Eastern Mediterranean world. And, while the current tendency among New Testament scholars is to emphasize the Jewish background of both the Gospels and the Pauline corpus, we would do well to be a bit open-minded on the issue. Even a quick visit to the ruins of one of Herod the Great's pet projects, Caesarea Maritima, will graphically demonstrate the presence of Greco-Roman customs on Palestinian soil. Further, Jesus' home town of Nazareth sat on a hill overlooking the Valley of Jezreel, which served as a major trade route in that part of the world, and across this trade route passed Greeks and Romans as well as Jews. Who knows what ideas passed from the soldiers and merchants to the villagers on the mountain?

In any case, general ideas are always hard to grasp clearly and can be clothed in diverse linguistic and cultural patterns. It is not impossible that some of Plato's ideas had, over the centuries, passed into the general life of various groups in the Near East and that, quite divorced from the name of Plato, they influenced Jesus as he grew up.

23. Strong, *Systematic Theology*, 715.

For Strong, however, the historical and factual elements constitute only half the truth. The other half is that the historical events revealed something about the universal structure of the human/divine and human/human relations. This other half of Strong's truth is difficult to label. Probably most modern theologians would call it "mythic" (not "mythological").[24] The term myth, however, is sometimes reserved for the stories which point to factors beyond the phenomenal world. But Strong is not telling a story in this second half of his truth; rather he is spelling out the nature of the universal elements to which the story points—elements which will structure the experience of any person who understands himself Christianly. And so, perhaps we should call Strong's second half the existential and universal truth.

> Those six hours of pain could never have procured our salvation if they had not been a revelation of eternal facts in the being of God. The heart of God and the meaning of all previous history were then unveiled. The whole evolution of humanity was there depicted in its essential elements, on the one hand the sin and condemnation of the race, on the other hand the grace and suffering of him who was its life and salvation. . . . The historical sacrifice of our Lord is not only the final revelation of the heart of God, but also the manifestation of the law of universal life—the law that sin brings suffering to all connected with it, and that we can overcome sin in ourselves and in the world only by entering into the fellowship of Christ's sufferings and Christ's victory, or, in other words, only by union with him through faith.[25]

From Whitehead's point of view, there are three basic inadequacies in Strong's discussion. First, Strong hangs too much on the cross; he places too much emphasis on the six hours of pain, and not enough on what they represent. Second, when Strong does consider what they represent, he does not see that the ideas represented are, in theory, detachable from their concrete embodiment. Third, in discussing what the historical facts represent, Strong does not generalize broadly enough. That is, Strong ought to be interested in God's relations to all actuality—human and nonhuman, organic and inorganic—and not just in God's relation to people.

When, in his discussion of rational religion, Whitehead's interest focuses on the concrete facts of history, the reason is always pragmatic. For example, Whitehead observes that general ideas take a long time to emerge into popular awareness. Therefore, if we can develop our philosophy and theology from a basis which has long been in the popular mind—such as the life of Christ—then we will considerably increase the chances of our theology or philosophy having a practical effect on the

---

24. Compare Chapter IV, "Epilogue: Myth, Philosophy, and Theology" in Langdon Gilkey, *Religion and the Scientific Future*, 101-36.
25. Strong, *Systematic Theology*, 716.

common life of our society within the reasonably near future (cf. AI 220b). Moreover, the fact that an idea of profound generality has been concretely illustrated in history gives that idea a considerably increased power to command attention and interest (AI 219b).

Whitehead himself does not take specific historical events as the final norm for his theology and philosophy. There are basically two reasons for Whitehead's position. First, as we have seen, Whitehead holds that rational religion is primarily a matter of general ideas (that is, patterns of coordinated value), where these general ideas articulate a concern for *all* actuality, for being as a whole. In this sense, particular historical events—e.g., the concrete life and death of Jesus—cannot be normative for either a rationalized religion or for a metaphysics because they are only a small part of the whole of actuality. Second, Whitehead is a radical empiricist. He insists that the general patterns of metaphysics and theology be found in our experience, but our present experience is the only experience we have! We can experience the past only insofar as it has survived into the present, and we can experience the future only insofar as we have a present anticipation of that future. Rational religion, therefore, must speak of truths which communicate with our *present* experience.

> It is a curious delusion that the rock upon which our beliefs can be founded is an historical investigation. You can only interpret the past in terms of the present. The present is all that you have; and unless in this present you can find general principles which interpret the present as including a representation of the whole community of existents, you cannot move a step beyond your little patch of immediacy (RM 82b).

> In so far as your metaphysical beliefs are implicit, you vaguely interpret the past on the lines of the present. But when it comes to the primary metaphysical data, the world of which you are immediately conscious is the whole datum (RM 82d-83a).

C

Did Whitehead himself fully exploit all the possibilities for understanding the theological significance of specific past historical events? If the answer is yes, then there would be an extremely wide, and perhaps unbridgeable, gap between Whitehead's philosophy and the Christian tradition, both in its Biblical foundations and in its various elaborations in history. It is a fundamental mark of most of the Christian heritage—including the New Testament—to assert that the significance of Jesus rests, at least in part, on his very historical particularity. Our salvation, says this significant stream of Christian tradition, rests on *this* Jesus and not merely on the general character of the image or picture of Christ.

Bernard E. Meland dealt extensively with this problem. His solution is to look for resources in Whitehead's metaphysics which Whitehead himself did not use in interpreting the life of Jesus Christ. In his book, *The Realities of Faith*,[26] Meland points out that, in our post-Darwinian, post-Einsteinian, and post-Freudian world, we must conceive the world as too complicated for any final scheme of ideas to comprehend it totally. Thus, we must be open to a variety of ways to thematize our world. This variety of thematizations, however, is not merely—or even primarily—an intellectual matter. Our experience, both unconscious and conscious, comes to us in organic or aesthetic wholes. Therefore, a new thematization of our experience is, in fact, a new mode of experiencing. In other words, within our felt experience, there are various implicit possibilities for its organization, and the different thematizations of that experience can actualize these different possibilities. We can re-express this in technical terms—although Meland does not much use Whitehead's specialized vocabulary. We may say that, at the first stage of concrescence, the data of our experience are infinitely complex; and within that first stage, there is a multitude of possible ways in which the actual entity can structure this material as it concresces. Thus, given its initial stage of concrescence, there are many possible satisfactions (i.e., thematizations of its experience) which an actual entity can achieve.[27]

Meland's Christology depends on these considerations. In Jesus Christ a new mode of experience broke into human affairs. This new mode of experience offered a new freedom and power. In Meland's own words,

> Thus the historical reality that looms as the focal point of the Revelatory event is the new life made vivid and transforming of human existence in the early Christian community. This, one will see, alters the nature of the Christological discussion. The focus of inquiry shifts from a concern with the nature of the person of Jesus who was called the Christ to the appearance of a saving reality experienced as the New Creation in an entire community within history following his death and the Resurrection experience. The reality discerned, then, is a depth within historical experience which loomed as a resource of new freedom and power in individual lives and in the group response as these transformed individuals intermingled with one another.[28]

For Meland, the historicity of Jesus is significant because it was in Jesus of Nazareth—as well as in the response of his community to him—that this new mode of sensitivity broke into the world. A new level of

26. Meland, *The Realities of Faith*.
27. We may restate this in terms of our discussion in Section I, Chapter Seventeen. Each actual entity, given the Reality which is present at its first stage of concrescence, can create a variety of work-a-day worlds out of that Reality. Each such work-a-day world which could be created from a given Reality would be a particular thematization of that Reality.
28. Meland, *The Realities of Faith*, 254.

humanness emerged at a particular time in history: a few years after the Romans established the institution of the emperor.

> The first point to make, then, in moving toward an explanation of what happened in the situation reported by the Gospel story is that real novelty, real mystery, was encountered in the historical process.[29]

Meland repeats this point:

> The initiating vehicle of agape, releasing the matrix of sensitivity or creative ground of spirit into full actuality as a historical being, was the person of Jesus. All one can say is that this structure of consciousness became the bearer of sensitivity in which this love was dominant.[30]

We can point to three main differences between Meland and Whitehead on these matters. First, Whitehead's rational religion points to certain general patterns of the coordination of values, whereas Meland's theory of religion points to a certain mode of experience. We must be careful, however, not to overstate the disparity between them. For Whitehead, these patterns are ideals which can mold and shape experience. They are factors in experience, and they make possible certain developed modes of experience. Stated in this fashion, Whitehead may not seem so far from Meland. Nevertheless, the difference in emphasis between Whitehead and Meland ought not to be understated either. Second, for Whitehead the patterns of rational religion are metaphysical in their generality and are highly abstract. But Meland is thinking of a specific mode of experience, concretely realized, for the first time, in the Middle East about two thousand years ago. Meland's mode of experience has not been achieved by everyone; and while he does not discuss technical metaphysics in his book, it does seem clear that this mode of experience has not been a realistic mode for everyone at all times. Rather, for Meland, we are given the possibility of this mode of experience as a form of grace.[31] Third, for Whitehead, Jesus embodies the eternal ideals of rational religion; for Meland, Jesus initiates a mode of experience at a specific time and place. Of course, as Meland himself hints in the first of our quotations from his book, in orthodox Christology the emphasis is on the person of the God-man and not merely on the mode of experience which he initiated. Nevertheless, in emphasizing the historical Jesus as the initiator of a new form of sensitivity—that is, of the New Creation—and in emphasizing the essential continuity of the church with Jesus as its initiator, Meland is far closer to the tradition of Western theology than is Whitehead. But the metaphysical basis on which Meland draws closer to the Christian tradition is itself to be found in Whitehead's system.

29. Ibid., 257.
30. Ibid., 259.
31. Ibid., 300ff.

19 God and Religion

IN THIS CHAPTER, we will discuss Whitehead's doctrine of God. We will not, however, consider the entire set of roles which the notion of God plays in Whitehead's metaphysical system. Our purpose in this chapter is much more limited. We will discuss God only to the extent that Whitehead has used the notion of God to provide a theoretical explanation for the intuitions of religion. That is, for Whitehead, religion has primarily to do with the coordination of values and the permanent side of the universe, and not so much with God. Although nothing in Whitehead's writings suggests that religion's direct concern with the coordination of values excludes a concern for God, it remains true that, in Whitehead's view of religion, God is introduced primarily in the attempt to explain this coordination of values. Of course, God is also introduced into Whitehead's metaphysical system to explain many other factors. Whitehead calls the use of God to explain non-religious factors in our experience the secularization of God (PR 315c). But, as we mentioned above, in this chapter, we will not discuss all the roles which Whitehead has God play within his system. We will consider only those roles which serve as an explanation of the religious data.[1]

---

1. Numerous studies concentrate on the complete set of God's roles in Whitehead's metaphysical system—though none of them, to our knowledge, clarifies how God functions as the explanation of the religious datum. For the interested reader, we may cite the following examples of full-scale studies of Whitehead's doctrine of God as it functions metaphysically: "Part Three: God and the World" (pp. 281-413) in Christian's book, *Whitehead's Metaphysics*; Kenneth F. Thompson, Jr., *Whitehead's Philosophy of Religion* (The Hague: Mouton, 1971); Cobb, *A Christian Natural Theology*. Despite the title of Thompson's book, it deals almost entirely with Whitehead's doctrine of God in its metaphysical context. Cobb develops his own position using Whitehead's philosophy as a framework, thereby offering a fairly complete exposition of Whitehead's doctrine of God.

I

In the previous chapter, we mentioned that one of the basic intuitions of religion was the insight that there exists a permanent side of the universe in which process does not entail loss. In part, this intuition is justified by pointing to the patterns of coordinated value, but it is also justified by pointing to God.

A

God is an actual entity (PR 168a) which does not perish (PR 521d, 523c-24a, and 524c). As an actual entity, God is both physical and mental. His mental side is called his primordial nature. His physical side is called his consequent nature.

Let us turn first to the physical side, to the consequent nature. As an actual entity, God must prehend each actual entity in his past. Since God does not perish, it follows that every finite actual entity eventually becomes a part of God's past, is prehended by God, and, thereby, becomes a part of God. Since God does not perish, it also follows that the finite actual entities, having become a part of God, will not perish either. This is one of the ways in which God serves as the theoretical basis for the religious intuition of permanence.

Let us now turn to God's mental side. God's vision of all eternal objects is the foundation of his primordial nature. In this sense, the general potentiality of the universe is in God. In addition, God has a subjective aim. We may associate God's subjective aim with his mental side, but we must also qualify that association. This is because a subjective aim is, in fact, a propositional prehension; but, as we saw in Part One, a propositional prehension is an integrative prehension which weaves together subordinate physical prehensions with subordinate conceptual prehensions. Therefore, while God's subjective aim involves his conceptual prehensions—and may thus be associated with his mental side—it is also the case that God's subjective aim is not one of the purely conceptual prehensions constitutive of his primordial nature.

God's subjective aim is at intensity of experience both in himself and in his relevant future (PR 41c). The specific character of the divine aim depends on the fact that all possibilities are envisioned in his primordial nature. According to Christian's interpretation, God's subjective aim is for "the actualization of *all* possibilities."[2] In this sense, God's subjective aim

---

2. Christian, *Whitehead's Metaphysics*, 352. There are some problems with Christian's interpretation. For example, does God aim at the actualization of an endless repetition of actual entities without novelty, at infinite ennui, or at deep agony and pain in little children? If the answer to any of these questions is negative, then God does *not* aim at the actualization of *all* possibilities. Christian is right, however, at least to this extent: God does aim at the

is perfect. The perfection of God's subjective aim endows God's consequent nature a unique capacity: in God's consequent nature each finite actual entity is prehended as a complete whole, without any loss or elimination due to negative prehensions.

> The perfection of God's subjective aim, derived from the completeness of his primordial nature, issues into the character of his consequent nature. In it there is no loss, no obstruction (PR 524e).

We can now expand our discussion of the theoretical basis of the religious intuition of permanence. Not only does God's everlasting consequent nature include each finite entity without perishing, but it includes the entirety of each entity. That is, because God's subjective aim is perfect, he prehends the entire finite entity and not just some portion of that entity. And because neither God as a whole nor any of his parts will ever perish, it follows that the entire finite actual entity is everlastingly preserved in God.[3] In this sense, therefore, God is the theoretical foundation for the intuitions of religion.

Whitehead roots God's ability to prehend entire finite entities in the perfection of his subjective aim. This, however, leaves us with a further question: *How* does the perfection of the divine subjective aim generate this capacity to prehend an entire finite entity without eliminating any portion of that entity? Although Whitehead spreads numerous hints throughout his writings, he never explicitly states the solution. These hints, however, have been collected by Christian, and he gives the only plausible answer. According to Christian, God can prehend finite entities without loss because he is able to supplement his prehension of any finite entity by comparing it with a relevant alternative. In other words, the unlimited wealth of potentiality in God's conceptual nature allows him to compare any concrete entity with another possibility. This comparison takes the form of a contrast, a contrast between what is and what might have been. Such a contrast can become an element in God's satisfaction, an element promoting intensity of feeling in the divine satisfaction. Therefore, God can use any finite entity whatsoever in support of his own intensity of experience. This is true even when the original finite entity, by itself and apart from being an element in such a contrast, would detract from the intensity of God's satisfaction.[4]

When an actual entity becomes an element in God, it is being put to

---

eventual realization of an infinity of possibilities—at more possibilities than any other entity can even envision. That is, at the very least, God aims at the eventual actualization of all possibilities which are commensurate with his own drive at an aesthetically balanced intensity of feeling.

3. By "preserved" we mean that the finite entity is the objective datum of a divine prehension. We do not mean that the finite entity continues to concresce or that it retains its subjective immediacy in God.

4. *Whitehead's Metaphysics*, 351-56.

its maximal usefulness in promoting intensity of feeling. That is, a particular finite entity—call it F—will be prehended by many future entities, including God. Each of these future entities will use F, so far as possible, to produce an intense satisfaction. Moreover, each of these future entities, in attempting to attain an intense satisfaction, will integrate its prehension of F with prehensions of other entities and eternal objects. In short, each of these future entities will use F in the production of a contrast, however trivial that contrast may be. God, too, will use F to promote the greatest possible intensity within himself. But, since God can draw upon the unlimited wealth of his primordial nature for the creation of contrasts, it follows that God's use of F will be productive of the highest possible intensity of feeling.

Therefore, not only will a particular entity be *permanently* present in God, and not only will that entity be *wholly* present in God, but also that entity will be a permanent factor in God's production of the *maximum possible intensity* of experience. Whitehead expresses it this way:

> Each actuality has its present life and its immediate passage into novelty; but its passage is not its death. This final phase of passage in God's nature is ever enlarging itself. [That is, God is always prehending new finite entities.] In it the complete adjustment of the immediacy of joy and suffering reaches the final end of creation. This end is existence in the perfect unity of adjustment as means, and in the perfect multiplicity of the attainment of individual types of self-existence. The function of being a means is not disjoined from the function of being an end. The sense of worth beyond itself is immediately enjoyed as an overpowering element in the individual self-attainment. It is in this way that the immediacy of sorrow and pain is transformed into an element of triumph. This is the notion of redemption through suffering which haunts the world. It is the generalization of its very minor exemplification as the aesthetic value of discords in art (PR 530d-31a; bracketed material added).

B

In the previous chapter of this book, we observed that rational religion's pattern of coordinated value will help a concrescing entity to anticipate its role in future actuality; and the more a concrescing entity can anticipate its future usefulness, the greater will be its present intensity of experience. Now, although Whitehead never explicitly states as much, it does seem clear that the patterns of coordinated value also help a concrescing entity to judge its usefulness to God. And the greater its usefulness to God, the greater will be the present intensity of the concrescing entity's experience. We explain as follows.

If we assume that the intensity of God's experience can vary from time to time, then it is obvious that the patterns of coordinated value, which help the concrescing entity to maximize its usefulness to future actual entities, will also help to maximize its usefulness to God. Some authors claim, however, that God's satisfaction does not vary from moment to moment or from age to age. Whitehead never explicitly commits himself one way or the other. But, for the sake of argument, let us agree that there is no variation in the intensity of God's satisfaction.[5] Would it follow from this admission that the self-identity of a finite entity makes no difference to the standing of that entity in the divine satisfaction? The answer is no; the self-identity of the finite entity does make a difference to its standing in God. The reason may be stated as follows.

Although the strength of the final contrast in the divine satisfaction would not vary, still the strength of the self-identity of that finite entity in that contrast might very well vary. That is, a particular finite entity might enter a contrast in which its specific self-identity is a matter of the highest importance, whereas another finite entity might enter a contrast in which its self-identity is relatively unimportant. The overall strengths of the two contrasts might be identical (because of the infinity of God's conceptual resources in constructing the contrasts), while at the same time the relative importance of each finite entity to its respective contrast may vary considerably. Again, consider an evil actual entity, that is, an entity which, because of its lack of coordination with its fellows, is destructive of harmonious intensity of experience in its future entities. Because of the wealth of his conceptual resources, God can create a contrast containing the evil entity which does not detract from the depth of his intensity of satisfaction. But it might very well be that, in creating this contrast, God relegates the evil entity to the status of a mere example of evil, to the status of a mere example of what to avoid, and to the status of an example of what other entities have avoided. On the other hand, God may very well weave a good actual entity into a contrast in which the individual identity of the good entity is valued for its own sake; indeed, God may very well weave the good actual entity into a contrast with the evil actual entity in which the evil actual entity merely serves to heighten the appreciation of the individuality of the good actual entity.

Our discussion thus far has assumed that the entirety of each actual entity is present in God's consequent nature. We turn now to several passages in which Whitehead seems to contradict this assumption. For example, Whitehead speaks of the "purged" and "transformed" self-identities of the finite actual entities in God (PR 527c) and of a finite actual entity having a "corresponding element in God's nature," where this corresponding element is "the transmutation of that temporal actuality"

5. Christian maintains this position in *Whitehead's Metaphysics*, 356-60. We doubt that he is correct in this claim, but we will not argue the issue. Rather, our explanation of how the self-identity of a finite entity can make a difference to a God whose intensity of satisfaction could not vary would apply all the more to a God whose intensity of satisfaction did vary.

(PR 531d). On the interpretation we have outlined in this section, we need not construe these passages as denying that God prehends the entirety of each actual entity into his consequent nature; rather, we may construe Whitehead as claiming that the use to which God puts each finite entity will vary according to the strength of that entity—the self-identity of strong, harmonious entities being much more prominent in God's satisfaction than the self-identities of weak or evil entities.

> The wisdom of [God's] subjective aim prehends every actuality for what it can be in such a perfected system—its sufferings, its sorrows, its failures, its triumphs, its immediacies of joy—woven by rightness of feeling into the harmony of the universal feeling, which is always immediate, always many, always one, always with novel advance, moving onward and never perishing. The revolts of destructive evil, purely self-regarding, are dismissed into their triviality of merely individual facts; and yet the good they did achieve in individual joy, in individual sorrow, in the introduction of needed contrast, is yet saved by its relation to the complete whole. The image—and it is but an image—the image under which this operative growth of God's nature is best conceived, is that of a tender care that nothing be lost.
>
> The consequent nature of God is his judgment on the world. He saves the world as it passes into the immediacy of his own life. It is the judgment of a tenderness which loses nothing which can be saved. It is also the judgment of a wisdom which uses what in the temporal world is mere wreckage (PR 525b-c).[6]

C

Before leaving Section I, we must consider one last problem of interpretation. Whitehead explicitly states in a number of passages that the finite entity is prehended into God's consequent nature without the loss of immediacy—or, in different words, without the loss of the 'unison of immediacy', of 'mutual immediacy', of 'immediate unison', or of the 'unison of becoming' (PR 517b, 525a, 530d, 531a, 531d, 532b, and 533a). Normally in the Whiteheadian corpus the term 'immediacy' refers to the self-functioning of an actual entity as it concresces; in fact, this is how the term is officially defined in the opening statement of the categorical scheme (PR 38d). This is called 'subjective immediacy'. Is, then, Whitehead saying that an actual entity survives in the consequent nature of God as a still functioning entity? This would seem to be most unlikely; Christian outlines

---

6. The inclusion, in the first line of this quotation, of the word "God's" is suggested by Kline in "Corrigenda for *Process and Reality*," 207. Since this is Kline's third list, it is only a tentative suggestion. Griffin and Sherburne's Corrected Edition of *Process and Reality* does not add the word "God's" to the text.

the reasons for the rejection of the survival of a finite entity's subjective immediacy in God.[7]

We cannot accept Christian's position that, in all the passages cited, Whitehead is merely using misleading expressions in his attempt to apply his system to ordinary experience.[8] Whitehead is too consistent and repetitious in his claim that a finite entity survives into the consequent nature of God without the loss of immediacy for this to be an accidental use of a misleading expression.

We have no completely satisfactory explanation for what Whitehead does mean in these passages. We can, however, mention some possible interpretations. The most plausible way to start, in our opinion, is to suggest that, in these passages, Whitehead has in mind some form of immediacy other than subjective immediacy. Consider the following passage, in which Whitehead *may* be using immediacy in a sense other than subjective immediacy.

> Objectification involves elimination. The present fact has not the past fact with it in any full *immediacy*. The process of time veils the past below distinctive feeling. There is a unison of becoming among things in the present. Why should there not be novelty without loss of this direct *unison of immediacy* among things? In the temporal world, it is the empirical fact that process entails loss: the past is present under an abstraction. But there is no reason, of any ultimate metaphysical generality, why this should be the whole story (PR 517b; emphases added).

In this passage, Whitehead may be using 'immediacy' to mean something less than 'subjective immediacy' and something more than 'objectification' or 'repetition'. (A) In this passage, if immediacy meant subjective immediacy, then the distinction between actual entities would be lost; and Whitehead can hardly want to say that. (B) At the same time, immediacy must mean more than repetition, that is, the repetition in the concrescing entity of the character of the objective data. In several passages, Whitehead contrasts immediacy with repetition (PR 206c, 234c-35a); and it would be quixotic for Whitehead simply to collapse this contrast without any hint or explanation.

Having stated what Whitehead probably does not mean in this passage by immediacy, can we provide any tentative clues to what he does mean? Let us consider a particular concrescing actual entity, X; and let us consider one of X's prehensions, P. Now the total significance of P within X can be known or felt only to the extent that X as an entire actual entity is known or felt. On the one hand, since for finite entities objectification entails elimination, it follows that when later entities prehend X, they will not be able to know the full significance which P had for X. On the other

---

7. Christian, *Whitehead's Metaphysics*, 339-42.
8. Ibid., 342.

hand, since God prehends no portion of X negatively, it follows that God can feel the complete significance which P had for X. Thus God does not merely repeat in himself the individual prehension P, but God fully feels the entire significance which P had for X.

Lewis Ford offers a rather radical set of suggestions which, if accepted, would also lead to a solution to this problem of God's prehension of finite entities without the loss of immediacy.[9] Ford makes two claims. First, God occupies every region in the extensive continuum. Second, God can prehend finite entities *during* their concrescences.

Ford's first claim would make God omnispatial rather than transspatial. Each site of concrescence, thus, would be occupied twice, once as a subregion in God and once as the region serving as the location of the concrescence of a finite entity.[10] Ford's second claim, that God can prehend finite entities during their concrescences, depends on the first. The reason, according to Ford, that objectification means elimination among finite entities is that the new, finite concrescence has a limited standpoint from which to begin its development. That is, the region of the extensive continuum occupied by a finite concrescence is always limited. Since its spatio-temporal standpoint is always limited, it follows that there will be some aspects of each past actual entity which the new entity cannot positively prehend. Therefore the new concrescence must negatively prehend those aspects of the past entities which it cannot assimilate.[11] God's perspective, however, is not finite. Since, according to Ford, God occupies the entire extensive continuum, God shares the finite perspective of every finite entity. Therefore God has a spatial-temporal perspective which allows him to eliminate nothing from his prehensions of finite entities.[12] Since God can prehend an entity without "disturbing" that entity, there is no reason why God cannot prehend a finite entity while it concresces. The conclusion is that God can prehend finite entities without any loss of immediacy.

Ford's position is certainly clever. It may even be an improvement on Whitehead's own position. It does not, however, seem to be White-

9. Ford, "Whitehead's Conception of Divine Spatiality," 1-23.

10. We should note a series of debates between John Cobb and Donald Sherburne in *Process Studies* 1 (Summer, 1971) 91-113; 2 (Winter, 1972) 277-95; 3 (Spring, 1973) 27-40. In these debates a principal point of contention is whether the notion of "regional inclusion" is coherent. Since Ford asserts that God occupies the entire continuum and that a finite entity also occupies a portion of that same continuum, we clearly have a case of regional inclusion. Thus the debate on the coherence of this notion is relevant to Ford's position.

11. We note the more customary reason why a finite entity must negatively prehend some portions of the past world: no finite entity has the conceptual resources to turn every potentially destructive conflict among past entities into positive contrasts.

12. We note the more customary explanation for why, in God's feelings of the universe, there are no negative prehensions: God has the conceptual resources to turn every conflict among finite entities into a positive contrast. Consequently, God need eliminate no aspect of any finite entity in his prehension of that entity.

head's. Whitehead holds that God does not occupy the extensive continuum—not even the continuum as a whole. And we can find no passage in which Whitehead suggests that God prehends the finite actual entities *during* their concrescences.[13] Thus we believe that our more modest proposal comes closer to Whitehead's own understanding of how finite entities can be prehended by God without a loss of immediacy.

II

From a metaphysical point of view, there is the dual problem of permanence and flux. Thus far in Part Four, we have stressed the religious intuition into the permanent side of the universe; and, indeed, the connection of religion with permanence is a typically Whiteheadian motif. From the perspective of metaphysics, however, this permanent side of the universe must be connected with the world's fluent side. Otherwise, our religion would deal with one factor in the world; in short, our religion would not be rational.

There is a sense in which permanence and flux achieve their final coordination in God. In support of this theme, Whitehead writes,

> Creation achieves the reconciliation of permanence and flux when it has reached its final term which is everlastingness — the Apotheosis of the World (PR 529a).

Whitehead does not completely explicate this passage. In part, he may have in mind the fact that God's concrescence never perishes. Thus any object prehended by God—which includes the entirety of each finite entity since God has no negative prehensions—will remain a permanent feature in God forever.

Another way in which flux and permanence are reconciled in Whitehead's thought is this: God gives each finite actual entity its initial subjective aim. In obtaining its subjective aim from God, each finite entity is drawing upon the permanent riches of God's primordial nature, and each finite entity is also drawing upon God's permanent consequent na-

---

13. In conversations with colleagues and students about Ford's proposal for the divine prehension of finite entities during their concrescences, I have several times encountered the following objection. If God can prehend an entity during its concrescence, how is it possible for that entity to have any freedom in its concrescence? At least in part, the objection continues, the reason for the independence of contemporary entities is to give each new entity the freedom to create its own self-identity. If God prehended the concrescing actual entity, would not this freedom be lost?

There is a simple but adequate response to this particular objection. As long as God added no new factors to the finite entity during its concrescence, and as long as God's prehension of that new entity did not subtract or eliminate any element from that concrescence, it is hard to see how the freedom of the new actual entity is being compromised.

ture, in which each past finite entity is prehended without loss. Thus we read:

> The theme of Cosmology, which is the basis of all religions, is the story of the dynamic effort of the World passing into everlasting unity, and of the static majesty of God's vision, accomplishing its purpose of completion by absorption of the World's multiplicity of effort (PR 529c-30a).

At this point we wish to expand our discussion of the theme that the permanent factors in the universe are mediated to the flux by God's gift of an initial subjective aim (PR 434b). We have three basic points to make about this divine gift of a subjective aim. First, this subjective aim is an ideal self-identity; it is a possible goal of concrescence. Moreover, this ideal must be specific enough to be unique for each new finite entity. Otherwise, the subjective aim for a particular finite entity—call it F—would not be a possible way in which F could define *itself*. As our second point, we note that in the very act of giving a new entity its *unique* subjective aim, the *general* patterns of coordinated value also become available to the new entity. We explain as follows. As we saw in the previous chapter, rational religion's patterns of coordinated values are abstract elements in each new entity's ideal self-identity, that is, they are abstract elements in each new entity's subjective aim. Therefore, in giving each new entity its own, unique, and particular initial subjective aim, God is also providing that entity with the general and everlasting patterns of coordinated value.

We come now to our third point about the nature of the subjective aim, which we will introduce with a question. On what basis does God choose this-and-not-that subjective aim for a new concrescence? In part, of course, God chooses on the basis of his desire to produce actual entities with the greatest depth of experience (RM 97a). In addition, for God to know which subjective aim is likely to promote the maximum intensity in a finite entity, he must know what materials are available to that new entity; that is, God must know the composition of the new entity's actual world. God, however, does know the new entity's actual world because he has prehended that actual world—and he has prehended that actual world without loss, without negative prehensions. Thus God has chosen the initial subjective aim for a new entity on the basis of his consequent nature.

Corresponding to these three observations about the nature of a subjective aim, there are three specific ways in which we can explicate our previous claim that the permanent side of the universe is mediated to the flux through the subjective aim. (In this context, the flux is represented by the multitude of finite entities, both those which are now concrescing and those which have already perished.) First, each entity's subjective aim draws upon the primordial nature of God (PR 373a). But God's primordial nature is permanent and eternal. As Whitehead observes, "God's conceptual nature is unchanged, by reason of its final completeness" (PR

523c). Second, the subjective aim mediates rational religion's patterns of coordinated value to the new actual entity. We saw in Sections II and III of Chapter Eighteen the many senses in which these patterns are permanent. Third, God gives a finite entity a specific subjective aim on the basis of his prehension of the actual world of that entity, that is, on the basis of his consequent nature, which is everlasting.[14] Thus the specific identity of each subjective aim results, at least partially, from this permanence of the divine consequent nature.

In summary, the permanent enters the world of flux through God's gift of a unique subjective aim to each new concrescence. And the flux enters the realm of the permanent through God's prehension of every finite entity into his consequent nature.

III

In the previous section, we stressed God's role in the interaction of permanence and flux. We noted that God overcomes the evil of perpetual perishing in the world through his prehension of the entirety of each actual entity into the everlasting permanence of his consequent nature.

There is, however, another way in which God overcomes evil in the world. Suppose a particular actual entity or group of actual entities is evil, that is, out of harmony with its relevant neighbors. Let F stand for the evil actual entity or group of entities. God, having prehended F into his consequent nature, knows in complete detail the extent of the evil. God then gives the later actual entities subjective aims which take that evil environment into account. Those subjective aims may allow the later entities to prehend most of the content of F negatively and to focus on alternative, less evil entities in the environment. Or, if this is not possible (because, for example, F and all F's contemporaries are evil), those subjective aims may simply allow the new entities to blot out most of their actual worlds, that is, to blot out most of the specific character of F and F's contemporaries. (This would result in rather low intensities of experience for the new concrescences.) Perhaps, in the more distant future, God will be able to begin building a new, kinder environment to support higher levels of experience. In this sense, God overcomes the evil in the world (RM 115a).

> Thus the initial stage of the aim is rooted in the nature of God. . . . This function of God is analogous to the remorseless working of things in Greek and in Buddhist thought. The initial aim is the best for that *impasse*. But if

14. By calling God's consequent nature everlasting, we do not mean that it is changeless. God's consequent nature constantly changes as he prehends new actual entities. The point is that God's consequent nature will continue to be an element in a concrescence that never loses its subjective immediacy. Since it never ceases, God's consequent nature is everlasting.

the best be bad, then the ruthlessness of God can be personified as *Atè*, the goddess of mischief. The chaff is burnt. What is inexorable in God, is valuation as an aim towards 'order'; and 'order' means 'society' permissive of actualities with patterned intensity of feeling arising from adjusted contrasts (PR 373a-74a).

For the same reason that God's presence in the world means that evil can be overcome, so also God's presence in the world guarantees that the universe cannot be blasted into total chaos. "The immanence of God gives reason for the belief that pure chaos is intrinsically impossible" (PR 169c).

IV

In this section, we will examine some arguments for the existence of God. These will not be the classical arguments for the divine existence. Nor will we even concentrate on those arguments which are most prominent in Whitehead's own metaphysical discussion. Rather, we will consider those arguments which stem most directly from Whitehead's analysis of religion. That is, we will try to discover the ways in which Whitehead's description of rational religion requires the introduction of God for its completion, for its overall coherence.

Before discussing the actual arguments, we will make a methodological observation. The basic structure of these arguments is this. First, Whitehead discovers some way in which his description of experience is incoherent (in Whitehead's technical sense), and that this description needs to be supplemented before it can be said to be coherent. In each argument, it is the introduction of God which provides the required coherence and completeness to the description of experience. In other words, the best analysis of experience which we can make reveals a "need" or a "gap." It is then asserted that the introduction of God meets that need and fills that gap better than any other available device. Thus the arguments are not so much lists of premises from which the conclusion "God exists" deductively follows; rather, they are more adequately considered indications of hiatuses in our analysis of experience which are best bridged by God. (To say that God "best" bridges the hiatus or that he fills the gap "better" than any other device is simply to say that the introduction of God is the most "coherent" way of doing these things.)

A

In Whitehead's scheme, the many finite actual entities represent the theme of flux. Each entity has the opportunity, at least to some extent, to mold its own final identity. We should expect, therefore, that as time passes the many finite actual entities — which *are* the flux — would become more chaotically varied in their identities. We should also expect that they would become less and less related to each other in the sense that any one finite entity would lack aesthetic harmony with its neighbors. In short, we should expect the world to be "running down" and to be exhibiting ever increasing randomness. Moreover, Whitehead assumes that the universe —that is, the total aggregate of finite entities past and present—is infinitely old. If the universe is infinitely old, and if only the finite entities existed, then the universe should have long ago descended into the monotony of random variations of entities which are as trivial as possible. If the flux alone is final, then entropy should be king.

But entropy is not king. The fact is that each finite entity finds its world—its past entities—so arranged that *some* intensity of experience can be attained. That is, the past entities have some degree of aesthetic coordination among themselves, however small.[15] How are we to account for this? The answer, of course, is that we need a factor which (A) is permanent, (B) involves the drive after intensity of experience, and (C) is immanent in the flux so that the permanent drive after intensity can be transmitted to the flux. This factor is God.

Someone might object to this argument for the existence of God as follows.[16] Granted, says the objector, that we need a permanent factor expressing the drive after intensity of experience. Why could not, asks our objector, the patterns of coordinated value be that factor? Rational religion's patterns of coordinated value are permanent in the sense that they are present in the initial subjective aim of *every* finite entity; and, since they are pat-

---

15. Moreover, we should also point out that, in Whitehead's opinion, there exist evolutionary forces tending toward ever increasing patterns of complexity and ever new patterns of intensity of experience. (This theme permeates his entire book, *The Function of Reason.*) And, as the complexities and the intensities of one epoch become boring, another epoch arises with new patterns of complexity and intensity. If we assume with Whitehead that the evolutionary motif has always been present in the universe, then there is a conflict between the theme of entropy —that the universe is running down—and the theme of evolution—that new patterns of order and new modes of intensity are arising. This conflict points to the need of a factor beyond the flux, beyond the many finite entities.

Suppose, however, that we deny that the universe has always expressed an evolutionary thrust among the finite entities. (Whitehead would strongly object to this arbitrary limitation of the theme of evolution.) Even in this case, it is still *incoherent* to affirm *both* the running down of the universe as a whole *and* the evolution of complexity and intensity of experience within selected portions of it. The affirmation of both of these is incoherent in the sense that Descartes' affirmation of body and soul in human beings was, according to Whitehead, incoherent. That is, the fact that the universe as a whole is entropic gives us no reason to suspect that certain portions of it are evolving toward increased complexity and intensity of experience. Likewise, the fact that some portion of the universe is evolving upwards gives us no reason to suspect that the whole universe is running down. To overcome this incoherence, we need some factor beyond the flux of the many finite entities.

16. Compare Sherburne's and Cobb's "Whitehead Without God Debate." While not expressing any specific position represented in that debate, our imaginary objector does represent the general kind of antitheistic position which is espoused there.

terns of *value*, they will involve by definition the drive after intensity of experience. Our objector continues: Consider a finite entity, F. The patterns of coordinated value will be exhibited in each of F's past finite entities. Since F must incorporate these past finite entities into its own self-identity, F will thereby incorporate these patterns of coordinated value into itself. Consequently, F will be in aesthetic harmony, at least to some extent, with its neighbors, all of whom have incorporated these same patterns into their identities. Therefore we do not need God to account for the aesthetic harmony which F finds in its past world nor do we need God to account for the aesthetic harmony which F passes on to its own future entities.

We respond to the objector as follows. First, the patterns of coordinated value are ideals. As such they are universally present in every finite entity only as part of that entity's subjective aim. The new entity, F, needs to incorporate into itself some part of each past entity, but F is not required to incorporate that part of each past entity which contains the past entity's subjective aim. Therefore, there is no reason to think that the permanence and the universality of the patterns of coordinated value can be explained solely by reference to the objectification of past finite entities.

Second, the patterns of coordinated value are not tautologies nor are they otherwise logically necessary. It is quite possible to imagine other patterns. (Indeed this is typical of most and maybe all metaphysical patterns.[17]) If other patterns are conceivable, then surely various finite entities in the infinite history of the universe would have imagined—that is, conceptually prehended—one of these alternatives. The result would be a variety of patterns of value, at least some of them mutually contradictory. These contradictory patterns, rather than accounting for the evolutionary thrust towards order, would themselves contribute to the flux and to the trend towards chaos. Thus the patterns of coordinated value cannot adequately account for the fact that the flux of the universe has not resulted —or is now resulting—in the universe's running down into the monotony of random variations of totally trivial entities. Rather, the permanence and generality of these patterns are themselves in need of explanation. Thus we are forced again to consider God as the factor needed to balance the flux of the universe and to account for the permanence and universality of the patterns of coordinated value. In short, we need God to account for such harmony and coordinated value as we do find present throughout the universe.

B

We turn to a second, and closely related, argument for the existence of God. Each finite actual entity, in its final self-identity (its satisfaction), en-

---

17. See Chapters Fifteen and Sixteen.

visions a specific role for itself in the future. These anticipations take the form of propositional prehensions of the future. There is no reason to think that each entity's anticipation of its future role will be compatible in every detail with all the anticipations which its contemporary entities have of *their* futures. Indeed, in human experience, we often find that our habits, customs, and hopes for the future conflict with our neighbors' habits, customs, and hopes for the future. If human experience is a clue, we may expect many finite entities to have anticipations of the future which seriously conflict with the anticipations of their contemporary actual entities. At least there will be a mild incompatibility.

A new concrescence, therefore, will find that in its actual world there are incompatibilities and conflicts which it must resolve. We are in need, therefore, of a principle by which the new actual entity can choose among the various conflicting demands which its past entities have laid upon it. This principle is the new entity's initial subjective aim.

The ontological principle, however, requires that the new entity's initial subjective aim must have come from somewhere, from some actual entity. It could not have emerged from the finite past entities because the initial subjective aim is, among other things, the principle according to which the new entity decides whether to meet or to reject the anticipations which those past entities had for it. Nor could the initial subjective aim come from the new entity itself. This is because the new entity *is*, at its first stage, a collection of past entities, where this past world is *already* organized according to the initial subjective aim. Thus, to say that the initial subjective aim comes from the new entity itself is equivalent to saying that the initial subjective aim appears *ex nihilo*. Such a doctrine of creation *ex nihilo*, however, violates the ontological principle. It would also violate the ontological principle to say that creativity entirely by itself produced the initial subjective aim, because creativity "entirely by itself" is not an actual entity but is only a factor in actual entities. Last, we cannot say that the initial subjective aim comes from the new entity's finite contemporary entities nor from its future entities. As for the future entities, they simply are not actual and never have been; thus they cannot be the source of anything. As for the contemporary entities, it is a well-established principle in Whiteheadian metaphysics that finite contemporary entities cannot directly prehend each other.

Therefore, either we must give up the ontological principle or there must exist a non-finite actual entity which provides the subjective aim. Whitehead chooses not to abandon the ontological principle. Therefore, there must exist a non-finite actual entity. By "non-finite" actual entity we mean an entity which can give each new finite entity a subjective aim which becomes *the* principle for determining how the new entity should adjudicate the conflicting claims of its past entities.

The antecedent environment is not wholly efficacious in determining the initial phase of the occasion which springs from it. There are factors in the environment which are eliminated from any function as explicit facts in the new creation. The running stream purifies itself, or perhaps loses some virtue which in happier circumstances might have been retained. The initial phase of each fresh occasion represents the issue of a struggle within the past for objective existence beyond itself. The determinant of the struggle is the supreme Eros incarnating itself as the first phase of the individual subjective aim in the new process of actuality (AI 255d-56a).

In short, we need God to provide a means of overcoming those conflicts which each actual entity finds in its past.

C

For Whitehead, novelty is a dominant feature of our existence. Genuinely new events emerge in the passage of time. Here Whitehead is a modern, and he will have no truck with the ancient view of time as cyclical or with views which make all novelty simply the result of rearranging previously existing elements. According to Whitehead, some things emerge into actuality which have never before appeared in this world.

The ontological principle requires that these genuinely novel possibilities be located in some actual entity. Since the universe has neither beginning nor end, and since genuine novelty always has and always will emerge in the universe, it follows that the actual entity in which these novelties are located must be infinite in its capacity to prehend such novelties. In short, this actual entity must be God. For this reason Whitehead writes:

> The scope of the ontological principle is not exhausted by the corollary that 'decision' must be referable to an actual entity. Everything must be somewhere; and here 'somewhere' means 'some actual entity.' Accordingly the general potentiality of the universe must be somewhere; since it retains its proximate relevance to actual entities for which it is unrealized. This 'proximate relevance' reappears in subsequent concrescence as final causation regulative of the emergence of novelty. This 'somewhere' is the non-temporal actual entity. Thus 'proximate relevance' means 'relevance as in the primordial mind of God' (PR 73a; cf. PR 102a).

There is a possible objection to Whitehead's approach. An objector might ask why we could not locate these unrealized potentialities within the world itself without reference to God. The objector notes that Whitehead's system provides a mechanism for making the world's own unrealized possibilities relevant to the new concrescences. We will let the objector explain as follows. Each finite entity—say F—reaches its satisfaction with a propositional prehension of the future. F's prehension of the future involves a suggestion (the predicate) for the future entities (the logical subjects). This suggestion concerns the self-identities of those future entities. Now, the eternal objects in the predicate need not have been actualized before; that is, it is possible that these eternal objects have existed previously only as the data of conceptual prehensions (including propositional prehensions). Thus, if the future actual entities should decide to actualize F's suggested self-identity (i.e., to actualize the predicate of F's propositional prehension), then those future entities would have introduced a novelty into the world *without* the intervention of God. Our objector concludes: Novelties can, therefore, emerge in the world without any connection to God.

We respond as follows. It is not enough to account for the emergence of an isolated novelty here and there. Rather, given the everlasting existence of the universe, we must account for endless novelty and boundless variety over an infinite expanse of time. The objector could say that *each* finite entity reaches a satisfaction which involves the conceptual prehension of *every* eternal object. Such a solution has problems, however. First, if each finite entity has conceptual resources of that magnitude, then why does not each finite entity reach a profound depth of satisfaction? Second, in Whitehead's metaphysics, a finite entity must negatively prehend some portions of its past world. But, if each new entity negatively prehends some portion of its past world, then the survival through an endless expanse of time of an infinity of eternal objects in each new entity becomes inexplicable. To say the least, it is strange that the infinity of eternal objects in each past entity should never be among those portions of the past which the new entity prehends negatively. It does not seem, therefore, that the objector can account for endless novelty and boundless variety over an infinite expanse of time by saying that each finite entity reaches a satisfaction which involves the conceptual prehension of every eternal object.

In an attempt to account for the endless novelty and boundless variety of the universe, the objector may wish to maintain that each finite entity prehends only a portion of all the eternal objects, but that some set of finite actual entities, considered as a whole, has prehended all eternal objects. Thus, according to the objector, we can account for the endless novelty which emerges in the universe without recourse to God.

This solution also has drawbacks. First, it immediately resurrects the problem of the coordination of values which led us, in the first argument, to assert the need for a God. That is, given that there is an infinite number of fresh possibilities, and given that these possibilities are scattered throughout the universe, then the question arises, How does it happen that contemporary entities coordinate their developments with each other so as to allow the new actual entities in their future to create at least some intensity of experience? That is, each new finite entity can develop its intensity of experience only on the basis of the materials present in its past world;

and it does seem strange that these past entities would coordinate their development despite an infinite number of possibilities for uncoordinated development scattered among them. Second, the issue of negative prehensions, which we discussed two paragraphs previously, also applies here. Specifically, if each new entity can, and must, prehend negatively some portion of its past world, the survival through an endless expanse of time of an infinity of eternal objects becomes inexplicable. The mystery is not lessened—indeed, it is deepened—when the objector asserts that this infinity of eternal objects does not survive in each actual entity, but that it survives only as scattered throughout some group of actual entities.

We may conclude that genuine novelty requires the introduction of God into the metaphysical scheme.[18]

18. The first draft of these arguments for the existence of God was completed before the 1984 appearance of *The Emergence of Whitehead's Metaphysics: 1925-1929,* Lewis Ford's study of Whitehead's personal philosophical development from his writing of *Science and the Modern World* through the final printed form of *Process and Reality.* We strongly felt that the arguments presented in this book are genuinely Whiteheadian in spirit, and yet these arguments without doubt are fairly creative in dealing with the Whiteheadian text. We were therefore glad to find that Ford's description of the stages of Whitehead's composition of *Process and Reality* mirrors, almost perfectly, our arguments for the existence of God and especially our third argument.

According to Ford, in the first stage of the composition of *Process and Reality,* Whitehead took seriously Hume's comment that we can imagine novel ideas (such as a shade of blue) which have not been a part of our past. Whitehead then introduced the notion of 'reversion' to account for this emergence of novelties into our experience. The problem is that reversion gives us no hint of where these novelties come from.

The next stage, according to Ford, was Whitehead's introduction of 'hybrid physical prehensions'. The novel idea thus could be said to emerge from a hybrid physical prehension of the unrealized concepts in past entities (i.e., a prehension of a past actual entity which focuses on eternal objects felt by, but not necessarily physically exemplified in, the past entities). Thus the entire realm of unrealized concepts becomes available to a new concrescence through its hybrid physical prehension of God. Ford writes: "With hybrid prehensions the category of reversion becomes superfluous, since all relevant novelty can be directly derived from God" (p. 235).

After the introduction of hybrid physical prehensions of God, Whitehead's first move was simply to restrict the notion of reversion to past finite entities. That is, reversion (the appearance of novelties without reference to their physical source) applies only "to transmission within the world, leaving God out of account" (p. 235).

At the next stage, Ford argues, Whitehead saw that reversion was not only superfluous but also deficient because it violated the ontological principle. Whitehead now understood that, with the notion of a hybrid physical prehension of God's conceptual wealth, it was possible in principle to eliminate reversion entirely and to preserve the ontological principle in its strictest form. Ford comments:

> "Since the reason for the relationship among unrealized eternal objects can only be found in God's primordial envisagement, a reason which is lacking for purely mundane reversion, and since hybrid prehension can supply all the novelty that reversion could, reversion is simply replaced by hybrid prehension. 'The category of reversion is then abolished' (PR 250)" (p. 237).

If Ford's analysis is correct, Whitehead followed a chain of argument in his own development which is very close to our third argument for the existence of God.

D

The fourth argument is closely related to the third. Each finite entity finds that the eternal objects are *graded* in their relevance to that entity. Moreover, this grading is unique for each new actual entity; no two finite actual entities will have their eternal objects organized into exactly the same pattern of relevance.[19] How are we to account for this unique grading of eternal objects in each actual entity except by saying that God provides it?

Suppose that our third argument for the existence of God failed. Suppose, that is, that we could figure out a way of saying that the entire set of eternal objects is present in the finite entities—either that the entire set is present in each actual entity or that the entire set is present in an appropriate group of finite entities. We would still be faced with the question we are raising in this section, namely, how are we to account for the fact that each new entity finds that the eternal objects are *graded* in their relevance to that entity? If we say that each new entity has its eternal objects organized for it by its antecedent finite entities, then we run immediately into the problem discussed in the second argument, that is, that different past entities will present the new actual entity with different— and even contradictory—expectations. Thus different past entities will suggest to the new entity different patterns of relevance among its eternal objects. This variety of suggested gradings requires a principle whereby the new entity may make a selection among them. Whitehead finds this principle in God, where God gives this principle to the new entity as a part of its subjective aim (PR 64a).

E

From a strictly metaphysical point of view, we may say that the basic argument for the existence of God is this: Creativity by itself is formless. It has no characteristics apart from its creations. Creativity is the "drive" of the universe which underlies the process of concrescence, and creativity is the "drive" of the universe which underlies the transition from entity to entity.

We have two final comments. First, in our book, we have used "reversion" in the mundane sense. That is, we have used reversion to describe the process by which a concrescence introduces a novelty which is new in relation to its past finite entities but which the concrescing entity derived from God through a hybrid physical prehension of God. Second, the elimination of reversion (or its downgrading to a handy way of speaking, apart from reference to God) and the introduction of the notion of hybrid physical prehensions confirm our analysis in Part One in which we claimed that *all* of a concrescing entity's purely conceptual prehensions are derived from prior physical prehensions, including hybrid physical prehensions of God, at that entity's first stage. (See especially Section I.C [and note 2] of Chapter Two.)

19. See Christian, *Whitehead's Metaphysics,* 360-62.

Since, however, creativity has no form of its own, it cannot "drive" either the process of concrescence or the transition from entity to entity unless it is given some form. Thus there is another need which God fulfills: God provides the characterization of, the limiting of, and the forming of creativity so that creativity can drive the creation of a new actual entity (transition) and so that it can drive the development of that entity towards its final satisfaction (concrescence) (RM 86c-91a).

V

Our previous discussion of Whitehead's theory of religion has made clear that rational religion requires the immanence of God in the world.[20] In this section, we will discuss some additional aspects of this immanence.

We have already presented the theoretical explanation for the immanence of God: God is present in the world through his gift to each new entity of its subjective aim. We ought not, however, to think of this subjective aim as something apart from God which God transfers to the new entity. The initial subjective aim is a part of God which becomes a part of the new actual entity. God is present in the entity as a proposition *(at least)*, where a proposition is a lure for feeling. Therefore, (this objectified portion of) God *is* the lure for feeling guiding the concrescence of the new entity. We read, "The primary element in the 'lure for feeling' is the subject's prehension of the primordial nature of God" (PR 287d). Whitehead also writes about God:

> He is the lure for feeling, the eternal urge of desire. His particular relevance to each creative act, as it arises from its own conditioned standpoint in the world, constitutes him the initial 'object of desire' establishing the initial phase of each subjective aim (PR 522c).

In Whitehead's opinion, this emphasis on the immanence of God accords well with the Christian tradition—or at least certain portions of it. In Section IV of Chapter Eighteen, we discussed the three stages of religious growth: Plato's intuition of certain general ideas, Jesus' exemplification of those ideas, and the theologians' elaboration of those ideas. At the stage of Jesus' exemplification of these ideas, Whitehead claims that Jesus modified the traditional Semitic emphasis on the transcendence of God in favor of a more immanent God. For example, in Jesus' teaching, God is coupled with the Kingdom of Heaven, with the

---

20. Of course, God is also transcendent in all the ways that Christian elaborates (*Whitehead's Metaphysics*, 371-80). Moreover, religion needs that divine transcendence for many purposes. For example, religion needs both the primordial and the consequent natures of God as they have entered into the divine satisfaction. The attainment of such a satisfaction, however, is one of the ways in which God is transcendent.

further explanation that the Kingdom of Heaven is "within" you (RM 70b). Again, Jesus conceived of God as a "father." This emphasis on immanence was continued by John—although it is difficult to know whether to connect John with Jesus' exemplification or with the theologians' explication. In any case, John understood Christ as the "logos," where this divine structure (the logos) is present throughout all creation (RM 70c). This emphasis on the direct immanence of God continues into the stage of the theologians' exemplification. As we saw in Section IV of Chapter Eighteen, the theologians opted for the direct immanence of God in Christ (i.e., the two natures in one person) and for the direct presence of God generally throughout the world, that is, the third person of the Trinity (AI 216b). In summary, Whitehead maintains that his doctrine is consonant with important sections of the Christian tradition, including the very teachings of Jesus himself.

The real presence of God in the world, however, must be understood carefully. Whitehead does not think that this real presence extends to the personhood of God.[21] That is, God is present through his gift of the subjective aim, through the patterns of coordinated value, and as a source of eternal objects; but God is not directly present as a person who thinks, wills, and hopes. Whitehead's reason for this position is simplicity itself. Very few people have a direct intuition of a personal God, but there is a widespread intuition into "a character of permanent righteousness" (RM 60d-61b). Therefore, on the real presence of this permanent rightness, Christian and Hindu can agree, as well as Jew and Buddhist, Muslim and Confucianist. When we leave the realm of direct intuition, however, and head towards the realm of the rational interpretation of religious experience, then the existence of (or the lack of) majorities is beside the point (RM 64b). Rather, if the coherence of our description of religious experience—as well as other forms of experience—demands that God be a person, then we should certainly assert the existence of a personal God. And, for all the reasons analyzed in this chapter, Whitehead himself does, in fact, assert the existence of such a deity.

---

21. We should observe that we are using the term "person" in its everyday sense, in which a person is an agent who thinks, is conscious, makes decisions, and is responsible. We are not using the term in the technical sense in which a person would be a nexus with 'personal order' as defined at PR 51c.

20 *The Language of Religion*

IN THIS CHAPTER, WE WILL CONSIDER the application of Whitehead's theory of language to his theory of religion. Although the chapter will not be short, neither will it be very long in light of its importance. We will use the materials previously developed.

I

Religious language is no different metaphysically from any other form of language. Here also we have perceptions of sounds and shapes—the squeaks and squiggles—which are used to educe or express propositional prehensions. If we follow Whitehead's threefold classification of rational religion, there will be three types of rational religious language: the language of intuition, as with Plato; the language of exemplification, as with the stories by and about Jesus; and the language of explication, as with the early Christian theologians. In each case, the language elicits or expresses an appropriate propositional prehension.

A

Let us turn to the stories about Jesus to illustrate this. At one level, these stories are similar to any other story about a historical figure. Consider the story of Jesus' calming the storm, Mark 4:35-41. So far as we are aware, Whitehead never offers an extended analysis of any specific passage in the New Testament. Therefore, rather than recording Whitehead's (non-existent) exegesis of this passage, we will construct a Whiteheadian type of exegesis. Generations of Christians have construed this story as, among other things, a literal report of an actual historical event. They have formed propositions having as logical subjects the actual entities in the body of Jesus, in the storm, in the boat, in the lake, and in the bodies of the disciples. And these Christians have applied various predicates to these logical subjects, including 'speaking', 'calming the storm', 'terror', and 'sleeping in the boat'. These propositions may or may not be true; there is no way of knowing apart from the normal methods of verification to be found in the discipline of history. There is also, perhaps, an additional proposition which some Christians may have formed in reading this story. All actual entities whatsoever are the logical subjects of this proposition, and the predicate would be something to do with a pattern of cooperation and mutual adjustment between the "natural" and the "personal" worlds. This predicate, in turn, may be merely one aspect of a still more abstract pattern of coordinated value. Of course, someone who had heard only this story and possessed no knowledge of the rest of the Bible or of the Christian tradition would be most unlikely to form any such proposition about the coordination of value. But a Christian, familiar with the rest of the Bible and/or the Christian tradition, might entertain precisely such a proposition.

We should make clear that the Christian's prehension of such a proposition need not be fully conscious. As we have observed throughout this book, propositions may enter into various degrees of consciousness, and language may elicit such propositions into any of these levels. That is, sometimes language elicits a proposition into the noontime clarity of full consciousness, sometimes into the evening twilight of semiconsciousness, and sometimes into the midnight of unconsciousness. But a proposition may be a significant factor in the concrescence of an actual entity no matter what level of consciousness it achieves. An actual entity builds its satisfaction on the basis of *all* its prehensions, and a proposition which remains at the early, preconscious stages of concrescence, may yet be a significant factor in determining the shape of that satisfaction.

Let us return now to our exegesis of Mark 4:35-41. It would be absurd to say that most Christians have ever consciously prehended the proposition about the cooperation and mutual adjustment of the physical and the personal worlds, although a good many Biblical commentators and preachers may have done precisely so. A larger number of Christians, however, may have elicited this proposition into the hazy shadows of the semiconscious realms. That is, suppose someone were to have a conversation with these Christians and, during that conversation, were to articulate this proposition in clear language. Further suppose that these Christians were then asked if they thought this proposition were true. Such Christians would probably answer yes, although it would not have occurred to them to formulate the words for themselves. In the case of a still larger number of Christians, however, the story of Jesus in the boat may have elicited this proposition, but not into any form of consciousness. Thus, these Christians have brought the proposition in question to the third phase of concrescence, but not to the fourth phase, where consciousness dwells. Nevertheless, the satisfaction of each actual entity is built upon the third phase just as much as it is built upon the fourth, and thus these Christians can live on the basis of their religion even if they cannot formulate its principles, or even recognize direct verbal statements of its abstract principles. One of the ways in which rational religion progresses is the gradual raising of such propositions from the realm of the subconscious to the realm of the conscious, either in society as a whole or in the life of a single person. The story of Jesus in the boat, however, must elicit this type of proposition—e.g., about the patterns of coordinated value— into *some* stage of the hearer's concrescence or else the story is not functioning as a part of a *rational* religion.

B

According to Whitehead's theory of religion, the subjective aim is the primary locus for the patterns of coordinated value. This is because the patterns of coordinated value are abstract elements in each new entity's subjective aim. We wish now to discuss somewhat further the relationship of the subjective aim to the propositions which, for example, the story of Jesus in the boat may be said to educe.

First, we may note that the patterns of coordinated value are not themselves propositions—at least not insofar as they are elements in the subjective aim. Thus, one of the functions of the story of Jesus in the boat is to promote the prehension of propositions which have these eternal objects—that is, the patterns of coordinated value—as their predicates. Such a proposition cannot emerge in the new actual entity prior to the third stage of concrescence.

Second, there is some ambiguity as to the logical subjects, both in the proposition felt in the subjective aim and in the propositions involving the patterns of coordinated value. Let us turn first to the subjective aim. In the proposition associated with the subjective aim, the primary logical subject is the entity entertaining that subjective aim. The predicate of this proposition, however, contains the patterns of coordinated value, where these patterns can be found in *every* actual entity. Thus, in a sense, all actual entities whatsoever ought to be the logical subjects of the proposition in the subjective aim. And so we have a problem. What is (are) the true logical subject(s) of the proposition in the subjective aim, the entity having that subjective aim or all actual entities whatsoever?

The solution to our problem is this. The primary logical subject is, of course, the concrescing entity itself. There is, however, a sense in which all actual entities whatsoever are present in that new actual entity. Specifically, all past actual entities are present as objective data, while all contemporary entities—including the concrescing itself—and all future entities are present as regions in the extensive continuum. Thus the entire set of actual entities is present in the new actual entity as a part of the "real internal constitution" of that new entity. It is a convention, thus, whether we claim that the proposition felt in the subjective aim has the set of all actual entities as its logical subjects (as the presence of the patterns of coordinated value would incline us to say) or whether we claim that this proposition has the new actual entity as its logical subject (as the fact that it is the subjective entity for *an* entity would incline us to say). In the first case, the proposition of the subjective aim would be a metaphysical proposition, with all actual entities whatsoever as its logical subjects; in the second case, the proposition of the subjective aim would be an ordinary proposition, exceptional only in the fact that it has a single actual entity as its logical subject.[1]

A similar ambiguity lurks in the propositions having the patterns of coordinated value as their predicates, which emerge at the third stage of concrescence. In the most straightforward sense, these are metaphysical propositions which have all actual entities as their logical subjects. Since, however, all actual entities are present in the concrescing actual entity as a part of its own very identity, it follows that we may construe these propositions as having the concrescing entity as its logical subject.

Lastly, we may recall that the subjective aim is derived from God. While, in Whitehead's theory of religion, God is introduced primarily as an explanation of certain data, Whitehead also allows that religion has a direct, albeit subsidiary, concern with God himself. We have, therefore, another class of religious propositions: those with God as their logical subject. Like the proposition of the subjective aim, this proposition is also unusual in having a single logical subject.

C

Rational religion deals with factors which are universally present, that is, factors which are available to all actual entities. This, in turn, requires that the insights of rational religion be communicable. If these insights were not communicable, then one of the primary tests of rational religion would be impossible: namely, it would be impossible to test for the presence of these factors in other occasions of experience, in other emotional states, and in other types of environment. That is, if the insights of rational religion were not communicable, then their metaphysical nature would be open to profound doubt. Nor would it be any escape from this conclusion to argue that each person must individually experience the truth of religion, and that a person, even though unable to communicate the truth of religion to others, can still know its truth individually and personally. (Something like this seems to be operating in many forms of mysticism.) The reason this argument will not work is that a person *is* a nexus of ac-

---

1. This paragraph represents an application of the discussion in Section II of Chapter Fifteen.

tual entities, and we are faced with the problem of communicating the religious insight from an earlier to a later occasion within a single person. There is no metaphysical difference, as we saw in Chapter Twelve, between communication from one person to another and communication from an earlier to a later entity within a single soul thread.

> The emergence of rational religion was strictly conditioned by the general progress of the races in which it arose. It had to wait for the development in human consciousness of the relevant general ideas and of the relevant ethical intuitions. It required that such ideas should not merely be casually entertained by isolated individuals, but that they should be stabilized in recognizable forms of expression, so as to be recalled and communicated. You can only speak of mercy among a people who, in some respects are already merciful (RM 32b-33a).

To the extent, therefore, that systematic theology wishes to deal with rational religion, it necessarily involves the study of language—especially language insofar as it symbolizes these sorts of propositions which are (for most people) so unhandy, vague, and hard to pin down. Whitehead writes:

> I suggest that the development of systematic theology should be accompanied by a critical understanding of the relation of linguistic expression to our deepest and most persistent intuitions (AI 209b; cf. 2787b).

II

In this section, we will discuss the sense in which religious language works *ex opere operato*.

A

Although the patterns of coordinated value may be present in every subjective aim, most entities do not use them as the predicates of distinct propositions. It seems most unlikely, for example, that an actual entity in an electron can detach the abstract patterns of coordinated value from their role in the subjective aim and then, at its third stage of concrescence, prehend the metaphysical proposition which has these patterns as the predicate and which has all actual entities as the logical subjects. Moreover, since most entities do not form such propositions at all, there must have been some actual entities which elicited these propositions "on their own", that is, without the aid of any relevant examples of such a proposition and without the aid of an established symbolism designed to evoke such a proposition. There must also have been occasions when such a proposition was elicited into the realms of the semiconscious without any previous examples and without the aid of an established symbolism. Lastly, there must have been occasions when such a proposition was elicited into the full daylight of complete consciousness without examples or established symbolism—that is, where such symbolism as may have been employed had not been previously used for this precise purpose.

When an actual entity elicits such a proposition "on its own"—or when an entity raises such a proposition to a new level of consciousness "on its own"—it will need to express that proposition in some symbolic form. Whitehead calls this 'original expression' (RM 127b). Original expression is primarily into words (RM 127c). Thus original expression is primarily a linguistic phenomenon.

There are inexhaustible opportunities for original expression. First, no finite entity has ever yet brought into full consciousness (or, perhaps, even into preconsciousness) a metaphysical proposition in which the complete pattern of coordinated value serves as the predicate. Rather, finite entities have only created propositions with a portion of the pattern of coordinated value serving as the predicate. Thus, as new propositions having predicates containing novel portions of the pattern of coordinated value are periodically elicited, and as they are brought to various degrees of consciousness, it follows that there will be many opportunities for additional cases of original expression. Second, as the various relations among these many propositions are perceived, there will be still further opportunities for original expression into language. Third, since religious language is concerned with God, insights into the divine nature and into his relation to the world provide still more situations in which original expression may occur.

Whitehead also speaks of 'responsive expression' (RM 129a). What Whitehead has in mind is that most of us have elicited—and some of us have brought to conscious light—at least a few metaphysical propositions about the patterns of coordinated value. And most of us have consciously entertained some propositions about God. We have usually done so, however, with a language designed for this purpose and under the influence of examples of such activity. Nevertheless, we still wish to express our insights—even though they are "second hand"—in some symbolic form. Usually this symbolism is language. Whitehead calls expression of our insights under these conditions 'responsive expression'.

B

Language when used by a person to express religious insights has the power to elicit those same insights in the listener. It makes no difference whether this language is the result of original or of responsive expression. And it makes no difference whether the listener is another person or a later member of the speaker's soul thread. As we saw in Section I of Chapter

Seventeen, language has the power to affect deeply the structure and content of our experience. That is, the "what" and the "how" of our lived world are, to a very great extent, the results of the creative power of language. In Chapter Fourteen, we discussed the theoretical basis for this capacity of language to shape our experience. The fundamental point was that there is an infinity of data at the first stage of each new entity which is simplified as the concrescence progresses, and that language is one of the factors guiding that entire development. Some portions of the original data are ignored in the full conscious stages of concrescence, and other portions of these data have been "edited" so that many of the original details are "smoothed over" in the later stages.

Now religious language is meant to elicit propositions about such items as the coordination of values and God. The materials for creating these propositions, however, are present at the initial phase of every new actual entity. For example, consider the propositions about the coordinated patterns of value. Since these are metaphysical propositions, it follows that all actual entities are the logical subjects. But, in one way or another, all actual entities are present as objective data in each new concrescence. Likewise, the predicates of these propositions are present at the initial stage of each new entity as abstract elements in that entity's subjective aim. Therefore, the materials with which to create the propositions of rational religion are present in every new entity. For example, in a proposition about God, both the logical subject (i.e., God) and the predicate (e.g., something about the relations among God, the subjective aim, and the finite entity) are present in the new entity.

Since the materials for creating religious propositions are present at the initial phase of every new actual entity, it follows that the task of religious language is to help the new entity actually to form them. In other words, religious language does not guide us towards some "mystical" or special experience which is available only to the "enlightened" or the "elect." Rather, religious language helps us to organize our ordinary experience so that certain implicit factors are made explicit.

Whitehead thus claims that religious language has the power to evoke propositions about the coordination of values and to evoke propositions about God. When Whitehead speaks of religious language as working *ex opere operato*, however, he has still more in mind. Religious language has the power to evoke the insights necessary to verify or confirm those propositions. To see how this is so, let us consider any one proposition about the pattern of coordinated values. This is a metaphysical proposition which is meant to apply everywhere. Now every actual world exhibits some pattern of order. Thus this metaphysical proposition either applies to the actual world of the entity entertaining that proposition or it does not. That is, either the proposition applies to *every* entity in that actual world or it does not.

Consequently, the proposition about the coordinated values either applies to the most recent of events—including those of the last quarter of a second—as well as those of the ancient past, or it does not. But the actual entities of the very recent past have not been relegated to the vague chaos of the ever present background; they have survived into the new actual entity with much of their individuality intact. Therefore, the actual entity entertaining the proposition could, in principle, compare the proposition with the actual pattern of coordination which it discovers in its environment. (Also, since God and his gift of the subjective aim is present to each new entity, the same logic holds for saying that religious language not only can help us elicit propositions about God but also can help us to verify those propositions.)

One may be inclined to ask the following question. If the patterns of coordinated value are present in every subjective aim, then why is it necessary to have a special religious language to help us "discover" those patterns? The answer is that the patterns of coordinated value are only one of many factors present in the initial stage of an actual entity, and the actual entity may choose to emphasize other factors in its later stages of concrescence. Thus the materials for the verification of these propositions are present at the initial stage but usually need the stimulus of religious language for their promotion into greater prominence in the later phases of concrescence.

> But the expressive sign is more than interpretable. It is creative. It elicits the intuition which interprets it. It cannot elicit what is not there. A note on a tuning fork can elicit a response from a piano. But the piano has already in it the string tuned to the same note. In the same way the expressive sign elicits the existent intuition which would not otherwise emerge into individual distinctiveness. Again in theological language, the sign works *ex opere operato*, but only within the limitation that the recipient be patient of the creative action (RM 128b).

C

Whitehead makes some comments on the evolution of religion which we will discuss in this section. Whitehead claims that the concrete language which is capable of educing significant religious insight was not produced instantaneously. Rather, it grew over a long period of time. At the beginning of *Religion in the Making,* Whitehead constructs a history of the evolution of religion, making numerous comments about the growth of language. Religion has had four stages, according to Whitehead. At first, religion is a matter of ritual. But ritual releases energy from the pursuit of immediate needs, and religion enters its second stage of emotion. In order to promote this emotion, men create myths and tales about their rituals, and thus religion enters its third stage of belief. Lastly, the myths and legends generate thought which is not tied to the pursuit of immediate needs. When such thought is maintained over a sufficient length of time, we enter the fourth stage, rational religion (RM 18-43).

It is not clear exactly how to interpret these comments. If one accepts Whitehead's positive orientation to evolution, these four stages are a plausible hypothesis concerning the development of religious insight. Whitehead has certainly helped his own cause by restricting his comments to general stages of religious development. He makes no assertions about particular events in prehistory. In this regard, Whitehead is far more careful than many other late nineteenth and early twentieth century thinkers, such as Sigmund Freud. Freud suggested that, before the dawn of written history, a group of brothers murdered their father and ate him. Then, lacking a leader, they projected the image of their dead father into the sky in an effort to find a leader, and this is the origin of the "reality" of God. Since there is no historical or archaeological evidence of such a murder, Freud's re-creation of history certainly does not stand up to serious examination.

Ought we to interpret Whitehead as intending his four stages of religious development to include not only prehistory but also early history? Frankly, we do not know. The reader may find it helpful to know that in our personal conversations with Whiteheadian scholars we have found sharply divergent opinions. On the one hand, some scholars argue that all four stages must be placed in prehistoric times. Their argument depends on the claim that all human societies, as we know them either through anthropology or archaeology, have reached the stage of rational insight into religion. For example, we may refer to the work of Jan de Vries, *The Study of Religion,* translated by Kees W. Bolle (New York: Harcourt, Brace & World, 1967). In this book, de Vries considers the views of a wide variety of scholars, from the Greeks to living contemporaries. Since many of these men had suggested various evolutionary schemes to account for the rise of religion, and since these evolutionary schemes typically assert that "thinking" or "reason" is the last element to arise in the development of religion, de Vries writes at length about the fact that all historical, archaeological, and anthropological evidence points to the existence of "thought" among people as soon as they are religious. If de Vries is correct, then Whitehead's evolutionary scheme must be interpreted as applying strictly to the evolution of the earliest societies.

On the other hand, other Whiteheadian scholars argue that at least the fourth stage of religious evolution may include well-documented developments in literate societies. Their argument is that, in all the cultures with which we are familiar (e.g. Hindu, Chinese, Greek, Hebrew), there is a point, long after the religion appeared with its myths, rituals, etc., when systematic and critical reflection, metaphysics, and rational speculation appeared. That primitive men think, these scholars conclude, is undoubted; that they make a *rational system* out of their religion is another issue. In this scenario, Whitehead's last stage of rationalization may be illustrated by Confucius's organization of the communal practices of early China or the emergence of Buddhism and Vedantism within Indian culture.

However we interpret Whitehead's four stages of religious evolution in relation to prehistory and history, there is another perspective which is very helpful to us. Whitehead's four stages of ritual, emotion, belief, and rationalization may also serve as his description of the various dimensions of religious experience as it exists now. In Whitehead's view, a rational religion (the fourth stage) tends to be rooted in myth and legend (the third stage). That is, the myths and legends of religion are typically the language which, in appropriate circumstances, may be used to elicit the metaphysical propositions of rational religion. For example, both the stories by Jesus and the stories about Jesus depend on—as well as continue—the mythic and legendary language of the ancient Hebrew tradition. Yet it is this language, rooted in the Hebrew heritage but modified by Christian experience, which has supported the rational insights of many Christians down to the present day. Moreover, the use of such materials to produce the insights of rational religion is facilitated by the presence of certain moods and emotions—namely, those emotions (the second stage) which the ritual and liturgy (the first stage) tend to produce.

D

Whitehead holds that certain emotional states are more efficacious for the development of religious insights than are others (RM 121b). That is, religious language works best in conjunction with certain emotional states. Whitehead does not describe these emotional states, but the fact that he places ritual at the beginning of the evolution of religion would indicate that he is thinking of the kinds of emotions which are developed in a liturgical setting. Whitehead's (rather Anglican) assumption that liturgy underlies the production of religious insight comes to the surface when he uses incense as an ordinary mode of symbolizing religious emotions (PR 278b-79a)! The determination of the most effective settings for the production of religious insight, however, is an empirical matter. It may vary from person to person and from time to time. We ought not to eliminate a priori the possibility that for some people—perhaps the majority — religious insight is best evoked in a Pentecostal speaking in tongues, in a Billy Graham crusade, in private daily Bible reading and meditation, in singing camp-meeting Gospel songs, or in a typical "low church" Methodist or Baptist Sunday service. In any case, religious insight often dawns on us in special circumstances of some sort. In fact, the religious appeal to history, according to Whitehead, is really the appeal to exceptional moments in lives of exceptional people when they had an unusually firm grasp upon the intuitions of religion (AI 207c-8a).

Although, as an empirical matter of fact, certain moods are the most propitious for the eduction of religious propositions, it is still the case that these propositions are metaphysical. We need therefore to test our religious insights in all sorts of moods and in all sorts of circumstances (RM 53c, 81a). In all thought and in all developed experience, there is the possibility of error. That is, there is a massive influx of conceptual novelty at the second stage of concrescence. This novelty allows us to feel propositions having predicates which correspond to "nothing in reality." Furthermore, this same wealth of conceptual novelty allows us to structure (the later phases in) our experience in ways which are not rooted "in reality," and thus there is the possibility of concocting "out of thin air" a verification of a proposition. In ordinary life we often use one experience to check on another, but in the case of a metaphysical proposition it is especially appropriate to use our experiences as checks on each other. After all, a metaphysical proposition is meant to apply everywhere and to be verifiable in all experiences. Therefore, as Whitehead says,

> Here a distinction must be drawn. Intuitions may first emerge as distinguished in consciousness under exceptional circumstances. But when some distinct idea has been once experienced, or suggested, it should then have its own independence of irrelevancies. Thus we may not know some arithmetical truth, and require some exceptional help to detect it. But when known, arithmetic is a permanent possession. The psychological interpretation, assigning a merely personal significance, holds when objective validity is claimed for an intuition which is only experienced in a set of discrete circumstances of definite specific character. The intuition may be clearer under such circumstances, but it should not be confined to them (RM 63c-64a).

III

Religious language elicits propositional prehensions and not just propositions. Thus religious language also elicits the subjective forms with which we prehend the specified propositions. All propositions are lures for feeling, but the propositions of religion have an unusually powerful attraction because the propositions about the coordination of values, when developed to their maximum potential, connect the new entity with *all* actuality. In addition, religious propositions point to God as the source of the initial subjective aim, where it is this initial subjective aim which establishes the new entity with its own potential self-identity. An entity's relations with its future entities as well as its suggested self-identity have a most profound influence on the capacity of that entity to attain depth of experience. Consequently, because the propositions of religion have unusually powerful attraction, we should also expect the subjective forms with which they are prehended to be unusually intense.

A

The central point which we wish to make is that, because language also elicits subjective forms, and not just propositions, it follows that religious language is central in *living* the religious life. As we have repeatedly observed, the role of language is not restricted to describing facts or communicating bits and pieces of information. This is true of religious language also. For example, religious language may educe the propositions about the coordination of values with a subjective form which helps us to organize our entire lives in terms of them. And, since we can instantiate these patterns with various degrees of awareness, religious language may educe these patterns so that they become more explicit in our lives. Or language may merely help us savor "with refreshment" the sense of purpose which we find in these patterns (PR 47a). Or we may find the language of religion eliciting these propositions with subjective forms which promote an attitude of thanksgiving, worship, or adoration. In addition, religious language may help us to respond to the "lures for feeling about God" with the subjective forms appropriate to prayer, gratitude, and companionship. In short, religious language elicits the prehension of these propositions in a way that affects the whole of our personhood.

> Your character is developed according to your faith. This is the primary religious truth from which no one can escape. Religion is force of belief cleansing the inward parts. For this reason the primary religious virtue is sincerity, a penetrating sincerity.
>
> A religion, on its doctrinal side, can thus be defined as a system of general truths which have the effect of transforming character when they are sincerely held and vividly apprehended.
>
> In the long run your character and your conduct of life depend upon your intimate convictions (RM 15a-c).

In Section IV of Chapter Seventeen, we discussed language as a social phenomenon. Since religious language elicits the subjective forms of propositional prehensions, it follows that it will tend to promote certain ways of being religious. That is, the subjective form of a prehension is *how* the prehending entity reacts to its world; or, in other words, the subjective form is the *way* in which the prehending entity is in its world. Therefore, in promoting certain subjective forms, religious language will promote certain ways of being in the world. There are, however, many different religious languages. To the extent that different religious languages suggest different subjective forms, it follows that a variety of religious languages will support a variety of different life-styles.

It is somewhat difficult to illustrate this point without appearing to offend someone. Surely, however, at least part of the mutual incomprehensibility between Hindu and Muslim stems from the articulation of different religious visions in quite different linguistic forms. For example, when reading the Koran, the Muslim finds a story in which temporal sequence is essential. God (or Allah) created the world. There is a sequence of prophets culminating in Muhammed. And there will be a final judgment. When reading one of the Hindu stories (or, more likely, watching it enacted at the local temple), the Hindu will find literal temporal sequence largely irrelevant. The resulting difference in attitudes to communal history, personal decision-making and ethical action (in light of the coming judgment) will be profound. Even within a single religion, the articulation of different religious languages will tend to elicit different life-styles and different religious communities. Consider this rather obscure issue in Protestant Christianity: Is baptism primarily a sign of God's promise to us or is it primarily a sign of our acceptance of those promises? The first case is the classical Augustinian/Lutheran/Calvinist perspective. In this case, there is likely to be more emphasis on the baptism of infants, because God can surely make a promise to a child. Along with this baptism of infants will be a stress on the family and the congregation as primary bearers of the Christian faith. The second case is typical of the more Arminian and Baptist groups. In this case, there is likely to be less emphasis on the baptism of infants, because it is nonsense to say that an eight-day-old child can respond in faith to God's promises. In this case there will likely be a stress on the individual's personal faith and on the congregation as a secondary—albeit necessary—tool for the promotion and maintenance of individual faith.[2]

We may note that we have found at least a partial explanation for the bitterness which often marks theological battles about terminology. Different words may denote the same factual material and yet evoke entirely different life-styles. It is not merely that different words have differ-

---

2. We are well aware of the many exceptions to these broad generalizations. Methodism, for example, is surely Arminian with an emphasis on personal conversion, but Methodists will baptize infants. Note, however, the following fact: there are several newer denominations—such as the Church of the Nazarene—which claim to be a more consistent application of Wesleyan principles. While the traditional Methodists may tend to practice infant baptism, the newer groups, such as the Nazarenes, tend to downplay infant baptism (without officially eliminating it). The author of this book has, through marriage, four relatives who are Nazarene ministers. None of them has ever performed an infant baptism.

There are also some Baptists who claim, except on the issue of baptism, to be good Calvinists. For example, the Primitive Baptists as a denomination maintain many of the Calvinist tenants. And Karl Barth is a classic illustration of a Calvinist gradually heading towards a Baptist position. Nevertheless, most Baptist churches and denominations, including the Southern Baptist Convention (the largest Baptist group in the United States), are oriented to individual conversions and tend to maintain an Arminian emphasis on an individual's freedom to respond to the Gospel.

ent connotations—although that also may be true. Rather, the variance in vocabulary may reflect a variance in "lived worlds," that is, in the satisfactions which human actual entities create out of their initial data. An interesting possibility for further research would be to analyze the great theological debates of Christian history from this perspective. The Homoousian-Homoiousian controversy, the Augustinian-Pelagian debate on the correct definitions of "grace," "sin," and "free-will," and the Evangelical-Romanist struggle—all these are more than disagreements about "what is the case;" rather, they also reflect conflicting ways of "being in the world."

B

Ever since A. J. Ayer published the first edition of *Language, Truth, and Logic* in 1936, there has been a widely publicized debate in the English-speaking world about the cognitivity of religious language. We will not discuss that debate here, but we will observe how Whitehead stands on this issue. A sentence is supposed to be cognitive when it states "what is the case about the world." Thus, when Ayer and the others propose verifiability, falsifiability, confirmability, etc., as tests for the cognitivity of ordinary sentences (as opposed to the tautologies of mathematics and logic), they are really saying that these tests will pick out all those sentences which state "what is the case about the world," and that these tests will pick out only such sentences. Sentences which do not meet these tests (and which are not tautologies) are noncognitive, that is, they do not say anything about the world. The early writers such as Ayer tended to dismiss all noncognitive sentences as nonsense and as meaningless. Later writers, however, tended to stress that language has many legitimate uses other than stating what is the case; for example, we also use language to ask questions, give orders, tell jokes, write poetry, make promises, and express our feelings.[3]

From Whitehead's point of view, the problem with this entire debate is that it is conducted on a false assumption: either language is wholly cognitive or it is wholly noncognitive. But on Whitehead's analysis, all language has both a cognitive and a noncognitive element. The linguistic forms elicit propositional prehensions. Every propositional prehension can be divided into two parts: the proposition, which is the datum of the prehension, and the subjective form, which is *how* the proposition is felt. Every propositional prehension *must* have both parts. Thus the felt proposition gives each propositional prehension a "cogni-

---

3. There are several examples of appeals to the "legitimate" non-cognitive uses of religious language in Antony Flew and Alasdair MacIntyre, *New Essays in Philosophical Theology* (New York: Macmillan Co., 1964). Also, Paul M. van Buren discusses this topic at length in *The Secular Meaning of the Gospel* (New York: Macmillan Co., 1963) and *The Edges of Language: An Essay in the Logic of a Religion* (New York: Macmillan Co., 1972).

tive" aspect, while the subjective form gives each propositional prehension a "noncognitive" aspect.

Let us turn first to the felt proposition and see how it introduces the aspect of cognitivity. A proposition always is the hypothetical attribution of an eternal object to a set of actual entities. If these actual entities are in the past, then the proposition is either true or false, that is, the eternal object either does, in fact, qualify the actual entities serving as the logical subjects or it does not qualify them. The proposition's truth or falsity remains a fact, no matter how that proposition is felt. The proposition may be felt in such a way that its truth of falsity is irrelevant, but that does not take away from the fact that it is either true or false. But let us suppose that the logical subjects are in the prehending entity's present or future. Then the proposition is merely possible, that is, the eternal object, which in the proposition is hypothetically attributed to certain logical subjects, may or may not come to qualify those logical subjects in fact.[4] Like propositions about the past, propositions about the present or future may be felt in such a way that their (possible) truth or falsity is irrelevant, but that does not take away from the fact that the proposition itself will become either true or false. We may conclude by observing that every propositional prehension has an essential reference to what is the case, that is, every propositional prehension includes an element which either is, or may become, true or false. In this sense, we may say that all language has a cognitive aspect because all language elicits prehensions of *propositions*.[5]

In every propositional prehension, the subjective form introduces noncognitive elements. The subjective form involves the noncognitive elements because the subjective form is *how* the prehending entity reacts to the world. The subjective form is not in any sense a hypothesis about that world, nor it is a "tale that might be told" about the world. In propositional prehensions which are questions, commands, or desires, the subjective forms clearly introduce noncognitive elements, that is, an "attitude towards" the proposition, or the feeling-tone "with which" the proposition is felt.[6]

We said, however, that *all* propositional prehensions have a noncognitive element. In what sense, then, does the subjective form of a "declarative" propositional prehension introduce a "noncognitive" ele-

---

4. See Section III.D of Chapter One.

5. We add the following word of caution. In this section, we associate propositions with the "cognitive" side of language. It should be remembered, however, that every proposition is first and foremost "a lure for feeling." While each proposition without exception must be either true, false, or possible, its truth status is not an intrinsic part of its nature but is only external. Therefore, while we remain committed to our thesis that all language has a cognitive aspect because it symbolizes propositions, we also remain committed not to associate those propositions solely with their cognitive functions.

6. See Section VI.B of Chapter Twelve.

ment? (By a declarative propositional prehension, we mean a propositional prehension which would be elicited by an ordinary declarative sentence and in which the symbolized proposition is meant to be a clear statement of fact.) The answer is simple. In a declarative propositional prehension, the subjective form is the urge towards believing or disbelieving the constituent proposition, or towards suspending belief; or it is the urge towards considering the proposition or towards wondering about the proposition; or it is the shock of recognition; or it is the delight of appreciation; and so forth.[7] The possibilities are endless. In each case, however, the subjective form involves a response to the proposition, that is, a psychological attitude towards the "tale which might be the case." In short, we have even in "declarative" propositional prehensions, in which the symbolized proposition is meant to be a straight description of fact, a noncognitive response to a cognitive lure. Thus all language, since it elicits *prehensions* of propositions, has a noncognitive element as well as a cognitive element.

What is true of all language in general is also true of religious language in particular. Consider the religious language which symbolizes the propositions about the patterns of coordinated value. The propositions are hypotheses about the coordination of values among all actual entities. Either the eternal objects serving as the predicates of these propositions genuinely qualify each actual entity or they do not. That is, the propositions are either true or false. Therefore, even though religious language may elicit propositional prehensions whose subjective forms take us into the very act of living religiously, nevertheless, that religious language will have a cognitive element because the elicited propositional prehensions have a proposition as their datum. This cognitive element will remain no matter how far the subjective forms direct our attention away from the explicit consideration of "what is the case."

Likewise, even when we use religious language to state "what is the case" in the most straightforward manner possible, we will still have a noncognitive element in our language. This is because the religious language can symbolize propositions only insofar as those propositions are the object of some prehension; but such a propositional prehension *must* have a subjective form of some kind. In addition and quite beyond such purely technical considerations, we previously observed that debates about religious terminology — which appear to be paradigm cases of religious debates about "what is the case" —may well reflect conflicting ways of "being in the world."

Therefore, debates whether religious language is cognitive or noncognitive are quite misplaced. The only significant question, in White-

7. For a fuller discussion of the subjective forms of belief, consideration, wonder, etc., see Section VI.A of Chapter Twelve.

head's view, is this: In a specific instance of religious language, what are its cognitive elements and what are its noncognitive elements?

IV

In this section, we will consider Whitehead's notion of dogma. In his view, dogma is a central type of language for rational religion.

A

We have already observed the dependence of religion on propositions and language, according to Whitehead. At one point, he offers a definition of religion which includes, among other items, the claim that religion is "a system of general truths" (RM 15b). A religious dogma is the attempt to state as precisely as possible the general truths disclosed in religious experience (RM 57b). It should be observed that any area of life which deals explicitly with general truths will have its dogmas. Whitehead gives the example of scientific dogmas (RM 57b), but he could have mentioned metaphysics, political ideology, military science, and economics. Thus the word "dogma" carries no negative connotations for Whitehead; indeed, in his eyes, it is something of an honorific term. A dogma is simply an exact statement of a general truth which is "divested so far as possible from particular exemplification" (RM 122b).

While the notion of a dogma may be simple, there is no reason to think that the dogmas themselves will be simple. In at least two different books, Whitehead warns against assuming that religious dogmas—or any other kind—will be simple or easy (AI 207b-c; RM 73f). All dogmas will necessarily be complicated because, in their full generality, dogmas are metaphysical statements and, therefore, anything but simple. The immense complexity of metaphysical statements is guaranteed by their complete generality, their high abstraction, and their interaction with each other over all areas of human experience.

Dogmas participate in the typical structures common to all language. There are the linguistic forms—that is, the aural squeaks or the visual shapes—which symbolize the propositions. More generally, perceptions of such squeaks and shapes elicit the various propositional prehensions. Lastly, we must be able to test the propositions by appeal to our experience (RM 123b). In Part Three, we observed how language is essential for a developed consciousness, memory, and thought-life.[8] Thus, to the extent that we wish to develop our consciousness of, our memory of, or our thought-life about the propositions of rational religion, we must

8. See Section VI.A and Section VII of Chapter Twelve.

develop linguistic forms with which to symbolize them. We must, that is, construct dogmas.

> Such precise expression is in the long run a condition for vivid realization, for effectiveness, for apprehension of width of scope, and for survival.
>
> For example, when the Greeks, such as Pythagoras or Euclid, formulated accurately mathematical dogmas, the general truths which the Egyptians had acted upon for more than thirty generations became thereby of greater importance (RM 122b-c; cf. AI 207b).

The central function of dogmas is to aid communication. Earlier in this chapter (Section I.C), we emphasized that the insights of rational religion cannot be easily communicated without the aid of language—not even from actual entity to actual entity within a single soul thread. Dogma is merely a very special kind of language which, in its attempt to state a truth precisely, avoids the story-telling quality of most religious literature and which also distinguishes explicitly between the general principle and its concrete exemplifications. Therefore, the dogmatic statement of a general truth allows the direct communication of the general truth. Such communication means that dogma is to be associated with the stage of religious life in which the solitary act of concrescence becomes available to the larger community (RM 132d).

Such communication is also necessary if we are to recognize this same general religious truth in areas other than that in which we first discovered it (RM 139c). This ability to recognize the same religious truth in many different areas is essential for the verification of that truth. That is, since the truths of rational religion are metaphysical in scope, they must be exemplified in all actual entities. However, ordinary religious discourse —for example, the stories by and about Jesus—elicits the propositions of rational religion in a concrete setting, and it does not clearly distinguish between the general principle and the concrete example. Therefore, if we are to check for the presence of the same general truth among its many different concrete instantiations, we must make clear the nature of that general truth apart from any particular exemplification. Ordinary religious language elicits the concrete example and does not place our attention squarely on the general principle—although the general principle must surely be present in that concrete example, if the religion is to be at all rational. The very essence of dogma, however, helps in the discovery and verification of the presence of the same general religious truth in many moods—both by many different actual entities in the same soul thread and by many different people entirely.

> The great instantaneous conviction in this way becomes the Gospel, the good news. It insists on its universality, because it is either that or a passing fancy. The conversion of the Gentiles is both the effect of truth and the test of truth (RM 133b).

B

Whitehead often reiterates that every dogma is set within a metaphysical system (e.g., SMW 190b; RM 76b). We observed, in Section III of Chapter Fifteen, that this is true of any proposition whatsoever. With a dogma, however, we are dealing explicitly with a truth of complete generality and high abstraction, which makes our recognition of the metaphysical setting of dogmas rather important. To illustrate this, consider the fact that all the truths of a metaphysical system ought to be coherent; consequently, the metaphysical truths, which, on the surface, seem to apply to one area of human experience, should require, for their complete exposition, some reference to the metaphysical truths from other areas. Thus the metaphysical dogmas which seem to be associated primarily with science must require, for their complete exposition, the metaphysical dogmas associated primarily with religion; and, similarly, the dogmas of religion ought to need the dogmas of science for their exposition. If the metaphysical dogmas of science and religion do not thus require each other, then the overall metaphysical system is incoherent.

> It seems an easy solution to hold that each type of idea is within its own sphere autonomous. In that case, the controversies arise from the illegitimate poaching of one type over the proper territory of some other type. For example, it is fashionable to state that religion and science can never clash because they deal with different topics. I believe that this solution is entirely mistaken. In this world at least, you cannot tear apart minds and bodies. But as soon as you try to adjust ideas you find the supreme importance of making perfectly clear, what you are talking about (AI 50a).

This brings us to the dogmatic fallacy. The dogmatic fallacy is the assumption—or in religious contexts, occasionally, the explicit statement —that this-or-that dogma is the perfect expression of a particular truth and cannot be improved. This is a fallacy because every dogma is set in a metaphysical system, and we cannot claim finality for that dogma without a corresponding claim for the finality of the metaphysical system (RM 126a). Since no metaphysical system can ever be final or complete or beyond improvement, it follows that no dogma can ever be final—including religious dogmas (RM 126b). Any verbal form will always disclose previously hidden ambiguities after it has been before the world for some time (SMW 190b). The other side of the coin, however, is that no dogma which has been before the world for some time is likely to be entirely wrong. It is not usually a question of such dogma's being right or wrong. Instead, it is usually a question of the dogma's degree of adequacy or inadequacy (cf. PR 13d-14b, 15d-16a, and, most significantly, 20c-22a).

A corollary of the dogmatic fallacy is that a single dogma—or even the complete set of dogmas which have been formulated at any one particular time—cannot be taken as the "whole story" (RM 140b). Of course, this position is a corollary of the doctrine that a metaphysics ought to be coherent so that no truth can be fully explicated without reference to the other metaphysical truths, but it is also an implication of Whitehead's position that no religious, scientific, or metaphysical system can ever be final. There may be ways of looking at any given fact which do not fit any of the current schemes of analysis and which, nevertheless, may prove to be quite fruitful.

> A dogma—in the sense of a precise statement—can never be final; it can only be adequate in its adjustment of certain abstract concepts. But the estimate of the status of these concepts remains for determination.
>
> You cannot rise above the adequacy of the terms you employ. A dogma may be true in the sense that it expresses such interrelations of the subject matter as are expressible within the set of ideas employed. But if the same dogma be used intolerantly so as to check the employment of other modes of analyzing the subject matter, then, for all its truth, it will be doing the work of a falsehood (RM 126b-c).

We note that, for Whitehead, the interpretation of religious experience requires systematic theology, and a systematic theology will be quite complicated. The real enemy of the "liberal spirit" is not a systematic theology which employs religious dogmas; rather, the true enemy is the attitude of dogmatic finality (AI 208b). Curiously, while in former times the theologians have been most guilty of harboring an attitude of dogmatic finality, it is now primarily the scientists who are most unwilling to consider fundamental shifts in the underlying structures of their systems (AI 185a).

As a consequence of his view of the nature of dogma, Whitehead insists that there must be a process of growth in our understanding of the various particular dogmas. Earlier dogmas are not so much wrong as limited in ways which had escaped the observation of earlier generations (RM 144b). Thus, if a particular dogma is not altered as the generations pass, it may well happen that the growth in the insights of a particular community will make the unchanged dogma an anachronism. And as an anachronism which is not put into contact with the deepest of the newer insights, the unchanged dogma begins to lose the power to attract the attention of the more knowledgeable members of the community. Something like this, according to Whitehead, has happened to the dogmas of the Christian and Buddhist communities. To the extent that these religious dogmas are considered unalterable and final, they have not been brought into contact with the deeper insights of modern science. And lacking such contacts, these unchanged religious dogmas have become anachronistic and unrelated to the dogmas of science. Thus, the older religious dogmas have "lost contact" with our enlarged insights into our experience, and the unaltered religious dogmas have lost their influence in modern scientific cultures (RM 140c-43).

It is interesting to speculate whether modern science, through its own attitude of dogmatic finality, may be losing some of *its* contact with the wider areas of human experience. For example, consider the reaction of orthodox psychology to parapsychology and of orthodox medicine to acupuncture—to say nothing of the tendency of many scientists to exclude a priori the interaction of their sciences with the West's own religious modes of knowledge. Surely as we Westerners try to live in a complete world, and not just in a world of scientific abstractions, the scientists will have to come to grips with these other modes of knowing or they themselves will become anachronistic and irrelevant to the "real" world.

Neither religion nor science, however, is fated to become anachronistic and irrelevant. Both can retain their timeliness and relevance if only they will be open to the continual growth and improvement of their dogmas.

> Progress in truth—truth of science and truth of religion—is mainly a progress in the framing of concepts, in discarding artificial abstractions or partial metaphors, and in evolving notions which strike more deeply into the root of reality (RM 127a).

C

The importance of religious language is very real, but it can be easily overestimated. No set of dogmas can ever probe the depths of reality. There is always more to learn. The purpose of rational religious language is to promote our prehension of the propositions about the patterns of coordinated value and to promote our prehension of the proposition serving as the initial subjective aim. We also hope to gain, with the help of religious language, some knowledge of the actual instantiation of the patterns of coordinated value. Religious language is important, thus, because it helps to bring such propositions and facts into prominence, but it is the propositions and facts themselves which are truly essential to the religious life and not the language about them.

Our basic point is that we live our religious lives on the basis of our total experience and not just that portion of it which can be encompassed by religious language—whether that language be the Jesus stories or the metaphysical dogmas of religion. Let us turn first to the dogmas of religion. We cannot live on the basis of our dogmas alone, because, in part, there are genuine limits to the ability of any metaphysical system to symbolize the basic structures of our experience—as we mention in Section E below. There is another reason why we cannot live on dogmas alone: religious dogmas point to such factors as the subjective aim, the patterns of coordinated value, and God's victory over the perpetual perishing of the finite entities, but these factors interact with all the details of our experience. Therefore, since it is beyond the capacity of any language—

metaphysical or otherwise—to symbolize all the details of our experience, our religious life will always be richer than our religious language.

There is, however, still another reason why our religious experience is necessarily broader than our dogmas. In Section II.A of this chapter, we observed that actual entities may on occasion prehend the propositions of rational religion without the stimulus of language, and we further noted that on occasion actual entities may be able to emphasize—at least to some degree—a pattern of coordinated value quite without the aid of language. And yet these propositions and these patterns in the environment may well be the basis on which a person lives the religious life and the basis on which the truth about the world is known.

It is for these reasons that Whitehead, in the midst of a discussion of the nature of dogma, writes,

> We can know more of the characters of those who are dear to us than we can express accurately in words. We may recognize the truth of some statement about them. It will be a new statement about something which we had already apprehended but had never formulated (RM 123b).

Although not occurring directly in a discussion of dogma, the following comments are clearly relevant to his view of dogma. Whitehead writes about our intuition into "the concept of a rightness in things, partially conformed to and partially disregarded:"

> This intuition is not the discernment of a form of words, but of a type of character. It is characteristic of the learned mind to exalt words. Yet mothers can ponder many things in their hearts which their lips cannot express. These many things, which are thus known, constitute the ultimate religious evidence, beyond which there is no appeal (RM 65c).

As a preliminary to another discussion of dogma, Whitehead writes:

> The final principle of religion is that there is a wisdom in the nature of things, from which flow our direction of practice, and our possibility of the theoretical analysis of fact. . . .
> According to religion, this discernment of relationships forms in itself the very substance of existence. The formulations are the froth upon the surface (RM 137c-138b).

In fact, Whitehead is willing to stake everything on the principle that we can live out of and "know truth" on the basis of our total experience, where this totality of our experience extends beyond that portion of it which is dominated by language.

> The importance of rational religion in the history of modern culture is that it stands or falls with its fundamental position, that we know more than can be formulated in one finite systematized scheme of abstractions,

however important that scheme may be in the elucidation of some aspect of the order of things (RM 137b).

D

Whitehead is well aware that religious faith in its everyday settings does not live by dogmas alone. Whitehead spoke of the need for "intermediate imaginative representations" (RM 141c). The phrase "intermediate imaginative representations" seems to refer to the concrete historical facts to which a particular religion may point as a part of its heritage. This phrase also seems to refer to the stories about these facts. In Whitehead's opinion, the metaphysical commitments and central dogmas of Christianity are implicit in these imaginative representations, but the followers of Christ must discern those perspectives and articulate those dogmas for themselves.

> Buddhism and Christianity find their origins respectively in two inspired moments of history: the life of the Buddha, and the life of Christ. The Buddha gave his doctrine to enlighten the world: Christ gave his life. It is for Christians to discern the doctrine. . . .
> We do not possess a systematic detailed record of the life of Christ; but we do possess a peculiarly vivid record of the first response to it in the minds of the first group of his disciples after the lapse of some years, with their recollections, interpretations, and incipient formularizations.
> What we find depicted is a thoroughgoing rationalization of the Jewish religion carried through with a boundless naïveté, and motivated by a first-hand intuition into the nature of things (RM 55b-56a).

Again we read,

> Christianity took the opposite road. It has always been a religion seeking a metaphysic, in contrast to Buddhism which is a metaphysic generating a religion. The defect of a metaphysical system is the very fact that it is a neat little system of thought, which thereby over-simplifies its expression of the world. Christianity has, in its historical development, struggled with another difficulty, namely, the fact that it has no clear-cut separation from the crude fancies of the older tribal religions.
> But Christianity has one advantage. It is difficult to develop Buddhism, because Buddhism starts with a clear metaphysical notion and with the doctrines which flow easily from it. Christianity has retained the easy power of development. It starts with a tremendous notion about the world. But this notion is not derived from a metaphysical doctrine, but from our comprehension of the sayings and actions of certain supreme lives. It is the genius of the religion to point at the facts and ask for their systematic interpretation. In the Sermon on the Mount, in the Parables, and in their accounts of Christ, the Gospels exhibit a tremendous fact. The doctrine may, or may not, lie on the surface. But what is primary is the religious fact (RM 50b-51a).

E

The fact remains that religious language is not the most successful form of language. This is because it does not elicit the desired proposition with the same degree of regularity as other forms of language elicit *their* desired propositions. And even if the religious language does elicit the desired proposition, a person may not be able to assent to it, either in the sense of being intellectually able to judge it as true or in the sense of being practically able to organize the whole of life in terms of it.[9]

In Chapter Sixteen, we discussed the reasons why it is difficult for metaphysical language to symbolize its propositions. Perhaps the best way of applying that discussion to religious language is to compare religious language with ordinary language. Let us note the following two characteristics which apply to everyday language. First, everyday language deals with simplified versions of the infinity of data present at the initial stage of concrescence. Second, it deals with elements which are sometimes present and sometimes not present in our experience, such as thunder, tigers, intentions, and moods. Elements which are constantly present in our experience are much more difficult to grasp clearly. For example, we are constantly in air and we are constantly in space, but even adults who have the benefit of a high school education are often hard-pressed to state clearly in their own words the exact difference between air and space.

When we turn to the propositions of religion—or at least of rationalized religion—we find that these characteristics do not apply. The propositions of religion usually involve either the patterns of coordinated value or else God's relation to the world. As for the propositions about the coordinated values, we may note that (A) they apply directly to the infinity of actual entities present at the conformal stage of concrescence and not merely to some selection of these entities, and (B) they are present in every individual moment of experience. In such propositions, all actual entities in the actual world of the new concrescence as well as all actual entities in the contemporary world and the actualities which will occur in the future—all these actual entities will serve as logical subjects. In contrast, in most of the propositions of our everyday language, only a portion of those actual entities will serve as logical subjects.

Other religious propositions refer more specifically to God. God is

9. Of course, this is a matter of degree. For most people in most contexts, the "intermediate imaginative representations" seem to function more successfully than strictly dogmatic language. Moreover, even at the level of these "intermediate imaginative representations," some stories convey—preconsciously or consciously—the propositions of rational religion better than other stories. Whitehead, as we have seen, apparently held a very high view of the ability of the stories by and about Jesus to elicit the desired propositions—as well as the ability of these stories to organize our experience so that we "see" that the world does, in fact, exhibit the coordinated patterns which the propositions describe.

present in the conformal stage of each actual entity. In this respect, God is quite unlike a tiger, a bolt of lightning, or a headache. In this sense, both religious propositions about the coordinated patterns of value and the religious propositions about God are alike; they both involve factors which are constantly present. Moreover, God is a single actual entity. A proposition about God, therefore, will have a single actual entity serving as the logical subject. In this regard, a proposition about God will differ not only from the other religious propositions, which have all actual entities serving as logical subjects, but it will also differ from everyday propositions, which have a selection of actual entities serving as logical subjects.

Therefore, whether our religious language involves the coordinated patterns of value or whether it involves God, it is still the case that it will be significantly different from our ordinary language. It will differ in that it will involve factors which are universally present in our experience, and it will differ in that it will not have a selected portion of the available actual entities serving as the logical subjects. Thus, to the extent that we are accustomed to dealing with everyday language, in the sense in which we have defined it, it follows that we have discovered at least some of the reasons for the fact that religious language is not as successful as many of the other forms of language.

V

To complete our book, we wish to indicate briefly another theological application of Whitehead's theories of language and religion. Whitehead's system can provide us with a systematic interpretation of the traditional Christian affirmation that God creates by speaking his word. In no sense is this an exegesis of the Whiteheadian corpus; rather, it is an indication of the theological possibilities of the perspective which we have developed on Whitehead.

God provides each actual entity its initial subjective aim. This subjective aim governs the concrescence of the new entity and is a determinant of the final identity of that entity. In the subjective aim, we find God's purpose and hope for the new finite entity. It is to be noted that this initial subjective aim originates as one of God's propositional prehensions. By means of a 'hybrid physical prehension', the new entity incorporates this divine prehension, making this prehension a part of itself. Thus the initial subjective aim is fundamentally a propositional prehension (divine in origin) within the new concrescence.

Language elicits propositional prehensions, including the initial subjective aim, into greater prominence within the new concrescence. The initial aim is the key to many things. It not only contains God's purpose for that new entity, but is also the way in which God is most directly present in the new entity. Thus to elicit the initial subjective aim into greater prominence is to elicit God's purpose and presence into greater prominence within the concrescence. And so, language has the power to elicit God's presence and purpose into greater effectiveness within the new concrescence.

Each entity's initial subjective aim is quite specific in its suggested identity for that entity. Of course, each entity has more or less freedom to deviate from the ideal inherent in the initial aim, but the initial aim remains the original guide in accordance with which a particular entity's process of creation must begin. Eliciting its initial aim into greater prominence within itself allows the new entity to employ more effectively that initial aim as a guide during its process of self-creation.[10] To the extent, therefore, that language has helped to elicit the initial subjective aim, it follows that such language has aided God in the creation of the world.

Where does such language come from? What is the source of language with powers to help the very creation of the universe? To answer this question, let us note once again Whitehead's claim that any adequate religious, ethical, metaphysical, or scientific language can be developed only over a long period of time. We may also note his claim that the successful functioning of language emerges along a circular path; that is, in some sense, the requisite experience must first be attained and then the language can symbolize it; but in another sense, the language helps to elicit that experience. Thus a mode of experiencing and a language create each other, in a gradual process over a long period of time. From this discussion, we wish to draw the following conclusion: the language which aids God in creating the world is not a magical language. Rather, we may assume that such a language is the product of a considerable period of development.

We may consider the language of the Christian Gospel—as well as its extension in the theological tradition of reflection upon that Gospel—as an example of a language capable of aiding God in the creation of the world. The sources of this language are such things as listening to preachers, meditating upon the Bible, and reading devotional literature. In the last section of Chapter Seventeen, we discussed the mutual dependence of a language and a community. On the basis of that discussion, we should expect the Christian language to be most effectively learned within the context of the Christian community, that is, the church. We ought not, however, to be dogmatic on this point. There are numberless stories of persons, even entire villages, being converted to Christianity solely by reading the Bible

10. Of course, the concrescing entity could also elicit the initial subjective aim for other reasons. For example, the new entity could elicit the initial aim in order to reject it, in an effort to increase the sense of rebellion.

—although, in such cases, these people learned to use a language within their respective communities, and, upon reading the Bible, they merely gave their linguistic abilities a new orientation. In any case, after a person has learned the language of the Christian Gospel, then memory may also be employed by that person as a source of this Gospel language.

Once we have acquired the Gospel language, we must apply it in concrete situations in the effort to elicit and elucidate God's purposes in our lives. The precise reasons (and/or causes) for the various specific applications of the Gospel language are as manifold as human motivations, and the discovery of these motivations is primarily a job for empirical psychology. Nevertheless, God's will is done, and God's creative vision for the world is effected.

So far we have assumed that the person has learned the Christian language and uses that language to enhance an insight into the will of God. This is, by far, the most common situation. In certain persons of unusual sensitivity, it may, however, be possible for God to suggest a new linguistic form or, at least, a new meaning for an old linguistic form. Suppose that the person has used the Gospel language sensitively over a period of time, and yet this person has not "fallen into a rut." Now God may give this person, already alert to the nuances of the divine will, an initial aim which suggests a particular linguistic form for symbolizing this new aspect of the divine will. At first, this person, who has intuited this new element only darkly and hazily, will fumble and search for words. As God continues, however, to give the new entities in the soul thread similar initial aims, and as God continues to suggest a particular linguistic symbolization for the new insight, the person will gradually find the new element in God's will becoming clearer and will gradually find the words with which to express this new element. Further, if this new insight is of general interest, the person will find linguistic forms with which to communicate this new insight to other people. Presumably the most effective way to communicate the new insight would be to illustrate it in a story or parable, or to act out this new truth in a "lived parable."

To conclude, let us note three ways in which the motif of God's creation through his word may be further developed in Whiteheadian terms. First, language liberates us from the past.[11] Language helps us to perceive alternative possibilities from those already exemplified in the actual world. Language thus helps the development of the art of deliberation, enhances the effectiveness of the memory, and sharpens our consciousness. Of course, being one type of language, religious language also does all this. In addition, religious language can be applied directly to the elicitation of the initial aim. It is God, however, who presents each new entity *in its initial aim* such new possibilities as are appropriate for its situation. Thus, while

11. See Section VIII.A of Chapter Twelve.

all language liberates us from the past, religious language does so supremely by making that initial aim an effective factor within the concrescence. Through "the word," therefore, God creates a new world.[12]

Second, language has a deep power to shape our perception of the world.[13] Language deeply influences not only the interpretation we place upon our experiences, but it even shapes the content of our experiences. The initial stage of concrescence is infinitely complicated and offers numerous possibilities for different kinds of perceptions at the later stages. God's goal is to create an intensity of experience within each new entity. Since the depth of each entity's intensity of experience will be very much influenced by how it perceives the world, the subjective aim will contain a suggested way of perceiving the universe. Moreover, to focus, by means of religious language, upon the initial subjective aim *is* to make the divine suggestion for perceiving the world more readily available. As a result, religious language can deeply shape our perceptions of the world in the way God suggests. This, in turn, may result in our seeing the hand of God throughout nature and history, in a way that a strictly secularized person will find incomprehensible. Also, since God's gift of the initial aim promotes intensity of experience, we will find the quality and satisfaction of our lives increasing as we perceive the world in the way that God suggests. Thus, God not only creates the world, but he also creates our perception of the world through his word.

Third, the spoken word carries with it the overtones of our basic existence in the world.[14] The spoken word reinforces the speaker's sense of being an efficacious agent in a world of such agents. By giving all entities their initial aim at the first stage of concrescence, God is working at the very basic depths of all actuality. Thus it is significant that the Bible uses the analogy of God *speaking* his word and, thereby, creating the universe.

In all these ways, then, we find an explanation of the Biblical theme that God creates the world by speaking forth his word. Whitehead's sys-

---

12. The theme of liberation from the past by means of religious language must be put into perspective. The novelties which God offers the new entity are always genuine possibilities in terms of that entity's past world, where the new entity must conform to that past world to some degree. The effectiveness of religious language in liberating us from the past is therefore very much related to its long history of development. In other words, because religious language has a long history in a particular setting, it also has been *formed* in *that* past; and, because it was formed in that past, it also has the power to express novelties which are genuinely possible in relation to that past. Whitehead was no reactionary, but neither was he a revolutionary. A novelty introduced without regard to the past history of an actual entity is merely destructive. Such a novelty liberates from nothing. It is a curse. If the liberation announced in the Gospel is to be truly *good* news, it must be rooted—either naturally by germination or artificially by transplantation—in the genuine soil, in the concrete past, of the people to whom it is being presented.

13. See Section I of Chapter Seventeen.

14. See Section IV of Chapter Twelve.

tem can offer us an interpretation of how the word of God can elicit God's purpose, presence, and creative power in the world. We also find that his system gives us some explanation of how the word of God can be a liberating force, a source of our perception of the world, as well as a spoken word.

Selected Bibliography

Berger, Peter L., and Luckman, Thomas. *The Social Construction of Reality.* Garden City, New York: Doubleday & Co., 1966.

Christian, William A. *An Interpretation of Whitehead's Metaphysics.* New Haven: Yale University Press, 1959.

Cobb, John B., Jr. *A Christian Natural Theology.* Philadelphia: Westminster Press, 1965.

————. *Beyond Dialogue: Toward a Mutual Transformation of Christianity and Buddhism.* Philadelphia: Fortress Press, 1982.

Cobb, John B., Jr., and Sherburne, Donald W. "Regional Inclusion and the Extensive Continuum." *Process Studies* 2 (Winter 1972): 277-95.

————. "The Whitehead Without God Debate." *Process Studies* 1 (Summer 1971): 91-113.

————. "Regional Inclusion and Psychological Physiology." *Process Studies* 3 (Spring 1973): 27-40.

de Vries, Jan. *The Study of Religion,* Translated by Kees W. Bolle. New York: Harcourt, Brace & World, 1967.

Eliade, Mircea. *The Sacred and the Profane.* New York: Harcourt, Brace & World, A Harvest Book, 1959.

Emmet, Dorothy. *Whitehead's Philosophy of Organism.* 2nd ed. New York: St. Martin's Press, 1966.

The Encyclopedia of Philosophy. S.v. "Propositions, Judgments, Sentences, and Statements," by Richard M. Gale.

Fitzgerald, Paul. "Relativity Physics and the God of Process Philosophy." *Process Studies* 2 (Winter 1972): 251-76.

Flew, Antony, and MacIntyre, Alasdair, eds. *New Essays in Philosophical Theology.* New York: Macmillan Co., 1964.

Ford, Lewis S. "Genetic and Coordinated Division Correlated." *Process Studies* 1 (Fall 1971): 199-209.

————. "Introductory Remarks." In *Two Process Philosophers: Hartshorne's Encounter with Whitehead,* pp. 1-9. Edited by Lewis S. Ford. N.p.: American Academy of Religion, 1973.

————. "Is There a Distinctive Superjective Nature?" *Process Studies* 3 (Fall 1973): 229-30.

————. *The Emergence of Whitehead's Metaphysics 1925-1929*. Albany: State University of New York Press, 1984.

————. "Whitehead's Conception of Divine Spatiality." *Southern Journal of Philosophy* 6 (Spring 1968): 1-23.

Gilkey, Langdon. *Naming the Whirlwind*. Indianapolis: Bobbs-Merrill Co., 1966.

————. *Religion and the Scientific Future*. New York: Harper & Row, Publishers, 1970.

Hocking, William Ernest. "Whitehead as I Knew Him." In *Alfred North Whitehead: Essays on His Philosophy*, pp. 7-17. Edited by George L. Kline. Englewood Cliffs, N.J.: Prentice-Hall, A Spectrum Book, 1963.

Janik, Allen, and Toulmin, Stephen. *Wittgenstein's Vienna*. New York: Simon & Schuster, A Touchstone Book, 1973.

Kline, George L. "Corrigenda for Process and Reality." In *Alfred North Whitehead: Essays on His Philosophy*, pp. 200-207. Edited by George L. Kline. Englewood Cliffs, N.J.: Prentice-Hall, A Spectrum Book, 1963.

Kraus, Elizabeth M. *The Metaphysics of Experience: A Companion to Whitehead's "Process and Reality"*. New York: Fordham University Press, 1979.

Lawrence, Nathaniel. *Whitehead's Philosophical Development*. New York: Greenwood Press, Publishers, 1968.

Leclerc, Ivor. *Whitehead's Metaphysics: An Introductory Exposition*. London: George Allen & Unwin Ltd., 1958.

Lindbeck, George A. *The Nature of Doctrine: Religion and Theology in a Postliberal Age*. Philadelphia: The Westminster Press, 1984.

Loomer, Bernard MacDougal. "The Theological Significance of the Method of Empirical Analysis in the Philosophy of A. N. Whitehead." Ph.D. dissertation, University of Chicago, 1942.

Lowe, Victor. *Alfred North Whitehead: The Man and His Work*, Vol. 1. Baltimore: Johns Hopkins Press, 1985.

————. *Understanding Whitehead*. Baltimore: Johns Hopkins Press, 1966.

Lundeen, Lyman T. *Risk and Rhetoric in Religion: Whitehead's Theory of Religion and the Discourse of Faith*. Philadelphia: Fortress Press, 1972.

Meland, Bernard E. *The Realities of Faith*. New York: Oxford University Press, 1962.

Otto, Rudolf. *The Idea of the Holy*. New York: Oxford University Press, A Galaxy Book, 1958.

Palter, Robert M. *Whitehead's Philosophy of Science*. Chicago: University of Chicago Press, 1960.

Pols, Edward. *Whitehead's Metaphysics: A Critical Examination of Process and Reality*. Carbondale, Ill.: Southern Illinois University Press, 1967.

Schmidt, Paul F. *Perception and Cosmology in Whitehead's Philosophy*. New Brunswick, N.J.: Rutger's University Press, 1967.

Sherburne, Donald W. *A Whiteheadian Aesthetic: Some Implications of Whitehead's Metaphysical Speculation*. N.p.: Archon Books, 1970.

————. "The 'Whitehead without God' Debate: The Rejoinder." *Process Studies* 1 (Summer 1971): 101, 106-8.

————, ed. *A Key to Whitehead's "Process and Reality"*. Bloomington: Indiana University Press, 1966.

Smart, Ninian. *The Philosophy of Religion*. New York: Random House, 1970.

Spencer, John Bunyan. "The Ethics of Alfred North Whitehead." Ph.D. dissertation, University of Chicago, 1968.

Strong, August Hopkins. *Systematic Theology*. Philadelphia: Judson Press, 1907.

van Buren, Paul M. *The Edges of Language: An Essay in the Logic of a Religion*. New York: Macmillan Co., 1972.

————. *The Secular Meaning of the Gospel*. New York: Macmillan Co., 1963.

Whitehead, Alfred North. *Adventures of Ideas*. New York: Macmillan Co., 1933.

————. *Concept of Nature*. Cambridge: Cambridge University Press, 1920.

————. *Essays in Science and Philosophy*. New York: The Philosophical Library, 1947.

————. *The Function of Reason*. Princeton: Princeton University Press, 1929. Cited from 1958 reprint (Boston: Beacon Press).

————. *An Introduction to Mathematics*. London: Oxford University Press, 1911.

————. "Mathematics and the Good." In *The Philosophy of Alfred North Whitehead*, pp. 666-81. Edited by Paul Arthur Schilpp. LaSalle, Illinois: Open Court, 1951.

————. *Modes of Thought*. New York: Macmillan Co., 1938.

————. *Process and Reality: An Essay in Cosmology*. New York: Macmillan Co., 1929.

————. *Process and Reality: The Corrected Edition*. Edited by David Ray Griffin and Donald W. Sherburne. New York: The Free Press, 1978.

————. *Religion in the Making*. New York: Macmillan Co., 1926. Cited from 1960 reprint (Cleveland: World Publishing Co., Meridian Books).

————. *Science and the Modern World*. New York: Macmillan Co., 2nd ed., 1926. Cited from 1953 reprint.

————. *Symbolism: Its Meaning and Effect*. New York: Macmillan Co., 1927.

Index

Absolute, the 115
Abstraction 71-72, 86, 182, 188-89
  and bifurcation 261-65
  and generality 267-68, 290
  and language 261, 266-72
  and metaphysics 286-89
  obscurity of metaphysical language
    289-92
  and religion 315-17
  as a part isolated from a mechanical
    whole 266, 287
  as a part isolated from an aesthetic whole
    267, 287
  as simplification 266, 286
  geometricized space as 170-71
  philosophy as critic of 286-89
  substance as 64, 290n.7
  third sense of 267, 275-77, 288-89
  three senses of 266-67
Action at a distance 88
Actual entity
  and future 35, 311-14
  and locus of a proposition 107-8, 111
  and order of the universe 111-13
  as fully determinate at its satisfaction 42
  as partially determinate and partially in-
    determinate at the first stage of con-
    crescence 42
  as subject-superject 72
  as ultimate metaphysical actualities 64
  causal efficacy universally present in 128
  conceptual side of 48
  contemporary actual entities 166, 187
  contiguous actual entities 88
  creates the strain locus 170
  eternal objects graded by God into
    degrees of relevance to each new ac-
    tual entity 349
  formal existence/nature of 94-100, 188-
    89, 191, 193, 195, 219
    and coherence of judgments 102

    and order of the universe 112
    and truth of propositions 101
    compared with existence as an objec-
      tive datum 94, 96
    justification of 94n.2
  full form of 106
  God as an actual entity 332
  God's prehension of contemporary ac-
    tual entities 338
  identity of each actual entity never lost 89
  important differences extend only a
    finite distance into the past 88
  inclusion/incorporation of one actual en-
    tity in another. *See* Inclusion/incor-
    poration
  indication of logical subjects 106-10, 275
  internal growth of 30
  introduced 2
  isolation of concrescing actual entity 305
  not an Aristotelian substance 72
  objectified in God without loss 333, 335-
    36
  objective existence of 31
  particularity of the whole actual entity
    extends to each part of that actual en-
    tity 75
  past actual entities. *See also* Past
    as "being-there," as retaining actuality
      for the new actual entity 70-75, 84
    externally related to future actual enti-
      ties 72
  past, present, and future defined for each
    actual entity 153
  perishing of 30-31
  physical side of 48
  present (concrescing) actual entity inter-
    nally related to its past actual entities
    72. *See also* Present
  present "in" the extensive continuum
    145, 166-69
  preserved everlastingly in God 333

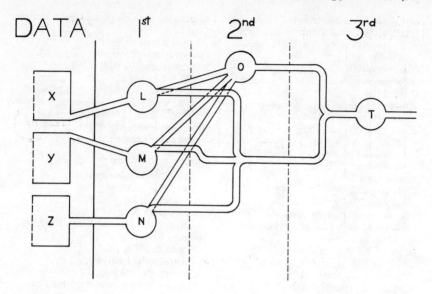

1. *Transmutation*

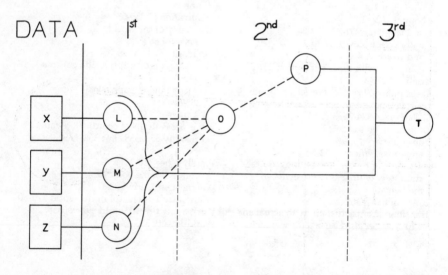

2. *Transmutation with Reversion*

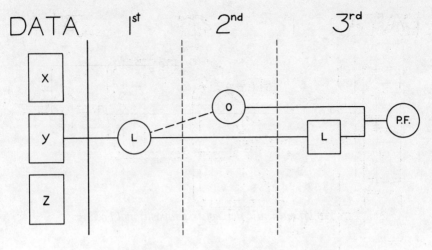

3. *An Authentic Perceptive Propositional Feeling*

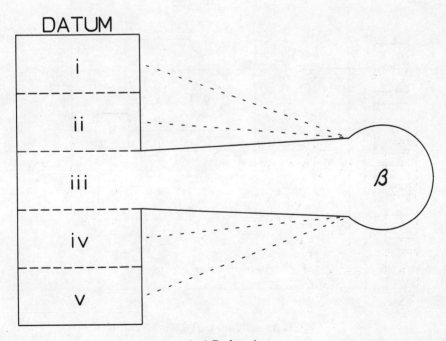

4. *A Prehension*

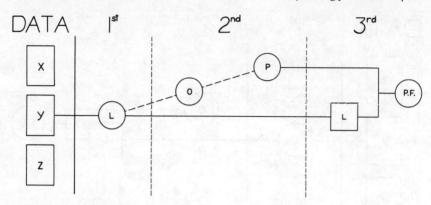

5. An Unauthentic Perceptive Propositional Feeling

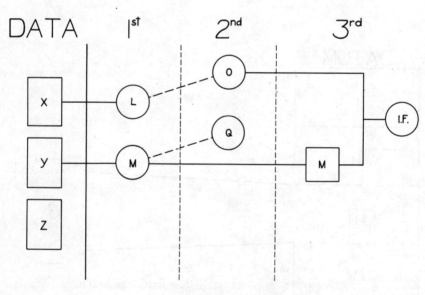

6. An Imaginative Feeling

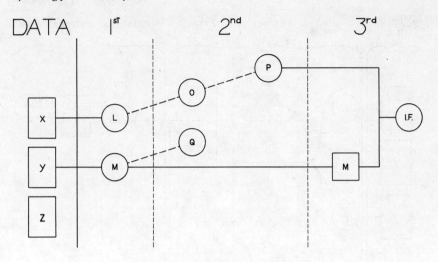

7. *An Imaginative Feeling with Reversion*

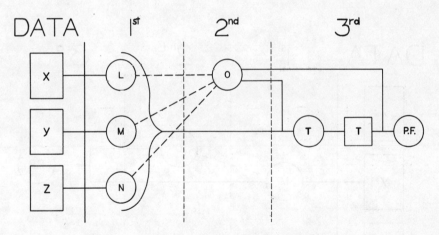

8. *A Perceptive Propositional Feeling with Transmutation*

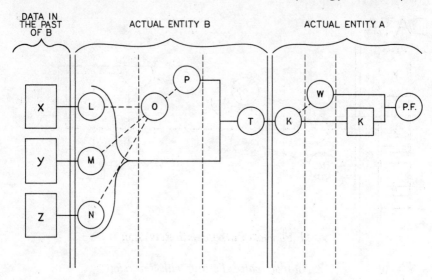

9. Transmutation and Reversion in a Dative Actual Entity

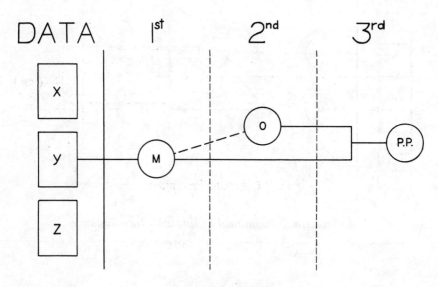

10. Physical Purpose

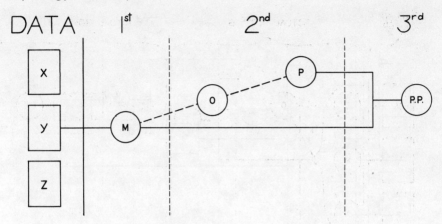

11. *Physical Purpose with Reversion*

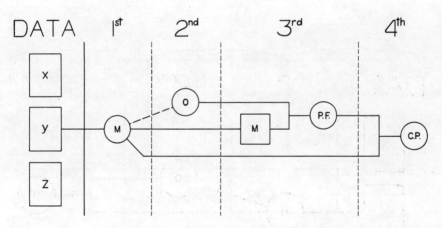

12. *A Conscious Perception*

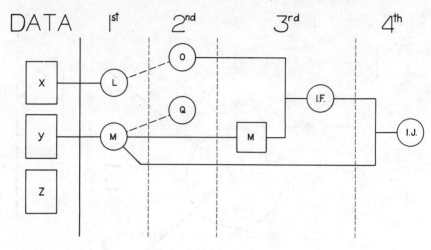

13. An Intuitive Judgment

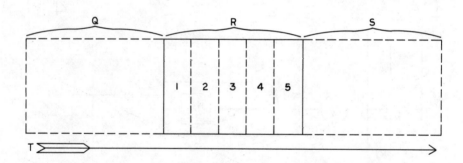

14. Three Successive Actual Entities

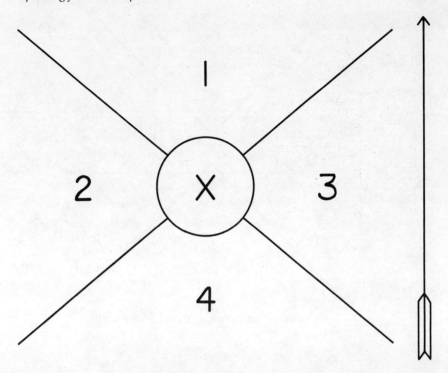

15. *An Actual Entity and Its Past, Present, and Future*

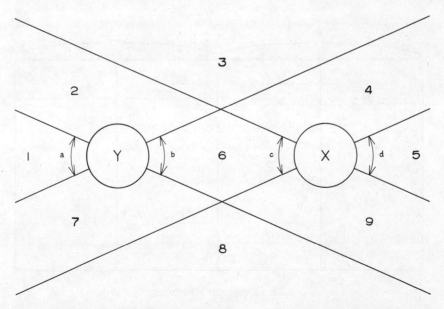

16. *Two Actual Entities and Their Pasts, Presents, and Futures*

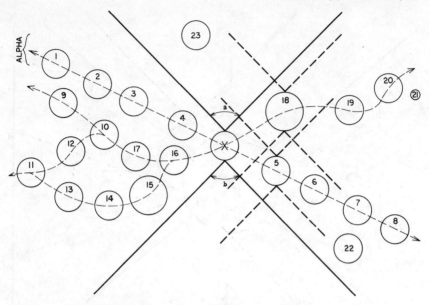

17. Durations Passing through an Actual Entity

18. Overlapping Regions

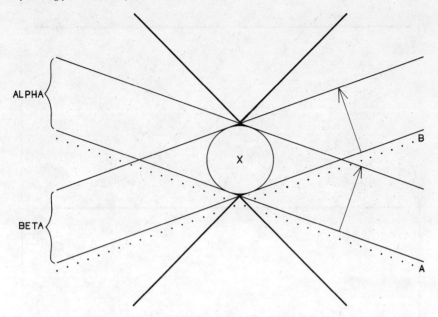

19. *Two Strain Loci (and Durations) Passing through an Actual Entity*

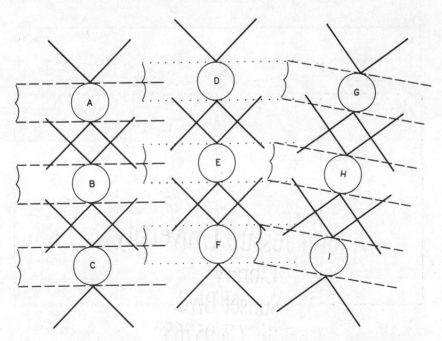

20. *Movement of Enduring Objects Defined in Terms of Their Strain Loci*

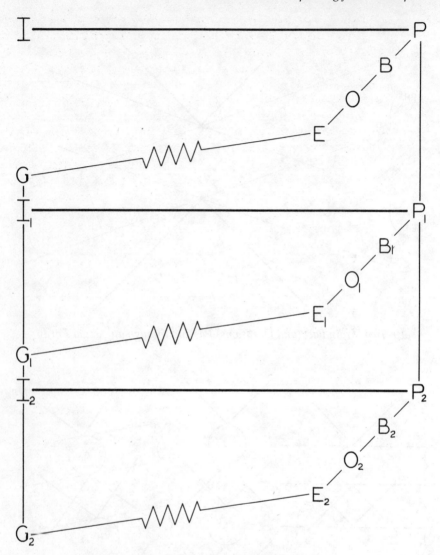

21. *Perceptions in Presentational Immediacy*